International theory: positiv

International theory:
positivism and beyond

Edited by

Steve Smith
Ken Booth
Marysia Zalewski

CAMBRIDGE
UNIVERSITY PRESS

CAMBRIDGE UNIVERSITY PRESS
Cambridge, New York, Melbourne, Madrid, Cape Town, Singapore,
São Paulo, Delhi, Dubai, Tokyo

Cambridge University Press
The Edinburgh Building, Cambridge CB2 8RU, UK

Published in the United States of America by Cambridge University Press, New York

www.cambridge.org
Information on this title: www.cambridge.org/9780521479486

First published 1996
Tenth printing 2008

A catalogue record for this publication is available from the British Library

Library of Congress Cataloguing in Publication data
International theory: positivism and beyond / edited by Steve Smith,
Ken Booth and Marysia Zalewski
p.   cm.
Includes index.
ISBN 0 521 47418 3 (hardback) ISBN 0 521 47948 7 (paperback)
1. International relations – Philosophy. 2. Positivism.
I. Smith, Steve, 1952– . II. Booth, Ken. III. Zalewski, Marysia.
JX1391.I6394 1996
327.1'01 - dc20 95–44524 CIP

ISBN 978-0-521-47418-4 Hardback
ISBN 978-0-521-47948-6 Paperback

Transferred to digital printing 2009

Contents

Contributors

RICHARD ASHLEY is Professor of Political Science at Arizona State University

KEN BOOTH is Professor of International Politics at the University of Wales, Aberystwyth

BARRY BUZAN is Professor of International Relations at the University of Westminster

CYNTHIA ENLOE is Professor of Government at Clark University

FRED HALLIDAY is Professor of International Relations at the London School of Economics

MARTIN HOLLIS is Professor of Philosophy at the University of East Anglia

ROBERT JACKSON is Professor of Political Science at the University of British Columbia

STEPHEN KRASNER is Professor of Political Science at Stanford University

ANDREW LINKLATER is Professor of International Relations at Keele University

RICHARD LITTLE is Professor of Politics at Bristol University

MICHAEL MANN is Professor of Sociology at the University of California, Los Angeles

MICHAEL NICHOLSON is Professor of International Relations at Sussex University

JAMES ROSENAU is University Professor of International Affairs at George Washington University

STEVE SMITH is Professor of International Politics at the University of Wales, Aberystwyth

CHRISTINE SYLVESTER is Professor of Political Science at Northern Arizona University

OLE WÆVER is Senior Research Fellow at the Centre for Peace and Conflict Research at the University of Copenhagen

IMMANUEL WALLERSTEIN is Director of the Fernand Braudel Center at the State University of New York at Binghamton

MARYSIA ZALEWSKI is Lecturer in International Politics at the University of Wales, Aberystwyth

Preface and acknowledgements

This book results from a conference held to celebrate the seventy-fifth anniversary of the world's first department of international politics. We wanted to celebrate the institutional birth of a separate discipline by examining an issue that relates not only to all aspects of the discipline but also brings to centre-stage the meta-theoretical positions within the subject. After all, it was precisely a concern with the importance of ideas that led David Davies to set up the Woodrow Wilson Chair of International Politics at Aberystwyth in 1919. The holder of that chair was expected to travel the world to spread the message that war was not some inevitable feature of the international body politic, but, rather, was something that could gradually be eradicated by knowledge working on practice. In this sense, today's central theoretical debate, which concerns the strengths and weaknesses of an international theory based on positivist assumptions, mirrors the origins of the discipline.

The main intellectual concern of the book, reflected in its subtitle, is to examine the state of international theory in the wake of a set of major attacks on its positivist traditions. Note that this subtitle does not claim that positivism is dead in international theory, only that there is now a much clearer notion of its alternatives. But the centrality of the debate between positivism and its alternatives is one that dominates the entire discipline, and it was this which led us to focus on this issue rather than any other for such an important anniversary.

The origins of this volume go back to early 1993 when a small working party of Ken Booth, Tim Dunne, Steve Smith, Nick Wheeler, Howard Williams, Pete Moorhead Wright, and Marysia Zalewski started to look at the question of how to commemorate the department's seventy-fifth anniversary. It was quickly agreed that we should hold a conference and produce a book, following the precedent set by the commemoration of the 50th anniversary in December 1969. That occasion, marked by a conference which brought together scholars such as E. H. Carr, Charles Manning and Hans J. Morgenthau to Davies's old family estate at Gregynog Hall, resulted in a volume, *The Aberystwyth*

Papers: International Politics 1919–69, edited by Brian Porter, and published by Oxford University Press in 1972.

The working party decided to use the anniversary celebrations to investigate the contending and contentious approaches to international theory as the century draws to a close. Two specific questions seemed to us to relate to the core of contemporary theoretical debate. The first concerns the extent to which broadly positivist assumptions continue to dominate the discipline despite the massive attacks on positivism in the social sciences in recent years. The second concerns the disputed achievements of the various 'new' approaches which have entered into international relations since the early 1980s. Investigating these questions would help us to take stock of where the discipline stands. But, what, these days, counts as 'the discipline'? We do not hide behind any notion that our planning decisions were 'objective' or 'neutral', but we do believe that we have identified issues and debates which will be familiar to all students of international politics whatever their particular approach. Additionally, we hope that the overview of the discipline which results will be helpful to a wider audience than those centrally involved in the theoretical debates themselves.

Having agreed on the overall themes, we prepared a detailed outline of the intellectual issues involved. We identified five issues that the conference and book needed to address. First, we wanted to give an overview of the strengths and weaknesses of positivism and the emerging set of 'new' approaches that are challenging its dominance. Second, we wanted to have a series of reflections on the legacies of the three paradigms that have dominated the literature in the last twenty years (realism, pluralism and globalism), and on the nature of the debate between them, the so-called inter-paradigm debate. Third, we wanted to speculate about the silences in the mainstream international politics literature; in other words, what has been marginalised or ignored by the inter-paradigm debate? Fourth, we saw the need to examine the theoretical openings that have emerged since the early 1980s, and to ask explicitly what they have achieved. Finally, we thought it would be interesting to provide a set of short conclusions on the possible future directions of the discipline and of the social sciences generally. How the discipline evolves will play a part, however small, in shaping future debates about the practice of politics on a global scale.

At this point we approached Cambridge University Press, and they and their anonymous readers gave us a set of constructive suggestions. Surprisingly, the single main objection was to the working title of the volume and conference, *After Positivism?* It was felt that this, even with a question mark, was misleading since it implied that positivism was dead.

Nevertheless, the conference went ahead with the working title, but we agreed to the current title for the book since we were persuaded that it more accurately reflects the state of the discipline and the views of the contributors; it is meant to indicate that positivism and its alternatives continue to vie as competing accounts of international politics.

A very successful conference was held in Aberystwyth in July 1994 where the contributors presented the first draft of their papers in front of an audience made up of staff and postgraduates from the department at Aberystwyth and about twenty invited scholars from elsewhere. The editors sent each contributor an outline of the questions that needed to be addressed, in order to ensure that the individual papers dealt with the general themes of the volume, as well as specific areas. The result, we believe, is a collection of papers that gives an interesting and controversial overview of the central debates within contemporary international theory.

We have incurred many debts in undertaking this project. We would like to thank the Cadogan Research Initiative of the Higher Education Funding Council for Wales for giving us the bulk of the money necessary to run the conference. Other funds came from the College Research Fund of the University of Wales, Aberystwyth (UWA) and from the Department of International Politics. We would like to thank the staff of the department who gave their support and those wives/husbands/partners who were actively involved in the conference. The success of the conference owed a lot to the work of Jim Wallace in UWA's conference office and the often unrecognised work of the staff of the Pentre Jane Morgan conference venue and the catering staff in Penbryn Hall. We would also like to record our appreciation of the Principal of UWA, Professor Kenneth O. Morgan, who kindly provided a reception at his home. The conference ran exceptionally smoothly, thanks in great part to the work of Donna Griffin. She did most of the hard work behind the scenes and we could not have run the conference without her cheerful and efficient help. Thanks are also due to the other departmental secretarial staff, Doreen Hamer and Elaine Lowe, for their help and support. John Haslam of Cambridge University Press supported the project from an early stage and showed his commitment by attending the conference. We thank him and also the four anonymous referees he approached: their comments were helpful in fine tuning the project. Finally we want to thank all those who took part in the conference. In addition to nearly all the staff in the department who attended the conference, there were also the twenty or so graduate students. Of the graduates, Steve Hobden and Alan Macmillan gave considerable administrative help during the conference. Academics from other universities who attended the conference, and contributed to its success were: Michael Banks, Chris Brown, Chris Hill, Mark Hoffman, Jill Krause, John Maclean, Marianne Marchand, Nick Rengger, Justin Rosenberg, Jan Aart Scholte, Roger Tooze, Andrea Williams, and Gillian Youngs. Finally, we were delighted that two retired members of the department, who had also been key participants at the 1969 anniversary conference, Brian Porter and Ieuan John, were able to attend. We hope that the combined efforts are a fitting tribute for the 75th anniversary of both the department and the discipline.

STEVE SMITH
KEN BOOTH
MARYSIA ZALEWSKI

Introduction

Steve Smith, Ken Booth, Marysia Zalewski

The real world begins here, though the contents page of this book contains no reference to an actual place or event in international history. But the reader should not be thereby misled into thinking that this is one of those books about something called 'theory' which is removed from what is usually understood to be the 'real' world. This book, we would argue, is fundamentally concerned with places like Bosnia and Rwanda, and with events such as world wars and also with the prospects for world politics in the twenty-first century. Even if – in these pages – these issues are mentioned only briefly, they are what we think the discipline is *about*. What we think about these events and possibilities, and what we think we can do about them, depends in a fundamental sense on *how* we think about them. In short, our thinking about the 'real' world, and hence our practices, is directly related to our theories. So, as people interested in and concerned about the real world, we must be interested in and concerned about theory: What are the legacies of past theories? Whose facts have been most important in shaping our ideas? Whose voices are overlooked? What can we know and how can we know it? Where is theory going? Who are *we*? The real world is constituted by the dominant answers to these and other theoretical questions.

Part I, *Debates*, begins with a chapter by Steve Smith which attempts to set the context for the rest of the volume. This chapter was shaped by the discussions of central concerns at the conference and, in particular, the problems surrounding the concept of positivism. Is it a clear epistemological position, or is it a slippery, contestable concept? The chapter also discusses the major theoretical disputes within contemporary international theory, namely the so-called post-positivist attack on the assumptions and methods of the dominant approaches. It assesses the extent to which there has been a move away from a positivist international theory, discusses the character and assumptions of the main competitors to positivism, and examines the epistemological terrain of the various approaches.

After the first chapter, the structure of the rest of the volume is broadly chronological, beginning with the inter-paradigm debate of the early 1980s. That debate has had important effects on the discipline, mainly because it has made it appear as if there was theoretical choice and diversity, but also because it has proved to be such a neat and tidy way of subdividing theoretical approaches to international politics. Suffice to say that it has been a standard way of teaching the subject throughout the world. Thus, for any overview of the discipline, it is useful to start with the three approaches that comprise this influential structure.

Accordingly, Part II, *Legacies*, starts with three chapters that discuss the continued importance of the individual paradigms of the inter-paradigm debate. In chapter 2 Barry Buzan provides a defence of the contemporary relevance of realism, arguing that it remains the best place to start the study of international relations, that it is theoretically relatively coherent and that its logic of security applies across time and cultural boundaries better than the assumptions of its main rivals. For Buzan, realism provides a firmer foundation on which to build an understanding of international relations than any other account.

In chapter 3, Richard Little traces the history of pluralist accounts of international politics, and then argues that the rise of pluralism in recent years has not been accompanied by the demise of realism. The central claim of Little's chapter is that, although pluralism and realism have increasingly overlapped (especially in the neo-realism/neo-liberalism debate), they remain quite importantly distinct. Critically, pluralism, like realism, rests on a positivist epistemological and methodological foundation; this has led many theorists to see hopes of a reconciliation between the two theories, but their unstated views of the social world make such a reconciliation impossible.

In chapter 4, Immanuel Wallerstein reviews the contribution of globalist theory by offering a summary of the main pillars of the modern world-system. It leads to the conclusion that the modern inter-state system is coming to an end. He lists seven trends which together call into question the viability of the system, and notes that the most deeply established feature of the modern geoculture, the faith in a form of positivist science, is now under profound cultural attack. He implores us to construct our own future utopias or others will do it for us.

Precisely because the rest of the volume focuses on what are seen as alternatives to or reactions against a positivist conception of international theory, we thought it necessary to ask two proponents of positivism to reflect on its achievements. In chapter 5, Stephen Krasner traces the contributions of international political economy, looking in particular at the conflict between realist and liberal (pluralist) accounts. His main theme is that the achievements of international political economy have been possible due to its being embedded in a rationalist epistemology; in contrast, he sees little utility, and considerable danger, in post-modernist theory and methods. The chapter concludes with a plea for the maintenance of the Western epistemological tradition in international theory.

In chapter 6, Michael Nicholson presents a defence of positivism in international relations. Pointing out that he dislikes the term 'positivism', since it implies a stark form of logical positivism which few social scientists would accept, he prefers instead to see the more accurate term for what has dominated international relations as empiricism. He then proceeds to give a detailed account of empiricism in the social sciences and concludes by noting that policy-making and implementation require a form of positivist belief in the underlying regularity of human affairs. If this regularity did not exist then effective political action would be impossible, and we would have no control over our lives.

Part III, *Silences*, focuses not so much on the content of the individual paradigms dealt with earlier, but rather on the issues and agendas that are ignored in the mainstream debate. The chapters address the different silences in both the inter-paradigm debate between realism, pluralism and globalism, and in the positivist orthodoxy in international theory. In chapter 7, Ole Wæver analyses the inter-paradigm debate, showing how it differed from other 'great' debates in the history of international theory. He sees the debate as having ended by the late 1980s, to be replaced by what he calls the 'neo-neo synthesis', epitomised by Robert Keohane's 1988 presidential address to the International Studies Association, in which he saw neo-liberalism and neo-realism as the two components of a 'rationalist' approach to international relations. Wæver argues that by the late 1980s and early 1990s, this 'neo-neo synthesis' confronted a series of what Keohane has termed 'reflectivist' opponents (including post-modernism and Critical Theory). He concludes that we have probably gone beyond that debate as well.

In chapter 8, Cynthia Enloe confronts students of 'power politics' with the view that international relations scholars traditionally have held a simplistic view of power. In particular, they have underestimated the amount and character of power it takes for the international system to operate. She examines the margins, silences and bottom-rungs of power relations, arguing that conventional analysis treats them as given; as a result international relations specialists are constantly in danger of being surprised by events. She shows how the 'facts' necessary to explain international political outcomes are to be found far deeper down in any political system than is imagined by mainstream accounts. Only by looking rather deeper than is usually the case can we begin to understand how power really operates in world politics.

Chapter 9, by Robert Jackson, examines another area ignored by the inter-paradigm debate, namely the linkage between international and political theory. Starting from Martin Wight's famous 1966 question 'Why is there no international theory?', Jackson argues that Wight's question was misconceived, because his account of 'international theory' applied only to realism. Jackson sees far more of a linkage between international and political theory in what he terms the classical tradition of international theory. This tradition attempted to deal with the perennial problems of human relations; in this sense there has in fact been a long history of international theory, one which has not ebbed and flowed according to the latest intellectual fashions. This being so he doubts whether what he sees as the current fads and fashions among international relations theorists are likely to have much long-term impact on the discipline. Jackson suggests that the understanding of inter-national relations will be aided more by attending to the long history of speculation about international society (the 'classical' approach) than by importing a rag-bag of currently fashionable theories from other disciplines such as philosophy and sociology.

If the previous two sections of the volume addressed the first concern of the project, namely to look at the impact of the inter-paradigm debate and the continued dominance of positivism in international theory, Section IV, *Openings*, turns to deal with the second main aim of this volume, which is to ask what have been the achievements of the new theoretical accounts of international relations of the last decade. Together these alternative approaches are commonly grouped together under the heading of post-positivism.

In chapter 10 Michael Mann starts by pointing out that he is no fan of theory, either within his own discipline, sociology, or international relations. This is because he does not get from theory what he wants, namely a substantive account/explanation of war and peace. He is openly sceptical about the chapters of many of the other contributors to the book, since he sees them as having too little to do either with the empirical world or with providing test cases which might allow the evaluation of rival theories. The bulk of his own chapter, which is explicitly located within an empiricist tradition, examines the relations between states, and between states and their civil societies, that produce patterns of war and peace. He concludes by noting how all modern ideologies have led to militarism and exclusion (for example by near-genocide), and how this cannot be explained by an international relations, or a sociology, that remains state-centric and assumes that military and political power are one and the same. The achievement of empirical historical sociology is that it offers an account of how modern forms of societies and states result in patterns of militarism and exclusion; it does this by treating power as a complex and multi-dimensional phenomenon.

Richard Ashley, in chapter 11, surveys the achievements of post-structuralism. He begins by noting how the language of international relations is strategic, and how 'the IR boys' seem to be constantly on the move, eschewing fixed locations and battles between positions. All this is in marked contrast to the traditional empirical and theoretical focus of the discipline of international relations on sovereignty and the sovereign state. Assessing the achievements of post-structuralism is, for Ashley, problematic because it requires an ahistorical judgement on conversations that are themselves still on-going. Moreover, he points out how judgemental and partial are the prevailing attitudes towards post-structuralism; these attitudes rely on a canon of argumentation that post-structuralism simply refuses to acknowledge. Nonetheless, he goes on to list twenty achievements of post-structuralist interventions in international relations. Finally, he proposes seeing the conversational battlefield of international relations as necessitating a mobile approach, with the international theorist a kind of itinerate condottiere. He concludes by identifying the tasks and *modus operandi* for such a theorist.

The achievements of feminist theory in international relations are looked at in chapter 12, by Christine Sylvester. Even a decade ago, she claims, such a volume as this would have had no place for a discussion of gender and international relations. She then outlines four mainstream (male?) responses to feminist interventions in the discipline. These range from a 'fanged' opposition to any feminist interventions, to a second group which seeks to discipline feminist work, to a third group who acknowledge it but do not actually use it, to a final small group which actually dares to use feminist work. Sylvester then embarks on a genealogical history of feminist theorising in international relations, tracing the stages of its development and offering extensive and intensive examples of its impact. She illustrates her case with a number of statements from women working in international relations, and by pointing to the wide range of feminist work being done on international relations. Like other contributors to the volume she concludes by drawing attention to just how limited is international theory as presently constructed; it is narrow in its view of what relations are involved, and unworldly in its definition of what constitutes the 'international'.

Chapter 13, written by Andrew Linklater, looks at Critical Theory. He starts by arguing that Marxian-inspired Critical Theory has, in the last decade, emerged as a serious alternative to the orthodoxy in international relations. The main part of his chapter involves a discussion of the approach's four main achievements. First, is its rejection of positivism and the notion that there can be such a thing as a politically neutral analysis of external reality, and its replacement by a social constructivist, and emancipatory, conception of knowledge. Second, Critical Theory refuses to accept existing structures as immutable, and it develops, by contrast, a view of human potentialities and a focus on enhancing human freedom. Third, it has proved able to move beyond Marxism and devise post-Marxist views of exclusion and the determinants of history, via the development of a discourse ethics that makes unconstrained communication possible. Finally, it is concerned to replace realist notions of territorial exclusion and the currency of military power with the notion of unconstrained discourse as the determinant of moral significance. In conclusion, Linklater sees Critical Theory as both moving beyond positivism and at the same time maintaining its faith in the Enlightenment project, thereby opening up the possibility of universal identities and obligations among the entire human race.

Part V, *Directions*, finally, offers a series of brief concluding chapters. In chapter 14, Martin Hollis, a philosopher, comments on the confusion that accompanies the use of the term 'positivism', and offers four versions of what may be meant by a rejection of positivism. It is, furthermore, by no means clear just what post-positivism means, and he points out how difficult it is to be a post-positivist and still avoid the dangers of relativism, by which he means the inability to offer criteria for choosing between rival accounts. In short, he is worried that in rejecting empiricism as epistemology, and in rejecting a naturalist view of the social world (which means that the social can be studied by using the methods of the natural sciences), post-positivists may also be rejecting any hope of objectivism.

James Rosenau, in chapter 15, then underlines the problems involved in trying to comprehend the complexity of contemporary international relations, but adds that a failure to do so is even more dangerous. The mechanisms for seeking comprehension are our sense of humility and puzzlement, and the use of theorising to reveal patterns out of the endless details. Rosenau is interested in what he calls 'genuine puzzles': these exist when significant outcomes that affect the bulk of humankind cannot be adequately explained. He wants international theorists to avoid an undue preoccupation with methodology and to start with puzzles rather than rehearse existing theories. He notes that this volume is preoccupied with the discontinuities represented by the attacks on positivism, but hopes that the 100th anniversary conference will concentrate instead on the continuities of world politics that make theorists want to continue to probe 'genuine puzzles'.

Fred Halliday, in chapter 16, offers a balance sheet of the discipline of international relations after seventy-five years. It is now a well-established discipline, he argues, both in terms of its institutional base and its intellectual attraction, yet there is no distinctive corpus of international theory to match that of, say, sociology or economics. Moreover, these other disciplines rarely pay much attention to the work going on in academic international relations: in this sense, international relations remains an invisible discipline. Within the discipline itself, there is a significant distortion due to the dominance of scientific methods and epistemologies, but at the same time Halliday sees a serious flight into forms of post-modernism. International relations suffers from what Geertz has called 'epistemological hypochondria'. Halliday then moves on to look at the empirical and theoretical issues likely to dominate international relations in the future. He concludes by listing four hopes: a more thorough grounding for international relations students in the philosophy of the social sciences; a renewed emphasis on history widely defined; a turn away from a concern with meta-theory towards a focus on substantive analysis; and a call for rigorous ethical work in international relations.

In the final two chapters, Ken Booth and Marysia Zalewski offer other concluding perspectives. In chapter 17, Ken Booth offers some ideas about the history of the department at Aberystwyth, suggesting that it has been dominated by foundational myths which together have shaped and disciplined the range of inquiry. All this he argues is now much more contested. He sees the current intellectual agenda of the discipline and the department as truer to the beliefs of both David Davies and E. H. Carr, each of whom has been the subject of one of the foundational myths of the department. He offers his view of what might be the major changes in the discipline of international relations in the years ahead.

In chapter 18, Marysia Zalewski concludes the volume by commenting on the relationship between theory and practice; specifically she asks what is the purpose of international theory. To examine this issue she poses three questions: What is theory? How does theory relate to the real world? Which is the best theory, and why? Using the contributions to the volume she discerns three uses of the term 'theory': theory as a tool, theory as critique and theory as everyday practice. She concludes by examining these questions as an example of the split between modernist and post-modernist conceptions of the theory/practice relationship. If we accept that international politics is what we make it, then, she argues, it matters enormously for the 'what' just who 'we' are. In this important sense the book ends by discussing the very same theory/practice relationship with which we started this introduction.

Taken as a whole we think that this volume addresses the central questions in contemporary international theory. Many of the contributors of the early chapters explicitly or implicitly accept a positivist conception of knowledge, thus justifying our initial judgement that positivism remains a very powerful, even dominant, force in international theory. But if the first two parts of the book show how dominant positivism is, the rest gives clear indications of why many are dissatisfied with it as an epistemological foundation. We leave it to the reader to decide how influential positivism is, exactly what positivism is, whether the discipline can move beyond positivism, and if there are dangers of relativism in so doing. Whether one agrees more with those who seek to sustain a positivist international theory, or whether one wants to move towards more social constructivist international theory, we hope that the essays in this volume offer an excellent summary of the strengths and weaknesses of the various positions. Because we see international theory and international practice as intricately and immutably interconnected, we believe that, whatever the outcome of this debate, it will not remain 'merely' an exercise in theoretical speculation but will also have a profound influence on the future of international relations. With the real world always in mind we hope that the essays in this book will contribute to this central debate in international theory.

I

Debates

1 Positivism and beyond

Steve Smith

For the last forty years the academic discipline of International Relations has been dominated by positivism. Positivism has involved a commitment to a unified view of science, and the adoption of methodologies of the natural sciences to explain the social world. The so-called 'great debates' in the discipline's history, between idealism and realism, traditionalism and behaviouralism, or between transnationalism and state-centrism, have not involved questions of epistemology. The discipline has tended to accept implicitly a rather simple and, crucially, an uncontested set of positivist assumptions which have fundamentally stifled debate over both what the world is like and how we might explain it. This is not true of those who worked either in the so-called 'English school' or at the interface between international relations and political theory, because these writers never bought into the positivist assumptions that dominated the discipline. But it has been the dominance of positivism that has accounted for both the character, and more importantly, the content of the central debates in international theory.

Viewed in this light, even the inter-paradigm debate of the 1980s looks very narrow, because all three paradigms, (realism, pluralism and globalism/structuralism) were working under positivist assumptions. This helps explain just why they could be seen as three versions of one world, rather than three genuine alternative views of international relations. Similarly, the current 'debate' between neo-realism and neo-liberalism becomes much clearer when it is realised that both approaches are firmly positivist. My central claim in this chapter will be that positivism's importance has been not so much that it has given international theory a method but that its empiricist epistemology has determined what could be studied because it has determined what kinds of things existed in international relations.

What's at stake in the epistemology debate?

The reason why a concern with positivism in international theory is particularly timely was explained in the Introduction: the one feature that the new 'critical' approaches to international theory have in common is a rejection of the assumptions of what is loosely described as positivism. By 'critical' here is meant the work of post-modernists, Critical Theorists (in the Frankfurt School sense), feminist theorists and post-structuralists. There can be little doubt both that these various approaches represent a massive attack on traditional or mainstream international theory, and that this traditional or mainstream theory has been dominated by positivist assumptions. I do not think that either of these assertions is in the least bit controversial, but a reader who needed convincing of each judgement might look at George (1988, 1994), George and Campbell (1990), Sjolander and Cox (1994), Sylvester (1994), Sisson Runyan and Peterson (1991) for support for the first contention, and simply refer to any recent issue of the (US) International Studies Association house journal *International Studies Quarterly* for the latter.

It is because of these two features of contemporary international theory that Lapid writes of the current period constituting the 'post-positivist era' of international theory; indeed he adds that the debate between traditional and post-positivist theory is so important that it is the third 'discipline-defining debate' in international relations' history (1989, pp. 235–9), following the two earlier debates between idealism and realism in the 1930s and 1940s, and between traditional and scientific approaches to studying the discipline in the 1960s. In essence, then, because much contemporary 'critical' international theory self-consciously portrays itself as being *post*-positivist, this makes it rather important to be clear as to what positivism means and what might be involved in speaking of a post-*positivist* international theory.

The stakes are high in such a debate. This much is clear from the way that mainstream theorists have responded to the rise of the approaches that Lapid groups together as post-positivist (and which I above called 'critical theories'). One particularly important response has been that of Robert Keohane, who, in his Presidential Address to the International Studies Association in 1988, spoke of the need to evaluate the rival research paradigms of rationalist (i.e. traditional neo-realism and neo-liberalism) and reflective (i.e. what I termed 'critical') approaches in terms of their 'testable theories', without which 'they will remain on the margins of the field . . . [since] . . . it will be impossible to evaluate their research program' (1989, pp. 173–4). As is noted below, this form of response reveals the dominance of positivism, since Keohane issues the challenge on grounds that are themselves positivist. Thus, positivism is precisely what is at issue in what Lapid calls the third debate because of its role in underpinning theory and, ultimately, serving as the criterion for judging between theory. Crucially, Keohane's central move is to propose that judgement between rationalist and reflective theories takes place on criteria that not only favour rationalism, but, more importantly, are exactly the criteria that reflective accounts are attacking. But note that a failure to come up to the (positivist) mark will result in reflective work being confined to the margins. Important consequences follow, then, from whether or not theories are positivist, and these consequences are not confined to questions as to what counts as knowledge but also involve the standing of theories and theorists within academia. All of this makes it very important to be clear as to how positivism operates in international theory, and to show how it is seen not merely as one explicit alternative among many but rather as the implicit 'gold standard' against which all approaches are evaluated.

But the stakes are also high because of the links between theory and practice. International theory underpins and informs international practice, even if there is a lengthy lag between the high-point of theories and their gradual absorption into political debate. Once established as common sense, theories become incredibly powerful since they delineate not simply what can be known but also what it is sensible to talk about or suggest. Those who swim outside these safe waters risk more than simply the judgement that their theories are wrong; their entire ethical or moral stance may be ridiculed or seen as dangerous just because their theoretical assumptions are deemed unrealistic. Defining common sense is therefore the ultimate act of political power. In this sense what is at stake in debates about epistemology is very significant for political practice. Theories do not simply explain or predict, they tell us what possibilities exist for human action and intervention; they define not merely our explanatory possibilities but also our ethical and practical horizons. In this Kantian light epistemology matters, and the stakes are far more considerable than at first sight seem to be the case.

Having pointed out just how much is at stake in any discussion of epistemology in international theory, it is necessary, before examining the present debate about whether we can characterise the current situation in international theory as one of 'positivism *and* beyond', or simply 'beyond positivism', to look at the history of positivism in the social sciences and then to examine various alternative epistemological positions. This will provide the intellectual context for the debates in international theory, as well as serve as an introduction to the language and contexts of these wider philosophy of social science debates.

The history of positivism

Positivism has a long history in the social sciences (see Keat and Urry, 1975, pp. 9–26; Lloyd, 1993, pp. 11–31, 66–88; Bryant, 1985; Kolakowski, 1972; Outhwaite, 1987, pp. 5–18; Halfpenny, 1982; Bernstein, 1976, pp. 1–54). There are three main chronological variants of positivism in the history of the social sciences, with the third of these being the most relevant for international relations. What unites them is a strong commitment to a specific way of gaining knowledge about the world, as will be discussed in more detail below.

The first variant is that developed by Auguste Comte in the early nineteenth century (indeed it was Comte who coined the word 'positivism', as well as 'sociology'). Comte's aim was to develop a science of society, based on the *methods* of the natural sciences, namely observation. Its aim was to reveal the 'evolutionary causal laws' that explained observable phenomena. For Comte, positive science was a distinct third stage in the development of knowledge, which progressed first from theological to metaphysical knowledge and then to positivist knowledge. He saw the sciences as hierarchically arranged, with mathematics at the base and sociology at the top, and thought that each of the sciences passed through the three stages of knowledge. Crucially, he therefore thought that all sciences (including the sciences dealing with society) would eventually be unified methodologically. This view was enormously important in the development of the social sciences throughout the nineteenth century, fundamentally influencing writers as diverse as Marx and Engels, and Durkheim. It is an assumption that still dominates the discipline of International Relations insofar as scholars search for the same kinds of laws and regularities in the international world as they assume characterise the natural world.

The second variant is that of logical positivism (or as it is sometimes called logical empiricism), which emerged in the 1920s in what was known as the Vienna Circle. This variant dominated English-speaking philosophy into the late 1960s, and is the starkest variant of the three summarised here. The central shared proposition of the members of this circle was that science was the only true form of knowledge and that there was nothing that could be known outside of what could be known scientifically. Hence, statements were only cognitively meaningful if they could be falsified or verified by experience. Moral and aesthetic statements were seen therefore as cognitively meaningless since they could not be in principle verified or falsified by experience. Such statements are merely expressions of preferences or feelings and emotions, but they are not knowledge (see Ayer, 1946, 1959). Thus, for instance, logical positivists rejected Comte's notion of causal laws explaining observable phenomena as metaphysical and therefore unscientific. In international relations, such a view would mean that it was simply not possible to speak of unobservables such as the structure of the international system or the 'objective' laws of human nature.

The third variant is the one that has been most influential in the social sciences in the last fifty years. It emerged out of logical positivism, but moved away from its extremely stark criteria for what counts as knowledge and its reductionist view (contra Comte) that all cognitive knowledge should be based on the principles of physics. Christopher Lloyd has summarised its four main features as follows (1993, pp. 72–3): first, *logicism*, the view that the objective confirmation of scientific theory should conform to the canons of deductive logic; second, *empirical verificationism*, the idea that only statements that are either empirically verifiable or falsifiable (synthetic) or true by definition (analytic) are scientific; third, *theory and observation distinction*, the view that there is a strict separation between observations and theories, with observations being seen as theoretically neutral; finally, *the Humean theory of causation*, the idea that establishing a causal relationship is a matter of discovering the invariant temporal relationship between observed events.

This view was extremely important in the social sciences, where the orthodoxy of the 1950s and 1960s was one of trying to apply the ideas of the main proponents of this view, Carnap, Nagel, Hempel and Popper, to the fledgling social science disciplines. Particularly important was the work of Carl Hempel (especially 1966 and 1974) because he developed an extremely influential account of what is involved in explaining an event. He argued that an event is explained by 'covering' it under a general law. Usually this takes the form of a deductive argument whereby (1) a general law is postulated, (2) antecedent conditions are specified, and (3) the explanation of the observed event deduced from (1) and (2). This model is known as the 'deductive-nomological' model, and Hempel argued famously that it could be applied to the social sciences and to history (1974). He also put forward an alternative, the 'inductive-statistical' model, whereby statistical or probabilistic laws are established inductively and are used to show how a specific event is highly likely given the established law (1966, p. 11).

This third variant underpins much of the literature of international relations since the 1950s. Its features seem to me to have become somewhat detached from their philosophical roots as they have taken hold in international relations. In my judgement, positivism in international theory has had four underlying and very often deeply implicit assumptions, which deal with many of the points raised in Lloyd's four-point summary noted above but in an altogether less philosophically conscious and explicit way. The first is a belief in the unity of science (including the social sciences). This was especially influential in international relations, and many would argue continues to be so. Accordingly, the slow pace of development of international theory could be explained by comparing it to the development of physics, which took centuries to create powerful theories. In short, the same methodologies and epistemologies apply to all realms of enquiry. In philosophical language this is known as naturalism, of which there are strong and weak versions; the strong view is that there is no fundamental difference between the social and the 'natural' worlds; the weaker version is that despite differences between the two realms the methods of the natural sciences can still be used for the analysis of the social world. In international relations an example of the strong version might be the view that the international system is essentially the same as the systems of the natural world; the weaker version is illustrated by the claim that scientific methods can be used to understand the beliefs of decision-makers even though this does not mean that these beliefs follow some (strong) laws of behaviour.

The second influential assumption is the view that there is a distinction between facts and values, and, moreover, that 'facts' are theory neutral. This fitted particularly well into the rush towards behaviouralist quantification in the 1960s, and was a position very much to the fore in the USA during the debates over US involvement in Vietnam. In philosophical terms this is an objectivist position, one that sees objective knowledge of the world as possible despite the fact that observations may be subjective. Thirdly, there has been a powerful belief in the existence of regularities in the social as well as the natural world. This, of course, licenses both the 'deductive-nomological' and the 'inductive-statistical' forms of covering law explanation. Again, in international relations terms, this kind of assumption lies at the heart of debates about polarity and stability, or about long cycles in world history. Finally, there has been a tremendous reliance on the belief that it is empirical validation or falsification that is the hallmark of 'real' enquiry, a position we have already seen explicitly taken by Keohane; in philosophical language this is the adoption of an empiricist epistemology.

The impact of positivism on international theory has been surprisingly unreflective, with the canon of positivism significantly shaping the discipline since the 1950s. But there has been little in the way of a discussion of what positivism actually means. Michael Nicholson's chapter in this volume offers a clear survey of the ways in which the terms 'positivism' and 'empiricism' are conflated and confused in international relations, although as will become clear his characterisation of positivism as epistemology is controversial. But it is certainly evident that in international relations positivism has tended to involve a commitment to a natural science methodology, fashioned on an early twentieth-century view of physics; that is to say a physics before the epistemologically revolutionary development of quantum mechanics in the 1920s, which fundamentally altered the prevailing view of the physical world as one which could be accurately observed. Accordingly, positivism in international relations, as in all the social sciences, has essentially been a methodological commitment, tied to an empiricist epistemology: together these result in a very restricted range of permissible ontological claims. Thus whilst the terms 'positivism' and 'empiricism' are used interchangeably, in both the philosophy of social science and the philosophy of natural science, I think that it is absolutely necessary to maintain a conceptual distinction between the two. However, this is not easy to do because whereas for the logical positivists (or logical empiricists) positivism operated as an epistemological warrant about what kinds of knowledge claims might be made, in the third variant of Hempel, Popper *et al.* summarised above, positivism was much more than just a commitment to an empiricist epistemology. If it is difficult to differentiate between the use of the terms in the philosophy of natural and social science, in international relations and the other social sciences the two terms are virtually synonymous.

An answer to the question 'what does positivism mean in international relations?' can now be given. Positivism is a methodological view that combines naturalism (in either its strong (ontological and methodological) or its weak (methodological) sense), and a belief in regularities. It is licensed by a strict empiricist epistemology itself committed to an objectivism about the relationship between theory and evidence. Whilst the usage of terms such as 'epistemology', 'methodology' and 'ontology' may be various and inconsistent it is important that we separate 'epistemology' conceptually from both 'ontology' and 'methodology', and then separate positivism from empiricism. Thus, as to the latter, I do not accept the view that empiricism = positivism = epistemology + methodology; rather positivism is a methodological position reliant on an empiricist epistemology which grounds our knowledge of the world in justification by (ultimately brute) experience and thereby licensing methodology and ontology in so far as they are empirically warranted.

As to the separation of epistemology, methodology and ontology the three are indeed fundamentally interrelated (see Hollis and Smith, 1990,

1991, 1992, 1994, 1996, and Smith, 1994a, 1994b). Methodology (why use that method?) needs the warrant of an epistemology (answer: because this method discriminates between 'true' and 'false' within the range of what we could know to be 'true' or 'false'); whereas ontological claims (what is the world like and what is its furniture?) without an epistemological warrant is dogma and will not itself license a methodology. Now I want to be clear in precisely what is being claimed here, because this position is widely disputed, most famously by Richard Rorty (1980) and Roy Bhaskar (1978, 1979). My argument should not be taken as meaning that just because I have come to this point in this chapter via an analysis of empiricism this means I think the epistemological warrant is or should be empiricism, although this is the assumption that has underpinned much of the literature of international relations for the last forty years. But I do maintain that epistemology matters because it determines of what we can have knowledge; moreover, it is not possible to wish it away, or undermine its importance, by arguing, as is fashionably the case amongst post-modernist philosophers and (philosophical) realists, that ontology is prior to epistemology. All of this is very tricky ground but my main claim is simply that I see neither ontology nor epistemology as prior to the other, but instead see the two of them as mutually and inextricably interrelated. Thus, just as epistemology is important in determining what can be accepted ontologically, so ontology affects what we accept epistemologically. In this light, prioritising one or the other, as has certainly been the case in work on the philosophy of knowledge (prioritising epistemology) and in post-modernist work (which prioritises ontology), misses the point because such a move sets up a false distinction between the two and implies that one is separable from the other.

Three epistemological positions

The next task is to clarify the main epistemological alternatives to the empiricism that underpins positivism in order to open up epistemological space for any attempt to construct an international theory not dependent on the very restricted warrant of empiricism. There is of course a massive and exciting literature on these alternatives and the interested reader would do well to follow up these debates in any of the major sources (see Hollis, 1994, or Chalmers, 1982, for excellent introductions to the philosophy of social science and science respectively; see also the work of Ryan, 1970, 1973, and Lessnoff, 1974, for accounts of the philosophy of the social sciences; for a good guide to contemporary epistemology see Dancy, 1985; for an overview of the history of epistemology see Aune,

1970; Lloyd, 1993, is very good on the relationship between history and epistemology, while Outhwaite, 1987, and Keat and Urry, 1975, remain excellent and illuminating studies of the relationship between epistemology and the social sciences).

Empiricism, as noted above, is the view that the only grounds for justified belief are those that rest ultimately on observation. Based upon the work of philosophers such as David Hume and John Locke, its central premise is that science must be based on a phenomenalist nominalism, that is to say the notion that only statements about phenomena which can be directly experienced can count as knowledge and that any statements that do not refer to independent atomised objects cannot be granted the status of justified knowledge (Kolakowski, 1972, pp. 11–17). Empiricists believe that science can rest on a bedrock of such pure observation, and from this bedrock can be established, by induction, the entire scientific structure. Put simply, basic beliefs, warranted by direct perception, provide the basis for induction so that we can move away from a very narrow foundation for knowledge to much wider inductive generalisations. Of course, it is much more complicated than this, and both Hollis (1994) and Aune (1970) go into considerable depth on this issue, while George (1988) offers a comprehensive and sophisticated overview of empiricism's history and its role in inter-national relations, and Nicholson (1983, 1989, 1992) and King, Keohane and Verba (1994) offer powerful defences of its role in international relations and the social sciences. The key point, however, is the simple one that if one grants that such a bedrock, however narrow, exists, then one can see how there might be an empirical foundation to knowledge.

But there are serious, and in my view insuperable, limitations to an empiricist epistemology. I will simply outline three fundamental ones. The first is that the epistemological warrant offered by empiricism is very narrow indeed, if in the end it has to be based on direct observation. Such a warrant rules out any consideration of (unobservable) things like social or international structures, or even social facts (to use Durkheim's phrase which refers to those shared social concepts and understandings such as crime, which he believed should be treated 'as things'). Thus, many philosophers point out that a strict empiricism actually allows us to *know* very little about only a very restricted amount of 'reality'. The second limitation is that, strictly speaking, empiricism does not allow us to talk about causes since these are unobservable. The best we can do, following Hume, is to talk about 'constant conjunctions', and therefore eschew notions of necessity. Causation is thus reduced to mere correlation, and our enquiry is therefore limited to that of *prediction* and cannot involve *explanation*. Hempel's covering law model, for example, can tell us what we might expect to happen, but not why it happens. Moreover, the logical structure of the covering law model allows us to make correct predictions from false premises. Overall, then, the kind of knowledge we can gain from an empiricism that refuses discussion of unobservables such as causes is very limited indeed.

But it is the final problem that really undermines empiricism most fundamentally: put simply it is the objection that the kind of pure unvarnished perception talked of by empiricists is simply impossible. There can be no 'objective' observation, nor any 'brute experience'. Observation and perception are always affected by prior theoretical and conceptual commitments. Empiricism, in other words, underestimates the amount of theory involved in perception or observation. To describe what we experience we have to use concepts, and these are not dictated by what we observe; they are either *a priori* in the mind, or they are the result of a prior theoretical language. The problems for empiricism arising out of its underestimation of the role of theory have been most clearly expressed in Quine's famous essay 'Two Dogmas of Empiricism' (1961), in which he disputed both aspects of the empiricist view of the relationship between theory and facts. First, he noted that there was no easy distinction between analytic and synthetic statements, and that even analytical statements (that is those deemed true by convention) are susceptible to revision by experience. For empiricists this matters because they treat theory (or, in Hume's phrase the 'relations of ideas') as 'merely' a series of tautologies, or to use Martin Hollis's phrase (1994, p. 52) a 'filing system'; no truths about the world can come from this filing system, such truths can only come from observation (or again to use Hume's phrase, from 'matters of fact'). Quine's first objection, then, punctures the neat distinction between analytic and synthetic statements that is central to the empiricist view of the role of theories.

His second objection is equally fundamental. Whereas empiricism rests on pure observation, Quine argues that this is simply not possible, since theory is involved in all empirical observation. Even the most simple acts of 'pure' observation involve a web of belief which is both far removed and far more complex than the individual act of observation. Our senses cannot give us access to 'the truth' since there is no way of describing experience independently of its interpretation. There are, therefore, no brute facts, no facts without interpretation, and interpretation always involves theory. Thus, whereas the empiricist view of knowledge clearly implies that if experience differs from our prior beliefs then we should change our beliefs (since these can never reveal any truths about the world), Quine shows that the web of belief in which individual acts of observation occur can give us reasons to think that it is our interpretation of observation that is mistaken. Any individual observation, therefore, can be revised or redefined. Theories define what the 'facts' are, and it is always an alternative to reject the 'facts' and thereby save the theory. Facts are always theory dependent, and not independent as empiricism maintains. To quote Quine 'it is misleading to speak of the empirical content of an individual statement . . . Any statement can be held true come what may . . . Conversely . . . no statement is immune to revision' (1961, p. 43).

These are absolutely fundamental objections to the empiricism that has dominated international theory, and, despite protests to the contrary by many contemporary empiricists, I think they apply to much of the work currently being undertaken in international relations. But if we wish to open up epistemological space for alternatives to an international relations based on empiricism, what other epistemologies are available? There are two historical contenders.

The first is *rationalism*. This view, originating in Plato but derived essentially from Descartes, Leibniz and Spinoza has been the historical counterpoint to the empiricism of Hume and Locke. The central argument is that the senses can never give us an understanding of the mechanisms that generate the observables we perceive. Very much influenced by the scientific revolution of Newton, Kepler and Galileo, rationalism subscribed to the view that the kinds of mechanisms discovered by the new science were quite different kinds of things to those which we could observe. Nature was seen as governed by laws, with mechanical forces producing the observed effects (for example, gravity cannot be seen but nonetheless produces observable effects). Accordingly, empiricism was wholly inadequate as an epistemology, and in its place rationalists offered the notion of reason, which is a property of the human mind, to work out the relationship between observables and deduce the causal mechanisms at work. This notion of reason, with mathematics as the exemplar, was based on a foundation of certain truth (note that empiricists also claim absolute certainty for observation), which for Descartes was an intuitive truth known by all minds; hence his famous *cogito ergo sum*. Reflective minds could doubt everything, except they could not doubt that they were thinking; this provides the basis for secure knowledge about the world. The knowledge which can be derived from this foundation comprises two related aspects, first general principles such as 'every event has a cause'; second, particular matters of fact, for example the belief that one exists as a doubter. By contrast, perception or observation is never sufficient on its own, and requires interpretation by reason. We can only gain knowledge of the world, then, by using reason to interpret what we observe or experience.

The problems with rationalism are numerous, complex and quite fundamental. I shall not summarise them here, but instead refer readers to accessible sources (see Dancy, 1985, pp. 66–84; Hollis, 1994, pp. 23–39; Bernstein, 1983, pp. 16–20; Aune, 1970, pp. 2–39). However, there are two important areas of difficulty which deserve special mention, one of which explains why rationalism has been long in decline in philosophical circles, another which poses peculiar and probably impossible problems for any rationalist attempt to explain the social sciences.

The first, more general, problem is that it is clear that there is more than one 'reason', if, in Cartesian spirit, we take it to mean a deductive system based on intuitive axioms. Different individuals might claim that their intuitions were different from those of others. How might we then choose between rival logically coherent deductive systems based on different intuitions? We know that such is certainly the case with Descartes's work on geometry, where he claimed that Euclidian geometry was absolute, being based on definitive axioms. Now, unfortunately for Descartes, there are rival accounts of geometry based on different intuitive axioms. How do we resolve these differences? In international relations terms, how do we resolve different accounts of why, for example, decision-makers in Britain in 1982 made the decision to use force to recapture the Falklands/Malvinas Islands when there are many accounts each of which claims to be able to make sense of or explain the 'facts'? Something other than intuition is needed if we are going to be able to decide between rival intuitions! In short, certain knowledge requires much more than rationalism can deliver because the rationalist project is wide open to the criticism that different social groups or genders or religions might have very different deductive reasoning systems. If this is so then there can be no secure foundation for knowledge claims based upon the criterion of reason.

The second weakness is particularly problematic for the social sciences, and it concerns the notion that there is *a* (in the sense of *one*) real world to explain. Consider the contrast between the social and the natural sciences on this point. Natural scientists can treat the external world as a reality independent of their understanding of it in a way that social scientists cannot. We can talk of the laws of nature, but do we really think that economic laws or the laws of international system are laws in the same kind of way? Is there in any sense a secure foundation or vantage point from which we can observe or reason about the social world, or are our observations, concepts and reasonings all constitutive of that reality? How, in short, can we observe the social world as it *really* is? There are two additional aspects of this problem; first, how do we know what is going on in other minds if we accept that intuitions may differ? Second, and even more problematically, are we really willing to accept in the wake of psychology's discoveries that individuals are the best source for interpreting their own reasoning? Thus, even if we accept that the natural world permits the exercise of reason to explain the relationship between observables, and this is itself very strongly attacked, there seem to be fundamental barriers to extending such reason to the social world, a world in which our reason is itself constitutive of and by the very social reality it is trying to comprehend.

Rationalism is, for these reasons amongst others, not much in fashion; empiricism has tended to dominate discussions of epistemology. But note that both empiricism and rationalism are each claiming secure grounds for judging knowledge claims; in philosophical language, they are foundationalist epistemologies. The third traditional epistemology to consider is *pragmatism* (see Aune, 1970, pp. 104–82; Diggins, 1994; Putnam, 1995), and its central figures are the American philosophers William James, Charles Peirce and John Dewey. More recently, there have been major pragmatist statements by Thomas Kuhn (1970) and Richard Rorty (1980), although each of these writers is ambivalent about accepting the label because each sees their work as adopting a different view of the relationship between theory and evidence than traditional pragmatism adopts. Pragmatism is the *via tertia* between empiricism and rationalism, in that it attempts to combine the notion that the mind is always active in interpreting experience and observation, with the thought that revisions in our beliefs are to be made as a result of experience. Theory and experience are therefore intimately interrelated, in a way that, pragmatists insist, transcends the opposition between empiricism and rationalism. Our theories are underdetermined by the evidence, so that we have to choose between a number of theories which may all be compatible with the available evidence. The concept of 'truth' therefore undergoes a significant change from the role it played in either empiricism or rationalism in that it loses its foundational role and is instead, as William James put it, 'only the expedient in the way of belief'. Although this maxim has been seriously misunderstood as equating truth with utility, notably by Bertrand Russell in his treatment of James, its meaning is simply that we need to adjust our ideas as to what is true as experience unfolds. Pragmatism, then, defines what is true as what is good in the way of belief, with good here meaning what is most useful.

Pragmatism differs from foundational epistemologies such as rationalism and empiricism in that it sees all our beliefs and assumptions as subject to revision and acceptable to us because they are useful to us in ordering our experience. Accordingly, pragmatists are fallibilists, in that they consider it possible that all our knowledge claims could turn out to be mistaken. Believing the empiricist's and rationalist's quest for certain foundations for knowledge claims to be no more than myths, pragmatists see knowledge as ultimately experimental, with the goal of epistemology therefore being not a search for a non-existent certainty but the construction of a web of belief that enables us to organise our experiences. Within pragmatism there is a split between those who see this web of belief as something that relates to notions of truth, in the sense that questions about truth content are not meaningless, and those, like Rorty, who see the fundamental problem to be philosophy's preoccupation with the concept of truth; for Rorty the problem comes from the fact that philosophy is centred on a concern with the theory of knowledge. Rorty says that philosophy has nothing special to say about truth; its task instead is to keep the conversation of mankind going; 'the philosophers' moral concern should be with continuing the conversation of the West rather than with insisting upon a place for the traditional problems of modern philosophy within that conversation' (1980, p. 394).

But there are obvious objections to the pragmatist position (see Diggins, 1994, pp. 386–493; Aune, 1970, pp. 104–78). The central epistemological difficulty is that pragmatism requires us to abandon the notion of 'truth' as either empiricists or rationalists know it, in the sense of being based upon firm foundations of either observation or reason. Consider for example the point that pragmatists give us no epistemo-logical reason for rejecting any statement that a community holds. In matters of belief, to paraphrase Paul Feyerabend, does anything go? Are we saying that whatever a community accepts is not just 'true' for that community but is '*true*'? Such a thought leads us into real problems when we consider contemporary international theory debates concerning human rights; are we saying that other cultures' views of the content of human rights are wrong, or that whatever the West accepts is right? Doesn't this make 'truth' solely a function of power? Similar problems come when we think about empiricism's reactions to pragmatism; put simply what are the rules for testing theories and how might we judge when it is appropriate to dispute the results of experience? In short, there are two main lines of criticism of pragmatism: first that it seems very flexible as to what it will accept as a knowledge claim; second, it runs the risk of treating questions of epistemology as questions of ethics, by allowing our choice of what counts as knowledge to be influenced or even determined by what a community thinks should be the case. Of course pragmatists have answers to these lines of attack, which usually show

how fundamentally mistaken are foundational notions of epistemology, but many empiricists and rationalists in particular have been deeply unconvinced that 'truth' can simply be determined as whatever a community wants it to be.

Contemporary epistemological debates

If, as I have claimed, positivism and its epistemological foundation, empiricism, are seriously flawed, if rationalism (empiricism's long-standing rival) is currently out of favour, and if pragmatism seems to run into a series of objections from those who want to retain notions of a foundational truth, then maybe there are other positions that might be of interest to those international theorists attempting to locate their work in an epistemology other than empiricism.

Broadly speaking there are five alternatives in the philosophy of knowledge that look particularly promising for post-positivist international theory. These are (a) scientific realism, (b) hermeneutics, (c) Critical Theory (in its Frankfurt School sense, hence the capital C and T to differentiate it from the more generic notion of 'critical theories' which is used to refer to all post-positivist approaches), (d) feminist standpoint epistemology, and (e) post-modernist epistemology. Some of these are related to the three approaches discussed above: notably, both scientific realism and Critical Theory share much with rationalism, and hermeneutics, feminist standpoint and post-modernism have close links to pragmatism.

Scientific realism is a position most closely associated with the work of Roy Bhaskar (1978, 1979, 1989; Collier, 1994; Outhwaite, 1987, pp. 19–44) and Rom Harré (1986). The central claim of scientific realism is that it makes sense to talk of a world outside of experience; that is to say, it is interested in uncovering the structures and things of the world that make science possible. Accordingly, the empiricist conception of the role of theories (as heuristic) is entirely wrong in that the existence of theoretical concepts such as electrons or classes are to be treated in the same way as so-called 'facts'. As a result, its epistemology is non-empiricist, with epistemology being the transitive objects of science which we create to represent and account for intransitive objects such as the structures and furniture of the world. Bhaskar distinguishes between the real, the actual and the empirical: the first refers to what entities and mechanisms make up the world, the second to events, and the third to that which we experience. The problem with empiricism is that it has looked at the third of these as a way of explaining the other two so that it reduces questions about what is (ontology) to questions about how we know what is (epistemology). As Bhaskar puts it: 'It is important to avoid the epistemic fallacy . . . [which] consists in confusing the ontological order with the epistemic order, priority in being with priority in deciding claims to being' (1978, p. 250). Similarly, Bhaskar rejects rationalism since it too reduces ontology to epistemology by its reliance on the role of theoretically necessary conceptual truths to make sense of the world. In contrast, realist science is an attempt to describe and explain the structures and processes of the world that exist independently of our perception of them. Indeed, for science to be possible, the world *must* be made up of real structures and processes. Bhaskar fundamentally disputes the primacy given to epistemology by both rationalism and empiricism, since they reduce ontology to epistemology. For Bhaskar, ontology is primary, but is nothing like as flexible as the pragmatists imply; in this sense scientific realism disputes the primacy of epistemology over ontology in rationalism and empiricism, yet sees pragmatism as mistaken in its claim (or more accurately its implication) that what is true is only what is 'good in the way of belief'.

Hermeneutics develops out of the work of Dilthey, Husserl, Weber, Heidegger, Wittgenstein and Gadamer. Its central claim is anti-naturalist in that it does not see the social world as in any sense amenable to the kind of treatment that empiricism, and especially positivism, assumes. Developing out of textual analysis, hermeneutics, as developed by Dilthey in the nineteenth century, starts from the premise that the analysis of nature and the analysis of the mind are very different enterprises. For Dilthey, each required a very different form of analysis, contra positivism, and these forms of analysis are what we now call explaining and understanding. Hermeneutics can at first sight be seen as a concern with how to understand a text or an actor, and the work of Collingwood (1946) and Skinner (see especially, Tully, 1988), are primarily concerned with this essentially methodological hermeneutics. However, the much more radical work of particularly Heidegger (1962), and Gadamer (1994) raises ontological questions about the nature of being: what does it mean for us to interpret and understand the world? Crucially, hermeneutics reverses the argument of traditional epistemology and instead of a being interpreting a world sees a being formed by tacit know-how which is prior to the interpretation of facts, events, or data. Individuals are caught up in a hermeneutic circle whereby we can only understand the world by our being caught up in a web of significance. Hermeneutics, in short, has ontological significance, which means that the traditional concerns of epistemology are inappropriate for understanding and making sense of our beliefs, since they posit the interpretive or observing subject as in some way prior to questions about the nature of being. In its place, Gadamer stresses the importance of the embeddedness of all analysis in language and history; individuals analyse and act within what Gadamer refers to as an 'horizon', by which he means their beliefs, preconceptions and situatedness and which both enables and constrains them. Crucially, for Gadamer, this embeddedness means that notions of truth and reason are themselves historically constituted, so that the kinds of claims about objective knowledge that have dominated epistemological discussions between rationalism and empiricism are fundamentally mistaken. What Gadamer proposes is an ontology of knowledge, reason and truth which shows how they are embedded in history rather than being above it. Epistemology, in its traditional sense discussed above, can therefore never be something prior, neutral, foundational or decisive, but instead has to be seen as secondary to ontology.

Critical Theory has a more recent history, emerging out of the work of the Frankfurt School in the inter-war years (see Held, 1980; Bronner, 1994; Wiggershaus, 1994). Its most influential thinker has been Jurgen Habermas (see McCarthy, 1984; Outhwaite, 1994). The main implication for epistemology has derived from his work on a broader conception of reason than the instrumental view which dominates Western science and his development of a non-positivist methodology for the social sciences. In his book *Knowledge and Human Interests* (1987, first published in 1968), Habermas puts forward the view that there are three types of knowledge: empirical-analytical (the natural sciences), historical-hermeneutic (concerned with meaning and understanding), and critical sciences (concerned with emancipation). Habermas claims that each of these types of knowledge has its own set of 'cognitive interests', respectively, those of a technical interest in control and prediction, a practical interest in understanding, and an emancipatory interest in enhancing freedom. The epistemological implication of this transcendental claim is that there can be no such thing as true empirical statements, for example in the realm of the natural sciences, independent of the knowledge-constitutive interest in control and prediction. Since the late 1960s, Habermas has moved away from this rather restricted notion of knowledge-constitutive interests towards the development of what he terms a theory of communicative action (1984; 1987), in which he is concerned with developing an epistemology based on the notion of universal pragmatics or discourse ethics, whereby he sees knowledge emerging out of a consensus theory of truth. Central to this is his idea of an 'ideal speech situation', which he sees as implicit in the act of communication, and as rationally entailing ethical and normative commitments. The 'ideal speech situation' is based upon the notion that acts of communication necessarily presuppose four things: that statements are comprehensible, true, right and sincere (see Outhwaite, 1994, ch. 3). It is not that Habermas thinks that the ideal speech situation is something that is commonly found in communicative actions, only that it is presumed by the very acts themselves. Habermas believes that we could in principle reach a consensus on the validity of each of these four claims, and that this consensus would be achievable if we envisaged a situation in which power and distortion were removed from communication so that the 'force of the better argument prevails' (Outhwaite, 1994, p. 40). Thus, his epistemological position is one which seeks to avoid the simple objectivism of positivism whilst at the same time stopping short of embracing the kind of relativism implicit in traditional hermeneutics. He proposes that the social sciences cannot proceed as do the natural sciences, and instead must see action from the perspective of the actor involved; but he maintains that this does not mean that the social sciences cannot criticise these perspectives on theoretical and ethical grounds. Crucially, Habermas's emphasis on the existence of foundations for making judgements between knowledge claims places his work as a direct descendant of the Kantian enlightenment project, a position that has been both a major source of criticism from post-modernists and yet a great source of strength to those who want to link foundational knowledge to emancipation.

Feminist work on epistemology is diverse, and only one variant of it will be dealt with here (for overviews see Hawkesworth, 1990, ch. 5; Code, 1991; Alcoff and Potter, 1993; Haraway, 1988; Stanley and Wise, 1993; Antony and Witt, 1993; Gunew, 1990, 1991; Lennon and Whitford, 1994; Harding and Hintikka, 1983; and Harding, 1986, 1987, 1991). Sandra Harding (1986) has noted three main strands in feminist work on epistemology: feminist empiricism, feminist standpoint and feminist post-modernism. The first of these ultimately rests on the kind of empiricist epistemology discussed above, while the third has much to do with the work on post-modern epistemology discussed in the next section. The central claim of feminist standpoint epistemology is well expressed in the work of Nancy Hartsock (1983), who set out to 'explore some of the epistemological consequences of claiming that women's lives differ structurally from those of men' (1983, p. 284). For Hartsock, the male (and Western, and white) domination of science and knowledge has produced knowledge which is partial and which excludes or marginalises women. Developing the Hegelian notion of the master–slave relationship, standpoint feminists argue that this marginality can be turned to epistemic advantage since women can have a better knowledge of male-dominated science than can the men involved; thus feminist standpoint knowledge will have both explanatory and emancipatory potential far greater than that created by feminist empiricists. The implication of feminist standpoint analysis for epistemology is enormous since it requires us to challenge the traditional epistemological assumption that the identity of the knower was irrelevant in the process of knowing, an assumption found in both rationalism and empiricism. Indeed, not only is a feminist standpoint epistemology corrosive of such a claim, but so is feminist empiricism, since each is claiming that there can be no 'master' narrative and that the situatedness of the mind is irrelevant. Moreover, feminist work on epistemology has made it abundantly clear that the knowing mind of traditional epistemology is axiomatically a male mind. This has radical consequences, since it requires us to abandon the idea of a disinterested and detached knowing subject, a move which is equally problematic for both rationalism and empiricism; in its place feminists propose the idea that knowledge is a social activity. In this light, the knowledge produced by this process cannot but fail to be influenced by the social location of those who construct it. The fundamental question for epistemology therefore becomes 'whose knowledge?'

Post-modern work on epistemology is extraordinarily diverse, and defies easy summary. Whilst such a claim can rightly be made about all the epistemological positions dealt with in this chapter, it is especially the case with post-modernism because its central tenet is one which seeks nothing less than the overthrow of virtually all preceding positions on epistemology. There are extensive debates over what is post-modernism and how it differs from post-structuralism, let alone quite what a post-modern epistemology looks like. It is a genre of work that has been attacked and dismissed, usually by people who have not bothered to engage with the complex issues involved (and maybe without reading the texts either!). I am going to point to three examples of post-modern work on epistemology, or, to be more precise, three writers whose work has enormous epistemological significance. The three writers are Michel Foucault, Jacques Derrida and Richard Rorty: interested readers are steered towards one of the several good introductory books on each author (on Foucault, see Smart, 1985; Hoy, 1986; Rabinow, 1986; Gutting, 1989, 1994; Dreyfus and Rabinow, 1982; Dean, 1994. On Derrida, see Norris, 1987; Dews, 1987, ch. 1; Culler, 1983; Kamuf, 1991; Johnson, 1993. On Rorty, see Haber, 1994, ch. 2; Malachowski, 1990; Bernstein, 1991, chs. 8 and 9).

The central implication of Foucault's work for epistemology comes from his concern with the historically specific conditions in which knowledge is generated. In his book *The Order of Things* (1970), he undertook 'an archaeology of the human sciences' to show how the human sciences were not 'natural' modes of enquiry but rather were made possible by an underlying structure of thought. His work on prisons (1977), on the rise of 'modern' medicine (1975) and on madness (1967) was concerned not so much with the content of the knowledge generated in these areas but rather on the relationship between knowledge and practice – that is to say on the relationship between power and knowledge – a relationship so intertwined that he referred to it as power/knowledge; each is always involved in the operation of the other. His later work on genealogy (1986) sought to show how specific academic 'discourses' emerged not as a neutral result of scholarly enquiry, but as the direct consequence of power relations. In short, power is implicated in all knowledge systems, such that notions like reason or truth are the products of specific historical circumstances. The concept of truth has to alter accordingly, since it can no longer refer to an underlying or foundational notion of truth, but rather to the idea of multiple truths. Epistemology is therefore decidedly not the centrepiece of philosophical enquiry, but is instead dependent on underlying power structures. This is a very radical move away from empiricism, rationalism or even pragmatism; it was also a source of considerable dispute between Foucault and Habermas. Finally, Foucault saw the concept of truth not as an empirically valid concept but rather as a tool for resisting power. Accordingly, the central feature of epistemology, a concern with the criteria for determining the truth, is replaced by a much more practical notion of truth-as-tool.

Derrida's work can be seen as an attack on one central assumption of traditional work on epistemology, what he calls the 'metaphysics of presence'. His claim is anti-essentialist and anti-foundationalist in that he refuses to see the knower as a given, and instead as merely one more construction of language and culture. Accordingly, he sees as flawed the central tenet of empiricist and rationalist epistemology, namely that the fundamental problem of epistemology is how to match the subjective self, or knower, with an 'objective' or external world. His work on deconstruction forces us to examine the 'reasonableness of reason', since he locates it within a specific cultural and historical setting of thinking and writing. His meticulous examinations of specific pieces of writing (see as examples, 1976, 1978, 1982) show how arbitrary and particular are the logocentric structures which mark language and thought; it is this which removes the foundations from rationalism and empiricism, since it completely subverts the idea of a prior presence (the metaphysics of presence). Instead, the knower is always caught up in a language and mode of thinking which, far from interpreting a world, instead constructs it.

The work of Richard Rorty was mentioned earlier when pragmatism was discussed, and I will not say much more about it here; except to note that Rorty has been an extraordinarily important writer on epistemology, and that his work falls somewhere between pragmatism and post-modernism. There really is no easy label to stick on him. The central point to stress here is that his work has been seen as celebrating a quite extreme epistemological relativism, arising out of his view that philosophy has nothing special to say about matters of truth. But this fundamentally misrepresents Rorty since he points out that the concern with relativism only makes sense within Enlightenment language. Indeed Rorty's main book, *Philosophy and the Mirror of Nature* (1980) amounts to an all-out attack on correspondence theories of truth and on the notion that it is possible to construct neutral foundations for knowledge. As his title makes clear, he is concerned to undermine the view, central to the history of the theory of knowledge, that the mind can mirror nature; instead, following Davidson, he sees truth as something that it is difficult to speak about, what matters more is coherence of beliefs. Thus, instead of spending time on fruitless searches for a foundational and non-relativistic epistemology, Rorty proposes that philosophers give up on the idea of truth, and instead play the role of 'liberal ironists' (1989, ch. 3), defending the values of 'we liberals' (those who live in North America, hence his self-description as a 'post-modern bourgeois liberal' (1991, pp. 197–202)). He extends this argument in his work on human rights (1993) to show that conceptions of such rights are not universal, but instead reflect particular views and identities.

Positivism in international theory

Having mapped out the terrain of the debate in the social sciences, this section will look at positivism in international theory, and the next will speculate about the possibilities open for developing a post-positivist international theory. The first question is whether international theory is currently dominated by positivism, or whether instead it has in some way moved *beyond* positivism.

At the outset I want to stress just how ill-defined 'positivism' is in international theory. Basically there are three common ways of using the term. The *first* treats positivism as essentially the same thing as empiricism, which is to say that each is seen as an *epistemology*. An epistemology deals with how it is that we might know something about the world. A *second* uses positivism in a *methodological* way, by which is meant a set of rules for the actual practice of science or study. *Thirdly*, positivism is often equated with *behaviouralism*, by which is meant a very restrictive reliance on quantitative data, and a disregard for what goes on inside actors' heads, as the basis for knowledge claims. Usually, it is the first of these uses that has characterised international relations, but the overlap of usages has been especially marked, and it is quite common to be able to discern more than one of the above usages in any given enquiry.

Within philosophy the term involves a series of different kinds of commitments. As Martin Hollis shows in his contribution to this volume, positivism is usually seen by philosophers as entailing both empiricism (an epistemology) and naturalism (the view that the natural and social worlds are one and the same kind of thing, a view which has both ontological and methodological consequences); positivism thereby entails methodological, ontological and epistemological assumptions and commitments. Indeed Andrew Sayer has remarked that the terms positivism and empiricism are so contested that he chooses not to use them in his (philosophical) realist rejection of these two associated positions (1992, p. 7).

The problem is not just that international theorists have tended to use the term in very free and easy ways, unaware of the depths of the philosophical waters involved, but, more importantly, that the vast majority of international relations research over the last 30 years has rested *implicitly* on positivist assumptions. Thus, while many of the leading behaviouralists were aware of their commitment to positivism (and indeed in many cases were powerful advocates of its strengths (see Hoole and Zinnes, 1976, which includes a particularly robust and tetchy defence by Singer)), many others adopted an unthinking positivism, and worked within a Kuhnian normal science thereby foreclosing debate or theoretical and philosophical self-consciousness. This has been especially problematic when the interrelationship of the epistemological, methodological and ontological entailments of positivism are ignored, and when theorists are unaware of the consequences of these. Moreover, there has been little in the way of discussion as to what an alternative to positivism might look like. It is often erroneously assumed either that 'we are all positivists now' or that positivism is now much more sophisticated than it once was, and that this 'neo-positivism' overcomes the inadequacies of the positivism-as-behaviouralism that characterised international theory in the 1950s and 1960s (such a position is well illustrated by Hermann, Kegley and Rosenau, 1987, pp. 18–22). In short, mainstream international theory has never really bothered to examine its positivist assumptions, nor what alternatives are available. Keohane's response to one such move to develop an alternative illustrates this poverty of imagination.

However, there have been notable exceptions to this silence about the role of positivism, but at first sight these seem to have been relatively ineffective in altering the orientation of the mainstream discipline. But on reflection such a view may simply reflect a massive (and very common) underestimation of the hold that positivism has had over international relations. One seemingly important reaction came in the so-called 'great debate' of the mid-1960s, when Hedley Bull attacked the 'scientists' for their methodological assumptions (see Knorr and Rosenau, 1969, for a collection of the main papers dealing with this 'debate'); in place of 'science' Bull proposed more traditional and historical analysis. Now the problem with the debate was that it ignored both epistemology and ontology; it was instead a very narrow dispute about what methods were appropriate for the study of international relations. A second celebrated debate came in the late 1960s with the induction/deduction dispute between Oran Young and Bruce Russett (see Young, 1969 and Russett, 1969); this was essentially a debate about whether enquiry was led by observation or by theory. But again this, although it seemed more important at the time, was really only another debate about the appropriateness of different methods. A third, and much more sub-stantive, response was the critique of Charles Reynolds (1973, 1992), which noted the weaknesses of empiricism and in its place proposed a form of Collingwoodian history whereby the task of the theorist was to understand events as perceived by the individuals involved in them. But this too was largely ignored in the mainstream literature. The reason seems to me to be that the mainstream was simply too wedded to positivism, and crucially, wedded in an implicit rather than an explicit way. On an anecdotal level, I recall many discussions with leading specialists in my own research area at the time (foreign policy analysis) who denied outright that they were positivists, associating it with a crude form of behaviourism which had failed 'to produce the goods'. This was very evident in the mid-1970s when the comparative foreign policy movement lost its impetus (see Kegley, 1980, Rosenau, 1976 and Smith, 1986). The response was *not* to abandon positivism, since this seemed untouched by the problems facing this sub-field of the discipline, but rather to reject the excessive reliance on quantitative data characteristic of behaviouralism, and also to question the belief in an inductive route to general theory. But, of course, neither of these moves involved a rejection of positivism, only one component of it, and a rather extreme one at that.

More recently, a series of post-modernist writers (most notably Jim George (1988, pp. 67–70 and 74–85; 1994, pp. 41–68) and Richard Ashley (1984)) have written about the limitations of positivism. But their work has been largely ignored by many traditionalists precisely because they write from theoretical positions that traditionalists do not accept as capable of providing 'real' or 'proper' knowledge. Kenneth Waltz's (1986) response to Ashley's (1984) critique, John Mearsheimer's quite amazingly confused comments on 'critical theory' (1995), Kal Holsti's (1993) worries that such interventions do not lead to 'progress', Roy Jones's (1994) reaction to Rob Walker's work, and Kal Holsti's (1989) and Tom Biersteker's (1989) responses to Lapid's article on post-positivism discussed above, are very clear examples of the reaction to post-structural or post-modern attacks on positivism. Rare indeed is the attempt to engage with these criticisms, with Michael Nicholson's and Stephen Krasner's chapters in this volume and John Vasquez's recent paper (1995) being notable exceptions. Yet again the reaction is essentially that writers such as Ashley and George are not doing 'proper' international relations. Part of the reason for this quite consistent rejection of attacks on positivism in international relations is, as stated above, that many international relations specialists tend to think of it in a very narrow sense; in this light, the critiques mentioned above 'do not apply to them'. But there is more to it than that, and in my judgement the explanation lies in the epistemological and ontological features of positivism. Thus the methodological aspects of positivism can be rejected as unduly quantitative or behaviouralist, but doing so does not mean that positivism's epistemological basis, and thereby its range of possible statements about what exists (its ontological realm), are also rejected. Positivism-as-methodology may be rejected but all too often positivism-as-epistemology continues to play the same role as before.

My basic argument, then, is that positivism is usually equated with a specific epistemological position, but almost always involved method-ological commitments; together these result in a very limited range of possible ontological claims. It is precisely this linkage that lies at the heart of Keohane's view of what is at stake in the rationalist/reflective debate; and it is this linkage that explains just why his proposed test of the alternatives is so problematic. Keohane accepts as settled exactly the kind of epistemological and methodological questions that non-positivists want to problematise, and therefore his proposed test results in only a small range of ontological statements being deemed acceptable. Positivism is therefore used in a variety of ways, lacks a common definition, conflates and confuses very distinct philosophical concepts (so that positivism is sometimes used to refer to an epistemology and at others to refer to a methodology), is implicitly and explicitly powerful, and through the 1980s has come to be increasingly criticised. All of which begs the question of whether we can move beyond positivism, and what might such theories look like; or, perhaps, whether there can now only be post-positivist theory?

Positivism and beyond

At the outset I want to claim that there is really no such thing as *a* post-positivist approach, only post-positivist approaches. I have written about this before (Smith, 1995), pointing out that there were two main debates concerning post-positivist international theory, between explanatory and constitutive theory and between foundational and anti-foundational theory. I called traditional international theory as overwhelmingly explanatory in character, and post-positivist theory as constitutive, and among post-positivist approaches saw critical theory, historical sociology, and some feminist theory as foundational and post-modernism and some feminist theory as anti-foundational. This classification can now be improved on so as to take account of the fact that the various post-positivist approaches operate within very different epistemological positions.

My claim is that whilst the vast bulk of international theory is indeed explanatory because it is positivist, and though a lot of post-positivist work is constitutive (or reflective to use Keohane's term), the post-positivist accounts are working with distinctively different epistemologies. It is this which explains why there is no prospect of them constituting an alternative. Rather, historical sociology, despite the fact that it has been central in undermining the realist conception of the state, seems to me now to be largely working within an empiricist epistemology, if not an outright positivism. The epistemological positions of the other three sets of approaches seem to fit within at least three of the five alternative epistemological stances summarised above. Thus, although the post-positivist approaches are united in an opposition to traditional international theory, one of them works within the same epistemology as traditional theory, and the others are operating in distinctly different epistemologies to each other.

To illustrate these differences I will broaden my recent division of approaches into foundationalist and anti-foundationalist. In its place I will use four criteria, those of *objectivism, empiricism, naturalism* and *behaviouralism*, to assess the precise commitments of the alternative epistemologies. Following Martin Hollis's definitions of these in the final chapter, *objectivism* can be defined as referring to the view that objective knowledge of the world is possible; *naturalism* as meaning that there is a single scientific method which can analyse both the 'natural' and the social worlds; *empiricism* as involving the claim that knowledge has finally to be justified by experience; and *behaviouralism* as meaning that we do not need to worry about what actors think they are doing to explain their behaviour. I offer an assessment of the five alternative epistemological positions on these criteria in Table 1.1, suggesting a single individual representative of each approach in order to limit questions of interpretation to one author as distinct from the entire approach!

What this table shows is that the five epistemological positions take importantly different stances on these criteria. Of course, there can be significant disagreement with several of my judgements; in particular I am aware that claiming hermeneutics as objectivist may at first sight seem mistaken, but I read Gadamer as claiming something rather more than merely that subjective interpretations of individuals are referent points of knowledge claims; he is saying something about the nature of 'horizons' which makes them features of the psychological make-up of individuals about which we might have objective knowledge. Similarly, feminist standpoint epistemology is classified as objectivist, despite the obvious point that it sees different standpoints as leading to different epistemologies; the issue, though, is that Hartsock decidedly is saying that, following Hegel, the oppressed does have more objective knowledge of her situation than does the oppressor. Finally, Critical Theory is classed as objectivist despite the fact that Habermas sees the simple objectivism of positivism as mistaken; the difference is that Habermas clearly does believe that there are secure foundations for knowledge, and that some versions of the social world are more objective than others. Thus, although I grant that there is room for debate about the classifications represented in Table 1.1, they do seem to bring into sharp focus the similarities, and, more importantly, the differences between the alternative epistemological positions.

The table shows that none of the alternative epistemologies is empiricist or behaviouralist, although the situation is rather more complicated than that in the case of both scientific realism and Critical Theory; each of these wishes to use empirical methods, but in neither case within an empiricist epistemology. The crucial differences come in whether the approaches are naturalist and objectivist. This in part explains why there has been no development of a post-positivist international theory. An epistemological position that is objectivist and naturalist is very different to one that is not; thus to call them both post-positivist may stress agreed points of departure more than underlying differences.

Although the five views have been influential in developing post-positivist international theory, it is interesting to note that some have been much more influential than others. Scientific realism has been used

Table 1.1 *The entailments of alternative epistemologies*

Alternative epistemologies	Criteria of assessment			
	Naturalism	Objectivism	Empiricism	Behaviouralism
Scientific realism (Bhaskar)	Yes	Yes	No	No
Hermeneutics (Gadamer)	No	Yes	No	No
Critical Theory (Habermas)	Yes	Yes	No	No
Feminist standpoint (Hartsock)	No	Yes	No	No
Post-modernism (Foucault)	No	No	No	No

very little (see Wendt, 1987; Dessler, 1989), which is rather surprising given that it has enormous potential for those who wish to construct an account of the influence of unobservable structures (such as the international system or the society of states?) on behaviour. Similarly, hermeneutics, as distinct from work on perceptions, has been little used, despite its obvious implications for the study of decision-making (for one important exception see Shapcott, 1994; see also the essays in Little and Smith, 1988). Feminist standpoint epistemology has been supported by Keohane (1991) as offering additional insights (to those of the mainstream), and used by Tickner (1992) in her book on international relations, but, as Zalewski (1993) argues, has otherwise been largely ignored in international theory. The other two epistemological perspectives, Critical Theory and post-modernism have been far more widely incorporated into international theory (for paradigmatic examples see, respectively, Cox, 1981, 1987; Hoffman, 1987; Linklater, 1990, 1992; and George, 1994; Ashley, 1987; Walker, 1993; Der Derian, 1987; Campbell, 1992). There is evidently still a large amount of epistemological space for the development of post-positivist approaches in international theory.

In conclusion, my task has been to show that positivism has had an enormous influence in international theory primarily because it has critically influenced what the discipline could talk about; in this sense it matters because its epistemological assumptions have had enormous ontological consequences. International theory now has a number of post-positivist approaches, which are opening up space not merely for other ways of thinking about international relations but also for other international realities. But there is no hope of a (single) post-positivist approach because some very distinctly different and mutually exclusive epistemological positions underlie post-positivist international theories. My aim has been to say something about both the nature of positivism and its traditional alternatives, and about the kinds of epistemological positions open to those who want to move beyond positivist international theory. This does not mean, however, that anything goes epistemologically, or that one can adopt a pick and mix approach to these alternative epistemological positions. Indeed, my main argument is that epistemological concerns are absolutely salient for contemporary international theory and to claim that the move away from positivism does not mean accepting a less rigorous epistemological warrant for theory. In my judgement, the weaknesses of positivism are so fundamental that the positivist project cannot be resurrected. At the same time, positivism's dominance of the discipline has been, and continues to be, so great that it has come to be seen as almost common sense. But more important still has been positivism's role in determining, in the name of science, just what counts as the subject matter of international relations. Its epistemology has had enormous ontological effects, and these have affected not only the study but also the practice of international relations. In positivism's place, international theory needs to develop strong post-positivist theories based on a variety of epistemologies because much more than epistemology is at stake.

REFERENCES

Alcoff, Linda and Potter, Elizabeth (1993), *Feminist Epistemologies* (London: Routledge).
Antony, Louise and Witt, Charlotte (1993), *A Mind of One's Own: Feminist Essays on Reason and Objectivity* (Boulder, CO: Westview).
Ashley, Richard (1984), 'The Poverty of Neorealism', *International Organization*, 38 (2), pp. 225–86.
   (1987), 'The Geopolitics of Geopolitical Space: Toward a Critical Social Theory of International Politics', *Alternatives*, 12 (4), pp. 403–34.
Aune, Bruce (1970), *Rationalism, Empiricism and Pragmatism: An Introduction* (New York: Random House).
Ayer, A. J. (1946), *Language, Truth and Logic* (London: Gollancz).
Ayer, A. J. (ed.) (1959), *Logical Positivism* (Glencoe, NY: Free Press).
Bernstein, Richard (1976), *The Restructuring of Social and Political Theory* (Philadelphia: University of Pennsylvania Press).
   (1983), *Beyond Objectivism and Relativism: Science, Hermeneutics, and Praxis* (Philadelphia: University of Pennsylvania Press).

(1991), *The New Constellation: The Ethical-Political Horizons of Modernity/ Postmodernity* (Cambridge: Polity).

Bhaskar, Roy (1978), *A Realist Theory of Science* (Brighton: Harvester).

(1979), *The Possibility of Naturalism: A Philosophical Critique of the Contemporary Human Sciences* (Brighton: Harvester).

(1989), *Reclaiming Reality: A Critical Introduction to Contemporary Philosophy* (London: Verso).

Biersteker, Thomas (1989), 'Critical Reflections on Post-Positivism in International Relations', *International Studies Quarterly*, 33 (3), pp. 263–8.

Bronner, Stephen (1994), *Critical Theory and its Theorists* (Oxford: Blackwell).

Bryant, Christopher (1985), *Positivism in Social Theory and Research* (London: Macmillan).

Campbell, David (1992), *Writing Security: United States Foreign Policy and the Politics of Identity* (Manchester: Manchester University Press).

Chalmers, Alan (1982), *What is this Thing Called Science?*, 2nd edition (Milton Keynes: Open University Press).

Code, Lorraine (1991), *What Can She Know?* (Ithaca, NY: Cornell University Press).

Collier, Andrew (1994), *Critical Realism: An Introduction to Roy Bhaskar's Philosophy* (London: Verso).

Collingwood, R. G. (1946), *The Idea of History* (London: Oxford University Press).

Cox, Robert (1981), 'Social Forces, States and World Orders: Beyond International Relations Theory', *Millennium: Journal of International Studies*, 10 (2), pp. 126–55.

(1987), *Production, Power and World Order: Social Forces in the Making of History* (New York: Columbia University Press).

Culler, Jonathan (1983), *On Deconstruction: Theory and Criticism After Structuralism* (London: Routledge).

Dancy, Jonathan (1985), *An Introduction to Contemporary Epistemology* (Oxford: Blackwell).

Dean, Mitchell (1994), *Critical and Effective Histories: Foucault's Methods and Historical Sociology* (London: Routledge).

Der Derian, James (1987), *On Diplomacy: A Genealogy of Western Estrangement* (Oxford: Blackwell).

Derrida, Jacques (1976), *Of Grammatology* (translated with an introduction by Gayatri Spivak) (Baltimore, MD: Johns Hopkins University Press).

(1978), *Writing and Difference* (translated with an introduction by Alan Bass) (London: Routledge).

(1982), *Margins of Philosophy* (translated with additional notes by Alan Bass) (Brighton: Harvester).

Dessler, David (1989), 'What's At Stake in the Agent-Structure Debate?', *International Organization*, 43 (3), pp. 441–73.

Dews, Peter (1987), *Logics of Disintegration: Post-Structuralist Thought and the Claim to Critical Theory* (London: Verso).

Diggins, John (1994), *The Promise of Pragmatism: Modernism and the Crisis of Knowledge and Authority* (Chicago: University of Chicago Press).

Dreyfus, Hubert and Rabinow, Paul (1982), *Michel Foucault: Beyond Structuralism and Hermeneutics* (Brighton: Harvester).

Foucault, Michel (1967), *Madness and Civilisation: A History of Insanity in the Age of Reason* (first published 1961) (London: Tavistock Publications).

(1970), *The Order of Things: An Archaeology of the Human Sciences* (first published 1966) (New York: Random House).

(1975), *The Birth of the Clinic: An Archaeology of Medical Perception* (first published 1963) (New York: Vintage Books).

(1977), *Discipline and Punish: The Birth of the Prison* (first published 1975) (Harmondsworth: Allen Lane).

(1986), 'Nietzsche, Genealogy, History', in Paul Rabinow (ed.), *The Foucault Reader* (Harmondsworth: Peregrine Books), pp. 76–100.

Gadamer, Hans-Georg (1994), *Truth and Method*, 2nd revised edition (New York: Continuum Books).

George, Jim (1988), 'The Study of International Relations and the Positivist/Empiricist Theory of Knowledge: Implications for the Australian Discipline', in Richard Higgott (ed.), *New Directions in International Relations* (Canberra: Australian National University), pp. 65–142.

(1994), *Discourses of Global Politics: A Critical (Re)Introduction to International Relations* (Boulder, CO: Lynne Rienner).

George, Jim and Campbell, David (1990), 'Patterns of Dissent and the Celebration of Difference: Critical Social Theory and International Relations', *International Studies Quarterly*, 34 (3), pp. 269–93.

Gunew, Sneja (ed.) (1990), *Feminist Knowledge: Critique and Construct* (London: Routledge).

(1991), *A Reader in Feminist Knowledge* (London: Routledge).

Gutting, Gary (1989), *Michel Foucault's Archaeology of Scientific Reason* (Cambridge: Cambridge University Press).

Gutting, Gary (ed.) (1994), *The Cambridge Companion to Foucault* (Cambridge: Cambridge University Press).

Haber, Honi Fern (1994), *Beyond Postmodern Politics: Lyotard, Rorty, Foucault* (London: Routledge).

Habermas, Jurgen (1987), *Knowledge and Human Interests* (first published 1968) (Cambridge: Polity).

(1984 [1991]), *The Theory of Communicative Action Vol. 1: Reason and the Rationalisation of Society* (Cambridge: Polity Press).

(1987 [1987]), *The Theory of Communicative Action Vol. 2: The Critique of Functionalist Reason* (Cambridge: Polity).

Halfpenny, Peter (1982), *Positivism and Sociology* (London: Allen & Unwin).

Haraway, Donna (1988), 'Situated Knowledge: The Science Question in Feminism and the Privilege of Partial Perspective', *Feminist Studies*, 14 (3), pp. 575–99.

Harding, Sandra (1986), *The Science Question in Feminism* (Milton Keynes: Open University Press).

(1991), *Whose Science? Whose Knowledge?* (Milton Keynes: Open University Press).

Harding, Sandra (ed.) (1987), *Feminism and Methodology* (Milton Keynes: Open University Press).

Harding, Sandra and Hintikka, Merrill (eds.) (1983), *Discovering Reality: Feminist Perspectives on Epistemology, Metaphysics, Methodology and Philosophy of Science* (Dordrecht, Holland: Reidel).

Harré, Rom (1986), *Varieties of Realism* (Oxford: Blackwell).

Hartsock, Nancy (1983), 'Feminist Standpoint: Developing the Ground for a Specifically Feminist Historical Materialism', in Sandra Harding and Merrill Hintikka (eds.), *Discovering Reality: Feminist Perspectives on Epistemology, Metaphysics, Methodology and Philosophy of Science* (Dordrecht, Holland: Reidel), pp. 283–310.

Hawkesworth, Mary (1990), *Beyond Oppression: Feminist Theory and Political Strategy* (New York: Continuum).

Heidegger, Martin (1962), *Being And Time* (Oxford: Blackwell).

Held, David (1980), *Introduction to Critical Theory: Horkheimer to Habermas* (Berkeley, CA: University of California Press).

Hempel, Carl (1966), *Philosophy of Natural Science* (Englewood Cliffs, NJ: Prentice-Hall).

(1974), 'Reasons and Covering Laws in Historical Explanation', in Patrick Gardiner (ed.), *The Philosophy of History* (Oxford: Oxford University Press), pp. 90–105.

Hermann, Charles, Kegley, Charles and Rosenau, James (eds.) (1987), *New Directions in the Study of Foreign Policy* (London: Allen & Unwin).

Hoffman, Mark (1987), 'Critical Theory and the Inter-Paradigm Debate', *Millennium: Journal of International Studies*, 16 (2), pp. 231–49.

Hollis, Martin (1994), *The Philosophy of Social Science: An Introduction* (Cambridge: Cambridge University Press).

Hollis, Martin and Smith, Steve (1990), *Explaining and Understanding International Relations* (Oxford: Clarendon Press).

(1991), 'Beware of Gurus: Structure and Action in International Relations', *Review of International Studies*, 17 (4), pp. 393–410.

(1992), 'Structure and Action: Further Comment', *Review of International Studies*, 18 (2), pp. 187–8.

(1994), 'Two Stories About Structure and Agency', *Review of International Studies*, 20 (3), pp. 241–51.

(forthcoming, 1996), 'Why Epistemology Matters in International Theory', *Review of International Studies*, 22 (1).

Holsti, Kal (1989), 'Mirror, Mirror on the Wall Which are the Fairest Theories of All?', *International Studies Quarterly*, 33 (3), pp. 255–61.

(1993), 'International Relations at the End of the Millennium', *Review of International Studies*, 19 (4), pp. 401–8.

Hoole, Francis and Zinnes, Dina (eds.) (1976), *Quantitative International Politics: An Appraisal* (New York: Praeger).

Hoy, David (1986), *Foucault: A Critical Reader* (Oxford: Blackwell).

Johnson, Christopher (1993), *System and Writing in the Philosophy of Jacques Derrida* (Cambridge: Cambridge University Press).

Jones, Roy (1994), 'The Responsibility to Educate', *Review of International Studies*, 20 (3), pp. 299–311.

Kamuf, Peggy (ed.) (1991), *A Derrida Reader: Between the Blinds* (Hemel Hempstead: Harvester).

Keat, Russell and Urry, John (1975), *Social Theory as Science* (London: Routledge).

Kegley, Charles (1980), *The Comparative Study of Foreign Policy: Paradigm Lost?* (Columbia, SC: University of South Carolina).

Keohane, Robert (1989), *International Institutions and State Power: Essays in International Relations Theory* (Boulder, CO: Westview).

(1991), 'International Relations Theory: Contributions of a Feminist Standpoint', in Rebecca Grant and Kathleen Newland (eds.), *Gender and International Relations* (Milton Keynes: Open University Press), pp. 41–50.

King, Gary, Keohane, Robert and Verba, Sidney (1994), *Designing Social Enquiry: Scientific Inference in Qualitative Research* (Princeton, NJ: Princeton University Press).

Knorr, Klaus and Rosenau, James (eds.) (1969), *Contending Approaches to International Politics* (Princeton, NJ: Princeton University Press).

Kolakowski, Leszek (1972), *Positivist Philosophy* (Harmondsworth: Penguin Books).

Kuhn, Thomas (1970), *The Structure of Scientific Revolutions*, 2nd edition (Chicago: University of Chicago Press).

Lapid, Yosef (1989), 'The Third Debate: On the Prospects of International Theory in a Post-Positivist Era', *International Studies Quarterly*, 33 (3), pp. 235–54.

Lennon, Kathleen and Whitford, Margaret (eds.) (1994), *Knowing the Difference: Feminist Perspectives in Epistemology* (London: Routledge).

Lessnoff, Michael (1974), *The Structure of Social Science: A Philosophical Introduction* (London: Allen & Unwin).

Linklater, Andrew (1990), *Beyond Realism and Marxism: Critical Theory and International Relations* (Basingstoke: Macmillan).

(1992), 'The Question of the Next Stage in International Relations Theory: A Critical-Theoretical Point of View', *Millennium: Journal of International Studies*, 21 (1), pp. 77–98.

Little, Richard and Smith, Steve (eds.) (1988), *Belief Systems and International Relations* (Oxford: Blackwell).

Lloyd, Christopher (1993), *The Structures of History* (Oxford: Blackwell).

Malachowski, Alan (ed.) (1990), *Reading Rorty: Critical Responses to 'Philosophy and the Mirror of Nature' (and beyond)* (Oxford: Blackwell).

McCarthy, Thomas (1984), *The Critical Theory of Jurgen Habermas* (Cambridge: Polity).

Mearsheimer, John (1995), 'The False Promise of International Institutions', *International Security*, 19 (3), pp. 5–49.

Nicholson, Michael (1983), *The Scientific Analysis of Social Behaviour: A Defence of Empiricism in Social Science* (London: Frances Pinter).

(1989), *Formal Theories in International Relations* (Cambridge: Cambridge University Press).

(1992), *Rationality and the Analysis of International Conflict* (Cambridge: Cambridge University Press).

Norris, Christopher (1987), *Derrida* (London: Fontana Press).

Outhwaite, William (1987), *New Philosophies of Social Science: Realism, Hermeneutics and Critical Theory* (Basingstoke: Macmillan).

(1994), *Habermas: A Critical Introduction* (Cambridge: Polity).

Putnam, Hilary (1995), *Pragmatism* (Oxford: Blackwell).

Quine, W. V. O. (1961), 'Two Dogmas of Empiricism', in his *From a Logical Point of View*, 2nd edition (Cambridge, MA: Harvard University Press), pp. 20–46.

Rabinow, Paul (ed.) (1986), *The Foucault Reader* (Harmondsworth: Peregrine Books).

Reynolds, Charles (1973), *Theory and Explanation in International Politics* (Oxford: Martin Robertson).

(1992), *The World of States: An Introduction to Explanation and Theory* (Aldershot: Edward Elgar Publishing).

Rorty, Richard (1980), *Philosophy and the Mirror of Nature* (Oxford: Blackwell).

(1989), *Contingency, Irony, and Solidarity* (Cambridge: Cambridge University Press).

(1991), *Objectivity, Relativism and Truth: Philosophical Papers Vol. 1* (Cambridge: Cambridge University Press).

(1993), 'Human Rights, Rationality, and Sentimentality', in Stephen Shute and Susan Hurley (eds.), *On Human Rights: The Oxford Amnesty Lectures 1993* (New York: Basic Books), pp. 111–34.

Rosenau, James (1976), 'Puzzlement in Foreign Policy', *Jerusalem Journal of International Relations*, 1 (1), pp. 1–10.

Runyan, Anne Sisson and Peterson, V. Spike (1991), 'The Radical Future of Realism: Feminist Subversions of IR Theory', *Alternatives*, 16 (1), pp. 67–106.

Russett, Bruce (1969), 'The Young Science of International Politics', *World Politics*, 22 (1), pp. 87–94.

Ryan, Alan (1970), *The Philosophy of the Social Sciences* (London: Macmillan).

Ryan, Alan (ed.) (1973), *The Philosophy of Social Explanation* (Oxford: Oxford University Press).

Sayer, Andrew (1992), *Method in Social Science: A Realist Approach*, 2nd edition (London: Routledge).

Shapcott, Richard (1994), 'Conversation and Co-existence: Gadamer and the Interpretation of International Society', *Millennium: Journal of International Studies*, 23 (1), pp. 57–83.

Sjolander, Claire Turenne and Cox, Wayne (1994), *Beyond Positivism: Critical Reflections on International Relations* (Boulder, CO: Lynne Rienner).

Smart, Barry (1985), *Michel Foucault* (London: Routledge).

Smith, Steve (1986), 'Theories of Foreign Policy: An Historical Overview', *Review of International Studies*, 12 (1), pp. 13–29.

(1994a), 'Rearranging the Deckchairs on the Ship Called Modernity: Rosenberg, Epistemology and Emancipation', *Millennium: Journal of International Studies*, 23 (2), pp. 395–405.

(1994b), 'Foreign Policy Theory and the New Europe', in Walter Carlsnaes and Steve Smith (eds.), *European Foreign Policy: The EC and Changing Perspectives in Europe* (London: Sage Publications), pp. 1–20.

(1995), 'The Self-Images of a Discipline: A Genealogy of International Relations Theory', in Ken Booth and Steve Smith (eds.), *International Relations Theory Today* (Cambridge: Polity), pp. 1–37.

Stanley, Liz and Wise, Sue (1993), *Breaking Out Again: Feminist Ontology and Epistemology* (London: Routledge).

Sylvester, Christine (1994), *Feminist Theory and International Relations in a Postmodern Era* (Cambridge: Cambridge University Press).

Tickner, J. Ann (1992), *Gender in International Relations: Feminist Perspectives on Achieving Global Security* (New York: Columbia University Press).

Tully, James (ed.) (1988), *Meaning and Context: Quentin Skinner and his Critics* (Cambridge: Polity Press).

Vasquez, John (1995), 'The Post-Positivist Debate: Reconstructing Scientific Enquiry and International Relations Theory After Enlightenment's Fall', in Ken Booth and Steve Smith (eds.), *International Relations Theory Today* (Cambridge: Polity), pp. 217–40.

Walker, Rob (1993), *Inside/Outside: International Relations as Political Theory* (Cambridge: Cambridge University Press).

Waltz, Kenneth (1986), 'Reflections on Theory of International Politics: A Response to My Critics', in Robert Keohane (ed.), *Neorealism and its Critics* (New York: Columbia University Press), pp. 322–45.

Wendt, Alexander (1987), 'The Agent–Structure Problem in International Relations Theory', *International Organization*, 41 (3), pp. 335–70.

(1992), 'Anarchy is What States Make of It: A Social Construction of Power Politics', *International Organization*, 46 (2), pp. 391–425.

Wiggershaus, Rolf (1994), *The Frankfurt School* (Cambridge: Polity).

Young, Oran (1969), 'Professor Russett: Industrious Tailor to a Naked Emperor', *World Politics*, 21 (3), pp. 586–611.

Zalewski, Marysia (1993), 'Feminist Standpoint Theory Meets International Relations Theory: A Feminist Version of David and Goliath?', *The Fletcher Forum of World Affairs*, 17 (2), pp. 13–32.

II

Legacies

2   The timeless wisdom of realism?

Barry Buzan

Realism is widely thought of as both the orthodoxy and the classical tradition of thinking about international relations. It is often contrasted to idealism, or more specifically to other so-called paradigms such as liberalism and Marxism. Unfortunately, there is no precise consensus on where the boundaries between these bodies of thought should be drawn. In this chapter I will try to provide an answer to those who have questioned why, given the nature of my writings, I continue to call myself a realist. Doing so will mean that I push the boundaries of realism further out than some people think appropriate. What follows is therefore a rather liberal interpretation. It will emphasise three qualities of realism: its continued relevance, its flexibility in coming to terms with many ideas from other approaches, and its value as a starting point for enquiry. The chapter attempts to provide a compact summary and evaluation of realism as an approach to the study of international relations. It starts by giving a brief overview of the intellectual history, and then sets out the main distinguishing features of realism. Next it looks at the place of realism within the discipline of International Relations, particularly how it relates to other paradigms. It concludes with an evaluation of realism, arguing that it remains the essential core of the subject even though it does not and cannot provide a full understanding of it.

A very brief intellectual history of realism

Realism claims a long intellectual pedigree going back to Thucydides, Machiavelli, Hobbes and Rousseau. This claim rests on the apparent durability of power politics as a feature of human civilisation, though Walker rightly questions whether this can be said to represent a coherent intellectual tradition (Walker, 1987). Realism dominated the study of international relations in the decades following the Second World War. It did not, however, dominate American policy which was driven by liberalism into an ideological confrontation with the Soviet Union. These liberals sometimes presented themselves as realists, but many leading realists such as Morgenthau, Waltz and Kissinger were critical of the crusading and paranoia that dominated the Cold War containment and arms racing policies of the United States, not to mention the Vietnam war (McKinlay and Little, 1986, chs. 8, 10). Despite numerous challenges, realism is arguably still the prevailing orthodoxy in the discipline. Like International Relations itself, realism is largely an Anglo-American theory (with substantial inputs from Central European immigrants). But realism was not the orthodoxy during the founding two decades of the 1920s and 1930s. When International Relations first emerged as a distinct field of study, it was in reaction to the carnage of the First World War, to the apparent casualness with which that war had been allowed to occur, and to the loss of control over the development of civilisation that it seemed to represent. The field was driven by the search for causes of war, and for prescriptions to prevent its recurrence. This first round ended with the catastrophes of the 1930s and 1940s, and the failure of the collective security mechanisms embodied in the League of Nations.

Post-war realism (confusingly referred to as 'classical') developed in reaction to both the practical and the intellectual failures of the inter-war period, and the experiences of the Second World War and the Cold War. It was concerned to rebalance the approaches of the inter-war idealists by giving priority to the need to study the international system as it was, rather than as one might like it to be. During the 1940s, 1950s and 1960s it was dominated by the writings of E. H. Carr (1946), Hans Morgenthau (1978) and John Herz (1951), all of whom gave primacy to power politics among states as the key to understanding the operation of the international system. The contrast between realists and idealists, though real, should not be overdrawn. Morgenthau looked forward to a world government, and there are strong idealist elements in the thinking of both Carr and Herz. Realism was accompanied in tandem by strategic studies, which concentrated on developing theories of nuclear deterrence. Driven by rapid changes in military technology, strategic studies quickly developed an analytical life of its own (Buzan, 1987), and dominated debates during much of the 1960s and 1970s. Strategic studies can be seen as continuing a Clausewitzian tradition of focusing on the military dimension ('other means') of power politics. During the later 1960s and 1970s the hold of classical realism on the study of International Relations looked like being broken. From the late 1960s onwards it began to be argued and accepted that the methodology and the theoretical and policy agendas associated with classical realism were anachronistic. Networks rather than billiard balls appeared to be the appropriate metaphor for an international system increasingly dominated by transnational relations, economic concerns, and an expanding web of international norms, rules and institutions (Burton, 1972; Keohane and Nye, 1977).

On the methodological front, behaviouralists were arguing that the work of classical realists did not satisfy the canons of scientific investigation. On the agenda front there were two lines of attack. One was a frontal assault coming from those concerned with interdependence, political economy and transnational relations. This included not only fundamental questioning about the centrality of the state and military power in realist thinking, but also an accusation that realism was unable to deal with either the issues or the character of international politics in an interdependent world, and a denunciation of the logic and the morality of realism's normative bias towards conflictual assumptions. The other came from the English school, whose main writers were Martin Wright (1977) and Hedley Bull (1977). It did not question the primacy of the state or power politics, but developed the concept of international society as a way of introducing both historical range, and a significant role for norm-based order, into the understanding of international relations. This latter idea was developed along narrower and more specific lines later in the United States by regime theorists (albeit with little reference to English school ideas).

A realist revival under the label neo-realism started in the late 1970s led by the work of Kenneth Waltz (1979). The term structural realism is preferred by those who seek to widen Waltz's analysis so that it can be combined with work in the liberal tradition that focuses on economic relations, regimes and international society (Buzan, Jones and Little, 1993), though the lines of identity here are not yet settled at the time of writing. Neo-realism was the counter-attack in this intellectual joust. It abandoned the conservative assumptions about human nature that underpinned classical realism, and reasserted the logic of power politics on the firmer foundation of anarchic structure. It defended the centrality of the state, and especially of great powers, exposing the partiality of some interdependence views of international relations, and reaffirming the primacy of American power in the international system. Its success was much aided by the onset of the so-called 'Second Cold War' in 1979, which caught off balance many of the advocates of interdependence and transnationalism, especially those who were still confidently generating explanations premised on the progressive redundancy of force in international relations and the fragmentation of state power. Work emerging from those perspectives during the 1980s in many instances bore more than traces of theoretical and methodological reassessment deriving from Waltz's critique (Gilpin, 1987; Keohane, 1984).

With the ending of the Cold War one might have expected another crisis for realism. Just as it had fed off the supporting realities of the Second World War and the Cold War, so realism might have been vulnerable to the ending of ideological and military rivalry between the superpowers. But although strategic studies has been hard hit, and has had to scramble to find a new and broader security agenda, realism is in pretty good shape, and remains the cornerstone of much theoretical debate within the discipline. It has largely come to terms with International Political Economy (IPE) (Gilpin, 1981, 1987), and has made partial common cause with neo-liberal institutionalism in pursuit both of a narrow rationalist agenda about the causes and conditions of co-operation under anarchy (Wæver in this volume; Niou and Ordeshook, 1994), and in the study of hegemony theory (Keohane, 1984; Grunberg, 1990). Of course important differences still remain: liberals see co-operation as potentially transforming of both states and the international system, whereas realists have a more restricted view of co-operation, and a much more restricted one of progress. As the dark side of the demise of communist power comes to the surface, much in the realist canon is being reaffirmed, though liberals can also point to impressive levels of institution-building. One new challenge comes from radical reflectivism, much of which takes its cue from post-modern forms of analysis, which eschew positivist logic and focus on language as the medium through which reality is constructed (Wæver, this volume). Another comes from global environmental concern whose very nature transcends the framework of state action and power politics.

The distinguishing features of realism

Realism in all of its forms emphasises the continuities of the human condition, particularly at the international level. Classical realists, most notably Morgenthau, tended to find the source of these continuities in the permanence of human nature as reflected in the political construction of states. Neo-realists find them in the anarchic structure of the international system, which they see as a vital and historically enduring force that shapes the behaviour and construction of states. On the basis of these continuities, realists see insecurity, and particularly military insecurity, as the central problem, and power as the prime motivation or driving force of all political life. Their analytical focus is on the political group rather than on the individual, and because it commands power, especially military power, most effectively, the key human political group is the state, whether understood as tribe, city-state, or national state. Because relations between states are insecurity-driven, and because the anarchic structure provides few constraints on states pursuing power to the best of their ability, realism emphasises the competitive and conflictual side of international relations. This is reflected in its core ideas, like the balance of power, which is one of the most long-standing analytical tools of realism, and the security dilemma, which provides the essential link between realism and strategic studies.

This focus on power politics provides the apparent continuity of the realist tradition, but continuity is not necessarily accompanied by intellectual coherence. Walker's critique exposes both static, structural, and dynamic, historical lines within the realist discourse (Walker, 1987). In addition, the concept of power lacks any agreed definition, and therefore encompasses a very wide range of quite different under-standings of what 'power politics' might mean (Nye, 1990; Stoll and Ward, 1989; Guzzini, 1993). Indeed, it is perhaps not going too far to say that the *debate* about power in international relations is the core of what realism is about. Its emphasis on the state derives from the sense that the state is the dominant wielder of power in the international system. Realism thus has not been, and may never be, either a single scientific approach or a single coherent theory. Power in its political sense will probably never be measurable, and consequently the idea of balance of power cannot be operationalised. Realism is not the only body of thought that focuses on power: Marxism and feminism also do, and they too have to deal with having an amorphous idea at their core. Having a debate rather than a hard concept at the core of one's analysis is offensive to positivists, but not difficult to live with for those of less rigorous (or less narrow) epistemological persuasion. Different conceptualisations of power will continue to lead to different explanations of events. Beneath the apparently smooth surface of realism lies not a single linear theory handed down from ancient times, but an ever-changing discourse about the nature, application and effect of power in an ever-changing historical environment.

It is clear that realism as a whole does not privilege any one level of analysis. Classical realists, most notably Morgenthau, emphasise the roots of power politics in human nature. Neo-realists focus on structure at the system level, but even Waltz freely acknowledges that this mode of analysis has to be accompanied by a unit level theory in order to get a complete explanation of events (Waltz, 1979, pp. 48–9, 78, 87, 126; 1986, pp. 328, 343). At the unit level, realists of all sorts give primacy to the state as opposed to other units, but it is not a characteristic of realism to treat the unit level itself as prime. Realism operates on all three levels – system, unit and individual (and on the sub-levels between them – sub-systemic/regional, bureaucratic), though it does favour the top and bottom ones. It should not be forgotten that the arch neo-realist Waltz is the author of a study in comparative foreign policy making (1967). One of the bitterest arguments within the discipline of International Relations has been between those stressing the importance of the system level as the key generator of behaviour (mostly neo-realists, but also varieties of liberals and Marxists), and those arguing in favour of the unit level (mostly foreign policy analysts) (Buzan, 1994; Rosenberg, 1990).

This eclectic attitude towards levels is not paralleled when it comes to sectors. Here realists of nearly all stripes privilege the military/political sector as opposed to the economic, societal or environmental ones. Most realists, both classical and neo (and with the notable exception of E. H. Carr), explicitly conceive(d) of themselves as political theorists. Note the titles of realism's two most famous texts: *Politics Among Nations*, and *Theory of International Politics*. Yet paradoxically, realists have borrowed methodology from economics in order to try to establish a distinctively political domain of theory, either explicitly, as Waltz (1979, pp. 89–94), or implicitly, as in the striking parallel between Morgenthau's rational actor pursuing 'interest defined as power' (1978, p. 5) and the assumptions about utility maximising individuals in economic theory. Both Morgenthau (1978, pp. 12–14) and Waltz (1979, p. 79) insist on the distinctiveness and separateness of the political realm. This obsession is both a cause and an effect of their preoccupation with the state and the dynamics of power, though one has also to read into this the peculiar effects of academic politics, and the fragmentation of the social sciences into organisationally distinct disciplines. Whether this obsession with the distinctiveness of politics is a necessary feature of realism, or merely a historical one, is an important question for understanding the potential scope of realism (Buzan, Jones and Little, 1993, esp. ch. 1). The borrowing of methodology from economics already opens a breach in the political dyke. I see no reason why the logic of power, self-interest and conflict cannot run in other sectors, nor, indeed, why the state should be seen as exclusively political. In my view, International Relations is a multi-disciplinary enterprise, and so is realism. The post-Cold War fate of realism's companion field, strategic studies, is perhaps suggestive of the possibilities. Having lost its military/nuclear focus, strategic studies is now busy metamorphosing into Security Studies, in the process picking up a multi-sectoral agenda that ranges from economic theory, through identity and society, to the environment. In this perspective, the more open, multi-sectoral, part of the realist tradition represented by Carr has more to offer to the future than that represented by either Morgenthau or Waltz.

Partly because of its political obsessions realism has, as brilliantly argued by Walker, constructed an 'inside/outside' view of the human condition (Walker, 1993). Inside the state there is relative order and peace. Change is expected in the form of development and progress, and because of this time is a meaningful measure of difference. Outside, in the realm between states, anarchy, disorder and war reign. This structure reproduces itself endlessly so that there is no progress, and time does not signify change. The inside and outside realms are each constructed by the other, making the whole assemblage extremely difficult to undo or escape from, both intellectually and practically (Hansen, 1996). The power of this separation practically defines the discipline of International Relations, and goes a long way towards explaining the durability of realism as its dominant orthodoxy. It also explains a persistent and potent two-pronged critique of realism. Firstly, critics argue that many states are too weak and ill-formed to sustain the inside–outside distinction. Somalia and Rwanda are only the latest in a long line of examples where the inside looks more like the outside is supposed to be. Secondly, critics argue that the state is now so penetrated by transnational actors and forces that the inside–outside distinction has become a meaningless blur. The question here is not whether these arguments are empirically sound: they are. Rather it is whether or not they undermine the realist model of world politics as an anarchic system of states. As any economist knows, simplifying models can tolerate a lot of deviance before they become useless as a way of understanding a complex reality. Walker's analysis also clarifies what otherwise seems a paradoxical view of history in realism. On the one hand, realists look to history, both intellectual and actual, to justify the permanence of power politics. But on the other hand, most strongly in the neo-realist tradition, they seem to deny history any autonomy, replacing it with the omnipresent operation of structural forces that are said to work identically in all times and places throughout history.

The focus on insecurity, power, the state and conflictual relations has for long made realism the target of a normative critique. Where realists see themselves as rationally pursuing the goal of studying what is (no matter how nasty it may be), both traditional idealists (mostly peace researchers and liberals) and various post-modernists see them as being an active part of the processes they describe. One way of seeing this issue is through Cox's distinction between 'problem-solving' theories, such as realism, which seek to work within the existing framework, and 'critical' theories which seek opportunities to change the existing framework (Cox, 1986). This means that far from being objective observers, realists in general, and the practitioners of strategic studies in particular, are accused of helping to legitimise and reproduce the hierarchical structures and conflictual relations that they talk about. By sanctifying in theory states, conflict and power politics, realists help to create self-fulfilling prophecies. If people believe that power is the key to human relations, then they will tend to behave in ways that make it so. This tension between the need to study what is, and the danger of reproducing it by doing so, is unresolvable. Although learning does occur, the essential dilemma is reproduced in each successive generation of people studying international relations. It is perhaps the main key to understanding the persistence not only of realism, but also of the dialectic between conservatives and radicals within the discipline (whatever their methodology) in each generation.

In methodological terms, realist analysis tends to model the state as a unitary rational actor operating under conditions of insecurity and imperfect information. In this both classical realism and neo-realism borrow consciously from microeconomic theory, seeing states as analogous to firms, anarchic structure as analogous to market structure, and power as analogous to utility. This analogy suggests a commitment to positivism, and there is indeed a strong thread of positivism in realism. But on this as on other methodological issues, realism, like most of International Relations, is divided and frequently confused. Because his concept of power was unamenable to measurement, Morgenthau did not conceive of realism as reducible to positivist science (Gellman, 1988, pp. 262–3). Waltz appears to want to go down the positivist route, but as Jones argues, is unable to complete the journey that he starts (Buzan, Jones and Little, 1993, part III).

Because the concept of power lacks a broad, quantifiable (if crude) indicator of the type that money is for wealth, it has so far proved impervious to quantification. Realism has therefore not had much opportunity to follow economics down the mathematical road. But inability to quantify key concepts has not much affected realism's commitment to the rationality assumption that it shares with economics. The assumption that actors are rational has been as prominent in realism as in economics, and for the same reason: without it there is no obvious way to model the behaviour of actors, and without models there is no obvious path towards coherent theory. Rational actor assumptions have been (notoriously) conspicuous in deterrence theory. They are also essential to the so-called 'neo-neo' synthesis (Wæver, this volume), and its use of game theory to investigate the logic of co-operation under anarchy. More broadly, the whole logic of power politics rests on the rationality assumption, albeit much tempered by imperfect information and the competing demands of domestic and international realms on the agents of the state. At bottom, the logic of power politics requires that statesmen (or more fashionably 'the agents of the state') do three things: observe and monitor the changing distribution of power; assess that distribution in terms of the threats it generates to their own interests and survival; and make policy within the limits of their resources and options so as to minimise their vulnerabilities and maximise their opportunities. Agents of the state who do not behave in this way risk elimination and replacement both of themselves and of their state by those that do. Rationality is thus not seen so much as a human attribute, but as a behaviourally engineered quality of actors within an anarchic political system.

The place of realism in the discipline of International Relations

Because realism has been seen as the dominant orthodoxy in International Relations since the Second World War, it has been, and remains, the favoured target of dissenters and radicals within the discourses of the discipline. But it is not wholly accurate to characterise realism in this way. In fact, the discipline is divided into a number of contending theoretical orientations, or paradigms, each of which represents an orthodoxy in its own right. There is some disagreement about how to classify and label these paradigms (see Wæver in this volume). All agree that realism is one, and most agree that liberalism is another (though it may be labelled 'pluralism', 'functionalism' or 'Kantianism'), and Marxism (or 'socialism') a third. The so-called 'English school' offers Grotianism (or 'international society') as a possible fourth, and their view is distinct enough from both realism and liberalism to warrant separate status. These paradigms are distinguished from each other mostly by what they choose to place at the centre of attention. They are distinct from the methodological debates about traditionalism, behaviouralism and post-modernism: it is possible to follow any one of these methodologies and still be a realist (or a liberal or whatever). All of the paradigms involve different normative predispositions, and in some cases (most notably liberalism and Marxism) reflect explicit ideological positions. Realism is not an ideological position as such (i.e. it does not necessarily represent a value preference), but it is the natural home of those disposed towards conservative ideology. Paradigms are schools of thought that have been built up by approaching the study of international relations in ways that favour some levels, sectors and norms over others. Each paradigm is a kind of composite lens, giving a selective view of international relations. Like any lens, looking through it makes some features stand out more strongly while pushing others into the background. This division has its uses, but like all academic specialisation, also leads to a certain amount of wasteful argument about boundaries, and unhelpful breaking up of subjects. Table 2.1 offers a crude suggestion as to what comes clearly into view, and what normative and political preferences shape that view, when one looks through these lenses.

Most of the work in International Relations can be located within one or another of these paradigms, though individuals often cross boundaries. Although all of the paradigms see the state as a unit, some do so much more clearly or exclusively than others. There is more disagreement on structure and process, and a very strong normative differentiation. Realism and Grotianism are located largely in the military and political sectors, though Grotianism has more overlaps into the economic and societal ones. Liberalism is centred in the economic sector with overlaps into political and societal, and Marxism covers both the societal and economic sectors. The paradigms are not mutually exclusive in any total way, though the core of each is distinct. Some realists and some liberals claim to include Grotianism as part of their paradigm. Marxism can be seen as a response to the logic and normative assertions of liberalism, which in return can be seen as a response to the logic and values of realism. International Political Economy (IPE) is a conscious attempt to fuse together major elements of all four paradigms, though this has succumbed to rifts among liberals, realists and Marxists (Gilpin, 1987, ch. 2).

One of the reasons why realism has remained central within the discipline, despite the numerous attacks upon it, is its relative success not only in revising and reinventing itself, but also in establishing an indispensable relevance for its perspective within the other paradigms. The liberal assault of the 1970s quite quickly had to abandon its 'sovereignty at bay' thesis in the face of the robustness of the state. Interdependence became not a substitute for power politics but a new framework for it. The idea that force was losing its relevance in inter-national relations proved to be an insight of Western rather than of global significance. Liberals increasingly accepted that the realist/neo-realist framework was an essential part of the picture. The whole field of IPE is an example of this synthesis, and even the neo-liberal institutionalist debate about co-operation under anarchy is being conducted largely within neo-realist assumptions about states and international system structure. At the risk of some exaggeration, it could be said that since the 1970s, liberalism has shifted its position from being an assault on realism, to being an extension of the realist framework into other sectors.

Table 2.1 *The inter-paradigm debate in International Relations*

Paradigm	Units	System structure	Process	Leading norms
	What one sees			
realism	– states – nations – (IGOs)	– anarchy	– struggle for power – security dilemma	– autonomy – security – balance of power – rationality – national interest
Grotianism	– states – civilisations – IGOs	– anarchy	– international society and regimes – balance of power	– international order and law – sovereignty – national self-determination
liberalism	– individuals – firms – IGOs – (states) – (nations) – (NGOs)	– market – (anarchy)	– world society – interdependence	– freedom – human rights – cosmopolitanism – co-operation – prosperity
Marxism	– classes – (states) – social movements – firms (MNCs)	– capitalism	– class struggle – language/discourse	– justice – equality – progress

Nothing could symbolise this more sharply than the title of Keohane and Nye's seminal 1977 book *Power and Interdependence*. The two main exceptions to this are: first the argument about the relative significance of units, with most liberals still much more inclined than realists to give more weight to multi-national firms and banks *vis-à-vis* the state (Stopford and Strange, 1991); and second, the assumptions about war, with liberals being much more confident that the regular recurrence of war can be broken.

Idealism more generally has lost some of its critical force against realism. Major schisms, such as the revolt of peace research during the 1950s, 1960s and 1970s against both realism and strategic studies have largely been healed. The peace research agenda has steadily merged into Security Studies, along the way adopting many aspects of neo-realist analysis. Although it remains organisationally, and to some extent normatively and philosophically, distinct, the merger of agendas means that there is not now much sense that it is primarily an oppositional exercise to realism.

Marxism, which along with liberalism provides the main underpinning for idealist thinking about international relations, has also accommodated with realism in a variety of important ways. Although remaining normatively and philosophically distinct, Marxist thinking now accepts some key aspects of the realist agenda. It has steadily accepted the relative autonomy of the state *vis-à-vis* class analysis, and in some branches of Marxian-inspired work (most notably historical sociology) the state has become the central object of enquiry. Because of its emphasis on hierarchy, power and struggle, Marxism was always open to many aspects of realist analysis despite its hostility to the state. Lenin's work on Imperialism is nothing if not a monument to the idea of the struggle for power as the driving force of international relations. Carr stands as an early testimony to compatibilities in realist and Marxist analysis.

The Grotian paradigm never had the quality of direct opposition to realism. As Little (1994) makes clear, its methodological assumption was that any system of states would display three qualities or elements: Hobbesian (realist) power politics; Grotian (English school) international society; and Kantian (liberal) world society. These qualities exist simultaneously, side-by-side, the question being what the relative strength among them was for any given time and place. Grotianism thus incorporates both the realist and the liberal positions, but seeks to interpose between them a third position based on the idea that states do construct orders amongst themselves. It is possible to link the idea of international society to neo-realist theory, seeing it in the same way as the balance of power, as a structurally generated consequence of both anarchic and hierarchic relations (Buzan, 1993).

In the same way that it has been able to accommodate, penetrate or absorb other paradigms, or at least create common ground with them, so also has realism been able to come to terms with, or outlast, methodological challenges. Neo-realism was in part a response to the behavioural challenge for more scientific method in International Relations. It can be argued (Buzan, Jones and Little, 1993, part III) that Waltz's response to this challenge was flawed. But it did suffice to hold the line, and in the meantime, the challenge from behaviouralism waned as the problems of applying positivist methods to social science began to be exposed. Traditionalists mounted an effective opposition, and now the behaviouralist project itself is under attack from post-modernism.

Post-modernists have adopted a 'tous azimuts' offensive against most aspects of International Relations (and much else), which also brings realism within their sights. But in principle, there is no reason why much of the post-modern discourse cannot eventually be merged into realism. There are traditions within realism that are receptive to the idea of language as power, and discourse as a major key to politics (Carr, 1946; Manning, 1962), and much of the post-modern debate is precisely concerned with issues of power, hierarchy and domination that are congenial to the realist tradition. Post-modernists such as Ashley and Der Derian have flirted with realism, registering a preference for the classical versus the neo version (Ashley, 1986; Der Derian, 1987). Wæver has gone further, actually constructing himself as a post-structuralist realist (Wæver, 1989a and b). As shown by Wæver's work, and by Jones's critique and reformulation of Waltz's analogy of international relations with economics (Buzan, Jones and Little, 1993, part III), post-modern approaches can be constructively at home right in the heart of realist theory. Because most methodologies can be applied to the realist agenda, realism has an inbuilt methodological eclecticism that keeps it relatively safe from epistemological attack.

The timeless wisdom of realism?

In sum, the insights of realism are substantial, though they are not as timeless or as uniformly distributed as some neo-realists would like to think. The common realist assumption that the basic structure and dynamics of international relations has remained unchanged through history survives mainly because almost nobody in the field has done the historical research which might put it to the test. At best there is a certain amount of selective raiding, looking for cases such as classical Greece, the 'Warring States' period in China, and Renaissance Italy, which do reproduce the anarchic quality of modern European inter-national relations. But a longer and more coherent historical perspective raises many questions about this image of the past (Buzan and Little, 1994; Watson, 1992). For most of history anarchic structure is not the prevailing organisation of international relations, balance of power is not the dominant behaviour, and units are neither structurally nor functionally alike within the system. Much of history is populated by international systems in which units are both structurally unlike (city-states, empires, barbarian tribes, national states) and functionally unlike (the unequal relations between suzerain and vassal units). Within these systems, balance of power behaviour is regularly overridden by successful empires that unify whole systems for extended periods (Rome, China, Persia, Ottomans), in the process creating structures that have strong hierarchic elements. Any attempt to understand this history cannot avoid the fact that when units are functionally and structurally differentiated, domestic structure plays at least as big a role as international structure in shaping state behaviour. If one takes the trouble to look at it, history is considerably more diverse than many realists suppose. At best it says that an anarchic, balance of power system populated by sovereign 'states' is one of the models for international relations that recurs in many different times and places.

With that qualification in mind, it also has to be said that other aspects of the realist canon do seem to have a timeless quality. No matter what the structure, or how differentiated the units, power politics, the logic of survival, and the dynamics of (in)security do seem to be universally relevant to international relations. At any period of history it is very hard to escape from the fact that the major powers do play the central role in defining international political and economic order. When great empires controlled the territory stretching from the Mediterranean to China, trade flourished. When those empires collapsed, trade was largely destroyed by the ensuing disorder. This tale can be told for dozens of different times and locations. Thus while the particular circumstances and conditions of history change from era to era, there does seem to be a certain continuity to some aspects of political life.

This aspect of realism's claim to timeless wisdom has been affirmed over the last couple of decades by the work done in historical sociology. In what amounts almost to an unintentional thought experiment, several historical sociologists writing macro-historical studies (Giddens, 1985; Mann, 1986; Tilly, 1990; Anderson, 1974a, 1974b; Gellner, 1988; and Hall and Ikenberry, 1989), have come to analytical conclusions remarkably similar to a rather crude view of classical realism. Few of these writers had much awareness of the realist tradition in international relations, yet all focus on war as crucial to the evolution of the modern state. One of their common themes is that the state makes war, and war makes the state (Tilly, 1990). Once centralised, mostly city-based, forms of political and economic order were invented, war became a regular feature of the human condition. War not only built empires and extended trade routes, it also shaped the internal development of states right down to the present day. Units that could not play successfully in this vicious game were steadily driven out of existence by those that could, with more primitive forms surviving only by dint of being located well outside the main arenas of civilisation. The question that animated most of these historical sociologists was the nature of the state. The result of their enquiries has been to support a harsh, social Darwinistic, interpretation of international history that shares much with the main assumptions of realism.

One even finds powerful echoes of this understanding in the writing of that most determined of liberal polemicists, Francis Fukuyama (1992, pp. 73–4):

The possibility of war is a great force for the rationalization of societies, and for the creation of uniform social structures across cultures. Any state that hopes to maintain its political autonomy is forced to adopt the technology of its enemies and rivals. More than that, however, the threat of war forces states to restructure their social systems along lines most conducive to producing and deploying technology. For example, states must be of a certain size in order to compete with their neighbors, which creates powerful incentives for national unity; they must be able to mobilize resources on a national level which requires the creation of a strong centralized state authority with the power of taxation and regulation; they must break down various forms of regional, religious, and kinship ties which potentially obstruct national unity; they must increase educational levels in order to produce an elite capable of disposing of technology; they must maintain contact with and awareness of developments taking place beyond their borders; and, with the introduction of mass armies during the Napoleonic Wars, they must at least open the door to the enfranchisement of the poorer classes of their societies if they are to be capable of total mobilization. All of these developments could occur for other motives – for example, economic ones – but war frames the need for social mobilization in a particularly acute way and provides an unambiguous test of its success.

Realism also finds seemingly endless affirmation in current events. One of its attractions, for some, is that it gives an odds on advantage to those who make gloomy predictions (i.e. more power politics, more conflict) about the future. Much of realism can be read as a sophisticated form of fatalism, and as Fukuyama (1992, p. 70) notes: 'a naive optimist whose expectations are belied appears foolish, while a pessimist proven wrong maintains an aura of profundity and seriousness'. The dialectics of order and conflict in the three world wars (two hot, one cold) of the twentieth century provide a good illustration of how current events reinforce realist pessimism. The wars themselves of course supported the realist view, as did their outcomes. Even the unusual Cold War can be seen as a classic demonstration of neo-realist power politics, with the unsuccessful challenger imploding, and its successors desperately trying to reform themselves on the model of the victors. The short-lived periods of euphoria following each war nourished more optimistic projections, but in each case the fairly rapid reassertion of power politics – the challenge of the fascist powers, the Cold War, the 'new world disorder' – reinforced realist views. This argument raises again the normative critique of realism: is it a rational response to observation, or does it block the path by which hope might triumph over experience? Even within the twentieth century, some learning has taken place, and significant restraints on the resort to force have developed for at least some of the states in the international system (James, 1992; Zacher, 1992). But there is still a very long way to go before power politics is expunged from human affairs. Although some of its old forms become less important, its basic logic seems to recur in a wide variety of historical conditions. The three tiers of the English school provide a useful way of looking at this dialectic. The Hobbesian, Grotian and Kantian dynamics all coexist but their proportions change. Grotius and Kant may have made some progress, but Hobbes still stands solidly in the background, and in many parts of the world indeed in the foreground.

In addition to the affirmations of realism by both past and present evidence, it also retains a powerful, and often neglected, normative attraction of its own. Realism can be taken as standing for an anarchic ordering of world politics. It can therefore be read as being in favour of such values as ideological and cultural diversity, political independence and self-reliance, and economic decentralisation. It can be seen as supporting political fragmentation (between states, but not within them) as the preferred expression of a human historical legacy of geographic, ethnic and cultural diversity. It can be taken as being against central-isation, whether imperial or federative, and political or economic; against cultural cosmopolitanism; and against homogenisation of the human race, both ethnic and cultural. In its normative clothes, realism reflects a preference for 'inside/outside' constructions of human life rather than attempts to construct some form of universalist 'inside'. It worries more about the costs and dangers of insecurity within hierarchy (tyranny, struggles over control, bureaucratisation), than about those under anarchy (security dilemma, war) (Waltz, 1979, pp. 111–14).

I also find realism intellectually attractive. As I hope is demonstrated in *The Logic of Anarchy*, realism possesses a *relative* (not absolute) intel-lectual coherence. It provides a solid starting point for the construction of grand theory, and as far as I can tell, allows sufficient flexibility to integrate main lines of argument from most other paradigms. Realism is a broad church. Its core ideas about power, struggle, domination and insecurity cross cultural boundaries more easily than those of its main rival, liberalism. Note how easily these ideas fit into the analysis of concerns as diverse as gender (see Enloe, this volume) and class (Marx and Engels, 1848). By contrast, many of the core ideas of liberalism, though unquestionably powerful and pertinent, seem more specifically to be bound into the Western cultural tradition. Although the market has now come close to achieving universal cross-cultural status, individualism, human rights and co-operation seem much more contested, much more like a new imperial 'standard of civilisation' than like a universal truth.

So why do I call myself a realist? Three reasons, not in order of priority. First, to provoke. I hope to make those both inside and outside realism reconsider the meaning and validity of their own labels. Second, to reduce fruitless conflicts within the discipline by working towards more unified theoretical frameworks. By expanding the logic of realism from within I hope both to broaden the perceptions of those within realist orthodoxy, and build bridges to those who, it seems to me, are unnecessarily outside it. Realism seems to me to be the most promising framework for this campaign, though I freely confess a bias in favour of top-down approaches to understanding that may not be shared by others. Third, is a matter of being consistent with my own feelings and beliefs. I remain firmly convinced that realism is the soundest starting place for constructing an understanding of international relations, and for building grand theory. Like it or not, it does reveal the foundations on which we have to build if we want to construct anything durable. I do, however, believe, both for theory and for practice, in the possibility of building something that rises well above the primitive and permanent nastiness of raw power politics. My sense is that for all its limitations and difficulties, this rather bleak and rocky terrain is firmer ground than sites which may initially look more attractive, but which will not support the ambitious structures that some want to construct on them. But perhaps I am just a fatalist with an unrequited streak of idealism.

NOTE

I am grateful to Lene Hansen, Richard Little, B. A. Roberson, Ole Wæver, Jaap de Wilde, Mark Zacher and the editors for comments on an earlier draft of this chapter

REFERENCES

Anderson, Perry (1974a), *Passages from Antiquity to Feudalism* (London: Verso).
  (1974b), *Lineages of the Absolutist State* (London: Verso).
Ashley, Richard (1986), 'The Poverty of Neorealism', in R. O. Keohane (ed.), *Neorealism and its Critics*, pp. 255–300.
Bull, Hedley (1977), *The Anarchical Society* (London: Macmillan).
Burton, John (1972), *World Society* (Cambridge: Cambridge University Press).
Buzan, Barry (1987), *An Introduction to Strategic Studies: Military Technology and International Relations* (London: Macmillan).
  (1993), 'From International System to International Society: Structural Realism and Regime Theory Meet the English School', *International Organization*, 47 (3), pp. 327–52.

(1994), 'The Level of Analysis Problem in International Relations Reconsidered', in Ken Booth and Steve Smith (eds.), *International Political Theory Today* (London: Polity Press), pp. 198–216.

Buzan, Barry, Jones, Charles and Little, Richard (1993), *The Logic of Anarchy: Neorealism to Structural Realism* (New York: Columbia University Press).

Buzan, Barry and Little, Richard (1994), 'The Idea of International System: Theory Meets History', *International Political Science Review*, 15 (3), pp. 231–56.

Carr, E. H. (1946 [1939]), *The Twenty Years' Crisis, 1919–1939: An Introduction to the Study of International Relations* (London: Macmillan).

Cox, Robert W. (1986), 'Social Forces, States and World Orders: Beyond International Relations Theory', in R. O. Keohane (ed.), *Neorealism and its Critics*, pp. 204–54.

Der Derian, James (1987), *On Diplomacy* (Oxford: Blackwell).

Fukuyama, Francis (1992), *The End of History and the Last Man* (London: Penguin).

Gellman, Peter (1988), 'Hans J. Morgenthau and the Legacy of Political Realism', *Review of International Studies*, 14 (4), pp. 247–66.

Gellner, Ernest (1988), *Plough, Book and Sword: The Structure of Human History* (London: Paladin).

Giddens, Anthony (1985), *The Nation-State and Violence* (Cambridge: Polity Press).

Gilpin, Robert (1981), *War and Change in World Politics* (Cambridge: Cambridge University Press).

(1987), *The Political Economy of International Relations* (Princeton: Princeton University Press).

Grunberg, Isabelle (1990), 'Exploring the "myth" of Hegemonic Stability', *International Organization*, 44 (4), pp. 431–77.

Guzzini, Stefano (1993), 'Structural Power: The Limits of Neorealist Power Analysis', *International Organization*, 47 (3), pp. 443–78.

Hall, John and Ikenberry, G. J. (1989), *The State* (Milton Keynes: Open University Press).

Hansen, Lene (1996), 'Deconstructing a Discipline: R. J. B. Walker and International Relations', in Ole Wæver and Iver Neumann (eds.), *Masters in the Making* (London: Routledge).

Herz, John (1951), *Political Realism and Political Idealism* (Chicago: University of Chicago Press).

James, Alan (1992), 'The Equality of States: Contemporary Manifestations of an Ancient Doctrine', *Review of International Studies*, 18 (4), pp. 377–92.

Keohane, Robert O. (1984), *After Hegemony: Cooperation and Discord in the World Political Economy* (Princeton: Princeton University Press).

Keohane, Robert O. (ed.) (1986), *Neorealism and its Critics* (New York: Columbia University Press).

Keohane, Robert O. and Nye, Joseph (1977), *Power and Independence* (Boston: Little Brown).

Krasner, Stephen (ed.) (1983), *International Regimes* (London: Cornell University Press).

Little, Richard (1994), 'Neorealism and the English School: A Methodological, Ontological and Theoretical Reassessment', unpublished manuscript.

Mann, Michael (1986), *The Sources of Social Power* (Cambridge: Cambridge University Press).

Manning, C. A. W. (1962), *The Nature of International Society* (London: LSE).

Marx, Karl and Engels, Frederick (1947 [1848]), *Communist Manifesto* (Chicago: Kerr).

McKinlay, Robert D. and Little, Richard (1986), *Global Problems and World Order* (London: Pinter).

Morgenthau, Hans (1978), *Politics Among Nations*, 5th edition (New York: Knopf).

Niou, Emerson and Ordeshook, Peter (1994), ' "Less Filling, Tastes Great": The Realist-Neoliberal Debate', *World Politics*, 46 (2), pp. 209–34.

Nye, J. S. (1990), 'The Changing Nature of World Power', *Political Science Quarterly*, 105 (2), pp. 177–92.

Rosenberg, Justin (1990), 'What's the Matter with Realism?', *Review of International Studies*, 16 (4), pp. 285–303.

Stoll, Richard and Ward, Michael (eds.) (1989), *Power in World Politics* (Boulder, CO: Lynne Rienner).

Stopford, John M. and Strange, Susan (1991), *Rival States, Rival Firms: Competition for World Market Shares* (Cambridge: Cambridge University Press).

Tilly, Charles (1990), *Coercion, Capital and European States AD 990–1990* (Oxford: Blackwell).

Wæver, Ole (1989a), 'Beyond the "Beyond" of Critical International Theory', *Working Paper 1/1989* (Copenhagen: Centre for Peace and Conflict Research).

(1989b), 'Tradition and Transgression in International Relations: A Post-Ashleyan Position', *Working Paper 24/1989* (Copenhagen: Centre for Peace and Conflict Research), forthcoming in Mark Hoffman and Nick Rengger (eds.), *Beyond the Inter-Paradigm Debate* (Hemel Hempstead: Harvester Wheatsheaf).

Walker, R. J. B. (1987), 'Realism, Change and International Political Theory', *International Studies Quarterly*, 31, pp. 65–84.

(1993), *Inside/Outside: International Relations as Political Theory* (Cambridge: Cambridge University Press).

Waltz, Kenneth N. (1967), *Foreign Policy and Democratic Politics* (Boston: Little Brown).

(1979), *Theory of International Politics* (Reading: Addison-Wesley).

(1986), 'Reflections on Theory of International Politics: A Response to My Critics', in R. O. Keohane (ed.), *Neorealism and its Critics*, pp. 322–46.

Watson, Adam (1992), *The Evolution of International Society* (London: Routledge).

Wight, Martin (1977), *Systems of States* (Leicester: Leicester University Press).

Zacher, Mark (1992), 'The Decaying Pillars of the Westphalian Temple: Implications for International Order and Governance', in James N. Rosenau and Ernst-Otto Czempiel (eds.), *Governance Without Government: Order and Change in World Politics* (Cambridge: Cambridge University Press).

3   The growing relevance of pluralism?

Richard Little

During the late 1960s and throughout the 1970s it began to be argued in the field of International Relations that the nature of international politics and the structure of the international system was undergoing a transformation. It was argued, in particular, that the division between international and domestic politics was breaking down and that, as a consequence, not only were the boundaries separating states dissolving, but also, that international politics was becoming domesticated in the process (Hanreider, 1978; Morse, 1970; Wagner, 1974). These developments were associated specifically with the evolution of transnationalism and interdependence and the analysts who focused on these putatively new features of the international system came to be labelled as pluralists. Initially, pluralists asserted that because state boundaries were becoming increasingly permeable it was no longer possible to understand international relations simply by studying the interactions among governments. Pluralists wished to focus on all the transactions which take place across state boundaries and many were committed to the view that these transactions would envelop states generating what Haas (1969) called a 'tangle of hope' within which it would be increasingly difficult for states to engage in war.

As well as providing the foundations for a new approach to the study of international politics this emerging school of thought was seen simultaneously to be mounting a significant attack on realism, widely considered to provide the dominant perspective on international relations. Although pluralist thought has evolved and diversified in subsequent years the one thing that pluralists continue to assert is that realism cannot provide an adequate account of contemporary international relations; its perspective is considered anachronistic and over-simplified. Realists were criticised initially for working on the basis of what Wolfers dubbed a 'billiard ball' model of the multi-state system, with the state being depicted as 'a closed, impermeable, and sovereign unit' (1962, p. 19). Later, however, the criticism was redirected and centred on the realists' preoccupation with the competitive relationship among these units generated by the attempt to maintain their autonomy. There was particular concern with Waltz's (1979) argument that the competition was structurally determined.

From the pluralist perspective, therefore, the realists adhered to a conception of international politics which could not begin to accommodate the growing complexities of the modern world. The pluralists saw it as an immediate priority to displace the billiard ball view of the international system and they began to draw on an alternative set of metaphors often representing world politics in terms of 'cobwebs' (Burton, 1968) which were seen to stretch across traditional state boundaries, linking together a complex array of interest groups and blurring or obscuring state boundaries in the process. It was this metaphor which was initially considered to provide the defining characteristic of pluralism.

Pluralists asserted that transnationalism and interdependence were global forces, but in practice, most of their analysis focused on developments in the Western hemisphere. They were primarily concerned with the role played by these global forces in the consolidation of a liberal world order, although it was accepted that the Soviet Union and its allies were successfully managing to prevent the web of pluralistic politics from being spun across the globe. After 1991, however, with the reputed death of communism, there seemed at first nothing to prevent the emergence of a world-wide liberal order (Fukuyama, 1992). As a consequence, it appeared as if pluralists would come to provide the dominant perspective on international relations by the end of the twentieth century.

But such an assessment is challenged in this chapter. Although there is no doubt that the pluralist perspective has become increasingly relevant during the course of the century, this has not been at the expense of other perspectives, and, in particular, realism. On the contrary, it will be argued that pluralism has become, over time, increasingly intermeshed with realism, and indeed it can be suggested that the evolution of pluralist thought can be related to the realist reaction to developments in international relations. Providing a description of this evolving relationship, however, is more difficult than might appear at first sight because it is only now beginning to be recognised that the historiography of political science and international relations is very underdeveloped (Gunnell, 1991; Schmidt, 1994). Although it has often been acknowledged that after 1945 the historiography of international relations was effectively hijacked and shaped to demonstrate the importance and relevance of realism, very little has been done to rectify this interpretation of how the discipline has evolved. According to the realists, for twenty years after the First World War, when the institutionalised study of international relations is considered to have initially taken root, the inchoate discipline is depicted as being held in the grip of idealists searching for blueprints to prevent the recurrence of another world war. But with the outbreak of the Second World War, the (self-styled) realists are depicted as pushing the idealists to one side on the grounds that, unlike idealists, the realists were willing to discuss the ineliminable role of power in international politics. In the 1960s, however, the realists themselves came under attack from the new breed of pluralists who were anxious to replace realism with a new approach.

This image of the discipline undergoing paradigmatic shifts resonated in the 1970s with Kuhn's (1970) account of how progress has been made in the natural sciences. The pluralists, anxious to follow in the wake of natural science, used Kuhn's ideas to account for the historical dominance of realism and simultaneously to legitimise the need for a pluralist turn in the discipline (Vasquez, 1983). The attempt by the pluralists to oust realism failed however and during the 1980s pluralism represented one side in a three-cornered debate with realism and Marxism (Little, 1981).

Unlike realists and Marxists, however, the analysts who have been located in the pluralist camp rarely if ever identify themselves as pluralists. They were grouped together under this heading largely for the pedagogical purpose of demonstrating that the discipline could be meaningfully divided into competing perspectives. The label itself is drawn from political science. It applies to a school of thought that defines politics in terms of the interaction among competing interest groups and largely deprives the state of any independent status. Pluralists, therefore, can be considered to adhere to an essentially liberal and anti-realist view of the state. The label was intended to establish a link between the expanding body of theorists who were opposed to the realists' state-centric approach in international relations and the long-established school of pluralism in political science. Closer inspection reveals, moreover, that some of the early pluralists in political science had already recognised that the logic of their analysis had international implications and attempts had been made before the Second World War to develop a framework which embraced domestic and international politics (Fox, 1975). After the Second World War, however, a bifurcation occurred; pluralists in political science now focused exclusively on domestic politics and it was another two decades before a pluralist perspective took hold among specialists in international relations. Despite the historic links, however, no attempt was made by the new pluralists in international relations to establish contact with the pluralist school in political science. Nevertheless, the pluralist label helps to draw attention to both continuities and discontinuities in pluralist thought which have been essentially ignored in the established historiography of the discipline.

A serious disadvantage, however, does potentially flow from the use made of the pluralist label. The disadvantage becomes apparent when attention is focused on how the thinking of analysts, ostensibly within this school of thought, has evolved. By the 1980s, some erstwhile pluralists are found to be no longer interested in attacking the state-centric nature of realism, because they themselves are now working within a state-centric framework. It would appear that these former pluralists have shifted their position and moved into the realist camp. But this is denied; although now more sympathetic to realism, these analysts continue to insist that the realists have an overly-simplistic assessment of international politics. Attention is drawn, in particular, to the importance of international institutions in the conduct of international relations and the ex-pluralists are often identified as neo-liberals (Baldwin, 1993).

A re-examination of the pluralist literature in political science, however, opens up a line of argument which suggests that it is still appropriate to think of these neo-liberals as pluralists. Despite the longevity of the approach in political science, it has been argued that pluralists have consistently failed to develop a coherent theory of politics. Instead, pluralism is identified as an anti-theory, designed to counter the views of others, and in particular Marxists (Jordan, 1990). Pluralists have been intent on demonstrating that the state is not an institution which is available to be controlled by any particular group or ruling class. According to this assessment, therefore, pluralism does no more than provide a critique of various approaches to political science, without offering a coherent alternative. It is demonstrated in this chapter that a similar line of argument can be extended to analysts working within the pluralist tradition in international relations. Pluralism represents a counter to realism and it is not possible to understand the evolution of thought in international relations without examining the interaction between realism and pluralism.

The first section in this chapter examines the intellectual heritage of pluralism which has been largely obscured by the willingness of the discipline to accept the attachment of the idealist tag to this seminal literature. The second section looks at the bifurcation of the pluralist tradition after the Second World War, with political science and international relations developing along independent tracks. In the final section there is an attempt to explain why the pluralist perspective abandoned its attack on state-centrism and thereby undermined its initial *raison d'être*.

The intellectual heritage of pluralism

To trace the intellectual heritage of pluralism it is necessary first to cut through the dense foliage of long-established views about the evolution of the discipline. Schmidt (1994) has started this task by questioning the familiar assertion that the institutionalised study of international relations was occasioned by the reaction of academics to the horror of the First World War. Schmidt argues that international politics was officially recognised as a section of the American Political Science Association as early as 1903. The precise date when international relations emerged as an independent field of study, however, is less important than the way that literature surrounding this development has been interpreted subsequently. It has become almost axiomatic to characterise this literature as idealist in form. But as Wilde (1991) has argued, a closer examination of some of the key writers of this period demonstrates that they were, in fact, precursors of the contemporary pluralists, providing lines of analyses which have a very modern ring to them. Nevertheless, current analysts more often than not continue to designate these proto-pluralists as naive idealists. According to Rosecrance, for example, in *The Great Illusion*, Angell 'neglecting past precedents, suddenly declared in 1912 that the economic interests and interdependence of the great powers would prevent war'. Rosecrance then goes on to suggest that 'this short term and limited perspective was shown to be wholly inadequate in 1914' (Rosecrance, 1989, pp. 45–50).

A close reading of Angell's text reveals that this is an erroneous rather than a contestable assessment. It was because Angell believed war could break out that he engaged in a polemical exercise to convince the advocates of war that the 'universally accepted axioms of international politics' (Angell, 1912, p. 12) needed to be overhauled. The overhaul was necessary because the world had moved on to a new stage of development. From Angell's perspective, war was a socially and economically counter-productive activity with states such as Germany now being capable of becoming successful world powers without requiring territorial gains.

At the heart of Angell's thesis was the assertion that during the previous forty years a revolution in communications had taken place in world politics resulting in the emergence of an interdependence which had had the effect of 'cutting athwart frontiers'. He pointed, for example, to a financial interdependence among the capitals of the world 'so complex' that a disturbance in London could force the co-operation of financiers in New York 'not as a matter of altruism, but as a matter of commercial self-protection' (1912, p. 50). As Angell saw it, the financial capitals of the world were more dependent upon each other than cities within a state had been in the past. In such an interdependent world, war could still take place, but no benefits could accrue because it was no longer possible for a state 'to enrich itself by subjugating another, or imposing its will on another' (1912, p. viii).

The historiographical assumption in the study of international relations that the discipline moved from an initial idealist phase through to a later realist phase is now so firmly established that the existence of a pluralist tradition has been largely overlooked. For the same reason, the historiographical link between contemporary pluralist writing in international relations and the pluralist literature in political science has also remained unexplored. The antecedents for the contemporary pluralist approach in political science can be found in both England and the United States (Nicholls, 1974). The English pluralists, headed by Laski and Figgis, writing during the first two decades of the twentieth century, argued that the state, particularly in France and Germany, was attempting to take responsibility for an increasing number of functional activities. The English pluralists wished to see this development resisted because they believed, as Laski argued, that 'at the root of our social system there is a contingent anarchy' (cited in Nicholls, 1974, p. 14). The English pluralists identified groups as the basic units which constitute society. In the absence of groups, it was argued, society would become atomised, and individuals would be left unprotected in the face of the growing power of the state. The English pluralists feared that this was what was happening in France and the legal historian Maitland referred to the 'macadamising' tendency of the French state which was obliterating all those features of society which intervened between the individual and the state (Nicholls, 1974, p. 7). The importance attached to groups was also emphasised by the American pluralists. Writing at the beginning of the twentieth century, Bentley argued in *The Process of Government* (1908) that the political arena must be defined in terms of the interactions among a wide range of interest groups.

These early pluralists, therefore, established an approach to political science which challenged the essential tenets of realism. In particular, they undermined the conception of the national interest which provides the starting point for most realist analysis. The American pluralists argued that the idea of the national interest did no more than serve as a useful tool for propaganda. Politics concerned adjustments among the array of interest groups that operated within the political system. The state, from the pluralist perspective, was deprived of any autonomous role; it was certainly not responsible for the formulation of a national interest. Dewey compared the state to an orchestral conductor whose role is not to make music, but to co-ordinate the activities of the musicians who do make music (Nicholls, 1974, p. 22).

These early pluralists did not consider that the absence of a strong or directive government gave rise to a disordered or conflictual system. From the pluralist perspective, individuals could be conceived of in terms of multiple roles. As a consequence, an individual could be a member of a range of different groups. Cross-cutting membership of groups, it was then argued, would have the effect of containing conflict. As Lippmann argued, because individual loyalties criss-cross it becomes 'inherent in the complex pluralism of the modern world that men should behave moderately, and experience amply confirms this conclusion' (Nicholls, 1974, p. 22).

Although rarely acknowledged now, this pluralist view of politics came to impinge directly on the study of international relations. The links were pointed out by Fox (1975) and they have been further investigated by Wilde (1991). Fox argues that a pluralist perspective came to dominate the Chicago school of politics between the two world wars under the influence of Merriam. From his perspective, the boundaries between domestic and international politics and between state and non-state actors were seen to be breaking down. Merriam observed that intra-state groups have developed 'extensions' across the boundary of the state on nationality, linguistic and religious grounds, forming an increasingly complex web of relationships. He went on to argue that

Commercial and cultural relations of many varying forms and types are found flourishing across state lines. Trading companies and modern cartels are sometimes more powerful than the smaller states, while 'internationals' of many colors stretch through the network of politics (quoted in Wilde, 1991, p. 161).

This pluralistic perspective was seen by Merriam to be reflected in the work of Wright (1942), Vagts (1937) and Earle (1943). And Fox argues that it was also present in Schuman's (1933) pioneering textbook on international politics and in the work of Lasswell (1935).

Although political scientists who adopted a pluralist perspective in the first half of the twentieth century were primarily interested in constraining the power of the state, by the start of the Second World War it was clearly recognised that there was an international dimension to the pluralist perspective. Analysts were aware of interdependence and transnationalism and acknowledged that these global forces were transforming the nature of the international system. These ideas have been largely overlooked, however, because the realists were so successful in having this literature characterised as idealist. Moreover, even when the realists themselves came under challenge, their characterisation of the inter-war literature was left largely undisturbed.

The re-emergence of pluralism in international relations

After the Second World War, the United States emerged unequivocally as the most powerful state in the international system. From the realist perspective, because of the power vacuum in Europe and the Far East, and the perceived threat posed by the Soviet Union, the United States had no alternative but to move to the centre of the world stage and begin to operate as a great power, willing to negotiate with the other great power in the international system – the Soviet Union. As the United States manoeuvred into this position, relations with the Soviet Union deteriorated (a development which realists were convinced was unnecessary) and, thereafter, the study of international relations began to focus on the implications of this development. From this point on, as Hoffmann (1977) has argued, because of the central role played by the United States in the creation and dissemination of knowledge, the evolving discipline of international relations came to be dominated by US concerns. And for the next twenty years, the emphasis was very much on the military and diplomatic dimensions of international relations.

But the emergence of the United States as a superpower and the onset of the Cold War also affected political science in the United States. The Soviet Union was seen to constitute an ideological threat to liberal democracy. The democratic system in the United States came under close scrutiny, and pluralists in particular were anxious to demonstrate the superiority of the democratic system as it operated in the United States. The need for the United States to be in a constant readiness for war, however, presented the pluralists with a problem, because it was difficult, under these circumstances, to deny that the state possessed an important, powerful and autonomous role. The field of international relations was left to examine this role, while the pluralists focused exclusively on domestic politics, portraying American society as 'fractured into congeries of hundreds of small special interest groups, with incompletely overlapping memberships, widely differing power bases, and a multitude of techniques for exercising influence on decisions salient to them' (Jordan, 1990, p. 289). These interest groups were assumed to be firmly contained within the shell of the state.

This disciplinary bifurcation encouraged what Easton (1981, p. 304) refers to as the 'double life' of the state, with political scientists exploring its internal features and specialists in international relations examining its external features. The joint impact of realists in international relations, stressing the role of the national interest, and pluralists in political science, asserting the priority of interest groups in politics, meant that the disciplinary divide was soon seen to correspond to a natural division of labour. The potential for interest groups to transcend state boundaries was ignored. The Second World War, therefore, acted as a firebreak for both political science and international relations. There was a lack of continuity with the pre-war literature and both fields of study lost sight of the international dimension of pluralism.

It has often been noted, however, that the doctrine of realism is 'antipathetic' to most Americans who are predisposed to believe in progress (Weltman, 1982, p. 37). As Western economies flourished, the Cold War persisted, and mistakes in US foreign policy proliferated, realism, directly or indirectly, came under attack from a number of different angles. Attention will be focused here on literature concerned with the fragmentation of the state, transnationalism and inter-dependence which are all seen to play a key role in the evolution of the pluralist perspective.

The fragmented state

The realist image of the state as a rational actor operating on the basis of the national interest became deeply entrenched in the study of inter-national relations after the Second World War. It represented the very antithesis of the pluralist image of the state as developed in political science. When the United States became mired in the Vietnam war, however, doubts began to be expressed about the validity of this model. Nascent pluralists began to argue that the image of the state as a rational and undifferentiated actor required a radical rethink and close attention began to be paid to the complexities of the governmental process. Neustadt (1960) had already made a seminal contribution which was then extended by Allison (1971). To understand foreign policy, it was argued, account must be taken of a bargaining process between competing bureaucracies. From this perspective, the major bureaucratic departments do not represent neutral agents supplying a president with impartial information and then implementing his decisions; bureaucracies represent fiefdoms constantly engaged in intense battles over policy, which emerges eventually as the result of the various parties pulling and hauling in different directions. Although this view was attacked by realists (Krasner, 1972), the pluralists have ensured that the image of a fragmented state persists as a constant challenge to the rational actor model initially propagated by the realists. Although Allison was primarily concerned with foreign policy analysis and was certainly not identifying with a pluralist conception of the state, the increasing awareness of state bureaucracies ensured that they were soon integrated into the pluralist approach.

Transnationalism

Attention also began to be paid to the growth of non-state, trans-nationally organised actors. It was argued repeatedly in the 1970s that the 'state-centric model has imposed research blinkers and has inhibited an accurate mapping of the increasingly complex global system' (Mansbach, Ferguson and Lampert, 1976, p. 28). Attention was drawn to the wide array of non-state actors which play a role in international politics (Keohane and Nye, 1971). These actors ranged from the giant multinational corporations to the universal Roman Catholic Church. Rosenau who wrote extensively on the issue argued that the existence of these transnational organisations was affecting the 'deep' structures of world politics (Rosenau, 1980, p. 97).

Most analysts working from a pluralist perspective, however, were less concerned with the impact of these transnational actors on the 'structure' of the international system and were more interested in how they were affecting the essential processes operating within the system. It was argued that it was no longer possible to think of international relations in terms of the interaction between governments. Instead, it had to be accepted that world politics involved transactions among a kaleidoscopic range of actors. Brown, for example, characterised this emerging situation as a 'polyarchy' (1974, p. 186) and later as a 'world polity' (1992, p. 170). Governments now found that they had no alternative but to interact with a wide range of non-state actors from terrorists to multinational corporations. And as pluralists highlighted the fragmen-tation of government, so it was recognised that state bureaucracies must also be depicted as transnational actors (Huntington, 1973; Keohane and Nye, 1974) which could establish links with their counterparts in other countries.

Although pluralists like Rosenau (1980, p. 134) were prone to argue that the emergence of transnationalism was symptomatic of a funda-mental transformation in international relations, realists insisted that transnationalism did nothing to change the basic anarchic structure of the international system (Waltz, 1979). But pluralists themselves were also concerned about the inability of the concept of transnationalism to provide theoretical insights. Keohane and Nye (1971), in drawing attention to the plethora of non-state actors now operating in the international system, were criticised by Rosenau (1980, pp. 31–2), for example, for failing to use their framework to formulate any interesting theoretical puzzles. It was accepted that although transnationalism was playing an important role in international relations, the concept had failed to generate a new research programme and it was soon accepted that transnationalism needed to be analysed within the context of the broader concept of interdependence.

Interdependence

Interdependence was considered to be a concept of considerable theoretical significance because it demonstrated so clearly the inadequacy of the realist assertion that states could be treated as autonomous agents within the international system. The meaning of interdependence, however, was often regarded as ambiguous or elusive; Rosenau feared that interdependence was simply being used as a label to characterise the growing complexity of the modern world (Rosenau, 1989). Although this is a danger, interdependence has drawn attention to two key features in the contemporary international system: the growing relevance of the global 'commons' and the rapidly increasing interconnectedness between states. Both of these features problematise the realist focus on states as autonomous units.

An awareness of the global commons being essential to the survival and well-being of humanity first began to surface with the realisation in the 1950s that because of radioactivity (and later the threat of a nuclear winter) nuclear weapons had the capacity to destroy the entire planet. This message was reinforced when images of the earth as a delicate and vulnerable planet floating in space were brought back after men landed on the moon. While realists were able to accommodate the emergence of nuclear weapons by drawing on the concept of mutual deterrence, it was much more difficult to process the evidence about the constant damage being done to the ecosphere. They had little to contribute to the debate sparked off in the 1970s by the assertion that there were 'limits to growth' and the resulting concern about the possibility that modernisation, designed to improve the life-style of everyone, was having the long-term effect of destroying the planet.

The ecosphere was seen by pluralists to represent a public or collective good (Ruggie, 1972) which appeared to escape the realist's mode of analysis premised on the conception of territoriality. The pluralist's recognition that we are globally interdependent meant that a failure to find planetary solutions to the problem posed by the 'limits to growth' would have consequences for everyone. By the same token, a solution to these problems would also be of universal benefit. The concept of interdependence drew attention to the wide range of collective goods, from satellite orbiting positions to ocean resources, which members of the international system have come to rely upon. The existence of these collective goods was seen to present problems for a perspective which treats the state as a competitive and autonomous actor. If states attempt to compete on the electromagnetic (radio) frequency spectrum, for example, then the possibility of successfully broadcasting on this spectrum is negated. By the same token, if the sea is over-fished, then all states are disadvantaged. Pluralists have stressed, therefore, that it is not possible for states to establish autonomy in the context of collective goods found in the global commons.

Interdependence has been linked in the second place to the rapidly growing transaction rates which have taken place between states. Holsti, for example, has pointed to the unprecedented 'interconnectedness' which has occurred as the result of the 'dramatic growth of means of transportation, communication and exchange of goods, money, and ideas' (Holsti, 1991, p. 53). Buzan goes further and suggests that interdependence is also a function of the rising levels of activity engaged in by every individual as the result of increases in 'human knowledge, productivity, mobility, education, consumption, wealth and organization'. This results, argues Buzan, in an ever increasing 'density' in the interactions across the international system (Buzan, 1991, p. 14). We are all now caught in a complex systemic web of interactions such that changes in one part of the system have direct and indirect consequences for the rest of the system. Governments constantly argue, for example, that their economic policies have been blown off course by events in the world economy. A familiar pluralist theme was that governments no longer had the capacity to achieve their objectives either inside or outside the state.

The basic ideas associated with pluralism had all been laid out by the early 1970s and their antecedents could be traced back to the start of the century. Pluralists were drawn to these ideas because they pointed to ways in which the autonomy of the state as a force in world politics was already being diminished and indicated why state autonomy would have to be further delimited if the human race was to survive. Pluralists, moreover, stressed their positivist credentials; they were not starry-eyed idealists but were simply stating the facts. From the late 1970s onwards, however, the position of the pluralists altered and diversified. This development will be explored in the final section of the chapter.

The growing relevance of pluralism?

During the course of the 1970s, pluralist thinking underwent a sea-change. At the start of the 1970s, the emphasis was on the diminishing autonomy of the state precipitated by the growth of transnationalism and interdependence. With the successful propagation of this position, realists, depicted as adherents to an outdated perspective, appeared to be losing ground to the pluralists. Although it was accepted that realism still had some purchase on East–West relations, there was a belief among pluralists that even Soviet–American relations would succumb to the forces of pluralism, an assumption epitomised by the image of 'vodka-cola'. But during the 1970s, pluralists were forced to re-evaluate their perspective with the emergence of increasing evidence that the economic power of the United States was on the wane. This loss of power was highlighted in 1971 when President Nixon declared that the dollar would no longer be convertible into gold. As the economic authority of the United States came under challenge, so there was a growing recognition that the pluralist forces associated with transnationalism and inter-dependence in the Western world had evolved within a framework of rules and organisations (identified in the literature as regimes) set up under the aegis of the United States at the end of the Second World War. Even more significant, the argument began to be aired that a liberal world order depended on the existence of a dominant or hegemonic state within the system, a 'benevolent despot', as Kindleberger (1974) put it, which was willing to police the rules underpinning this world order. With the emergence of evidence that the hegemonic position of the United States was being eroded, doubts began to be expressed about the capacity of this country to enforce these rules in the future.

While this reassessment was taking place, pluralists also had to face a counter-attack from realists who were reacting simultaneously to the perception of the United States' loss of status. Tucker (1977) attacked the pluralist notion that interdependence and transnationalism would promote a harmony of interests within the international system. Tucker insisted that there were enduring conflicts of interest between states and that order within the international system must be maintained on the basis of rules which favoured the interests of states with power because only states with a substantial stake in the system would have an incentive to police the rules and maintain international order. Tucker insisted that so long as it possessed the power to do so, the United States must resist attempts to modify established international rules which served US interests. If the United States' power did diminish, then it was certain that the rules in the international system would be altered to promote the interests of the new power holders and that these changes would unquestionably damage the long-term interests of the United States.

Tucker's concerns were fuelled at first by the threat to US interests reputedly posed by the Oil Petroleum Exporting Countries (OPEC) during the 1973 oil crisis. He developed his argument in highly polemical terms because he was deeply disturbed by what he saw as the passive response made by the United States. But a much more academic defence of realism was presented shortly afterwards by Waltz (1979) who argued that a scientific approach to the study of international relations must treat states as rational actors and couch explanations in systemic terms. One of the key insights was the demonstration that relations between states were inherently competitive because the competition was generated by the anarchic structure of the international system. But Waltz also showed that agreements could be reached between the Great Powers even in a competitive environment. Waltz's approach gave a new lease of life to realism and was quickly identified as structural or neo-realism.

It was against this background that the pluralists reassessed their own position. Initially they had assumed that the eroding autonomy of the state held the potential to generate a more co-operative global community. They now began to question this assumption from a number of different angles. It was necessary first to examine the possibility that the regulation of transnationalism and interdependence had been premised on the capacity of the United States to operate as a hegemon. Second, they began to contemplate the possibility that states, strenuously resisting attempts to have their authority transferred to global institutions, were going to remain the dominant actors in the international system. Finally, they continued to believe that the growth of transnationalism and interdependence was diminishing the capacity of governments to regulate both domestic and international politics. When these propositions were examined in conjunction, they began to raise serious doubts about the governability of the international system.

There have been two rather different responses by pluralists to this assessment. Both, however, have found it necessary to acknowledge the realist argument that states remain crucial actors in the international system. On the one hand, Rosenau (1990) argues at the level of grand theory that it is necessary to accept that contemporary world politics is bifurcated into the familiar state-centric world described by realists and the less familiar multi-centric world exposed by pluralists. In contrast to the early pluralist analysis which appeared confident that the authority of states was being eroded by the forces of pluralism, Rosenau now acknowledges the potential for the state to reassert itself and for a purely state-centric world to re-emerge. But Rosenau also insists that the forces of pluralism could still prevail, with the existing bifurcated world giving way to a multi-centric world society. As things stand, however, Rosenau accepts that the state-centric world co-exists with the multi-centric world and he argues that although there is some degree of overlap, the structures, norms and processes describing these two worlds tend to be 'mutually exclusive' (Rosenau, 1990, p. 11). Nevertheless, Rosenau makes clear that he does believe that the potential to transform world politics exists. The critical source of transformation is identified in the skills possessed by individuals. He argues that we are no longer habit-oriented creatures but are extremely adaptive with highly developed analytical skills and complex cognitive maps (1990, p. 211). Individuals are seen as a consequence to be much more sceptical of authority, making it increasingly difficult for states to maintain their autonomy. But Rosenau concludes that the turbulence in contemporary world politics is too great to make any accurate forecasts about whether a future pluralistic world society will actually emerge.

A second group of pluralists, eschewing grand theory, have become preoccupied with the question of how the international system can be governed in the absence of a hegemonic state. Central to the research agenda of this group has been the attempt to invalidate the neo-realist assertion that competition is a necessary structural feature of an anarchic system. But in following this route, the pluralists have accepted the state-centric orientation adopted by the neo-realists. It has proved, moreover, to be a complex and confusing theoretical undertaking for pluralists, previously concerned with the growing fragmentation of the state, to focus on the way that states, defined as rational actors, manage to co-operate within an anarchic arena. The difficulties confronted by these theorists is very evident in a transitional work such as Keohane and Nye's *Power and Interdependence* where there is an attempt to link the established pluralist concern with the declining autonomy of the state to the emerging interest in the way states, viewed as rational actors, establish regimes. The intention was to develop 'a coherent theoretical framework' which would 'blend the wisdom' of both realists and pluralists (1977, p. 4). The attempt to erase the boundary line between realism and pluralism, however, became the source of considerable confusion. Because of the book's prominence, moreover, the confusion has been transmitted through the discipline.

In line with established pluralist concerns, Keohane and Nye begin by providing a discussion of complex interdependence which identifies a hypothetical world where the role of force has been excluded and the autonomy of the state is being eroded by transnational forces. In a reassessment of the text, the authors admit that this conception of interdependence 'remained a relatively underdeveloped and under-valued concept' (1987, p. 733). Subsequently Keohane and Nye made it clear that they rely in the text primarily on what they later came to call 'strategic interdependence' (1987, p. 733) where the outcome of any bargaining situation is determined by the intersection of decisions arrived at independently by the participants. So, for example, if two states run into conflict over the terms of a regime to govern their future trading relations, then either state can threaten to implement a trade embargo. But, if one state is much less dependent on the trading relationship than the other, and will suffer less should the relationship break down, then it can use this asymmetry to generate power.

Although Keohane and Nye make clear that this conception of power is very different from the realist's fungible conception of power based ultimately on military capabilities, their interest in developing a new and more effective conception of power does indicate a clear desire to draw on the realist approach to develop a more theoretical focus for pluralism. They fail to note in doing so, however, that whereas for realists, power is used by states to gain an advantage in a competitive relationship, they are interested in showing how interdependence can generate a form of power which can be used to maintain co-operation among states in an anarchic arena. This conception of power certainly fits very neatly with their interpretation of events after the Second World War. Because the United States was in an asymmetrical trading relationship with many countries at that time, it moved into a hegemonic position within the international system and it was able to use its power to establish and police the regimes which established the mutually beneficial post-war liberal world order. In developing this interpretation, they fail to see, however, that this is not an assessment with which realists could concur (Krasner, 1985). In fact, it is by sleight of hand that Keohane and Nye given the impression that they have developed a coherent framework that conflates realism and pluralism.

The resulting confusion is extended in *After Hegemony* (1984), where Keohane goes on to explore how international regimes can be established without a hegemonic state. He argues that the realist's conception of the state as a 'rational and egoistic actor' can provide a useful starting point which discourages wishful thinking, but he asserts that hegemony is neither a necessary nor a sufficient condition to account for the emergence of international regimes. The willingness of states to co-operate is not simply related to the distribution of power within the system, but it is also seen to be vitally affected by 'the quality, quantity and distribution of information' available in the system because human

beings and governments 'behave differently in information-rich environ-
ments than in information-poor ones' (1984, p. 245).

From this perspective, then, the weakness of realism is not its state-
centrism, but its failure to appreciate the importance of the growing
number of international institutions which circulate information and
thereby ensure that states operate in an information-rich environment.
The information engenders trust and reduces uncertainty, thereby
making states more willing to co-operate in the creation and maintenance
of regimes. Realists, therefore, are shown to have ignored the fact that
'Information as well as power is a significant systemic variable in world
politics' (Keohane, 1984, p. 145) and as a result they come to the false
conclusion that competition is a structural feature of the international
system. But Keohane goes further and insists that the growth of international institutions undermines the realist, or as he puts it, realpolitik
ideal of the 'autonomous, hierarchical state that keeps its options open
and its decisionmaking processes closed' (1984, p. 259). In the end,
therefore, Keohane comes back to the familiar pluralist distrust of the
state.

Although the argument advanced by Keohane has been identified in
terms of neo-liberalism, it can be characterised, nevertheless, as a further
refinement of pluralism. Keohane argues that he is drawing on international institutions to rectify an inadequacy in the realist framework.
His position, however, has given rise to a debate with the neo-realists
who insist that even in situations where there is increased information,
co-operation is still more difficult to achieve than the neo-liberals
recognise because states are more concerned about relative than absolute
gains. As a consequence, an agreement which would secure mutual
benefits will still not be struck, according to the neo-realists, if it alters
the relative power positions occupied by the states seeking to establish a
regime (Grieco, 1988).

Keohane's claim that the neo-liberal institutionalists are simply
refining and strengthening neo-realist thought fails to acknowledge,
however, just how far removed he is from the realist perspective. By
assuming that regimes can be treated as collective goods in which everyone has a stake, Keohane is working from an essentially liberal posture.
From a realist perspective, this assumption throws a veil over inevitable
conflicts of interest which exist within the international system. By
contrast, the veil is removed in realist analysis where it is made quite clear
that international regimes benefit the states with power at the expense
of the weaker states who are forced to comply with the regime. In pre-
supposing that international regimes promote the interests of all,
Keohane ignores the possibility that weaker states may participate in

regimes under duress. Power, under these circumstances ensures compliance rather than co-operation.

Conclusion

This chapter has endeavoured to trace the evolution of pluralist thought through the twentieth century. It has been premised on the assumption that providing a historiographical account of a perspective is a complex task because the evolving study of international relations needs to accommodate the dynamics within different perspectives, the interaction between perspectives, and the impact of external events on perspectives. In the case of pluralism, the task is further complicated by the influence of widely accepted assessments which have the effect of defining pluralism out of existence. On the one hand, the evolution of pluralist thought in the first half of the twentieth century has been obscured by the persisting realist interpretation which characterises the literature of this period as idealist rather than pluralist. On the other hand, recent pluralist literature has been defined, even by pluralists themselves, as neo-realist in origin. Yet as Snidal (1985, p. 581) has noted, neo-liberals who claim affiliation with the neo-realism effectively turn realist thinking on its head, by suggesting that weaker states benefit from regimes more than the hegemon itself.

Strange (1985, p. 259) suggests that this debate is a product of 'academics in search of tidy models' and she insists that the world is 'far messier and full of contradictions' than academic bystanders appreciate. This analysis has been reinforced by her assertion that it is necessary to cut through the ideological claims of competing perspectives, which she sees as 'toy trains on separate tracks' (1988, p. 17), and promoting the erroneous impression that there are incompatible views of the world available for inspection. Such an argument, however, is obviously straining after a positivist ideal where it is assumed that different assessments about the nature of social reality can potentially be resolved.

Most pluralists also adhere to a positivist position which is why the neo-liberal institutionalists were so attracted by the idea of building on neo-realist foundations to form a bridge between apparently incompatible perspectives. Subsequent attempts to reconcile the obvious differences between neo-liberals and neo-realists (Niou and Ordeshook, 1994) are similarly straining after the positivist desire for a definitive interpretation of past events. The danger with these attempts at reconciliation is that they gloss over fundamental differences between the competing perspectives. They underestimate the extent to which these

84   *Richard Little*

perspectives offer interpretations which necessarily rest on judgements derived from deep-seated and ultimately untestable beliefs about reality.

REFERENCES

Allison, Graham T. (1971), *Essence of Decision: Explaining the Cuban Missile Crisis* (Boston: Little Brown).

Angell, Norman (1912), *The Great Illusion: A Study of the Relations of Military Power to National Advantage* (London: William Heinemann).

Baldwin, David (ed.) (1993), *Neo-Realism and Neo-Liberals: A Reader* (New York: Columbia University Press).

Bentley, Arthur F. (1908), *The Process of Government* (Chicago: Chicago University Press).

Brown, Seyom (1974), *New Forces in World Politics* (Washington: Brookings Institution).

— (1992), *International Relations in a Changing Global System: Towards a Theory of the World Polity* (Boulder, CO: Westview Press).

Burton, John W. (1968), *Systems, States, Diplomacy and Rules* (Cambridge: Cambridge University Press).

Buzan, Barry (1991), 'Interdependence and Britain's External Relations', in Lawrence Freedman and Michael Clarke (eds.), *Britain in the World* (Cambridge: Cambridge University Press), pp. 10–41.

Earle, E. Mead (ed.) (1943), *Makers of Modern Strategy* (Princeton: Princeton University Press).

Easton, David (1981), 'The Political System Besieged by the State', *Political Theory*, 9, pp. 305–25.

Fox, William T. R. (1975), 'Pluralism, the Science of Politics, and the World System', *World Politics*, 27, pp. 597–611.

Fukuyama, Francis (1992), *The End of History and the Last Man* (New York: Free Press).

Grieco, J. M. (1988), 'Anarchy and the Limits of Cooperation: A Realist Critique of New Liberal Institutionalism', *International Organization*, 42, pp. 485–508.

Gunnell, John G. (1991), 'Disciplinary History: The Case of Political Science', *Strategies: Journal of Theory, Culture and Politics*, 4/5, pp. 182–227.

Haas, Ernst B. (1969), *Tangle of Hopes: American Commitments and World Order* (Englewood Cliffs: Prentice Hall).

Hanreider, Wolfram F. (1978), 'Dissolving International Politics: Reflections on the Nation-State', *American Political Science Review*, 72, pp. 1276–87.

Hoffmann, Stanley (1977), 'An American Social Science: International Relations', *Daedalus*, 20, pp. 41–60.

Holsti, K. J. (1991), *Change in the International System: Essays on the Theory and Practice of International Relations* (Aldershot: Edward Elgar).

Huntington, Samuel P. (1973), 'Transnational Organizations in World Politics', *World Politics*, 25, pp. 333–68.

Jordan, Grant (1990), 'The Pluralism of Pluralism: An Anti-Theory?', *Political Studies*, 38, pp. 286–301.

Keohane, Robert O. (1984), *After Hegemony: Cooperation and Discord in the World Political Economy* (Princeton: Princeton University Press).

Keohane, Robert O. and Nye, Joseph S. (1971), *Transnational Relations and World Politics* (Princeton: Princeton University Press).

(1974), 'Transnational Relations and International Organizations', *World Politics*, 27, pp. 39–62.

(1977, second edition 1989), *Power and Interdependence: World Politics in Transition* (Boston: Little Brown).

(1987), 'Power and Interdependence Revisited', *International Organization*, 41, pp. 725–53.

Kindleberger, Charles (1974), *The World in Depression, 1929–1939* (Berkeley: University of California Press).

Krasner, Stephen (1972), 'Are Bureaucracies Important? (Or Allison in Wonderland)', *Foreign Policy*, 27, pp. 159–79.

(1985), *Structural Conflict: The Third World Against Global Liberalism* (Berkeley, CA: University of California Press).

Kuhn, Thomas S. (1970), *The Structure of Scientific Revolutions*, 2nd edition (Chicago: Chicago University Press).

Lasswell, Harold D. (1935), *World Politics and Personal Insecurity* (New York: McGraw Hill).

Little, Richard (1981), 'World Politics in Perspective', unit prepared for *World Politics* (Milton Keynes: Open University Press).

Mansbach, R., Ferguson, Y. and Lampert, O. (1976), *The Web of World Politics: Non-State Actors in the Global System* (Englewood Cliffs, NJ: Prentice Hall).

Morse, Edward L. (1970), 'The Transformation of Foreign Policies: Modernization, Interdependence and Externalization', *World Politics*, 22, pp. 371–92.

Neustadt, Richard (1960), *Presidential Power* (New York: John Wiley).

Nicholls, David (1974), *Three Varieties of Pluralism* (London: Macmillan).

Niou, Emerson M. S. and Ordeshook, Peter C. (1994), '"Less Filling, Tastes Great" The Realist–Neoliberal Debate', *World Politics*, 46 (2), pp. 209–34.

Rosecrance, Richard (1989), 'War, Trade and Interdependence', in James N. Rosenau and Hylke W. Tromp (eds.), *Interdependence and Conflict in World Politics* (Aldershot: Avebury).

Rosenau, James N. (1980), *The Study of Global Interdependence: Essays of the Transnationalization of World Affairs* (London: Frances Pinter).

(1989), 'Introduction', in James N. Rosenau and Hylke W. Tromp (eds.), *Interdependence and Conflict in World Politics* (Aldershot: Avebury).

(1990), *Turbulence in World Politics: A Theory of Change and Continuity* (New York: Harvester Wheatsheaf)

Ruggie, John G. (1972), 'Collective Goods and Future International Cooperation', *American Political Science Review*, 66, pp. 874–93.

Schmidt, Brian C. (1994), 'The Historiography of International Relations', *Review of International Studies*, 20, pp. 349–67.

Schuman, Frederick L. (1933), *International Politics* (New York: McGraw-Hill).

Snidal, Duncan (1985), 'The Limits of Hegemonic Stability Theory', *International Organization*, 39, pp. 579–614.

Strange, Susan (1985), 'Protectionism and World Politics', *International Organization*, 39, pp. 233–59.

(1988), *States and Markets: An Introduction to Political Economy* (London: Pinter Publishers).

Truman, D. B. (1971), *The Governmental Process*, 2nd edition (New York: Alfred Knopf).

Tucker, Robert C. (1977), *The Inequality of Nations* (London: Martin Robertson).

Vagts, A. (1937, 2nd edition 1959), *A History of Militarism* (New York: Free Press).

Vasquez, John A. (1983), *The Power of Power Politics: A Critique* (London: Frances Pinter).

Wagner, W. (1974), 'Dissolving the State', *International Organization*, 28, pp. 435–66.

Waltz, Kenneth N. (1979), *Theory of International Politics* (Reading: Addison Wesley).

Weltman, J. F. (1982), 'On the Interpretation of International Thought', *Review of Politics*, 44, pp. 27–41.

Wilde, Jaap H. de (1991), *Saved from Oblivion: Interdependence Theory in the First Half of the 20th Century* (Aldershot: Dartmouth Publishing Co.).

Wolfers, Arnold (1962), *Discord and Collaboration: Essays on International Politics* (Baltimore: Johns Hopkins University Press).

Wright, Quincy (1942), *A Study of War*, 2 vols. (Chicago: Chicago University Press).

4   The inter-state structure of the modern world-system

Immanuel Wallerstein

From the perspective of world-systems analysis, the inter-state structure of the modern world-system (conventionally the principal subject matter for students of international relations) is merely one institutional structure or plane of analysis among a number that altogether make up the integrated framework of the modern world-system. This world-system, like all world-systems, is an historical system governed by a singular logic and set of rules within and through which persons and groups struggle with each other in pursuit of their interests and in accord with their values. Pertinent analysis of geopolitics, in this perspective, can only be done within the context of the functioning of the modern world-system as a whole and in the light of its particular historical trajectory.

I shall therefore first outline the structure and historical development of the modern world-system as a whole, and then describe the functioning of the inter-state system in particular, ending with an analysis of the present and future trajectory of the modern world-system in general and its inter-state system in particular.

The modern world-system

The modern world-system is not the only world-system that has existed. There were many others. It is, however, the first one that was organised and able to consolidate itself as a capitalist world-economy. Although initially formed primarily in (part of) Europe, its inner logic propelled it to seek the expansion of its outer boundaries. Over some four centuries, it proved durable and strong enough to be capable repeatedly of incorporating new areas and peoples within its division of labour until, by the late nineteenth century, its organisation or integrated labour processes effectively covered the entire globe, the first world-system in history to achieve this.

The capitalist world-economy is a system socially structured by an integrated axial division of labour, whose guiding principle is the ceaseless accumulation of capital. The key mechanism to realise this principle has been the construction of extensive commodity chains of production that cross multiple political boundaries. The chains consist, conceptually and historically, of series of operations that are meaningful as nodes in a chain. The conditions prevailing within the many nodes of each chain vary over time of course, as do the conditions of any one node from that of other nodes. Some nodes have contained multiple producers in multiple countries; others have been relatively monopolised by a very few producers. In some nodes the labour force has been recruited primarily by paying wages. In others, employers have utilised a variety of more coercive and less costly modes of controlling labour. Profit is usually made at all the nodes along a chain, but greater profit is the consequence of a higher degree of monopolisation at a particular node.

The activities of the more profitable nodes have tended to be geographically concentrated in a few, relatively small areas of the world-economy, which we may call collectively the core zone. The less profitable nodes tend to have their units of economic activity more geographically dispersed, most of these units being located in a much larger area we may call the peripheral zone. But while core and periphery are terms of geographical origin and geographical consequence, they are not used here as primarily spatial terms but rather as relational terms. A core–periphery relation is the relation between the more monopolised sectors of production on the one hand and the more competitive on the other, and therefore the relation between high-profit (and generally high-wage) and low-profit (low-wage) production activities. It is a relation between world capital and world labour; but it is also a relation between stronger capitalists and weaker capitalists. The major consequence of integrating the two kinds of activities is the transfer of surplus-value from the peripheral sector to the core sector, that is, not merely from the workers to the owners but from the owners (or controllers) of the peripheral productive activities to the owners (or controllers) of the core activities, the big capitalists.

Coreness and peripherality, being relational, are not necessarily or always geographically separated. The two kinds of activity may well coexist within the same square mile. But there are a number of good reasons why, in practice, there has tended to be a high degree of spatial segregation, with a heavy concentration of core activities in a few places, with others housing primarily peripheral activities. Nor do coreness or peripherality have anything inherently to do with particular kinds of economic activity. It matters little whether the activity is trans-formational (agricultural, industrial) or service (merchandising, informational, transport, financial).

At given times, and under given conditions, any of these activities may be core-like or peripheral, high-profit or low-profit. What matters first and foremost is the degree to which the activity is (can be) relatively monopolised at a given point in time. The successful entrepreneurs (capitalists) discern which kinds of economic activities have the possibility in the short run of a high degree of monopolisation, and whose products have or can be induced to have a considerable demand. A successful capitalist has no intrinsic commitment to product, to place, to country, or to type of economic activity. The commitment is to the accumulation of capital. Therefore, the capitalist will shift locus of economic engagement (product, place, country, type of activity) as shifts occur in the opportunities to maximise revenues from undertakings.

This means that a capitalist market, by definition, can *never* be either an entirely free market or an entirely closed administered market. The ceaseless accumulation of capital precisely requires something in-between: a partially free market. This kind of market is the constructed result of the efforts on the one hand of some powerful economic actors to achieve relative monopolies by combining productive efficiencies and political influence and the contrary efforts of other actors to break or dilute these monopolies by combining alternative productive efficiencies and political influence. Monopolies are thus constantly being created and constantly being diluted. Nonetheless, at all points in time, some monopolies exist, and hence the world market has never been nor can it ever be more than partially free. If it were otherwise, high profit rates could not exist, and in this case the ceaseless accumulation of capital would no longer be possible.

Only the modern world-system (the capitalist world-economy) has evolved a political structure composed of states, each of which claims to exercise 'sovereignty' in a delimited geographical area, and which collectively are bound together in an inter-state system. Such a political structure is in fact the only kind of structure that can guarantee the persistence of the partially free market which is the key requirement of a system based on the ceaseless accumulation of capital. Capitalism and the modern state-system were not two separate historical inventions (or conceptions) that had to be fitted together or articulated with each other. They were obverse sides of a single coin. They were both part of a seamless whole. Neither is imaginable without the other. They were simultaneously developed, and neither could continue to exist without the other.

One of the crucial interfaces of world capitalist economic structures and the states is the perpetual moulding of a world labour force that is (a) available, (b) relocatable, and (c) not too costly. This is a very complicated structure to develop, especially since the labour forces have views of their own about how available, relocatable, and costly they should be. And needless to insist, the views of the world labour force on these subjects are quite often in direct conflict with the views of the owners or controllers of economic structures, as well as with the views of political leaders and bureaucrats. In reality, workers almost always have to be induced to do the work required by capitalist enterprises – by a combination of carrot, stick and ideology – especially if one wants them to work at a specific time in a specific place at a specific task for a specific remuneration.

The use of sticks on behalf of the enterprises by the states, who are the ones who control the majority of sticks, is obvious and has translated itself into the establishment of multiple forms of coerced labour, especially in the peripheral zone. State intervention has also taken the form of outlawing or hindering the class organisation of workers. But sticks have their costs, even if these costs are not all (or even for the most part) borne by the immediate employers of the coerced or bullied workers. Therefore, the creation of self-propelling institutions whose workings might achieve the same results has first complemented and later in considerable part supplanted the use of direct state coercion on behalf of employers.

The key institution that has been created is the income-pooling household, a unit, usually of 3–10 persons of all ages and both sexes, who pool income of multiple kinds over a long period of time. Obviously, persons enter and exit these households all the time, both by birth and death and by social decision. Such households are not the same as the various kinds of traditional kinship units (usually much larger) of previous historical systems.

These households are organised in terms of economic survival in a capitalist world-economy. Wage income is only one of five kinds of income such households acquire, and for the majority of households in the capitalist world-economy, wage income constitutes less than half its total income. The other four kinds of income brought in by household members are petty market income, self-produced (so-called subsistence) income, rents, and transfer payments. All members of the household from small children to the aged bring in some income, and many (even most) household members bring in several kinds of income.

The structure of the income pool of a household determines the availability, relocatability, and price of the labour any household will direct to wage-employment. The optimal situation from the point of view of those who hire the wage labour is to obtain their wage-labourers from households which are not in a position to devote most of their labour-effort in wage-labour. We call such households semi-proletarian. The wage-workers in the semi-proletarian household typically receive wages that are *below* the hourly return for labour effort necessary for household reproduction. In such a case, the household is in fact reproducing itself out of the higher hourly return coming from other income-producing activities. De facto, this means a transfer of surplus to the employer of the wage-worker from the other work activities in the household. This of course presumes that, despite the below minimum level of the wage, the household cannot forgo wage-work entirely, since it needs this wage-income, however poorly paid, for survival.

Such a system guarantees that the wage-worker will continue to receive a low level of pay, which in turn makes it possible for employers in peripheral activities to make profits despite the high level of competition in their sector. But to ensure that households are in such a position (needing to offer *some* part of their work time to wage-labour but not enabled to utilise *most* of their work time to wage-labour) requires not merely the active role of the state(s) in which the household is located but of the inter-state system as a whole. And, without such active and repeated intervention, the core–periphery relationship would collapse.

In turn, however, the fact that the large majority of the population in given states are located in such semi-proletarian households sustains the kinds of political structures which makes it extremely difficult for the governments of the world-system. Conversely, the fact that in other states the majority of households are proletarian sustains the kind of state structures which enable these states to assert their power in the world-system.

Semiperipheral states are those states which combine within their boundaries a significant mix of core-like and peripheral economic activities. To the extent that the governments intervene actively, they are generally able to maintain such a mix despite the ever-changing patterns of production activities which constantly threaten to redefine the internal mix of semiperipheral countries in the direction of peripheralisation. Semiperipheral countries regularly run very hard to stay in place. One way they do this is by seeking to maintain and expand the percentage of proletarian households within the state structure. Much of what has been called 'socialism' and 'economic development' in the last century has involved essentially such attempts to promote proletarianisation.

Proletarianisation has usually been thought of as a process imposed on reluctant workers. In one sense, this is surely true. Proletarianisation has in most cases required deruralisation and hence uprooting (over perhaps a generation or two) of previously agricultural populations. But proletarianisation of a household is not overall a negative process from the point of view of the household. For proletarian households typically have larger incomes than semi-proletarian households (whether urban or rural). For one thing, proletarianisation, by definition, limits the amount of surplus available from non-wage income and therefore makes essential higher hourly wages for the wage-work, if the household is to survive. For a second thing, (urban) proletarian households are in a stronger position to create syndical organisations to defend their interests. And this in turn makes them more available to participate in antisystemic movements.

The construction of an axial division of labour, the establishment of trans-state commodity chains, the rise of sovereignty as the defining characteristic of stateness, the creation of an inter-state structure, the development of income-pooling households were all features of the early history of the modern world-system (sixteenth–eighteenth centuries) and were all well in place before the so-called industrial revolution. Nonetheless, the overall structure was not yet complete. The system lacked a unifying geoculture which could contain its centrifugal forces. It was the French Revolution which catalysed the multiple pressures to establish such a geoculture.

For three centuries, the dominant values within the capitalist world-economy were in partial conflict with the dominant economic and even political forces in the modern world-system. The result was an increasing fragility of the principal structures which finally exploded in the French Revolution. The French Revolution changed relatively little in the economic structures of either France or the world-system. It changed little in the state structure of France (Tocqueville long ago demonstrated the degree to which the reforms of the Jacobins and of Napoleon were the continuation and furtherance of the work of Richelieu and Colbert) or in the inter-state system (the Congress of Vienna merely amplifying the structures set in place at the Treaty of Westphalia).

The earth-shaking effect of the French Revolution and its Napoleonic aftermath was in the transformation of mentalities. Two concepts gained wide popular acceptance: the normality of political change, and the sovereignty of the people. Neither concept was new, but previously neither one could be said to have had significant support. Political change had always been of course historically normal. But culturally it had traditionally been illegitimate. Whenever change did occur, the new powerholders denied that a change had occurred; they defined the happening as a restoration of an old order that had been usurped or corrupted. Suddenly, people were ready to say the opposite: political change is legitimate, normal, even desirable. And once this view became widespread, the consequence would be that, with every (even small) rotation in powerholding, the new powerholders would exalt the change, even if little real change had occurred.

Sovereignty was itself one of the defining concepts of the modern world-system. Each state was supposed both to be sovereign and to have a sovereign. For three centuries, the typical sovereign had been the absolute monarch, an invention of the sixteenth century. The French Revolution was a struggle against the absolute monarch as sovereign; the replacement sovereign the Revolution offered was 'the people'. This idea too caught on. Even with the defeat of Napoleon, the so-called Restoration of Louis XVIII, and the creation of the Holy Alliance, it was not possible to eradicate the growing commitment to the concept of popular sovereignty.

The geoculture of the modern world-system was forged in reaction to the ever-widening acceptance of the normality of political change and popular sovereignty. For the two ideas, when paired, represented the most serious danger to the survival of the capitalist world-economy: the danger of democratisation. The response of the powerful to the dangers of democratisation was pursued in three institutional domains: the invention of the ideologies; the reconstruction of the knowledge system and the triumph of scientism; and the taming of the antisystemic movements. The essential tool in doing this was the construction of a geoculture built around a symbiotic antinomy: universalism on the one hand and racism – sexism on the other.

The ideologies were basically a set of political strategies to cope with the pervasiveness of those two new ideas. The first one to emerge, almost immediately, was conservatism. In its original version, put forward primarily in the period 1789–1830, conservatism consisted of the total rejection of both ideas, in the name of preserving collective wisdom accumulated over time and incarnated in the practice and values of traditional social groups – the monarchy, the nobility (or more generally the orders), the church, the community, the family. The active state as a structure abstracted from the traditional groups, and *a fortiori* the state as the reflection of the sum of individual wills (popular sovereignty), was seen to be an aberration and an abomination. In the face, however, of massive social rejection of these premises, conservatism after 1830, and especially after 1848, took on a more moderate coloration. It preached the politics of prudence. It advocated the norm of minimal change to be undertaken only when carefully justified, and the guidance of popular will by the bearers of traditional messages.

Against conservatism emerged liberalism, as the ostensible defender of the two new ideas. The liberals accepted willingly the normality of change but did not assume that any and all change was desirable. Rather they put forward the theme of *rational* change, careful change (but the care was in its planning rather than in its justification, as for conservatives). The liberals proclaimed the Enlightenment faith in the desirability and inevitability of progress. For the liberals, the correct political strategy was therefore to embrace change by encouraging rational reform of outdated institutions and practices. For the liberals, individual liberty and technology were going forward hand in hand.

The liberals were unsure what to say about popular sovereignty. Against the conservatives they defended the concept in principle. But in practice they were dismayed by the prospect that uneducated (and therefore for liberals inevitably irrational, or at least not optimally rational) persons would control political decisions. They therefore preached expanding education (to make the masses more rational) and giving the leadership in the pursuit of reform to experts (in practice to technocrats), who would of course ensure that the reforms were rational (which in practice meant they were limited and not too rapid).

At first the liberals upheld the banner alone against the conservatives, but gradually a third ideology emerged as a reaction to liberal equivocation. There was no obvious name for this third ideology at first. This group was called variously republicans, radicals, socialists, but above all democrats. For the heart of their position was to take democracy seriously, truly to want political change and to want it to occur as quickly as possible, and truly to desire effective popular sovereignty (with no special place either for traditional leaders or for experts).

The world-system revolution of 1848 marked a turning-point in the history of the three ideologies. For a brief moment, the democrats seemed to gain ground, and then they were repressed. The proponents of all three ideologies learned great lessons from the political struggles of 1848–52. The conservatives learned the political explosiveness and strength of democratic forces. They drew two lessons from this. One was that they had to bury forever the extreme version of their ideology, the restoration of the *ancien régime,* and satisfy themselves with what we now call conservatism (maximal conservation amidst prudent limited change). This meant, among other things, that a Holy Alliance vision of the inter-state system was untenable. The second lesson they learned was that it was politically dangerous to allow liberals and democrats to coalesce. And in order to prevent such a coalescence, or coalition, it would be necessary to decrease their own ideological distance from the liberals, even to be more reformist than the liberals from time to time (the Peel–Disraeli–Napoleon III–Bismarck strategy).

The democrats learned in turn that political explosiveness was no guarantee of political success, and that spontaneity had many political drawbacks. They also learned that any alliance with liberals was fragile and that they had only two real choices: to break with the liberals with the risk of isolation, or to appease them with the risk of undermining the drive to democratise. The conclusion the democrats/socialists drew was that they needed to organise their own movements, as long-term structures (eventually bureaucratised) movements in order to create the pressure necessary to bring about the social transformation they advocated.

The liberals, however, drew the most important lesson of all. They learned that, in trying to manoeuvre a middle-of-the-road course for rational limited reform, they had a tiger by the tail. They drew the conclusion that, in the long run, they could only succeed by what came to be called in the twentieth century consensus politics. This meant that they had to pull both conservatives and democrats/socialists closer to the middle, that is, closer to the liberals. The secret of liberal success in nineteenth-century Europe/North America and in the twentieth-century world was this liberal strategy of consensus politics based on a coherent dosage of reforms. This liberal political strategy became one pillar of the geoculture of the world-system.

The second pillar was the reconstruction of the knowledge system. The displacement of philosophy by science as the organising model of knowledge had been more or less steadily occurring for three centuries, but it was only in the nineteenth century that the displacement was fully realised. The universities were revived to provide the institutional basis for the flourishing of scientism, which has been anchored by the creation of the 'disciplines' around specific courses in the university. The natural sciences contributed spectacularly to improving the production system in innumerable ways, which served to validate the legitimacy of these disciplines. The new versions of the humanities (particularly programmes in the national literatures which only at this point became legitimate objects of study) served to undergird the national conscious-ness which the liberal states were encouraging as a mode of reinforcing consensus politics and legitimating the authority of the state. And the 'in-between' social sciences were developed with the hope and expectation that they would be able to offer a scientific or knowledge basis for the rational manipulation of the social world, that is, for political and social reforms, and also for more efficacious repression.

The third pillar of the liberal geoculture was the depoliticised political incorporation of the dangerous classes, which might otherwise be called the taming of the antisystemic movements. These movements took two main forms in the nineteenth century: so-called social (or socialist) movements which organised urban workers; and so-called nationalist movements which organised 'nationalities' seeking political rights and/or autonomy/independence. While support for the two kinds of movements sometimes overlapped, in most cases they organised different constituencies. What they shared, however, was a strong sense that the current political regime in which they were located was oppressive and unjust, that the oppressed group needed to organise for 'revolutionary' change, and that obtaining state power was the essential first step to obtain the kind of change they wanted.

The liberals countered this programme with a programme of political change aimed at 'incorporating' these 'dangerous classes' into the political system, thereby removing their disaffection with the liberal programme of rational reform enacted by experts. The liberals framed a long-term programme of three elements: the suffrage, the welfare state, and citizen patriotism. As we know, by 1914, it was the case in Europe/ North America that most countries had universal (male) suffrage, the beginnings of a welfare state, and a developed code of popular patriotism inculcated largely via the (compulsory) school system and service in the armed forces (required in most of these countries for young men). This liberal programme was put in place not only by liberal political parties but often by the pre-emptive action of conservative parties and/or under the pressure of socialist parties. Nevertheless, it was a liberal programme, and represented the realisation by 1914 in these countries of the liberal consensus, serving in fact to turn the antisystemic movements in most cases into moderate parliamentary oppositions or even participants in the governmental regimes, without modifying in any significant way the ability of the states separately, and collectively via the interstate system, to guarantee the conditions for the ceaseless accumulation of capital.

The three pillars served as well to obscure the basic symbolic and symbiotic antinomy of this liberal consensus: the simultaneous pursuit of universalism on the one hand and racism – sexism on the other. By the middle of the nineteenth century, universalism had become the ostensible central organising value of the capitalist world-economy. Science was said to consist of the statement of universal laws, whose statements were equally true of all identical processes. Scientists were said to be disinterested researchers seeking to state such universal laws, preferably elegantly, in quantified and simple form. To the extent that such universal laws were known, scientists (and engineers) would then presumably use them to create applications of universal benefit.

The liberal state was said to be the application of such universal principles to the polity. The principle of universal individual rights eliminated in theory any irrelevant privilege (that is, any advantage that was not earned by current achievement). Suffrage was the reflection of this principle. And finally the free market presumably was the guarantor that only productive efficiency would be relevant to the exchange of commodities produced in the division of labour. The free market was in theory equally accessible to all as buyer or seller, and its rules were universally valid.

The results of such universal principles were manifestly unequal in terms of distributive justice, within and among the several states. (That the premises of science were implausible and harmful of long-term scientific advance was also true but not yet recognised.) Furthermore, as explained above, a truly free market and/or a truly democratic state would soon make unviable the underlying and unstated *raison d'être* of the capitalist world-economy, the ceaseless accumulation of capital, which requires monopolised markets, assignment of labour to unequally rewarded slots in the division of labour, and reasonable political stability.

Indeed, the very triumph of universalist values itself undermined the system insofar as it eliminated previous justifications for a hierarchical work place and a hierarchical political system. The problem was how to maintain/restore hierarchy without renouncing universalism, a necessary component of the geoculture. The answer was the institutionalisation of racism and sexism. Neither xenophobia nor gender oppression was new in the history of the world. But it is only with the rise of universalist values that there came to be an urgent need to institutionalise and theorise racism and sexism rather than merely to use traditional oppressive mechanisms.

Racism and sexism played analogous but distinctive roles in the geoculture. Racism was essentially the mechanism by which universalist values became in practice applicable *ad interim* only to an in-group, defined by race (colour of skin, religion, citizenship, or any other locally useful distinction). Racism was not a mechanism of exclusion, but rather a mechanism of justifying inclusion in the workforce and the political system at a level of reward and status sharply inferior to that of some large group. Sexism had the same objective, but reached it via a different path. By restricting women to certain modes of producing income, and by defining such modes as non-work (the concept of the 'housewife'), sexism promoted the semi-proletarian household and hence, as we have already discussed, worked to reduce wage levels in very large sectors of the world-economy. In addition, insofar as women (and children) were utilised as wage workers, they received far lower wages, which was justified by sexism.

As with racism, sexism was defined as not violating the principles of universalism, since the sexes were said to be essentially different, and hence men and women (as Whites and Blacks, or Whites and all others) were not comparable entities in terms of the application of universal laws. The antinomy of universalism/racism – sexism thus served to maintain a careful balance between two extremes, either of which was highly dysfunctional to capital accumulation, just as the partially free market remained in-between the extremes of the totally free and the totally administered market.

The inter-state system

The normal functioning of any historical system is simultaneously cyclical and secular, both systemic (and thus with homeostatic pressures) and historical (and thus moving in a direction far from equilibrium). The key cyclical rhythm in terms of the world production system is the so-called Kondratieff cycle (50–60 years in average length) which expresses the process of creating major monopolies (forming the cycle's A-phase) and undoing them as a result of excessive entry into the market by new suppliers (forming its B-phase).

The inter-state structures, however, are governed by a longer cyclical process we may call the hegemonic cycle. Just as capital accumulation is maximised in the modern world-system when it operates in the *via media* of a partially free market and within a value system governed by a tension between universalism and sexism – racism, so it is the case that capital accumulation is maximised when the inter-state structures veer neither towards the extreme of a world-empire (a single overarching political structure) nor towards the extreme of the relative anarchy that derives from a situation in which there are multiple 'great powers' all of somewhat equal overall strength (military/political/economic/social). The ideal situation in terms of capital accumulation for the system as a whole is the existence of a hegemonic power, strong enough to define the rules of the game and to see that they are followed almost all of the time. When rivalry is replaced by hegemony as systemic condition, it does not mean that the hegemonic power can do anything; but it does mean that it can prevent others from doing things that will significantly alter the rules.

The search for hegemony in the inter-state system is analogous to the search for monopoly in the world production system. It is a search for advantage never quite totally achieved. We can therefore ask three questions about hegemony. How does a given state achieve a position strong enough *vis-à-vis* other strong powers such that we may call it hegemonic? What kinds of policies do hegemonic powers pursue? Why does a hegemonic power lose its hegemony? The history of the 'international relations' of the modern world-system offers answers to each of these questions.

What is needed for a given state to have pretensions to hegemony in the modern world-system? Strangely enough, the primary requirement at the outset is not military strength, although the acquisition of military strength is a crucial achievement in the process. There have been only three hegemonic powers in the history of the modern world-system: the United Provinces in the mid-seventeenth century, the United Kingdom in the mid-nineteenth, and the United States in the mid-twentieth. Each was hegemonic only briefly. The most significant achievement for each on the road to hegemony was primacy in productive efficiency within the world-economy. One of the reasons each was able to achieve this superiority was the fact that it had not invested heavily during this period in creating a large army. However, each had created a large merchant marine which, in addition to its obvious economic function, supported the ability of this state to sustain a large naval force. It is indeed probably the case that a key factor in the ability of the state that won out in the struggle to achieve hegemony (won out against its major rival) was the fact that it had *not* invested in a large army.

Productive efficiencies historically made possible commercial efficiencies, which in turn supported the achievement of financial efficiencies. While this rise in relative efficiencies was partially a direct product of market transactions, it was never that alone. It always required the use of state power to create non-market-generated advantages for the putative hegemonic power. The process was one of cumulating advantages, and turning them into a structurally privileged position. In fact, in every case, the final phase of the struggle for hegemony involved a major military encounter, which we may call generically a 'thirty years' war'. Such a war is different from the frequent localised, usually two-power wars or the wars of strong states with very weak ones (wars of conquest or quasi-conquest). The 'thirty years' wars' involve over time (not always totally simultaneously) *all* the major military powers, and involve massive physical destruction (and consequently destruction of production facilities). Each of the three such wars we have had – the original Thirty Years' War, 1618–48; the Revolutionary and Napoleonic wars, 1792–1815; the First/Second World Wars, 1914–45 – were sporadic rather than continuous, saw states change sides in the middle belying their asserted ideological commitments, and ended in the definitive victory of one of the two main contenders. In each case, the sea(/air)-power defeated the land-based power. In each case, the power committed to maintaining the basic structure of a capitalist world-economy won out against the power that was pushing in the direction of transforming the system into a world-empire. In each case the thirty years' war itself was the decisive factor in achieving the necessary marked superiority in productive efficiency within the world-economy as a whole and in particular relative to the main rival. In each case, the war itself increased enormously the military strength of the putative hegemonic power. And in each case, the drive to achieve hegemonic status had been a very long process, stretching over many decades at least.

The end of each thirty years' war marked a significant stage in the construction of the inter-state system: the Treaty of Westphalia, the Concert of Europe, and the United Nations. Each time, the hegemonic power sought to create an order in the system that would guarantee its economic advantage over the long run. The dilemma for the hegemonic power was very simple. Because of their efficiencies, the producers of the hegemonic power benefited in the short run from a maximally free world market. But since productive efficiencies can be eventually matched, any advantages that its enterprises had in terms of productive efficiencies were vulnerable in the middle run insofar as the world market was truly free. A hegemonic power can maintain its hegemony over a middle run only as long as it can impose institutional constraints on the freedom of the world market that would work in its favour. Such constraints may include forcing open the markets of other countries to the products of the hegemonic power, while keeping its own markets relatively closed when necessary. Arrangements to funnel commercial and financial transactions via loci in the hegemonic power is another such constraint. The imposition of a currency of world transactions and last resort is still another. And the political demand to be involved in all decisions throughout the world-system without a reciprocal right for other powers is yet another.

The imposition of institutional constraints requires the judiciously combined use of force, bribery and ideological persuasion. It is at this point that military supremacy is essential. The force must be sufficient such that, in most cases, it is not necessary to use it; most of the time, the mere threat must suffice. The efficacy of force, when actively and repeatedly challenged, diminishes over time by virtue of the challenges, even if they are unsuccessful. The bribery involves the trade-off of rewarding allies (or pseudo-allies) against their contribution to the effective force, as well as their overall political support of course. And the ideological persuasion is a key element in persuading the populations of the hegemonic power to pay the price of military supremacy, to persuade the cadres and populations of the allied countries to consider the pluses of an alliance far greater than its minuses, and even to create doubts among the victims of the system as to the acceptability of their complaints. Successive hegemonic powers have been increasingly successful in this ideological task.

But, despite the relative success, the very policies of the hegemonic power which prolong economic advantage via political 'leadership' are in fact the eventual cause of the decline of hegemony. Force needs to be used on occasion, and the use of force delegitimises the user, even when it succeeds. Force has furthermore a price for the user, and each time it is paid reluctance to pay it grows. Strengthening allies allows allies to become stronger *vis-à-vis* the hegemonic power itself. And ideological justifications of leadership, inevitably specious, tend to wear thin. For all these reasons, there comes a moment when leadership is no longer automatic, when persuasion becomes very difficult, and perhaps most important when the hegemonic power can no longer demonstrate greater productive efficiency than its rivals.

The decline of hegemony is perceived simultaneously as very slow and quite rapid. On the one hand, suddenly, everyone seems to notice that the authority of the hegemonic power is under serious challenge, and that the achievement of its political will is no longer automatic. The hegemonic power seems to be in some economic trouble, after a long period of unquestioned prosperity. And of course the very perception of these weaknesses increases them, since others are then ready to act in the inter-state arena in ways that are markedly different from the ways in which they acted during the heyday of the hegemonic power. On the other hand, decline seems very slow. The hegemonic power, even when it begins to decline, is clearly still the strongest power (militarily, politically, economically, even culturally). If it does not automatically get its way, it remains hard for anyone to do things against its will. If its economic lead is cut, it still seems (and is) very wealthy.

Much of the debate about how long hegemony lasts, often phrased as the debate over whether or not a given power is in 'decline', results from the ambiguity of the early stages of decline. It is the old question of whether the glass is half empty or half full. It is in many ways a semantic debate. The fact is that it takes a long time for a given state to become a hegemonic power. Once it gets there, its power is at a height and on a sort of plateau. Then its power begins to wane. It takes almost as long for its power fully to wane as it does to achieve the power fully in the first place.

Analytically, it seems useful to distinguish between the period of the plateau and that of the decline. In this essay, we restrict the word 'hegemony' to the period of the plateau, considering that such a usage is clearer. But clearly, many of the mechanisms that the hegemonic power has put in place during its peak period survive in the period of decline, if with diminishing efficacy. That was always the hope and expectation of the hegemonic power. These mechanisms are ways of slowing the inevitable decline, and they do indeed slow it down. On the other hand, we think it important to underline how brief is the period of the plateau. The system of hegemonic cycles works such that true hegemony exists at most a quarter of the time. The statistically normal phenomenon is the existence of multiple rival 'great powers' – with, however, the proviso, that there are always two at least who are making strenuous efforts to become the successor hegemonic power.

We also restrict the use of 'hegemony' only to one power at a time, and in relation to the world-system as a whole. Thus, we do not term regional strengths 'local hegemonies' since that misses the point that the hegemonic power, if there is one, sets the rules for how regional blocs work as well. In the early nineteenth century, Metternich was dismayed by the capacity of the British to limit Austria's ability to impose its will on neighbours who defied the principles of the Holy Alliance. And in the post-1945 world, the USSR found itself effectively constrained by the rules of the Yalta world-order.

It has been the cyclical rise and fall of hegemonic powers that has provided the crucial degree of equilibrium to the inter-state politics of the modern world-system, thereby enabling the processes of capital accumulation to proceed without serious hindrance. A hegemony that lasted too long would have pushed the system towards its transformation into a world-empire. And a system that never saw the emergence of a hegemonic power would not have had the possibility of creating the stable interim orders needed to maximise accumulation. If the length of a hegemonic cycle has been far greater than that of a Kondratieff cycle, it is that the complexity of the hegemonic order is far greater than the monopoly of a leading sector. It takes far longer to establish and it is more disruptive to tamper with it. But the rhythm of the cycle has been crucial for the circulation of the collective psychic energy we call the social cohesion of the system as a whole.

The modern world-system, nonetheless, like all systems, has secular trends which are moving it far from equilibrium, and therefore towards a true crisis, in which there will be a bifurcation. The present system will come to an end, to be replaced by one or more successor systems. There are several reasons to believe that we have already entered that phase, and that it is consequently unlikely that there will be another hegemonic cycle in the further history of this system. The functioning of the modern world-system has been dependent on three international phenomena: a relatively stable inter-state system, of which the system of hegemonic cycles has been the motor; a highly profitable world production system, of which the monopoly cycles (the Kondratieffs) have been the motor; and the social cohesion of the sovereign states, especially those which are in the core zone. What has made this social cohesion possible has been the establishment of liberal states, offering suffrage, welfare, and a sense of racial/national superiority of its citizenry. Tying this all together has been a geoculture, founded on the illusion of universal development and the expectation of general prosperity and democratic equality on the horizon for everyone. There are at least seven major secular trends which combine to make it implausible that this interconnected web of structures will continue to be viable.

1 The process of capitalist development is a polarising process. The gap between those who are its beneficiaries and those who are not has been growing greater for 500 years. This fact has been obscured by looking at the wrong units of analysis, the individual states, rather than the world-system as a whole. Even in Kondratieff A-periods, when all measured phenomena seem to be moving upward, the relative gap has grown; and in B-periods, the growing relative gap reverts to being a growing absolute gap. While the polarising tendency has been constant, it has grown ever greater in extent. In addition, the economic/social gap has been reinforced, particularly in the last fifty years, by a demographic gap, which renders the polarisation not only more acute but also more visible. Among other consequences, it has created an enormous pressure for South-to-North migration which seems virtually unstoppable. But this in turn has serious political consequences for the functioning of the world-system.

2 A crucial element in the functioning of the system has been, we have argued, the creation of semi-proletarian income-pooling household structures, which have accounted for the transnational, so-called historical differential in wages, so necessary for high profit levels. However, the periodic needs of the world-economy for additional effective demand plus the pressures of the workers themselves have led to a steady deruralisation of the workforce which is in the process of depriving the world-system of its reserve labour force. A reserve labour force has not only been crucial to resolving profitability dilemmas, but it has been a key element in maintaining the social cohesion of the states, the newly socially incorporated workers tending to be a pillar of national patriotism. A deruralised workforce, insufficiently employed, leads instead to enormous so-called marginal populations in the cities of the world-system of all sizes, with an increasing policy problem not open to a structural solution.

3 The liberal developmentalist illusion has played itself out. Its last

and greatest flourishing was at the height of US hegemony, in the period from 1945–70, when everyone everywhere seemed to be sure that, one way or another, by one political/economic method or another, their state would 'develop' eventually. The one clear lesson of the last twenty-five years is that this is not so, and that most of the states which had made a seemingly significant push forward during the 1945–70 period have since lost relatively whatever they had gained. This is equally true of seeming gains made in the reduction of intra-state inequalities, which have been sharply resurgent in the post-1970 period. The ideological outcome has been a turning against the liberal geoculture, and its vision of the beneficent state, which was itself a major factor in the social cohesion of the states.

4 The disillusionment with liberal developmentalism, that is, with the whole ideological framework developed since the French Revolution and in response to it, has been accompanied by, or rather is reflected in, the disillusionment with the classical antisystemic movements (socialist and national liberation), which had been preaching liberal develop-mentalism in the guise of antisystemic revolution. The collapse of these movements has removed one of the major underpinnings of the system of liberal states. The collapse of these movements has removed one of the major restraining forces on the political impulses of the world's dangerous classes.

5 Meanwhile, however, liberalism has, despite its protagonists' best intentions, fostered the demand for democratic restructuring and measurable welfare. Thus, to put it very simply, the popular demands on the states to provide education, health and a reasonable lifelong standard of living for its citizens has been far greater than ever before, and shows no signs of slowing down. This has brought on the so-called fiscal crises of the states, since even the wealthiest states find they are in no position really to respond to these demands, however legitimate. Thus for the first time in at least 200 years, and probably in 500 years, there is a real attempt to reduce, both absolutely and relatively, state expenditures on welfare, broadly defined. But these cutbacks threaten to lead to the withdrawal of legitimation of the states by the group that has supported state structures most strongly, the so-called middle strata. In this way, the fiscal crises of the states become the political crises of the states. This in turn makes it far more difficult for a hegemonic power, or even great powers in general, to act to maintain order within the inter-state arena. The situation is then aggravated considerably by the inter-state migration, and is reflected in growing internal disorder, much exagger-ated in perception, but in any case destructive of cohesion. It is leading to the breakdown of citizenship as a category covering the overwhelming

majority of persons resident in a state; we are returning to a system in which the states are formally politically stratified, which in turn reinforces the internal tensions.

6 Five hundred years of expanded production (and enormous waste in the process) have led to an acute ecological problem, which can only be resolved even partially by an enormous expenditure of money, and a considerable amount of social dislocation as well. But who will pay this money, if this is done seriously? If it is the enterprises, it will vitiate the unending accumulation of capital. And if it is achieved by reducing popular welfare, this will be the last straw in the possibility of maintaining the social cohesion of the states. The greatest likelihood is that neither solution will be attempted, in which case the physical and health consequences will be destructive of the world-system.

7 Finally, the deepest pillar of the geoculture has been the faith in science that was difficult to construct and which was based very largely on the ability of the scientists to contribute to technological change that in turn sustained the expansion of the world production system. The (Newtonian) scientists of previous generations overplayed their hand, selling faith in expertise as objective rationality. Within the ranks of the scientists themselves, there has arisen a demand for a fundamental revision, a new science, based on the rejection of linearity, the impossibility of precision, the unpredictability of phenomena even if they are all explicable, and the arrow of time. At the same time disillusionment with the false universalism of Newtonian science has given rise to a profound cultural attack which has taken many forms (from integrist religiosity to deconstructionism to the equal validation of all truth-assertions). It is not to the point to discuss here the epistemological, philosophical and political issues under debate, but simply to notice the degree to which this pulls one final rug from under the edifice carefully constructed over 500 years.

The inter-state system, like the system of states, was part and parcel of a singular world-system, the capitalist world-economy, that was constructed initially in Europe beginning in the late fifteenth century. This system has been remarkably successful and was able to expand geographically to cover the entire globe, the first historical system to achieve this in the history of humanity. The system, like all historical social systems, has been a complex one. Its parts have not been isolated, autonomous entities, and cannot be intelligently analysed if they are so regarded.

The modern world-system is in the process of coming to its end. This is not *per se* good or bad; it all depends on what will be constructed in its place. It is, however, rather unlikely that the successor system will have an inter-state system of the type we now know, since it is rather unlikely that the structure of sovereign states will survive. Since we are at an early stage in this process of transition, and its course is not predetermined, our individual and collective inputs will matter significantly. We are in effect being called upon to construct our utopias, not merely to dream about them. Something will be constructed. If we do not participate in the construction, others will determine it for us.

NOTE

This text has been much improved thanks to the careful reading of Terence K. Hopkins.

BIBLIOGRAPHY

Elaboration of the world-systems perspective can be found in numerous volumes. On the historical structuring of the modern world-system, including its inter-state structures, see Immanuel Wallerstein, *The Modern World-System*, 3 vols. (Academic Press, 1974, 1980, 1989). See also Giovanni Arrighi, *The Long Twentieth Century* (Verso, 1994). Reading Fernand Braudel, *Capitalism and Civilization, 15th–18th Century*, 3 vols. (Harper & Row, 1981, 1982, 1984) will be immensely rewarding. And for a somewhat different approach from any of the above, see George Modelski and William R. Thompson, *Seapower in Global Politics, 1493–1993* (University of Washington Press, 1988).

For a discussion of whether or not the inter-state system operates on a different logic from that of the capitalist world-economy, see Christopher Chase-Dunn, 'Interstate System and Capitalist World-Economy', *International Studies Quarterly*, 25 (1) (March 1981). On the concept of hegemony, for three variant expositions, see Immanuel Wallerstein, 'The Three Instances of Hegemony in the Capitalist World-Economy', in *The Politics of the World-Economy* (Cambridge University Press, 1984); Giovanni Arrighi, 'The Three Hegemonies of Historical Capitalism', and Terence K. Hopkins, 'Note on the Concept of Hegemony', *Review*, 13 (3) (Summer 1990). For recent changes in the world-system, see Immanuel Wallerstein, *Geopolitics and Geoculture* (Cambridge University Press, 1991).

For structural analyses of the functioning of the world-system, see Christopher Chase-Dunn, *Global Formation* (Blackwell, 1989) and Peter J. Taylor, *Political Geography: World-Economy, Nation-State, and Locality*, 2nd edition (Longman/Wiley, 1989). For analyses of the geoculture and its present dilemmas, see Immanuel Wallerstein, *Unthinking Social Science* (Polity, 1991). For analyses of household structures in the world-economy, see Joan Smith and Immanuel Wallerstein, coord., *Creating and Transforming Households* (Cambridge University Press, 1992).

For discussion on cycles (both hegemonic and Kondratieff), see Joshua S. Goldstein, *Long Cycles* (Yale University Press, 1988). For another view on hegemonic cycles, see George Modelski, *Long Cycles in World Politics* (University of Washington Press, 1987). For the original presentation of Kondratieff cycles, see Nikolai Kondratieff, *The Long Wage Cycle* (Richardson & Snyder, 1984).

Finally, three older works should not be neglected: Ludwig Dehio, *The Precarious Balance* (Knopf, 1962), Frederic Lane, *Profits from Power* (SUNY Press, 1979), and Josef V. Polisensky, *The Thirty Years' War* (University of California Press, 1971).

5   The accomplishments of international political economy

Stephen Krasner

Introduction

International political economy (IPE) is concerned with the political determinants of international economic relations. It tries to answer questions such as: How have changes in the international distribution of power among states affected the degree of openness in the international trading system? Do the domestic political structures and values of some states allow them to compete more effectively? Is the relative poverty of the Third World better explained by indigenous politics and economic conditions in individual countries or by the workings of the international political economy? When can international economic ties among states be used for political leverage?

International political economy can be contrasted with conventional economics and with security studies. Conventional economists ask many of the same questions as do students of IPE but their answers are related to economic factors such as savings rates, labour markets, or technical knowledge rather than political factors like the international distribution of power or the relationship between the state and the private sector. Students of international security ask different questions like: what are the causes of war? or when are alliances likely to be stable? but offer explanations that are similar to those deployed by scholars who work on international political economy.

The study of international political economy has been guided almost exclusively by the canons of what John Searle has labelled the Western Rationalistic Tradition which is characterised by the assumption that reality exists independently of the way in which it is represented by humans and that the truth of a statement depends on how well it conforms with this independent reality (Searle, 1993, p. 57). The 'truth or falsity of the claims made is totally independent of the motives, the morality, or even the gender, the race, or the ethnicity of the maker' (Searle, 1993, p. 66). International political economy is deeply embedded in the standard epistemological methodology of the social sciences which, stripped to its bare bones, simply means stating a proposition and testing it against external evidence. Students of IPE have implicitly rejected the sceptical or anti-foundational post-modernist position which claims that there is no there there; that 'each society has its own regime of truth, its general politics of truth' (M. Foucault quoted in Rengger, 1992, p. 563).

Some history

During the 1950s and 1960s international relations was concerned primarily with security. The Cold War dominated the interest of scholars and the attention of policy makers. International economic issues were a secondary concern. Between the East and the West, economic transactions were highly politicised and tightly controlled while within the West economic disputes were muted. Setting the rules of the game and achieving the optimal configuration of international economic transactions were seen as technical issues. There were only a few isolated scholars working on questions related to the political determinants of international economic relations. Before the mid-1970s there were no courses, at least not in the Unites States, called international political economy.

The attention devoted to international political economy increased dramatically after 1970 for several reasons, some intellectual and academic, others related to political events. OPEC and the rise of oil prices in 1973–4, the collapse of the Bretton Woods monetary system in 1971, and the demands of the Third World for a New International Economic Order in the mid-1970s made it clear that the major issues related to international economic relations could not be explained solely by strictly economic considerations.

Attention to international political economy was further reinforced by developments within the academy. The old agenda of international politics had become exhausted. The most interesting arguments about nuclear strategy as a rational strategic enterprise had been made by the early 1960s (Schelling, 1960, 1966). The study of international organisations had not moved beyond an arid formality expounded by specialists in international law. Economics, as an academic discipline, came increasingly to reward its members for expertise in the development of formal models and to discount institutional analysis. Hence, in the early 1970s there was an absence of systematic investigations of increasingly troublesome global economic developments. The field of international political economy developed to fill this gap.

IPE has been dominated by four major perspectives – liberalism, realism, domestic politics and Marxism. Only the first three will be discussed in this essay.

The central debate in IPE has been between liberal and realist analysts. Liberal analysis has focused on the incentives and opportunities for co-operation. Realists have focused on the way in which power has influenced both the character of international regimes and conflicts among specific states.

Explanations which emphasise the interaction between domestic and international politics, the way in which domestic structures, values and groups influence international interactions and vice versa have, in some specific cases, been deeply illuminating, but no one has presented a coherent general theory.

Liberalism

Liberalism makes the following *assumptions*:

1 There are many different kinds of actors including state-owned enterprises, multi-national corporations, public international organisations, non-governmental organisations, private foundations, and terrorists, as well as states.
2 These actors are all rational and calculating but they pursue different objectives: corporate executives want profits or sales; the rulers of states want security and higher levels of well-being for their populations; environmental groups want to preserve the ecosphere. Furthermore, different actors have different power capabilities in different areas; specific actors can influence outcomes in some arenas but not others.
3 International relations and especially international political economy offer opportunities for everyone to gain at the same time. Actors are more concerned with their absolute well-being than with their relative position *vis-à-vis* others.

The *explanatory variable* for liberalism is the configuration of interests and capabilities associated with a given issue area; that is, outcomes, including the creating of institutions designed to secure Pareto optimal outcomes (situations in which no actor can be made better off without making some other actor worse off), are a function of the preferences and capabilities of a variety of different actors concerned with maximising their own individual utility.

The *evidence* that is needed for a liberal analysis involves specifying the relevant actors (states, multi-nationals, etc.), assessing their resources and signifying their objectives (including not only their interests but also the constraints and incentives that are presented by existing institutional structures and other actors).

Every theoretical perspective works with an *exemplary problem* which is assumed to be the most important kind of issue in the international system and which can be analysed using the theoretical tools (assumptions, evidence and causal arguments) of that approach. The exemplary problem for contemporary liberal analysts is market failure; that is, situations in which the purely individual calculation of interest does not lead to Pareto optimal outcomes.

Liberalism offers a basically benign image of the global economy. There are many different actors. They have different interests. There are opportunities for cutting deals. Everyone can be better off at the same time. Human ingenuity and intelligence can create new institutions that encourage behaviour that leads to Pareto optimal outcomes.

The most important empirical development for all variants of the liberal perspective is the growth of global interactions. Transportation and communications costs have dramatically declined because of changes in technology. These changes have opened many new opportunities for mutual gain. Automobiles or computers can be assembled from parts that are produced in many different countries. Billions of pounds or dollars can be moved around the globe with a flick of a computer switch. Individuals with e-mail can sit in Bombay, Athens and Silicon Valley and work on the same software program. The benefits of an open world economy have increased. More and more actors have a stake in a stable international economic order.

Liberalism, like all of the major theoretical approaches to IPE has several different variants: three of the most prominent are functionalism, transnationalism and co-operation theory. Functionalist and neo-functionalist theories were developed in the 1950s and 1960s primarily to explain the European Community. Functionalism was both an analysis and a prescription. As originally laid out by David Mitrany and others, the idea was to create institutions in Europe that would focus the interests and ultimately the loyalties of individual actors. Corporations, foundations, lawyers and individuals would see their economic interest and their self-identity increasingly tied up with European institutions rather than those of their national states. Neo-functionalist arguments put more emphasis on the role of the state arguing that integration would take place as a result of domestic political pressures to enhance regional institutions (political spillover), the inherent links between issue areas so that integration in one necessitated integration in another (functional spillover), and upgrading common interests by relying on integrative institutions to work out mutually beneficial issue linkages (Burley and Mattli, 1993, pp. 53–7).

The fate of functionalist arguments has waxed and waned with the degree of progress towards integration in Europe. The spillover effects that functional and neo-functional arguments expected were not obvious during the 1960s and early 1970s. Recently, however, functionalist arguments have been revived to explain the Single European Act, Maastricht and other manifestations of regional integration in Europe (Burley and Mattli, 1993).

Transnationalism is a second line of liberal analysis. Writing in 1971 Robert Keohane and Joseph Nye defined transnational interactions as 'the movement of tangible or intangible items across state boundaries when at least one actor is not an agent of a government or an inter-governmental organization' (Nye and Keohane, 1971, p. 5). While recognising that transnational relations had always existed Keohane and Nye went on to argue that governmental control had been restricted by changes in technology which facilitated interaction among societal actors in different countries (most notably, the subsidiaries of trans-national corporations), by the increasing agendas of governments which impinged on more and more groups in civil society, and by the flow of information from the mass media. Effective management of this increasingly transnationalised world would require higher levels of co-operation (Nye and Keohane, 1971, pp. 725–9; and Keohane and Nye, 1977).

Transnational relations is the most immediately obvious liberal perspective because it resonates with the everyday experiences of many individuals. Examples of transnational flows include international air flights; ATM machines that can supply pounds in London, or yen in Tokyo from a bank account in Des Moines; international phone, fax and e-mail; the live global coverage by CNN and other networks of news events; and the movement of undocumented workers across territorial borders. As a research programme, however, transnational relations failed because in most cases it could not clearly specify *ex ante* actors, their interests, or their capabilities. If all actors are relevant, and actors can have many different interests, and the ability of actors to pursue these interests is not well defined, then any outcome in international politics would be consistent with the theory; that is, after the fact it would be possible to find some group of transnational actors that supported public policy that was ultimately selected. But if a theory can be made consistent with every possible outcome then it explains nothing.

One major exception to this generalisation about the inability of transnational relations theory to generate an ongoing research effort is global finance. Richard Cooper, writing in 1968, argued that the size and mobility of international capital flows had severely constrained the ability of states to carry out an independent monetary policy. Efforts to raise interest rates, for instance, would only encourage the inflow of international capital, increasing the money supply, and driving interest rates down (Cooper, 1968; Krause, 1971, pp. 523–7). The advanced industrialised countries all abandoned efforts to permanently control short-term capital flows during the 1980s because the level of such flows had increased so dramatically (at an annual rate of 21.4 per cent from 1970 to 1985, compared with growth of 12.7 per cent for world trade), the ability of private multi-nationals to evade controls had increased as their operations had become ever more globalised, and because of the pressure from these same firms on their own governments to abandon regulations lest they be placed at a competitive disadvantage with their competitors who could more easily access international markets (Goodman and Pauly, 1993, pp. 51–2, 57–9).

The third, and now the most important line of liberal research is co-operation theory. Co-operation theory analyses market failure problems. States may fail to maximise their own utility because individual self-interested behaviour results, in some circumstances such as a prisoner's dilemma payoff structure or the provision of collective goods, in a Pareto sub-optimal outcome. These failures can often be resolved by the creation of institutional arrangements that provide information, monitoring and salient solutions (Keohane, 1984; Stein, 1990). Co-operation theory is based upon analytic techniques, especially game theory and rational choice, that have exploded in the discipline of economics over the last decade. These techniques are heuristically very powerful; that is, they provide a set of analytic tools that can be used to examine many different issues.

Co-operation theory has been applied to issues related to trade, finance, the environment and economic sanctions. For instance, in the absence of international institutions states could fail to engage in free trade, despite the fact that such a policy would (at least according to standard neo-classical trade theory) make all of them better off. The best policy for each individual state is to impose an optimal tariff. If, however, all countries attempt to impose such tariffs, then they would all be worse off. If one country refrains from imposing a tariff while others do so, it could be worse off. This potential market failure, in which every country imposes a tariff, can be overcome by establishing an international institution, such as GATT or now the World Trade Organisation, which can define standards for what constitutes cheating, provide rules that act as salient solutions, engage in some modest level of monitoring, and provide dispute settlement mechanisms.

A second example of the use of co-operation theory is international banking and finance. An individual country can maximise the business opportunities for its own financial institutions by having low capital requirements making it possible for their banks to loan more money. If all countries have low requirements, however, then there is a greater danger of an international financial collapse because the failure of one undercapitalised institution could lead to other failures. To overcome this potential problem of competitive undercapitalisation, central bankers from the major industrialised countries signed the Basle Agreement in 1988 which defines a common set of capital standards to which all signatories must adhere (Kapstein, 1989; Martin, 1992a, pp. 765–92 and Martin, 1992b).

In sum, liberal analysis in its various forms has provided explanations for a number of developments in the world political economy. Co-operation is manifest in many different areas despite the fact that the international system remains anarchical. Transnational flows have increased dramatically. The number of international institutions has exploded.

Liberal analysis is, however, much less adequate for addressing other questions. It has little to say about war. For military conflict, as opposed to international political economy, the basic liberal contention has been that the world is changing: the opportunities for mutual gain through exchange have increased and the cost of war has spiralled. It makes more sense to trade than to fight (Rosecrance, 1986; Doyle, 1983). This change in incentive structures does not, however, seem to have altered the behaviour of leaders in Iran, Iraq, Serbia, Bosnia, Croatia, Rwanda, Aden, Somalia and elsewhere. Liberal perspectives cannot explain the basic division of the global economy that existed during the Cold War with the United States and its allies working under one regime and the Soviet bloc under another. If changes in technology and the opportunities for mutual gain are driving national behaviour why not more integration between the East and the West? Realism, which focuses on power, security and distributional conflict offers answers to these questions as well as others.

Realism

Realism makes the following *assumptions*:
1 The constitutive actors in the international system are sovereign states. Other actors such as multi-national corporations, or non-

governmental organisations are subordinate to states in that they must operate within governing structures established by states and they can be ruined by states, albeit sometimes at considerable cost.

2 The international system is in a state of anarchy: there is no accepted political authority. States engage in self-help; they determine their own national policies although their options may be severely constrained by the power of other states.

3 States must be concerned with their own security. At a minimum, a state must act to protect its territorial and political integrity. States cannot be oblivious to relative gains because in some situations changes in power capabilities can put their security at risk (Powell, 1991).

4 States are rational unified actors. Domestic politics, individual irrationality, or organisational failures have only a marginal impact on outcomes.

The *explanatory variable* for realism is the distribution of power among states. The basic claim of realism is that given a particular distribution of power among states it is possible to explain both the characteristics of the system and the behaviour of individual states. For instance, in a bipolar world the two poles are bound to be adversaries. Realism makes no effort to probe the domestic determinants of foreign policy; what counts is state power and external constraints.

The *evidence* that realists utilise requires operationalising the power of states by, for instance, looking at the size of armies, aggregate economic output, or the ability to make credible threats.

For realism the *exemplary problem* is to explain how either zero sum or distributional conflicts are resolved given the power and interests of states (Waltz, 1979). The world remains a dangerous place. Economic transactions among specific states can, in some circumstances, be used for political leverage. States struggle to define international regimes because different regimes have different distributional consequences (Krasner, 1991).

Realist analyses of international political economy have addressed two kinds of issues: first, how national power has influenced relations among specific countries; and, second, how the distribution of power in the system as a whole has determined international regimes.

In 1945 Albert Hirschman published *National Power and the Structure of Foreign Trade* which remains one of the most illuminating discussions of the way in which power affects international economic relations among specific countries. He argued that there were two ways in which trading relations could be used to alter the capabilities or policies of another state: first, states could limit the availability of critical products or technology in an effort to weaken the resource base of their opponents; second, one state could attempt to change the foreign policy behaviour of another by threatening to change the rules of the game governing their economic transactions.

The policies of the Western alliance towards the Communist bloc during the Cold War are an example of an effort to limit the power capabilities of an enemy by restricting the flow of goods, loans and information. The Eastern bloc was almost completely excluded from international economic organisations – the international financial institutions (the World Bank, IMF, and the various regional banks), and the GATT (General Agreement on Tariffs and Trade). The Western alliance (including Japan and Europe) established the Coordinating Committee or COCOM whose members assembled a list of products whose sale to the Communist bloc was prohibited (Mastanduno, 1992; National Academy of Sciences, 1987, pp. 106–7).

Economic relations can also be used to change the foreign policy of a target state. If one state can credibly threaten to alter the existing pattern of exchange, the second state will acquiesce if the cost of the sanctions would be greater than the cost of compliance: better to go along with the preferences of the strong than to suffer economic harm. The critical question then is: what makes a threat credible? Hirschman provided a brilliant answer. A threat is only credible if the relative opportunity costs of change are asymmetrical. If the initiator can change its economic policies at little cost (cutting off trade for instance), but the cost of such a change would be high for the target, then the threat is credible. If, in contrast, the opportunity costs of change, or altering the present state of affairs, is symmetrical, then the threat is not credible: the cost of implementing the threat would be as high for the initiator as for the target. Opportunity costs provide a way of operationalising power, a problem that has plagued realist analysis. Hirschman demonstrated that Nazi Germany had used asymmetrical costs to make credible threats against the smaller countries of Eastern and Central Europe in the 1930s and had successfully constrained their foreign policy options (Hirschman, 1945, part II).

One basic expectation of realist analysis is that there will be tension, although not necessarily war, among the major states in the international system regardless of their domestic political structures. Economic interactions, for instance, between the Soviet Union and the United States were limited. With the end of the Cold War Japan has emerged as the major challenger to the United States and tension between the two countries has increased. In some issue areas American policy makers have become more concerned with relative gains, more attentive, for instance, to the ways in which different kinds of arrangements between the two countries would affect the transfer of technology and potentially even military capability. American trade policy has increasingly differentiated Japan from other countries. American officials have pressured Japan to open specific markets including government procurement, medical equipment, automobile parts, cellular telephones, and rice. The success of these efforts remains in doubt at least in part because the relative opportunity costs of change are not highly asymmetrical; the actual imposition of trade sanctions by the United States against Japan would be costly for both countries (Mastanduno, 1991). Hence, examining the relationship among specific countries with regard to the interaction between power, security and economic transactions has been one major focus of realist analysis.

The second major focus of realism has been the relationship between the distribution of power among states in the international system and the nature of international economic regimes. The most prominent argument along these lines is the realist version of hegemonic stability theory which asserts that a stable open international economic system is most likely when there is a hegemonic distribution of power; that is, when there is one state that is much larger than any of the others. (There is also a liberal version of hegemonic stability which focuses not on imposition, power and distributional gains but on the need for a hegemon to provide collective goods, especially acting as a leader of last resort in the financial sector (Kindleberger, 1973).)

Robert Gilpin argued in *US Power and the Multinational Corporation* that first Britain in the nineteenth century and then the United States in the latter part of the twentieth century strongly supported open regimes for international investment. As the most advanced economic powers with the largest amount of capital they would be the major beneficiaries of such rules. Other countries, with more limited resources, might have preferred a more restrictive regime, one that would provide their own corporate actors with a greater competitive advantage.

The realist version of hegemonic stability theory also argues that if there is a hegemonic distribution of power there is likely to be an open regime for trade. The dominant power favours such a regime because it increases its economic well-being and economic growth, and provides it with more political leverage. A hegemon would also have the resources to entice or coerce other states into participating in an open regime, and to provide the system with collective goods. International openness has been associated with two periods when there has been an economic hegemon – Britain during the last part of the nineteenth century and the United States (for the non-Communist world) during the second half of the twentieth century. There is, however, far from a perfect fit between changes in the international distribution of power and changes in international regimes. Openness continued into the first decade of the twentieth century even though British power had declined and was not restored until after the Second World War even though the United States became a hegemon after the First World War (Krasner, 1976).

Another realist explanation for trade policy examines the links between alliances, security and economic transactions. By exploiting comparative advantage states can increase their economic resources. With more resources they can increase their military power. In an anarchic world states must be alert to developments that could jeopardise their security. Hence, states are more likely to engage in open regimes with their allies than with their enemies, not only because openness provides economic benefits but also because it can strengthen the military capabilities of the alliance as a whole (Gowa, 1994, ch. 3).

More specific aspects of the trading regime can also be influenced by distributional (and even relative gains) conflicts. The Tokyo Round of trade negotiations, which was completed in 1979, included a number of codes dealing with non-tariff barriers such as subsidies, government procurement, customs valuation, import licensing procedures and dumping. Some of these codes were implemented in more effective ways than others. The variation, Joseph Grieco has argued, was the result of differences in American and European expectations about relative and absolute gains. For instance, the code on customs valuation was very effective while that covering government procurement had a much more limited impact. In the first case Europe and the United States expected balanced gains; in the second case Europe expected to lose. States acting as what Grieco has termed defensive positionalists were loath to cede greater benefits to a potential rival (Grieco, 1990).

Realist arguments can be applied in areas other than trade and capital flows. In the establishment of the International Monetary Fund, for instance, Britain wanted a large fund with liberal provisions for borrowing. The United States wanted a smaller fund with more restrictions on borrowing. Britain was a debtor; the United States was a creditor. The USA had more power because while Britain wanted to borrow, the United States was not compelled to lend. The Articles of Agreement of the IMF reflected American not British preferences.

In the area of telecommunications the development of satellites, a new technology initially controlled by the United States, led to the creation of new institutions. INTELSAT was established in 1964 to regulate communications satellites. It assumed activities that would otherwise have been under the purview of the International Telecommunications Union (ITU), the oldest established international organisation. The ITU was a one nation, one vote, organisation. Votes in INTELSAT were distributed in proportion to usage which meant that the United States got the largest share.

For realism this particular episode illustrates that changes in the distribution of power (in this case the development of a new technology by the United States) leads to changes in the international rules of the game. The United States wanted a new institution, INTELSAT rather than the ITU, because this would provide it with more control and a higher level of benefits. In this particular case relative gains were irrelevant; it was the distribution of absolute gains that counted (Krasner, 1991).

Realism and liberalism have defined the basic lines of debate in international political economy. Liberals see a rosy future. Technology is shrinking distance. The opportunities for mutual gain through international interaction are huge and growing.

Realism is pessimistic. While the United States remains the only global power, its capabilities in many important issue areas have deteriorated, suggesting that it will adopt a more narrowly self-interested policy. It will be less concerned about upholding international economic rules that are not optimal for itself, even if such rules would provide greater benefits for the system as a whole.

Liberalism predicts an increasingly integrated global economy. Realism predicts movement towards regional blocs, or greater differentiation across countries and sectors. Liberalism predicts the consolidation of universal international rules of the game which facilitate mutual interaction. Realism predicts specific rather than diffuse reciprocity with states focusing more on immediate than long-term benefits.

Domestic politics

The final theoretical focus of international political economy has been the relationship between domestic politics and the international system. One of the successes of international political economy as an area of study is that it has integrated international relations and comparative politics, fields that were much more distinct before 1970. There have been two general lines of inquiry. The first examines the impact of the international system on domestic political structures and groups. The second investigates how variations in domestic political structures, group interests, and values and ideas affect foreign economic policies and outcomes.

There is no dominant argument about the influence of the international system on domestic political structures. The works of Peter Katzenstein, Ronald Rogowski, and Jeffry Frieden are illustrative. In *Small States in the World Economy*, Katzenstein argues that the development of what he calls democratic corporatism in the small European countries (Austria, Sweden, Switzerland, Denmark, the Netherlands, Norway and Belgium) reflects their heavy involvement in the international economy. Democratic corporatist structures are functionally efficient modes of organisation for such states. In democratic corporatist polities distinctions between state and society are blurred and all important groups are incorporated into political decision making. Such inclusive political institutions are needed to lessen the risk of internecine quarrels that would be economically disastrous because they would preclude swift adaptation to rapidly changing external conditions. The small states of Europe cannot isolate themselves from external interactions nor (unlike more powerful states) can they control the external environment. They must be able to adjust.

Ronald Rogowski in *Commerce and Coalitions* shows how changes in the international opportunity for trade can impact on the power of domestic groups within a given political system. Countries export those products that use factors with which they are comparatively well endowed: countries with relatively large amounts of capital export capital-intensive goods; countries with large amounts of labour export labour-intensive goods. If trade becomes more open the position of abundant factors of production will be strengthened and that of scarce factors weakened. For instance, in advanced industrialised countries, which are generally capital abundant, open trading regimes have weakened the position of labour. Membership in labour unions has declined in many countries. Assuming that public policies reflect the preferences of groups in the society, the political influence of labour will also erode.

Jeffry Frieden has used a similar line of argument but emphasised sector specific factors. The more open the environment the more relative strength is gained by labour and capital in internationally competitive sectors. In an increasingly open global economy it is the holders of mobile international assets that have benefited the most (Frieden, 1991). The second line of inquiry relating domestic political factors and the international economic system examines the ways in which different domestic structures, values and ideas affect foreign economic policies. The most obvious argument points to the influence of domestic interest groups. International economic policy, like other policy, can be explained by the configuration of domestic pressures. Internationally competitive industries and factors will favour openness; import competing industries will favour closure. Large multi-national firms want to be able to freely transfer capital, goods and labour. In contrast, labour-intensive sectors in industrialised countries want protection from goods produced with lower cost foreign labour (Milner, 1988).

Other analysts have focused not on the simple configuration of interests but also on how domestic institutional structures affect foreign economic policy. One prominent example of this kind of approach distinguishes between weak and strong states, where the term 'state' refers to central decision-making institutions not to the polity as a whole. In weak states political power is fragmented among many institutions – the legislature, public bureaucracies, private pressure groups. It is difficult to formulate a coherent foreign economic policy. The United States is the most obvious example. Power is divided between the executive and a bicameral legislature. Political parties are weak. The judiciary and the central bank are relatively independent of direct political control. Specific bureaucracies have close ties with societal sectors (Krasner, 1978; Evans *et al.*, 1985).

In polities with strong states power is concentrated in the hands of a small number of actors in the executive branch who can set policy and secure, through coercion or incentives, the support of major groups in civil society. Japan is, arguably, the illustrative case. In Japan the Ministry of Finance and the Ministry of International Trade and Industry (MITI) have played a critical role in orchestrating and defining state policy. Since the conclusion of the Second World War Japan has focused on industrial development, a focus that can be attributed to a desire to reduce Japan's international vulnerability. The Liberal Democratic Party (LDP) governed from the early 1950s until the early 1990s. The central ministries had a more or less free hand in organising, albeit not dictating, the activities of the major internationally competitive Japanese industries on which economic growth depended. The LDP secured votes and political support from other sectors such as agriculture and construction (Johnson, 1982; Okimoto, 1989).

Aside from domestic political structures another line of argument has examined the impact of ideas. International political economy, like the rest of political science, has been primarily concerned with material interests and power even if the definitions of interest and power have been intensely debated. The influence of norms and ideas has received much less attention. The analytic problem in discussing the impact of ideas and values is that they often covary with other factors such as economic interests. When there is such covariance, it is impossible to make a compelling argument that ideas really matter, that they are anything more than rationalisations for more conventional concerns.

Recently, however, a number of scholars have demonstrated that ideas can be consequential; they have been able to isolate the independent impact of ideas. Peter Haas has developed the concept of epistemic communities. Epistemic communities are groups of individuals who share the same scientific understandings and the same policy agenda. Haas and his colleagues have been able to show that the presence of such a community within the policy-making apparatus of a country has altered public policy. For instance, donor countries stopped giving away international food aid because agricultural economists demonstrated that this destroyed the incentives for local production. The policies of north African governments towards pollution control in the Mediterranean changed when they established environmental ministries that were staffed by individuals with scientific knowledge (Haas, 1992).

Ideas can also be consequential because they become embedded in institutions, often for haphazard reasons, which then constrain the options available to policy makers. For instance, in the 1930s the United States opted for interventionist state policies for agriculture which included a high level of protection. At the same time, state intervention in the manufacturing sector failed in part because of rulings from the Supreme Court. These differences became embedded in American domestic legislation and were reflected in American foreign economic policy after the Second World War. Agriculture was excluded from GATT, largely as a result of initiatives taken by the United States despite the fact that America had the world's most competitive agrarian sector. Hence, decisions taken at one point in time that were associated with a specific set of ideas and interests persisted even though material circumstances had changed (Goldstein, 1989; Goldstein and Keohane, 1993).

Conclusion

The achievements of international political economy have been generated by an epistemology that conforms with the Western Rationalistic Tradition, not with those versions of post-modernism that reject any separation between the student and the object of study. The success of different approaches to IPE has been determined primarily by their ability to generate a progressive research programme. Theories have fallen from favour either because they did not conform with empirical evidence or because they could not be formulated in ways that were, in principle, testable.

Some arguments that were prominent in the literature twenty years ago have collapsed. The viability of dependency theory, for instance, which explained the poverty of the Third World in terms of the interactions between rich and poor countries, has been undermined by increasing variation in the economic performance of peripheral countries. Some, especially the east Asian newly industrialising countries (Taiwan, Korea, Hong Kong, Singapore, and now Thailand and others as well), have been spectacularly successful, growing at faster rates than any other group of states. At the same time other countries, most of the states of Africa, have become mired in poverty. If the most important explanation for the economic prospects of a state is its peripheral position in the world capitalist system, it is impossible to explain this variation.

The central debate between liberal and realist analysis has not, however, been resolved even though the research programmes of both of these paradigms has changed. For liberalism, co-operation theory, which focuses on the way in which institutions can overcome market failure, has supplanted functionalism, neo-functionalism, and transnationalism as the dominant mode of analysis because these earlier liberal formulations either failed to confirm with empirical evidence (functionalism) or could not generate testable hypotheses (transnationalism). For realism hegemonic stability theory has been superseded by theoretical arguments that have demonstrated that different distributions of power can also lead to open international regimes (Lake, 1988) and that security concerns may drive foreign economic policies (Gowa, 1994; Mansfield, 1994).

To a large extent the enduring debate between realism and liberalism is about the nature of the exemplary problem in the contemporary international economic system. Is marked failure the basic issue that states must address? In this case it is possible to make everyone better off at the same time by creating new institutions or cutting new deals. Or, are distributional conflicts or relative gains the basic questions that confront states? In this case outcomes will be determined by power; new institutions or strategies of issue linkage will reflect the preferences of the strong.

Issues related to the international environment, for instance, seem to cry out for liberal analysis since it appears that everyone can be made better off if institutions can be developed to deal with externalities including mechanisms for side payments. For example agreements banning the production of CFCs were reached quite quickly in the later 1980s when the scientific evidence for ozone depletion became unassailable and when, one must add, the major chemical companies, especially Dupont, were able to produce substitutes. Distributional conflicts were resolved by providing technical and material aid to tropical Third World states which stood to lose the most from the ban (Haas, 1992; Benedick, 1991). In contrast, the economic relationship between the Soviet bloc and the West during the Cold War was about distributional gains and relative power. Here, realism offers much better analytic tools.

If liberal and realist analyses, and the various approaches that attempt to integrate domestic and international politics, have not provided definitive answers, they have offered systematic frameworks within which issues can be addressed. They have made statements about causal variables (power, security, group interests, ideas, values) and they have suggested the kind of evidence that would be relevant for testing these alternative arguments.

What defines social science is a methodology based on argument and evidence. Even if the argument is not fully worked out and the evidence is muddy, social science is the best approach that we have to understanding social, political and economic phenomena. For IPE this conventional epistemology cannot be defended by arguing that some kind of breakthrough has been achieved which has provided answers that are so obvious that any reasonable observer must accept them. There has been no such breakthrough. The debates between liberalism and realism still rage as strongly as they did a decade ago albeit in somewhat different guises. The theories are rarely good enough to provide concrete guidance for policy makers. Conventional arguments have, however, demonstrated that some positions do not hold up in the face of empirical evidence: dependency theories are wrong; hegemony is not the only path to economic openness; private interests do not, as functionalism suggests, necessarily generate political integration; domestic political structures are not insulated from external economic interactions.

The conventional epistemology that has informed the study of international political economy stands in sharp contrast with those variants of post-modernism that reject the Western Rationalistic Tradition. For these post-modernists there are many analytic categories each of which contains its own truth. Testing can never be definitive and is often entirely irrelevant.

Given the weakness of the findings in international political economy, the failure to clearly demonstrate the superiority of one paradigm over another, why not throw it all up? Adopt a post-modern stance. It would be more fun if it were not necessary to muck through all that messy and ambiguous data.

Despite the failings of IPE and other literatures informed by conventional methodology, to embrace post-modernism would be to strip social science of the most important contribution that it can make to the betterment of human society: that contribution is to discipline power with truth. In some rare instances it is possible to show decision makers what their best course of action is. Economics, for instance, has improved the well-being of the world's peoples by elaborating the relationship between government policy and macro-economic perform-ance; a replay of the Great Depression is unlikely because economists, and the policy makers they advise, have a much better understanding of how monetary policy works. In most cases, however, including the work in international political economy, social science can hardly claim to provide a right answer which is supported by definitive empirical evidence. Nevertheless, conventional social science can show that some arguments that policy makers use to justify their actions are wrong because their assertions do not conform with empirical evidence. The Western Rationalistic Tradition can contest claims by testing them against empirical data. This check on the assertions of the mighty is one of the bulwarks that modern society has constructed against the ravages of political extremism. None of the evil regimes of the twentieth century – Hitler's Germany, Stalin's Soviet Union, Mao's China – has supported the Western Rationalistic Tradition.

Post-modernism provides no methodology for adjudicating among competing claims. There is no reason to think that post-modern pronouncements will exercise any constraint over those with power. If Lysenko's theory supported Stalin's beliefs, then Lysenko was right. Darwinian biology simply disappeared in the Soviet Union. If each society has its own truth – apartheid in South Africa, nazism in Germany – what is the basis for arguing that they are wrong? The Western Rationalistic Tradition, the stipulation that theories be tested against empirical data, is no panacea for the prevention of evil. Nevertheless it does offer the best hope for academicians to make a positive contribution to the larger society because it can in some instances suggest a wise course for public policy and in others demonstrate that a policy is wrong. Post-modernism, in contrast, in its more extreme versions provides no such check. On the contrary, it leads directly to nihilism which can produce an intense and burning flame but which hardly moves society towards peace and justice.

REFERENCES

Benedick, Richard (1991), *Ozone Diplomacy* (Cambridge: Harvard University Press).
Burley, Ann-Marie and Mattli, Walter (1993), 'Europe Before the Court: A Political Theory of Legal Integration', *International Organization*, 47, pp. 41–76.

Cooper, Richard (1968), *The Economics of Interdependence: Economic Policy in the Atlantic Community* (New York: McGraw-Hill).

Doyle, Michael (1983), 'Kant, Liberal Legacies, and Foreign Affairs', *Philosophy and Public Affairs*, 12, pp. 204–35.

Evans, Peter *et al.* (1985), *Bringing the State Back In* (New York: Cambridge University Press).

Frieden, Jeffry (1991), 'Invested Interests: The Politics of National Economic Policies in a World of Global Finance', *International Organization*, 45, pp. 425–51.

Gilpin, Robert (1975), *US Power and the Multinational Corporation* (New York: Basic Books).

Goldstein, Judith (1989), 'The Impact of Ideas on Trade Policy: The Origins of US Agricultural and Manufacturing Policies', *International Organization*, 43, pp. 31–71.

Goldstein, Judith and Keohane, Robert O. (eds.) (1993), *Ideas and Foreign Policy* (Ithaca: Cornell University Press).

Goodman, John B. and Pauly, Louis W. (1993), 'The Obsolescence of Capital Controls?: Economic Management in an Age of Global Markets', *World Politics*, 46, pp. 50–83.

Gowa, Joanne (1994), *Allies, Adversaries and International Trade* (Princeton: Princeton University Press).

Grieco, Joseph M. (1990), *Cooperation Among Nations: Europe, America, and Non-Tariff Barriers to Trade* (Ithaca: Cornell University Press).

Haas, Peter (1992), 'Banning Chlorofluorocarbons: Epistemic Community Efforts to Protect Stratospheric Ozone', in Haas (ed.), 'Knowledge, Power and International Policy', special issue of *International Organization*, 46, pp. 187–224.

Hirschman, Albert (1945), *National Power and the Structure of Foreign Trade* (Berkeley: University of California Press).

Johnson, Chalmers (1982), *MITI and the Japanese Miracle: The Growth of Industrial Policy 1925–75* (Stanford: Stanford University Press).

Kapstein, Ethan (1989), 'Resolving the Regulator's Dilemma: International Coordination of Banking Regulations', *International Organization*, 43, pp. 323–47.

Katzenstein, Peter J. (1985), *Small States in the World Economy* (Ithaca: Cornell University Press).

Keohane, Robert O. (1984), *After Hegemony* (Princeton: Princeton University Press).

Keohane, Robert and Nye, Joseph (1977), *Power and Interdependence* (Boston: Little Brown).

Kindleberger, Charles P. (1973), *The World in Depression: 1929–39* (Berkeley: University of California Press).

Krasner, Stephen (1976), 'National Power and the Structure of Foreign Trade', *World Politics*, 28, pp. 317–47.

  (1978), *Defending the National Interest: Raw Materials Investment and American Foreign Policy* (Princeton: Princeton University Press).

  (1991), 'Global Communications and National Power: Life on the Pareto Frontier', *World Politics*, 43, pp. 336–67.

Krause, Lawrence (1971), 'Private International Finance', *International Organization*, 25, pp. 523–40.
Lake, David (1988), *Power, Protection and Free Trade: International Sources of US Commercial Strategy, 1887–1939* (Ithaca: Cornell University Press).
Mansfield, Edward D. (1994), *Power, Trade, and War* (Princeton: Princeton University Press).
Martin, Lisa L. (1992a), 'Interests, Power and Multilateralism', *International Organization*, 46, pp. 765–92.
    (1992b), *Coercive Cooperation: Explaining Multilateral Economic Sanctions* (Princeton: Princeton University Press).
Mastanduno, Michael (1991), 'Do Relative Gains Matter? America's Response to Japanese Industrial Policy', *International Security*, 16 (1), pp. 73–113.
    (1992) *Economic Containment: Cocom and the Politics of East – West Trade* (Ithaca: Cornell University Press).
Milner, Helen (1988), *Resisting Protectionism* (Princeton: Princeton University Press).
National Academy of Sciences (1987), *Balancing the National Interest: US National Security Export Controls and Global Economic Competition* (Washington: National Academy Press).
Nye, Joseph S. Jr. and Keohane, Robert O. (1971), 'Transnational Relations and World Politics: An Introduction', *International Organization*, 25, pp. 326–50.
Okimoto, Daniel (1989), *Between MITI and the Market: Japanese Industrial Policy for High Technology* (Stanford: Stanford University Press).
Powell, Robert (1991), 'Absolute and Relative Gains in International Relations Theory', *American Political Science Review*, 85, pp. 1303–21.
Rengger, N. J. (1992), 'No Time like the Present? Postmodernism and Political Theory', *Political Studies*, 40, pp. 561–70.
Rogowski, Ronald (1989), *Commerce and Coalitions* (Princeton: Princeton University Press).
Rosecrance, Richard (1986), *The Rise of the Trading State: Commerce and Conquest in the Modern World* (New York: Basic Books).
Schelling, Thomas (1960), *Strategy of Conflict* (Cambridge: Harvard University Press).
    (1966), *Arms and Influence* (New Haven: Yale University Press).
Searle, John R. (1993), 'Rationality and Realism: What is at Stake?', *Daedalus*, 122, pp. 55–83.
Stein, Arthur (1990), *Why Nations Cooperate: Circumstance and Choice in International Relations* (Ithaca: Cornell University Press).
Waltz, Kenneth (1979), *Theory of International Politics* (Reading, MA: Addison Wesley).

Michael Nicholson

Introduction

It is sometimes claimed that a positivist approach to international relations is still dominant, implying that it not only is dominant now but has been for some time in the past. I am not sure how dominance would be defined in any strict way and would not be confident I would recognise it if I saw it. There is certainly a lot of work done in international relations which is not of a positivist nature. However, it is hard to dispute that a lot of research is being done currently using research strategies based on essentially positivist principles. These are widely regarded as appropriate to the tasks in hand and are widely practised by scholars who do not seem to doubt their legitimacy. This view of the position of positivism is probably generally accepted by scholars though they would be divided on whether this acceptance was with pleasure or regret. In confirmation there are a host of papers in the *Journal of Conflict Resolution* or the *International Studies Quarterly* where formal models are analysed, or quantified relationships are studied, and where the whole ethos is of one of firm positivism (except, of course, for one famous issue when the latter journal was handed over to the post-modernists). Most of the papers on conflict or international relations in the *American Political Science Review* are likewise in this mode. All these journals, it should be noted, are published in the United States, with a predominance of North American authors (with a disproportionate number of Canadians, given Canada's population) and a handful of Europeans, and an even smaller handful of other nationalities (a distribution of national origins which, in another context, would raise some interesting questions).

I use 'positivism' to mean an epistemological approach to international relations which implies the legitimacy of certain methodologies or methods of doing things. I regard the epistemology as the view that we can make generalisations about the social world, including our particular interest, the international system, which are verifiable (or, if preferred, refutable). Further, we have theories where at least some of these propositions are interrelated in a logical structure. Thus, some propositions imply other propositions. The methodology I regard as the actual practical procedures by which these statements are discovered and tested. 'International relations' and similar terms I assume to be understood externally to this essay.

The view I am arguing for is one of 'broad positivism' which might not be regarded as positivism at all. The label 'positivist' seems to incite misunderstanding, so in an ideal world I would rather be without it. (Though to be called a 'post-positivist' would probably be worse.) I shall use the term reluctantly, because it seems to be required, to express the views which justify the behavioural tradition in International Relations, though 'empiricism' seems closer to the standard philosophical labelling.

The fact that a certain epistemological position, such as positivism, and the methodologies which imply that position, are widely practised does not mean that they are right. Even if meaning were to be given to dominance and even were it to be dominant according to this meaning, behaviouralism (which I shall regard as being roughly the international relations as well as the political science version of positivism) could be meaningless. Those who work in a behaviouralist tradition may have been wasting their time producing nonsense (in a strict sense of nonsense, that is, without sense). Positivism may be widespread but wrong and a critic of positivism could write a paper with the same title as this one either as a lament or a challenge. In defence of the tradition, I could write a philosophical justification of positivism or elaborate my view that there is a lot of work still done in that tradition. I shall do something in the middle and discuss some aspects of research in the positivist mode, justifying their legitimacy, while suggesting that the links with other traditions are perhaps closer than they appear at first sight. I shall discuss the issues raised in two research programmes. First I shall discuss the quantitative tradition in international relations, particularly that which follows from one branch of the Peace Research tradition. Quantification is a widely misunderstood issue, often used to berate the positivists. Secondly I shall discuss the unfortunately named 'rational choice' research programme. These traditions are still vigorously pursued in international relations and elsewhere despite the objections of the post-modernists to their legitimacy.

There is some disagreement about what should count as positivism, in international relations. Some, indeed, appear to identify it with realism, which is most misleading. Realism (at least as understood in international relations) is a theory of how the world works, whereas positivism is an epistemology which prescribes how to investigate it. The movement was not a handmaiden of the realists. Lewis Fry Richardson, one of the first and greatest of the explicit positivists, defined his interests as the study of 'Deadly Quarrels', not inter-state quarrels, important though these were deemed to be. The collection of so much statistical data on a state basis often imposes a practical state-centricity on some of the work, but it is accidental rather than ideological. The realists in the classical tradition as defined by Hedley Bull (1966 [1969]) were staunchly anti-positivist in rhetoric, even if one could argue that their recourse to generalisation when talking of such things as the balance of power meant that, had they thought about it, they would have realised they were closer to positivism than they would have found comfortable. In this sense, the recent critiques of positivism are also critiques of the classical tradition, though it is not a critique that the classicists would welcome or, indeed, in many cases recognise. With a few exceptions, the British international relations profession treated the overtly social scientific approach with disdain as just another American fad. Though Peter Winch (1958), a British scholar, had been ahead of the field with his criticisms of the whole positivistic approach in the social sciences, there was at that time very little attempt to engage the positivists at a philosophical level amongst British international relations scholars. An exception was Charles Reynolds whose long campaign started in 1968 (Hedley Bull's 1966 attack was witty but superficial and damagingly rebutted by David Singer, 1966 [1969]). The story is very different now but that is the tale as it was. At that stage, the explicitly positivist approach flourished in the United States. It has never been more than a fringe movement in the United Kingdom, certainly in its quantified mode, and hardly central in any behavioural mode. Ironically it is probably as well-developed as it ever has been today when it is the object of much more serious philosophical challenge.

The nature of a moderate positivism

Basically positivism involves the view that the social sciences can be built upon the same model as the natural sciences and furthermore on a particular model of the natural sciences as expressed at various stages by Russell (1948), Hempel (1965), Braithwaite (1953), Ayer (1940) and so on. Fundamentally they argued that observation and experience were the central criteria by which one judged scientific theories. Some, such as Ayer, went so far as to argue that statements that could not be confirmed by observation (synthetic statements) or were not matters of logic (analytic statements, as in mathematics) were meaningless. Metaphysics, and perhaps with greater embarrassment ethics, were confined to the waste paper bin. Popper (1959), whose views on the characteristics of science (though not metaphysics) were not as far removed from the positivists as one might think from the rhetoric, argued that in highlighting and defining empirical statements he was proposing a criterion of *demarcation* which defined what was science and what was not. This did not imply anything particularly pejorative about non-scientific knowledge – indeed, in Popper's case, far from it. Many social scientists, particularly economists, embraced this view with enthusiasm. However, there are two possible difficulties. First, the view of the natural sciences which the positivists and empiricists proclaimed has been challenged in the work of people like Kuhn (1970) and Feyerabend (1975) and severely modified by Quine (1953, 1992) who would, nevertheless, be classed as a moderate critic. Secondly, as human beings are conscious and conceptualising beings, one can argue that there is a fundamental distinction between a study of them and a study of inanimate objects. Human beings are conscious of and interpret their situation and actions. It is part of our role to understand this – something for which there is no parallel in the analysis of inanimate matter. I argue that, while this is all true, the difficulties are surmountable within what is recognisably still a positivist framework.

The term 'positivism' is unfortunate, as I have already suggested. It raises images of logical positivism in its extreme form. Indeed what is presented as positivism by its critics is a doctrine of such severity as to have caused comment in the Vienna Circle itself. I do not want to defend such an extreme view – few would – though I do want to argue that experience is not such a frail vessel as is sometimes alleged and that the degree of subjectivity of beliefs about the natural or even the social world is much exaggerated. I wish to maintain the view that it is possible to have rational belief about the truth of propositions about which, at the minimum, there is a great deal of inter-subjective agreement.

The form of positivism I would defend in the social sciences is one which asserts the centrality of empirical propositions, that is, propositions where the reasons for believing them are grounded in observation. Further I argue that there is sufficient 'common understanding' (a phrase I highlight) for us to be confident of the existence of many social 'things' which are the content of those observations.

As an example, consider A. K. Sen's work on famines (Sen, 1981). Sen argues that the conventional view that famines were primarily due to an absolute shortage of food is severely misleading and that a common characteristic of famines has been that the distribution of entitlements to food had altered drastically. Thus, in 1943, a famine year in Bengal, the average amount of food per head was actually higher than in the non-famine year of 1941 when, though there was starvation, it was markedly less. It seems that this analysis of famines involves a lot of empirical propositions, which are generally and commonly understood. The experience of a famine was clearly very different from the point of view of a starving peasant mother desperately trying to keep her child alive, from the child itself for whom hunger was the totality of its experience, a trader who was doing rather well out of the shortages and not starving at all, or a British administrator, sympathetic but not personally hungry, trying to prize shipping space for food out of a reluctant Admiralty. It is even more different for us today looking at it as an abstract, historical experience. However, despite these different practical experiences, I suggest there is a common concept of famine (which we can define in a number of different but, to us, comprehensible ways). This can be used, in conjunction with other mutually comprehensible forms, such as the distribution of entitlements, to produce meaningful propositions about the world. In turn these can be confronted with evidence which is comprehensible to us all, such as aggregate food supplies and death rates. This evidence either confirms or refutes the propositions. I find no difficulty in thinking of these as 'facts' about a famine which it would be eccentric to deny, established by methods which it would be eccentric to deny. The analysis of famines is not done as an intellectual exercise but for its possible, indeed probable use in preventing or at least alleviating future famines. Such alleviation means intervening in a process which has been understood (positivisitically) where we have some strong reasons for assuming what the consequences of the intervention will be. But these reasons themselves are derived from positivistic analysis of what happens in the sorts of situations envisaged. We observe events and on the basis of these observations hope to predict the consequences of actions carried out now or in the future. The talk of 'alleviation' itself presupposes that we have some intuitions about how people feel in famine and are confident that they are feelings of hunger and distress. Furthermore, we are sure we can make them feel better – by their own criteria, not just ours. The motive for conducting our positivistic analysis is moral but this, in itself, is separate from the analysis.

I can summarise the general principles of positivism in the broad form which I am advocating. Whether all those who adopt this general position would be happy to call themselves positivists is another matter. First, international relations consists of empirically testable theories. A theory is a set of propositions such that from some postulates, which are assumed as the basis of the theory, a set of implications, logically deduced from these postulates, are derived. Sufficient of the propositions must be testable (refutable) by observations that the theory as a whole is confirmed or refuted by observations, in the sense that, if true, all propositions are confirmed either by direct observation or by logical deduction from those which are so confirmed. Thus, the confirmation of a structure does not imply that every proposition within it is directly confirmed by observation or even can be. Secondly, observations of international behaviour can be made which are unproblematic within the context of 'common understanding'. These are the central concepts. Along with them though is the view of Lakatosian research programmes (Lakatos, 1970) which are progressive rather than degenerating. In the context of international relations I would view the 'three paradigms' as research programmes, and, in the same way, rational choice 'theory' is a research programme. Finally, parsimony is a virtue, where this is a value judgement.

This form of positivism also permits as data such things as perceptions and other psychological states (including emotions such as hostility) which are not directly observable. Behaviourism (this is not a misprint for 'behaviourALism') exists but has receded in popularity in psychology. Behaviouralism in political science was never so austere a doctrine and has always permitted perceptions, misperceptions and such like mental events to be considered as data. It penetrated the mind by such daring stratagems as assuming speech had meaning though being willing to look a little below the surface, such as by content analysis, and attribute hidden meanings to some texts (in the common or garden, not the post-modern definition of text – my old-fashioned texts consist of words). Thus, the political science/international relations positivism has always permitted some considerable measure of interpretation into events and has never concerned itself simply with physical manifestations. Thus one might question whether it was positivism after all, or whether it was a closet, though rather pared down, hermeneutics with a few mathematical formulae thrown in to give it greater respectability. This is a tenable interpretation.

Earlier versions of positivism assumed that data was unproblematic or at least involved practical rather than conceptual problems. The 'understanding' school challenge this though I am counter-arguing that this is less severe a problem and not as damning to the theoretical enterprise as many assume. Thus, without arguing the case in detail, I would suggest that one can perfectly well have a positivist theory of voting amongst those people who share a concept of voting. They have a 'common experience' or 'common understanding'. It might be difficult to explain this to someone unfamiliar with the concept of voting but amongst those who are familiar there is no difficulty. Further one can make analyses such as relating voting behaviour to disposable income, which are perfectly respectable and objective analyses to all of those who share this common understanding and, here, a common vocabulary. I may be unsure of the stability of such a relationship but this is a different matter. Even in economics new variables have crept into the analysis and have disturbed many apparently stable relationships. It is unlikely to be any better in international relations.

In general, scholars in this tradition are not looking for relationships which cover all people in all societies, though they are delighted if they get them. In practice they are more concerned with temporary, socially limited relationships which give us guidance in our analysis of the world and hopefully also in our manipulation of it. Oddly it is the old traditionalists, who would be shocked to be called positivists, who really go for the long period relationships, though in a very informal manner. Thucydides, Machiavelli, Clausewitz and all the rest are constantly drawn to our attention as commentators on the (presumably timeless) human condition.

Quantification in International Relations

Though mathematical models and measured relationships do not define the positivist field, and it is a mistake to think of them as the same thing, a lot of work in the positivist tradition does involve one or the other or both. The positivist believes in the possibility of generalisation and once this mode is adopted, quantification cannot be far behind.

Quantification is not a simple concept. There are a whole variety of different forms such as ordinal measures, cardinal measures (of different strengths), index numbers and a range of others. An ordinal measure may be possible where a cardinal measure is not, but this restricts the strength of any mathematical operation which can be carried out. For instance, one cannot add ordinal 'numbers'. One distinction should be made for our purposes. Suppose we make a proposition such as that the balance of power preserves the peace, then, having defined 'balance of power' and 'peace', one counts up the instances favourable and unfavourable to the hypothesis to see whether it is confirmed or not (I have sympathy with those who object that the relevant terms are difficult to define but such people have no business making such an assertion in the first place). However, suppose we want to measure 'power' or 'capability' or 'arms levels', we are involved in a rather different activity. We are here measuring the factors we are dealing with in the theory not testing the theory as such (though it is presumably done with a view to a test at some point). Clearly these are very different uses of measures and numbers. The first is central to testing and I would argue even the meaning of a generalisation between two entities. Though the entities themselves may be measurable, they need not be. 'Red-haired people usually have blue eyes' is tested by counting instances but not by measuring red-hairedness. The central issue in my first case is that it is possible to identify cases of balance of power and peace in such a way that they can be classified as instances of the same thing. It requires neither balance of power nor peace to be measurable in themselves though without some sort of measure of power the notion of a balance is going to be very weak. The crucial requirement is a definition of 'sameness' which is not a requirement of quantification as such but of generalisation.

The move to quantification in international relations came in the 1950s and flourished in the 1960s following on from the work of Richardson (1960a, 1960b), initially neglected but now elevated to the position of patron saint, a position he still holds. Much of its earlier inspiration came from the Peace Research tradition and from the view that if one wants to cure something (such as war) one should first understand it. Medical analogies abounded. There was impatience with the then dominant classical realists, both for their apparent acceptance of a violent world without appearing to consider the possibilities of engineering (I use the word advisedly) something better with the materials available, and their indifference to the systematic testing of the generalisations about power and such like to which they were apparently wedded. The positivists came in as technicians to fix a system which did not work very well, just as other technicians had fixed poliomyelitis and other diseases. It involved both the collection of data on a large scale, such as in the Correlates of War project, and the analysis of a multitude of propositions using the newly arranged data. Cioffi-Revilla (1990) gives a useful survey of the data sets now available which concern peace and war.

The quantification and mathematisation of international relations did not come in intellectual isolation. The same trends were developing apace in sociology, psychology and the social sciences in general, following its perceived success in economics and the development of the computer, which was making hitherto undreamt of feats of computation a practicable proposition. The computer seemed to have laid to rest the concern that social systems were too complex to analyse successfully even if there was no reason to object to the possibility in principle. The developments of branches of mathematics such as the theory of games, which had the analysis of social systems directly in mind, seemed to free social scientists from the sense that they were a sort of residual user, picking up the crumbs from the physicists' table. Indeed the late 1950s and the early 1960s appeared to be the great glad morning for the social sciences. While its failures are not as calamitous as its critics maintain, its successes as methods for alleviating the human condition have undeniably been disappointing.

Quantification comes into play when one is trying to test theories. This is the case whether one is testing a theory in a strict sense of a set of deductively related propositions, or in a less formal sense where the propositions are more loosely related but regarded as 'interesting'. The propositions which are tested in international relations are frequently of this latter sort or are derived from what I shall call 'shallow theories'. I mean by a shallow theory one which consists of few deductive steps and therefore has few other propositions which are linked deductively with the tested proposition. Deep theories exist in international relations. Richardson's arms race theories are deep but the data required to test them in the original form would require data of a sort which is unavailable, and it is hard to see how it ever would be. The many tests done have been necessarily on what are effectively cruder versions of the model. Later developments in the Richardson tradition such as the work of Zinnes and Muncaster (1984) and Schrodt (1981) are likewise not easy to test. The more rigorous versions of the balance of power in the last few years (for example, Niou, Ordeshook and Rose, 1989; Wagner 1986) are quite deep and produce testable implications. Bueno de Mesquita (1981) bases his theory of war causation on a version of expected utility theory. Bueno de Mesquita lacks Barry Buzan's diffidence (in this volume) about the measurement of power.

A whole variety of statistical tests have been carried out which are relevant to the realist views, many of them using data from the Correlates of War project. Thus, Bremer (1980) finds a positive association between the possession of military capacity and its use. This, though it does not directly contradict any realist thesis, does not endear itself as a device for preserving the peace. Elsewhere Singer and Small (1968) find that alliances are more often followed by war than by peace. Again, though not a refutation, this is clearly not an implication of realism. Diehl (1983, 1985), while finding little to confirm Michael Wallace's finding (Wallace 1979, 1982) that arms races were followed by war (a proposition which fell at the definitional hurdle and has so far not managed to get up), found perhaps more surprisingly that unilateral arms build-ups prior to crises did not lead to war as compared with situations where there were no such arms build-ups. Vasquez (1983), using good behavioural methods, tests the implications of realism and finds them sadly wanting in many ways which have still to be fully addressed by the realists. But this is not using data which have meaning only to the realist or the anti-realist. It is data which retains its status as data for a very broad interpretation of 'common understanding' (which is why, elsewhere – Nicholson (1996) – I have denied that realism is a paradigm despite Vasquez's own views on the matter).

This is not to deny there are many problems facing the purveyor of quantitative relationships. Most empirical propositions are consistent with numerous different theoretical structures. Also relationships are rarely predominantly bivariate but usually involve lots of factors in a complex structure of mutual causation. Thus, Diehl's result initially would appear to indicate that an increasing preponderance of weapons does not induce war but it may conceal a number of other things. The reason for this may be that the weaker parties are too afraid of war and the threat is sufficient for them to accede to the dominant party's demands. It may also be that the threats are perceived as threats against someone else. Likewise, Bremer's result that heavily armed states are more likely to engage in armed conflict than lightly armed states is consistent with the view that arms provoke conflicts but also that states in a chronically conflictual situation are both more likely to fight and more likely to acquire arms. This does not invalidate the relationships but it is not clear in isolation what theory these relationships confirm. A bivariate relationship can refute only a bivariate assumption but it is comparatively easy to argue that third, fourth or fifth variables intervene in the structure to invalidate the refutation. This point is fully understood in the econometric literature – Leamer (1983) gives a particularly acute statement of it and a series of papers by Hendry (1994) point in the same direction. The test of an isolated proposition, however apparently compelling, is of limited use except in the context of a theory which has a number of different observable implications. It is not a problem of international relations but found in all the social sciences, or indeed any other science where one is observing natural as opposed to experimental situations.

A further problem comes with the actual measures themselves. I give two examples which are questions requesting numerical answers: what is the population of London? how many languages are spoken in the world? (Language is an oddly neglected study in international relations.) They raise different issues of a type which come up time and again in international relations testing. In the first case the units to be counted, people, are straightforwardly defined and raise no conceptual problems. The problem is to define 'London'. The boundaries will differ according to different criteria – postal, sociological, common usage – and are going to be arbitrary. However, having lighted on a definition, the population with respect to that definition can be estimated both conceptually and practically with considerable accuracy.

The second example likewise raises the issues of definition – this time of when closely related forms of speech are languages or dialects. There are no linguistic criteria which distinguish a dialect from a language and in practice the difference is determined more by political criteria than anything else. Glaswegian English and Texan English are regarded as dialects whereas Norwegian (in two varieties for political reasons) and Swedish are regarded as languages. Depending on one's definitions one can get answers to the question posed varying from 3,000 to 10,000 (Crystal 1990) and doubtless by either tightening or liberalising the definition of language we could extend the range further.

I give these apparently innocuous examples to show the enormous ambiguity of measurement when describing social factors. The definition of the entities involved is frequently difficult and arbitrary. One might be tempted to abandon the problem and say there is no meaning to measurement in such contexts, but this would be extreme. To abandon as meaningless a statement such as 'London is bigger than Oslo', would require an almost perverse unwillingness to draw arbitrary boundaries. However, if one does admit such a statement as meaningful, one is required to specify some procedures for establishing it, which means some form of measurement. Further, though arbitrary criteria are necessarily involved, there are limits to this. There are dangers in being so purist that one ends up by saying nothing.

Rational choice theory

Rational choice analysis is developing apace at the moment and appears a fruitful research programme. It has had a major impact in international relations particularly in forms derived from the theory of games, which go back to the early 1960s with Boulding (1962), Rapoport (1974) and Schelling (1960), and still flourishes today with the rather different work of Brams (1985) and Axelrod (1984). Work such as that of Bueno de Mesquita (1981), though dealing with war causation, does not deal directly with strategic views though it is directly within the rational choice canon.

'Rational choice' is an unfortunate term. The rationality involved is instrumental rationality which means little more than consistent choice under a coherent set of beliefs. However, 'rational' implies approval, at least in some people's minds. Its sophisticated practitioners recognise that no approval is implied but it is easy to slip into error. 'Goal-directed choice theories' would be a better term. Further, while it is extremely useful as a model of choice, it leaves a lot out, so, as an empirical tool, it must be broadened. Thus, its status as a model, describing a simple and artificial world, rather than a theory which is the model when developed further to describe the real world, needs to be constantly emphasised.

Rational choice theory has been applied to strategy and strategic analysts, particularly those from the United States, have seized upon it with joy. The joy, I often feel, is misplaced, as a great deal of rational choice theory in conflict (game) situations shows the ambiguity of following the rules of even the most modest forms of instrumental rationality. Many of the standard games, such as chicken and prisoners' dilemma, show that mutually satisfactory solutions in unmediated conflict can be hard to find. The application of rational choice theory to strategic studies has identified the field more with realism than some of its practitioners care for. Another approach is to recognise the difficulties of co-operation as illustrated in the game theory framework and from there to see how more co-operative behaviour can be induced. Prominent workers in this sort of field are Michael Taylor (1987), Robert Axelrod (1984) and Nigel Howard (1971) whose later work he and his collaborators call drama theory, regarding drama as a better metaphor than game. All these approaches stress the issue of co-operation or at least of using conflict to achieve generally beneficial rather than destructive outcomes.

All these approaches are in what is generally the positivist mode or certainly using the positivist methodology (or technology). Whether they are to be counted as strictly positivist or not is another matter. The central methodology of the empirical rational choice programme is to assume a set of circumstances in which decision makers of a certain sort (entrepreneurs, governments, individuals or whatever) operate, assume a set of goals which they pursue and then see what choices and what consequences follow from this as an issue of logic. The test of the theory is in how closely or otherwise the predicted consequences match up with the actual. Thus, in the case of Bueno de Mesquita's work, the theory posits certain conditions which will need to be fulfilled if a state declares war and then compares them with the actual initiation of war from 1815 onwards and finds a remarkably close relationship. If it had not been, then either the goals assumed or the measures of the other variables (capability and uncertainty) would be wrong. However, we can consider what the status of these assumed goals are. First, they are not directly observable. They are observable only in their implications. This is not worrying. The status of unobservables is perfectly secure in positivist theory. However, there is some level at which they have to be understood by the observer. In classical profit-maximising micro-economics the concepts of profit and maximisation must be understood, while in examinations of co-operation the concepts of co-operation have to be understood. This brings us back to the earlier question of the role of understanding even in positivist theory. Propositions can be empirical and refutable within the domain of those understanding the language, but they might be hard to follow outside that conceptual community. They are nevertheless objective, in the sense of commanding general inter-subjective agreement, within that community.

My basic issue here is that a belief held by a person is a fact about that person, just as an aesthetic judgement held by a person is a fact about them. If I believe in witches, hobgoblins and the like, then this belief is a fact about me. However, it does not presuppose that they objectively exist in that attributes can be given to the hobgoblins which are detectable to the outside community who understand them but do not believe in them. To incorporate a person's belief into a theory requires that observers understand that belief but not that they share it.

There are further developments of rational choice analysis such that the name of rational choice becomes less and less appropriate. It is not necessary that an actor consciously articulates the goals involved. In some analyses it is supposed that they could if they wished but it is quite possible to think of unconscious goals which might be accessible to the observer but only with difficulty to the actor. (One theory of schizophrenia is that it is a rational, in the sense of instrumentally rational, response to intolerable circumstances where the goal involved is psychological self-preservation (Laing, 1960), though, so far as I am aware, this has not so far been brought into rational choice theory.)

Not all rational choice analysis is empirical in the sense of endeavouring to provide testable theories of how people behave. Much of it is normative, either in the strategic sense of how to do as well as possible in a conflict, or in a peace research sense of how to induce co-operative behaviour in conflict situations. The empirical and the normative procedures are remarkably similar. However, they should be distinguished even if this injunction is as honoured in the breach as in the practice.

Morality and positivism

Positivism provides a demarcation principle between what is scientific and what is not. Of particular concern is morality. In itself, positivism concerns what is, not what ought to be, and, furthermore, it is argued that it is important to distinguish between the two. Thus it can be parodied as an amoral view of the world. It is amoral, of course, just as chemistry is, but this does not mean that its practitioners are amoral. On the contrary, many of them study international relations because of a desire to improve the world, but with the belief that effective action presupposes a good understanding of the system one proposes to change. Indeed much of the early Peace Research work was motivated by strong moral concerns but was sternly positivist in nature and was done by people who were impatient with the classical theorists' casual attitude to testing. Demarcation between facts and morality does not imply a lack of interest in morality either logically or empirically.

International relations concerns issues over which we have strong moral feelings. It concerns peace and war which, since the development of weapons of mass destruction, now involve the very existence of the planet as a place for life. Particularly through international political economy it also concerns the gross disparities in income and wealth throughout the world. This makes it all the more important that we have rigorous criteria for distinguishing between what is the case in the world and what we want to be the case. The temptations to self-deceit are so strong that an exceptional concern with the methodological criteria for determining what is and what is not the case is required. This is not itself an argument for positivism but it is an argument for making exceptional efforts to establish a pragmatic form of truth which will enable wars, famines, poverty, gross inequalities and the like to be alleviated and perhaps abolished. I believe this list of bads is perfectly comprehensible and we cannot escape by pleading that they mean different things to different people.

Though we can distinguish and demarcate the positive statements about the world from other statements, this does not end the contact between morality and science. A positivist argues that empirical statements are value-neutral, certainly in the sense of moral values. However, statements are uttered in a social context and may lead to consequences. For example, the fact that something is discussed might appear to give it some legitimacy even if the discussion is a critical one. This has been argued about strategic studies. Rapoport has held that engaging in a discussion was to imply the moral legitimacy of certain inherently immoral acts like large-scale nuclear attack. Thus it becomes wrong to talk about certain sorts of things even if these things are true according to positivist criteria. I think this view is misguided but understandable. The legitimacy argument, we should note, is different from the self-fulfilling prophecy argument in which the actors read about the theory and from there on act in accordance with the theory. Politicians learn about the apparent academic respectability of realism and act accordingly. Similarly monetarism and other economic doctrines have been believed to be better established than in fact they were. This can lead to these beliefs being either self-fulfilling or self-defeating.

This brings us into deep ethical water. Uttering a statement then implies responsibility for these consequences if these consequences could have been foreseen. Thus, a discussion of poison gases in Nazi Germany could have been conducted entirely in terms of well-confirmed empirical facts which in themselves are value-neutral. The discussion itself would not have been. Thus, though we can distinguish conceptually between the positive, value-neutral statements and the social context in which they are uttered, this is an academic exercise as all statements are made in a social context. Are there some statements which should not be made even though, in themselves, they are value-neutral? But is the failure to tell the truth a form of lying and, if so, how wide is the morally permitted range of lies-by-omission? (Poor Kant would be very unhappy here.) As I say, we are in deep moral water. However, we are in it only if we see positivism as a powerful tool which can tell us things about the world including those we wish were false. The moral dilemma is one for the positivists. Those for whom the social world is a collection of prejudices and purely private perceptions, do not need to worry.

Conclusion

It follows from the positivist's concern with generalisation that the world is viewed as having some pattern to it and further that this pattern can be discerned if we try hard enough. This does not logically imply that the behaviour of the world can be altered in foreseeable directions, with the concomitant hopes that its behaviour can be improved, though many positivists hope (and usually believe) that this is the case. What is perhaps more significant is that, if the social world does not have these characteristics, it is hard to see how we can have any control of it. We are destined to be the victims of impersonal forces about which we can do nothing, a rather depressing possibility in view of what impersonal forces have done for us so far where issues of war and violence are concerned. Thus, policy requires positivism and the avoidance of this issue by the classical school has been a severe case of scholars wanting their cake and eating it. Some, like Martin Wight, were diffident about offering policy advice and, indeed, might have accepted my picture of the impersonal forces with equanimity. However, others in that tradition, such as Hedley Bull, were only too ready to offer comments on policy despite the rather dubious philosophical basis on which these comments rested if the rest of his admittedly unclear epistemology was to be accepted.

This does not mean that positivism must be accepted. It merely means that if one is to have a philosophically coherent basis for policy it must be accepted. The reverse is not true. The methods which imply positivism do not guarantee a coherent basis for policy though they make it a bit more likely. In fact the generalisations about human behaviour may be very unstable and the patterns of behaviour very fluid. This may force us back to look for the rules which govern the changes in the rules but this gets very difficult. However, if this is the case it is an empirical issue which at some stage we should be able to discover. This is a very different position from that of Winch who seems to regard the instability of social behaviour as an *a priori* truth about behaviour. Probably most positivists hope that this is not the case as most would hope that policy is possible. However, this is an empirical proposition about the belief structures of positivists which is therefore subject to empirical test.

REFERENCES

Axelrod, Robert (1984), *The Evolution of Cooperation* (New York: Basic Books).
Ayer, A. J. (1940), *The Foundations of Empirical Knowledge* (London: Macmillan).
Boulding, Kenneth (1962), *Conflict and Defense: A General Theory* (New York: Harper and Row).
Braithwaite, Richard (1953), *Scientific Explanation: A Study of the Function of Theory, Probability and Law in Science* (Cambridge: Cambridge University Press).
Brams, Steven (1985), *Superpower Games: Applying Game Theory to Superpower Conflict* (Boulder, CO and London: Lynne Rienner).
Bremer, Stuart (1980), 'National Capabilities and War Proneness', in J. D. Singer (ed.), *The Correlates of War: Testing some Realpolitik Models* (New York: Free Press).
Bueno de Mesquita, Bruce (1981), *The War Trap* (New Haven: Yale University Press).
Bull, Hedley (1966 [1969]), 'International Theory: The Case for a Classical Approach', in K. Knorr and J. Rosenau (eds.), *Contending Approaches to International Politics* (Princeton: Princeton University Press), pp. 20–38.
Cioffi-Revilla, Claudio (1990), *The Scientific Measurement of International Conflict* (Boulder, CO and London: Lynne Rienner).
Crystal, David (1990), *The Cambridge Encyclopaedia of Language* (Cambridge: Cambridge University Press).
Diehl, Paul (1983), 'Arms Races and Escalation: A Closer Look', *Journal of Peace Research*, 20 (3).
    (1985), 'Arms Races to War: Testing Some Empirical Linkages', *Sociological Quarterly*, 27, pp. 311–49.
Feyerabend, Paul (1975), *Against Method: Outline of an Anarchistic Theory of Knowledge* (London: Verso).
Hempel, C. (1965), *Aspects of Scientific Explanation and Other Essays in the Philosophy of Science* (Cambridge: Cambridge University Press).
Howard, Nigel (1971), *Paradoxes of Rationality: Theory of Metagames and Political Behaviour* (Cambridge, MA and London: MIT Press).

Kuhn, Thomas S. (1970), 2nd edition, *The Structure of Scientific Revolutions* (Chicago: Chicago University Press).

Laing, R. D. (1960), *The Divided Self* (Harmondsworth: Penguin).

Lakatos, Imre (1970), 'Falsification and the Methodology of Scientific Research Programmes', in Imre Lakatos and Alan Musgrave, *Criticism and the Growth of Knowledge* (Cambridge: Cambridge University Press).

Lakatos, Imre and Musgrave, Alan (eds.) (1970), *Criticism and the Growth of Knowledge* (Cambridge: Cambridge University Press).

Leamer, Edward E. (1983), 'Let's take the Con out of Econometrics', *American Economic Review*, 73 (1), pp. 31–43.

Nicholson, Michael (1983), *The Scientific Analysis of Social Behaviour: A Defence of Empiricism in Social Science* (London: Pinter).

(1989), *Formal Theories in International Relations* (Cambridge: Cambridge University Press).

(1992), *Rationality and the Analysis of International Conflict* (Cambridge: Cambridge University Press).

(1996), *Causes and Consequences in International Relations: A Conceptual Study* (London and New York: Pinter).

Niou, Emerson S., Ordeshook, Peter C. and Rose, Gregory E. (1989), *The Balance of Power: Stability in International Systems* (Cambridge: Cambridge University Press).

Popper, Karl R. (1959), *The Logic of Scientific Discovery* (London: Hutchinson).

Quine, W. V. (1953), *From a Logical Point of View* (Cambridge, MA: Harvard University Press).

(1992), revised edn, *The Pursuit of Truth* (Cambridge, MA: Harvard University Press).

Rapoport, Anatol (1960), *Fights, Games, Debates* (Ann Arbor, MI: Michigan University Press).

Richardson, Lewis Fry (1960a), *Arms and Insecurity* (Pittsburgh: Stevens).

(1960b), *Statistics of Deadly Quarrels* (Pittsburgh: Stevens).

Russell, Bertrand (1948), *Human Knowledge: Its Scope and Limits* (London: Allen & Unwin).

Schelling, Thomas C. (1960), *The Strategy of Conflict* (Cambridge, MA: Harvard University Press).

Schrodt, Philip A (1981), *Preserving Arms Distributions in a Multi-Polar World: A Mathematical Study* (Denver: Monograph Series in World Affairs, University of Denver).

Sen, A. K. (1981), *Poverty and Famines: An Essay on Entitlement and Deprivation* (Oxford: Clarendon Press).

Singer, J. David (1966 [1969]), 'The Incompleat Theorist: Insight without Evidence', in K. Knorr and J. Rosenau (eds.), *Contending Approaches to International Politics* (Princeton, NJ: Princeton University Press), pp. 62–86.

Singer, J. David and Small, Melvin (1966), 'National Alliance Commitments and War Involvement, 1815–1945', *Peace Research Society (International) Papers 5*, pp. 109–40.

(1968), 'Alliance Aggregation and the Onset of War, 1815–1945', in J. David

Singer (ed.), *Quantitative International Politics: Insights and Evidence* (New York: Free Press), pp. 247–86.

Taylor, Michael (1987), *The Possibility of Cooperation: Studies in Rationality and Social Change* (Cambridge: Cambridge University Press).

Vasquez, John (1983), *The Power of Power Politics: A Critique* (London: Pinter).

(1993), *The War Puzzle* (Cambridge: Cambridge University Press).

Wagner, Harrison (1986), 'The Theory of Games and the Balance of Power', *World Politics*, 38 (4), pp. 546–76.

Wallace, Michael (1979), 'Arms Races and Escalation: Some New Evidence', *Journal of Conflict Resolution*, 23, pp. 3–36.

(1982), 'Arms and Escalation: Two Competing Hypotheses', *International Studies Quarterly*, 26 (1), pp. 37–56.

Winch, Peter (1958), *The Idea of a Social Science and its Relation to Philosophy* (London: Routledge and Kegan Paul).

Zinnes, Dina A. and Muncaster, Robert G. (1984), 'The Dynamics of Hostile Activity and the Prediction of War', *Journal of Conflict Resolution*, 28 (2), pp. 187–229.

III

Silences

7 The rise and fall of the inter-paradigm debate

Ole Wæver

> The separation of concepts applicable to groups from those applicable
> to individuals is a powerful tool for eliminating the solipsism charac-
> teristic of traditional methodologies. Science becomes intrinsically a
> group activity, no longer even idealizable as a one-person game.
>
> Thomas S. Kuhn (1993, p. xiii)

A standard textbook presentation of International Relations (IR) has it
that there are three paradigms, three dominant schools. The first is
realism, the second is alternately called pluralism, interdependence and
world society but it is in some sense always the liberal approach, and the
third is Marxism or more broadly radicalism, structuralism or globalism.
Some writers claim that this is the timeless pattern of International
Relations debate – even in the classics, we find these three types of
thinking (Kauppi and Viotti, 1992; Viotti and Kauppi 1993 [1987]).
Others will be more restrictive and say the discipline *became* like this at
some point, e.g. in the 1970s (Holsti, 1985). Not everyone, however,
cherishes this categorisation.

Is it vague and arbitrary? (Why these three? Why three? Where do you
place the Neo-realism/Neo-liberalism debate?) No, all typologies are
problematic – this no more than others. Such will not be my main line
of criticism. A fairly coherent construction can be made (and will be
presented in section 1).

But 'the debate' is a misleading map and a bad guide to introduce
students to. This is not the pattern of debate today. The story about an
'inter-paradigm debate' does not give a grip on the ongoing controversies
in the discipline. The debate has moved on; self-referential story-telling
in the discipline ought to move with it. We need to construct new, more
up-to-date stories and invent new images and metaphors to replace
the triangle of the late 1970s. (Sections 2, 3 and 4 will address the
peculiarities of this picture in contrast to alternative, contemporary
maps.)

Is the debate's self-conception of the *status* of the debate a useful
tool for self-appreciation of IR? No, the image of 'incommensurable'

paradigms is a block to scientific progress as well as to earnest, painful criticism, and its 'theory of science' basis is at least contestable (see the final section in this chapter).

What was the inter-paradigm debate?

The first great debate in IR was that of idealism versus realism in the 1940s and the second was behaviouralism versus traditionalism in the 1950s–1960s. In the late 1960s and throughout the 1970s, there was increasing criticism of the dominant realist paradigm, not primarily its methodology, but its image of the world, its alleged state-centrism, preoccupation with power and its blindness to various kinds of processes domestically,   transnationally   and   beyond   the   political–military sphere.

The challengers not only formulated a criticism of realism but tried to present alternative conceptions of the international system. These went in terms of regional integration, transnationalism, interdependence, and a pluralist system of numerous sub-state and trans-state actors who made up a much more complicated image than the usual state-to-state one. States did not exist as such – various actors in the state interacted to produce what looked like state policy and sometimes even went around it and had their own linkages across borders. Not only were there more actors than the state, the state was not the state but was to be decomposed into networks of bureaucracies, interest groups and individuals in a pluralist perspective.

Increasingly, it became clear that the new theories were to win no easy victory. The realist imagery had a solid hold on decision makers who kept to some extent operating in a world of states (Rothstein 1972), and the new formulations had difficulty consolidating into *theory* and not just complications *of* the realist theory.[1]

There was a general understanding, that an alternative image of international politics had materialised, but also that realism did not easily give in. The two paradigms had different strengths, there were things better explained by the one, and others better dealt with by the other. And more importantly: there was no way to *prove* one or the other right. Realists and pluralists (interdependence people) *saw* different realities. If they went out to 'test' their theories, they would test them against different material, for they each sorted the world according to different concepts and thus got different empirical material. This was not the conception of for instance Keohane and Nye, who actually tried to test the two models – and the ensuing four models of regime change – against each other. But the emerging self-perception in and of the

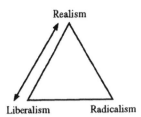

Figure 7.1 The inter-paradigm debate

discipline was that competing theories had emerged which each contained its own confirming stories, data and preferred issues.

Such an understanding was assisted by the contemporary criticism of positivism and especially Thomas Kuhn's theory of *paradigms*.[2] From here the idea was borrowed, that relations among competing general theories cannot be judged in any over-arching, neutral language. Each 'paradigm' constructs its own basic concepts/units and questions – and thereby its data, criteria and not least its stories about paradigmatic experiments or similar scientific events. Paradigms are incommensurable, because they each generate their criteria of judgement and their own 'language'. Realism and its pluralist challenger appeared to be such incommensurable paradigms.[3]

Meanwhile, a third paradigm had arisen: Marxism. Marxism was not new as a theory making powerful statements on international relations. Actually, it had done so at least as long as the discipline of IR had existed. (The first department of IR was – as all readers of this book have realised by now – established in Aberystwyth in 1919; Lenin wrote his *Imperialism, the Highest Stage of Capitalism* in 1916.) Theories of imperialism had been discussed vigorously – probably more blood was spilled here than in the debates of IR. But very few saw this as international relations (despite the dual allegiances of one of the founding fathers, Carr). In the 1970s, however, Marxism was increasingly seen as an alternative theory of international relations. It was not really equally well established within IR, but it became fashionable to present the discipline as engaged in a triangular debate (Marcusian 'repressive tolerance'?). Maybe it was triangular, but it was *de facto* mainly a debate along one side of the triangle (Figure 7.1).

It is easy to see that the three schools tell different stories of international relations. Numerous 3 times x schemes have been filled out with: key actor, concept of system, main sector, etc. (some of this is condensed in Table 7.1, but will not be rehearsed here). One might more interestingly ask: what are the essential features of the three schools?

One way to answer could be with Rosenau to emphasise the key level of analysis: the state-as-actor for realism, the many non-state (e.g. firms), sub-state (e.g. bureaucracies), supra-state (e.g. regimes) and trans-state (e.g. transnational bureaucracies) actors for liberalism, and finally the system for the neo-Marxists. It was this logic that led many in Britain to use the term 'pluralism' for the liberal strand and 'structuralism' for the Marxists. Pluralism because of the many actors and the link to liberal, political science,[4] and 'structuralism', because the whole system is much more organised and ordered according to the Marxists, than according to the other two. Following Rosenau, the system is fragmented to the realists, interdependent to the pluralist and integrated according to Marxists. (This was before attention was focused on *structural* realism, or neo-realism, whereafter 'structuralism' became more difficult as a code word for Marxism.)

One could also emphasise a difference regarding state/non-state and political/non-political. The realist's focus (in this story) on the states and their conception is political – relations from other spheres do not impinge deeply. The liberalists basically believe that all the interaction in other fields will eventually have an effect on international relations. The general evolution that has marked human affairs will also change the international. It is impossible that this sphere will remain the same (as claimed by the realists) while all other spheres change so dramatically. 'Non-political' relations will eventually transform this political set-up of states and conflict. The Marxists have a political, conflictual approach. There are conflicts of interest. But they do not operate between states, but within states and across states between oppressors and oppressed. By this formulation it becomes clear that this is not a continuum with two extremes and an in-between position (as the Wightian three traditions in some sense is). The two can line up against the third in all possible constellations depending on what is emphasised. Realists and radicals agree in recognising the role of power and struggle in contrast to the more harmony-oriented liberalism. Radicals and liberals together attack the narrow state universe of the realists. And of course the radicals on many issues meet a common front of realists and liberals who reject revolutionary change. You can keep travelling around in the triangle – it does not stabilise into a simple dichotomy.

Also it is clear, that the concept of time differs among the three: realism claims that fundamental change does not appear in international relations. The liberals find it hard to believe that in an era marked by accelerated change of almost everything else, international relations

Table 7.1 *Boxing the inter-paradigm debate*

	Realism	Pluralism/ interdependence	Marxism/radicalism
Level according to Rosenau	state-centric	multi-centric	global-centric
Basic actors	states	numerous sub-state, trans-state and non-state actors	the capitalist world economy (or forces and relations of production) and classes
Image (Banks)	billiard ball model	cobweb model	octopus model
View of the state	unitary actor	disaggregated into components	representing class interests (more or less directly)
Behavioural dynamic (Viotti and Kauppi)	State is rational actor seeking to maximise its own interest or national objectives in foreign policy	Foreign policy making and trans-national processes involve conflict, bargaining, coalition, and compromise – not necessarily resulting in optimal outcomes	Focus is on patterns of dominance within and among societies
Issues	National security is top	Multiple, not least welfare	Economic factors
Solidity of reality (objective/ subjective)	National interests exist objectively. The statesman has to ascertain these and to act them out. In some versions, the world of manipulation and intuition take on an independent life	Perceptions and roles often differ from reality. Academic analysis can help to find rational and optimal policy	Deep structures in the economy are very stable and consistent. Political actors are systematically misguided in their perceptions (ideology).
Repetition/ change	timeless laws, international relations is the realm of recurrence	change and possibly progress	stable and continuous pattern – until the break
conflict/ co-operation	relations among states are basically conflictual/ competitive	relations among states are potentially co-operative, non-state actors often mitigate conflict, but make the image confusing	Relations within and among states are conflictual, because the class struggle is the main pattern
Time	Static	Evolutionary	Revolutionary

Sources: Rosenau, 1982; Viotti and Kauppi, 1987; Keohane and Nye, 1977; Wilde, 1989.

should remain insulated from evolution/progress. And the radicals believe that everything could be different if just everything was different, i.e. there has to be one basic, revolutionary change, and then we can talk improvement. For Marxists this is of course a revolution in the relations of production, but to other versions of radicalism it is more often the states-system that has to be abolished.

As to terminology, there is agreement on the first corner: *realism* (except in the International Political Economy formulation of Gilpin where this is called *mercantilism* or *nationalism*). The second is called *pluralism* (e.g. Banks, 1985; Little *et al.*, 1981; Viotti and Kauppi, 1993 [1987]) to underline the multiple units disaggregation of the state and its affinity to non-statist approaches in political science, *liberalism* (which I will take as the most enduring label which links up to inter-war perspectives and which has returned in recent years as the preferred label in the US; cf. also McKinlay and Little, 1986), *globalism* (in for instance Maghrori and Ramberg, 1982) and *world society* (Groom, 1988; Rittberger and Wolf, 1988). The term *globalism* is used by some as designation for the third perspective as it points to the global, capitalist, world economy (cf. Viotti and Kauppi), but others prefer the term *structuralism* which stresses that the system is neither anarchic, nor equal, but structured in relations of super- and sub-ordination and actually quite 'organised' (e.g. Little *et al.* 1980; Banks, 1980). A more straightforward name would of course be *Marxism* (or neo-Marxism), but this corner contained also non-Marxist perspectives that were structuralist, dialectical and/or radical. One possibility is to use a label wide enough to capture all these 1970s–80s writings as well as 1980s post-modernism and critical theory which speaking in terms of 'discipline patterns' take the same location *vis-à-vis* the other positions. This might legitimise a rather vague covering term like *radicalism* for the third corner. James Rosenau rather precisely captured the late 1970s debate with the terms *state-centric, multi-centric* and *global-centric* (Rosenau, 1982). Alker and Biersteker in probably the most comprehensive overview used a 3 times 3 matrix where the three political perspectives (conservative, liberal-internationalist and radical/Marxist) were combined with three methodological approaches: traditional, behavioural and dialectical (1984). Numerous variations exist with authors adding a fourth or fifth, subdividing one or another of the basic paradigms, etc.[5] The image of the triangle, however, has been the one to be used most often as a guiding metaphor for the discipline. The term 'inter-paradigm debate' arouses in most scholars the image of three competing paradigms, and more important than the number is the form and content of debate, the meeting of incommensurable paradigms.

How did it differ from the other three great debates?

The debate took place mainly in the 1970s but gained its self-reflection *as* 'the inter-paradigm debate' or 'the third debate' in the beginning of the 1980s (Holsti, Rosenau, Banks).[6]

In contrast to the two previous debates, it increasingly was seen as a debate not to be won, but a pluralism to live with. In the first two debates, it was expected that one side would eventually win and International Relations would evolve as a coherent discipline in the winning camp. In the third debate, one increasingly (mostly implicitly) got the self-conception that the discipline *was* the debate. 'International Relations' was this disagreement, not a truth held by one of the positions. Each saw a side of reality that was important but could only be told from its perspective, not translated into the other two, nor subsumed in some grand synthesis. The discipline was thus in some sense richer for having all three voices, but also potentially in danger of fragmenting.

The yellow jersey of the leader who was in a position to define the discipline has travelled a complicated route. The discipline was invented in the inter-war period by liberalist theoreticians, while the first debate carried over the jersey to the camp of the realists (where now also they wanted to develop a specific discipline, International Relations). Realism had its palmy days in the 1940s and 1950s, and in a sense one might say the discipline did too. There was a clear focus, a relatively widespread consensus both on what IR was and that one had relevant things to say hereabout. Then followed the second debate, where the challengers were even more sure that the study of international relations was worthwhile and could be put to use (but possibly at times more doubtful whether there was a separate discipline). The movement of the new techniques hardly established a fixed, successful programme, and produced instead a confused situation. An assortment of empirical studies came from this wing, but no new paradigm. (Instead the behaviouralist challenge had a long-term impact on realism; more on this in a moment.) The behaviouralist programme with its fixation on method was not ready to *replace* realism (this the empirical findings were supposed to do!). The crux of the discipline came – if we stay with the metaphor of the yellow jersey – to hang fluttering somewhere near realism but in strong wind from the methodological challenge. After a period of extensive but diffuse belief in the new scientificness of the discipline, we returned to realism but a less focused, less self-assured realism. IR research could be conducted in a multitude of ways, many of which were on arch-realist premises (e.g. with power political, egoistic states fitted into models of a game theoretical or system theoretical nature). Thus the discipline flapped towards the 1970s when it definitely became triangular. With incommensurability, one no longer strived for ending debate, for finding who was right, but acknowledged that each 'paradigm' contained its own truth, and that they were all valuable. The debate is the discipline. This was definitely different from the two previous debates (as well as the one to follow it).

The debates have also differed as to arena or object of contest. The arena for competition in the inter-paradigm debate was largely 'basic assumptions' and 'basic images': what is international relations made up of – states, individuals, bureaucracies, a global economy, or what? Each paradigm was assumed to be locked, psychologically in its self-reaffirming conception which it could not convince the other of. The main issue of contention was 'the nature of international relations' (with ensuing political consequences) and the secondary one 'methodology'.

The fourth debate will be introduced in greater detail in section 4, but a brief way of presenting the distinction between the third and fourth debate could be via Lapid's article on 'The Third Debate' (1989). Yosef Lapid has given a summarising (and widely accepted) interpretation of the meta-theoretical debates of the 1980s as the third debate of the discipline. 'The third debate' has according to Lapid stimulated self-reflection in IR and by use of closer connections to meta-theoretical debates elsewhere in the social sciences furthered a revolt against positivist left-overs, and thereby pointed towards new measures for objectivity and science in IR. Beyond the detail that (unless this is assimilated into the inter-paradigm debate, or the latter is ignored) we must have reached the *fourth* debate, I see his attempt as problematic in content. In the Lapid version, the debate of post-structuralists (and others) with rationalists is turned into a question of epistemology (how do we know?) and something close to the second debate (on a higher level). This is too superficial in relation to the truly *philosophical* nature of the fourth debate. It is in contrast to the third debate not primarily about the character of the international system and contrary to the second debate it concerns more than how researchers could and should work. In some ways it is closer to the first in being about the relationship between 'reality' and 'utopia', about activist interventions versus a search for knowledge, about the relationship between language, politics and praxis. But first of all it is a much more fundamental challenge of basic assumptions regarding objectivity, subjectivity (the author, signature and the work), object/subject distinctions, the use of dichotomies, the rule by Western metaphysics over seemingly diverse ways of thought, and about referential versus relational conceptions of language, and much,

Table 7.2 *Themes of the four debates*

	Politics	Philosophy	Epistemology	Ontology (The nature of IR)	Methodology
first debate	XXX	XX		X	
second debate			XX	X	XXX
third debate	XX			XXX	X
fourth debate		XXX	XX	X	

Note: XXX = main form of debate. XX = secondary form, etc.

much more. If one accepts the challenge of the post-structuralists, this has consequences not only for the 'method' one uses (second debate), nor 'just' for one's perception of what international relations basically consists of (third debate), but it has consequences for how one perceives basic articles in the world we live in: language, society, praxis, politics, individuals and such like (see Table 7.2).

Politics was discussed in the first debate as balance of power versus rule of law and international organisations, and in the third as a debate over *détente* versus power politics, multilateral co-operation versus national policy. *Philosophy* was discussed, e.g. by Carr in the 1930s and 1940s, as utopia versus realism, and morality versus relativism, and again in the 1980s as questions of morality, relativism and activist theorising, of subject/object dichotomies and 'the death of the author'. *Epistemology* played a certain role in the second and the fourth debate; and *method* was at the centre of the second, whereas the third was basically about *the nature of IR (ontology)*, an issue that has always lurked in the background of all the debates.[7]

Thus, Table 7.2 should indicate that the fourth debate raises philosophical questions not reducible to those of the third. This is why one of the criticisms raised against Lapid was that he 'had lost sight of the critical purpose for which methodological pluralism and relativism have been pushed . . . It is not pluralism without purpose, but a *critical* pluralism, designed to reveal embedded power and authority structures, provoke critical scrutiny of dominant discourses, empower marginalized populations and perspectives, and provide a basis for alternative conceptualizations' (Biersteker, 1989, p. 264).

The third debate can be clearly singled out from the other three debates in three ways: its self-conception as 'incommensurable paradigms'; its area for locating the differences: 'ontologically' as different conceptions of the nature, units and content of international relations; and its 'participants': the three schools.

How did it start?

The specific parties to the inter-paradigm debate should not be explained here, they have their separate chapters in this book. What is important in this context is the *form* of the debate: incommensurability.[8] The paradigms could not have a real, normal 'debate'. They could not be tested against each other, since they basically did not speak the same language.

This at first had the 'liberating' function to allow weaker contenders to appear on the scene without being immediately bulldozed. It served a kind of 'infant industry' function and the reason for this pluralism was probably to be found in the weakened mainstream: American IR was marked by self-doubt after the Vietnam war, the student revolt and the oil shock. Without a sense of direction and a self-assured centre to control developments, without a voice of authenticity, there was suddenly room for more diversity in IR. In the longer run, however, the inter-paradigm debate might have had a conservative function. 'It became a welcomed barrier against any critique and a good legitimation for scientific routine. "Don't criticise me, we speak different languages"' (Guzzini, 1988, p. 13, 1992, p. 142).

Thus, the main explanation for this peculiar form for a discipline to take is to be found in a weakening of the centre (cf. Holsti, 1985, 1993). This can be explained by a combination of *discipline history* (the attacks on realism)[9] and *discipline external* developments (as mentioned: student revolt, Vietnam war, etc.). In this situation, the discipline avoided complete disintegration through the holding operation of the inter-paradigm debate. This was made possible by some inter-disciplinary (and some intra-disciplinary across-levels) borrowing. There is a clear meta-theoretical inspiration from the theory of science discussion around Popper, Kuhn, Feyerabend and Lakatos. To what extent this was misapprehended and misapplied will be addressed later – and is actually less interesting. Kuhn's theory was anyway not meant for the social sciences but mainly for the natural sciences. Thus, we are not really talking 'application' of a meta-theoretical, philosophical framework, but rather an inter-disciplinary borrowing which so often happens in science and which always means 'misunderstanding' but is often very fruitful (as when evolutionary ideas are applied beyond biology, complementarity beyond nuclear physics, Galilean physics by Hobbes, etc.). The metaphor of *paradigms* was useful for reconstructing a more decentralised but stabilised image of the discipline in a time of troubles.

I would further suggest that there was also a kind of sideways inspiration from within the discipline. Implicitly, one seemed to borrow from the 'perceptions' studies that proliferated in the same period (notably Jarvis, 1970, 1976; Snyder and Diesing, 1977; Janis and Mann, 1977): we are all caught by our view of the world, and this structures our way of importing new information and evaluating it. Ideas of perceptions, images, and cognitive psychology which found in those years their way into the discipline, were (implicitly) applied to the discipline itself.

When rereading the debates from then, textbooks from then and now, as well as Kuhn, it is striking how many of the participants in the debate actually employ something closer to the cognitive model of inertia in perceptions rather than paradigms in anything resembling Kuhn's sense. 'The new debate [the third debate] consisted of confrontation between opposing perspectives of the most general kind, variously known as frameworks, perspectives or paradigms. These were all terms intended to convey a world view more basic than theory' (Banks, 1984, p. 15). 'A paradigm contains within it a fundamental view of the world, and its assumptions act as lenses through which that world is perceived. "Facts" rarely speak for themselves and make sense only when interpreted in the light of the basic assumptions of a paradigm' (Mansbach and Vasquez, 1981, p. 71). Formulations like these miss the sociology of science and history of science argument by Kuhn (who is admittedly ambiguous on this; Masterman 1970), that paradigms are intrinsic to the *social* functioning of a scientific community.

The *perceptions* argument can be run on a purely individual basis ('we are all caught in our world views'). Why the discipline then coheres into three rather coherent 'paradigms' becomes something of a mystery. This often leads to a completely unKuhnian intrusion of naive realism (in the philosophical sense) suggesting that these three erupt because reality (international relations) actually consists of these three 'dimensions'. Alternatively, it is – in an instrumental and utilitarian manner – suggested, that 'we need' such shared images in order to organise our world and communicate about it (e.g. Holsti, 1988 [1967], pp. 11–13). With the more sociological approach of Kuhn, the emphasis instead falls on the production of questions or puzzles that are sufficiently closely tied to theories to be scientific. It is not that without paradigms, we could each be very wise but our images would be too complex for political advice and for debate among scholars. Without paradigms, there would be no *scientific* questions (Kuhn, 1970b, p. 9).

Progress can only appear in science within paradigms. Only paradigms can produce measures for this, and more importantly paradigms produce the puzzles on which to work. Participants can only be brought to accept such a framework by a process similar to a conversion, not by a rational argument – the argument would be one about what are the most important questions (questions framed in terms of concepts that mean different things in the different formulations). Only within a paradigm, there can be clear criteria for choosing competing explanations – among competing paradigms not, and therefore no logically definitive way of proving what paradigm is 'right'. This is the root of Kuhn's image of scientific 'evolution' as alternating periods of 'normal science' with agreement on a dominant paradigm, and 'revolutionary' periods with competing paradigms and/or paradigms crisis.

As the meaning of employing quasi-Kuhnian arguments increasingly became to explain and to some extent legitimise the simultaneous existence of several 'paradigms' without a way to settle their differences, the emphasis shifted from the sociological explanations (which were tied to an image of one dominant paradigm) to the more cognitive argumentation in Kuhn,[10] but fitted nicely into the literature emerging in the discipline at the time about 'perceptions' and 'images'. Quoting from the text that introduced the term 'the third debate': 'Although realists and globalists disagree on the essential character of the international system, they both accept one point: models do count. They agree that [quoting Keohane and Nye] "one's assumptions about world politics profoundly affect what one sees and how one constructs theories to explain events"' (Maghrori and Ramberg, 1982, p. 14). But note: when there is a debate, the most important question is in a sense always to ask 'what do the contestants agree on: how do they agree to frame the question over which they subsequently disagree? And here the agreement, Ray Maghrori claims, is that images of the world shape theories and theories shape images of the world. The inter-paradigm debate is the accord on seeing international relations theories as competing and incommensurable perceptional filters.

Some of the first applications of Kuhnian terminology to international relations were by optimistic pluralists who saw 'the decay of an old paradigm' (realism), looked for 'anomalies' which the old paradigm was unable to explain (which they easily found) and thought that the setting was ready for the arrival of *the* new paradigm which should according to Kuhnian logic then replace the old one (see e.g. Mansbach and Vasquez, 1981). Even Banks (1984) who coined the phrase 'inter-paradigm debate' ultimately presents the outcome as the victory for the world society paradigm (which will in the future develop its anomalies etc.). These authors are in fact closer to the classical Kuhnian presentation of the evolution of science in terms of one dominant paradigm followed by a revolutionary period and then replaced by normal science within another paradigm (which the pluralists employing this terminology, however, cannot resist presenting as a 'better' paradigm, which Kuhn would not say).[11]

Kuhn's own image of *social* science is that here, one often finds several paradigms operating simultaneously (or earlier, when the concept of paradigm was reserved for 'normal science', several competing schools). In this way, the debate in the social sciences comes to resemble that which is in natural science abnormal: the constant, critical attempts to question the believed.

[I]t is the tradition of claims, counterclaims, and debates over fundamentals which, except perhaps during the Middle Ages, have characterized philosophy and much of social science ever since. Already by the Hellenistic period mathematics, astronomy, statics and the geometric parts of optics had abandoned this mode of discourse in favour of puzzle solving. Other sciences, in increasing numbers, have undergone the same transition since. In a sense, to turn Sir Karl's view on its head, it is precisely the abandonment of critical discourse that marks the transition to a science. Once a field has made that transition, critical discourse recurs only at moments of crisis when the bases of the field are again in jeopardy. Only when they must choose between competing theories do scientists behave like philosophers. (Kuhn, 1970b, p. 7)

Kuhn himself has not much to say about more permanently 'multiple-paradigm sciences' (Masterman, 1970, p. 74). The most enduring contribution of the Kuhnian idea of paradigms to IR has been the image of a by definition inconclusive debate among competing schools of thought.

Did it exist, the inter-paradigm debate? Partly no, it was not actually an intense three-way debate occupying the minds of International Relationists, but an artificially constructed 'debate', mainly invented for specific presentational purposes, teaching and self-reflection of the discipline. (Just as the first and second debates to some extent were constructions.) Partly yes, it refers to a pattern of behaviour and an attitude which gradually emerged in the 1970s and was given a clarifying label as the 'inter-paradigm debate'.

How did it end?

In the mid and late 1980s we were no longer in the inter-paradigm debate, even if it was still used as a teaching tool and as schematism when some idea was to be evaluated 'across the discipline'. The 1980s constellation was different. Different because there was a change of fronts, and different because it moved to a different level (as argued above) and, not least, it moved beyond incommensurability.

In the triangular third debate, the three sides probably were never equal. The Marxist/structuralist side did not achieve full equivalence, and at least for a while the initiative was with 'interdependence' (the liberalist brand of the day). As often noted, Waltz's *Theory of International Politics* (1979) and Gilpin's *War and Change in World Politics* (1981) were the revenge of realism, an attempt to relaunch more 'scientific' versions of realism. Especially Waltz's version, which became known under the name Robert Cox and Richard Ashley gave to them: 'neo-realism' (Cox, 1981; Ashley, 1984).

What is 'neo' about it? What distinguishes the new realism from the classical one? Often the answer is given that the old one argued from human nature, whereas neo-realism bases its realism in the anarchic nature of the international system. If that is the criterion, neo-realism dates back to the 1950s, when Herz as well as Waltz emphasised strongly that they did not include any premises about human nature, that their arguments were based in social features peculiar to 'the international'.[12] There have all along been quite different versions of how to ground realism – human nature, international structure, philosophy of history, knowledge pessimism (Wæver, 1992, ch. 3). Thus the 'basis' can hardly be the defining criterion for neo-realism. The really new thing about neo-realism is its *concept of science*. General speculation and reflection is no longer sufficient, realism has to express itself in the form of *theory*, of a system of clearly specified sentences, cf. the title of a Waltz article: 'Realist Thought and Neo-Realist Theory' (1990). In this sense the shift from realism to neo-realism can be seen as a delayed and displaced victory for the 'scientific' side of the second debate.

This change has important and interesting effects on the relationship among 'paradigms'. (Neo-)Realism is no longer an ethico-philosophical position. Sweeping statements on the nature of life and politics are replaced by precise statements. Compare the rhetoric of classical realists like Morgenthau, Kissinger and Liska who generalise about the nature of human life (not necessarily human nature, but wisdom about the human condition) and tell stories about the inherently tragic nature of politics and other lessons at a level close to philosophy of history.[13] Neo-realism in contrast says only 'a small number of big and important things' (Waltz, 1986, p. 329), a conscious self-limitation. Becoming scientific implies a certain minimalism, and plenty of space is left for developing theory and empirical studies on a number of other factors.

Liberal theory underwent a parallel development. It moved away from being a general interpretation of the nature of international relations or an idea of overall developments, and concentrated instead on asking a few precise questions. Or maybe simply one: 'how institutions affect incentives facing states' (Keohane, 1989, p. 11). And the principal thesis is

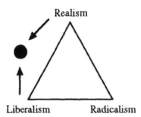

Figure 7.2 The neo-neo synthesis

that variations in the institutionalization of world politics exert significant impacts on the behaviour of governments. In particular, patterns of cooperation and discord can be understood only in the context of the institutions that help define the meaning and importance of state action. (Keohane, 1989, p. 2)

As a basis for investigating this, the anarchy assumption of neo-realism is taken as a useful starting point. As Keohane argues, if one smuggles on board cosmopolitan preferences it is not surprising that one reaches the conclusion that regimes are important. By basing instead the argument on (what is claimed to be) realist premises with states as egoistic, rational actors, it can be shown that institutions are possible and relevant *even* on these restricted premises. The neo-liberal institutionalists search in parallel with the neo-realists for still more limited, precise, formula-like assertions that can be reduced to simple analytical statements amenable to tests and theory.

This is not to say that neoliberal institutionalism gives us the answer – only that it gets the question right. (Keohane, 1989, p. 11)

As they are both extremely American, it might be appropriate to notice that neo-realism and neo-liberalism both became 'leaner and meaner'.

During the 1980s, realism became neo-realism and liberalism neo-liberal institutionalism. Both underwent a self-limiting redefinition towards an anti-metaphysical, theoretical minimalism, and they became thereby increasingly compatible. A dominant *neo-neo synthesis* became the research programme of the 1980s (Figure 7.2). No longer were realism and liberalism 'incommensurable' – on the contrary they shared a 'rationalist' research programme, a conception of science, a shared willingness to operate on the premise of anarchy (Waltz) and investigate the evolution of co-operation and whether institutions matter (Keohane). Inside this we saw both the emergence of direct attempts at synthesis (Ruggie, 1983; Buzan *et al.*, 1993) and a standard type of *International*

Organization article operationalising and testing realism and liberalism against each other in a specific field, but with a clear idea that they could be brought back into conversation.

My term 'neo-neo' does not refer to an idea that this is newer than the new, a reformulation of neo-realism for instance. It refers first of all to the synthesis between realism and liberalism that became possible, when realism was transformed into neo-realism and liberalism into neo-liberal institutionalism; it is the synthesis of the two neo-schools and became possible by their very neo-ness.

In this cross-field produced by their *rapprochement*, one can find much of the empirical studies of the 1980s, especially the typical 'theory guided' and/or 'theory testing' article in *International Organization*. Regime theory, co-operation under anarchy, hegemonic stability, alliance theory, trade negotiations, and Buzanian security analysis can all be seen as located in this field.

In this environment, the main line of controversy shifted to the opposite direction as one between rationalists and reflectivists, the post-modernism debate. As the previous line of debate 'dried out', the radicals entered to fill the vacuum. Thus the two main poles became on the one hand a neo-realist, neo-liberal synthesis and on the other reflec-tivism (cf. Figure 7.3, debate 4a in Table 7.3).

This constellation became authorised by Keohane's presidential address for ISA 1988 where he discussed 'two approaches to inter-national institutions'. The two approaches were on the one side the rationalist, clearly referring to the merged neo-realist neo-liberalist research programme of which he himself is one of the leaders, and the other side what Keohane united under the label 'reflectivists' which was to cover those inspired by French post-modernism, those with German hermeneutics as well as late-Wittgensteinian rules-perspectives and social constructivism. (Sometimes, the label reflectivist has – consciously or not – been changed to *reflexivists* in order to point to the self-reflective nature of the new critical approaches.)

Reflectivists, according to Keohane, are characterised by emphasising *interpretation*, the *reflections* of the actors as central to institutions. Norms and regimes cannot be studied positivistically but have to be seen as inter-subjective phenomena only researchable by non-positivist methods (Kratochwil and Ruggie, 1986). Institutions are not something actors rationally construct following from their interests, since they act in meta-institutions (such as the principle of sovereignty) which create the actors rather than the other way round. Institutions and actors constitute each other mutually.[14]

That this rationalist–reflectivist axis was the main line of struggle was

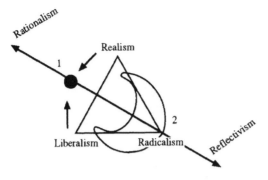

Figure 7.3 IR debate of the 1980s

to be registered in many ways in the 1980s. Many younger academics who were to be evaluated – for tenure or positions – or had articles refereed in this period will have stories to tell about the vehemence of resistance against especially post-structuralism. Also articles allegedly not dealing with this line of controversy reveal it. For instance Keohane in a presentation of the relationship between neo-realism and neo-liberalism argues like this:

Neoliberal institutionalism (. . .) shares some important intellectual commitments with neorealism. Like neorealists, neoliberal institutionalists seek to explain behavioral regularities by examining the nature of the decentralized international system. Neither neorealists nor neoliberal institutionalists are content with interpreting texts: both sets of theorists believe that there is an international political reality that can be partly understood, even if it will always remain to some extent veiled. (Keohane, 1989, p. 8)

It is visible here how the unity of the neo-neo position is partly argued by reference to some unnamed academics who 'are content with interpreting texts'.

In the new set-up it could finally be noted how the reflectivists carry out a flanking operation (see Figure 7.3). In their work to reshape themselves in scientific form, realism as well as liberalism had to leave behind some of their traditional fields, political statesmen in the case of realism, and ethics in the case of liberalism. Reflectivists attempted to articulate these classical issues against the two neo-schools, who had become too scientific for such matters. Post-structuralists have argued that classical realism was in many ways superior to neo-realism (cf. e.g. Ashley, 1984; Der Derian, 1987). Ethics, a traditionally liberalist theme, has in recent years been articulated more often from a reflectivist basis (Brown, 1992).

Why is reflectivism placed in the same corner as Marxism, why the vague covering term 'radicalism'? Reflectivists do not share many assumptions with the Marxists. Thus, if one wants to make an ahistorical model of different schools, they have to have clearly separate positions. But when the models are snapshots at a given time, they can be located in the same place – radicalism – since post-modernist approaches largely replaced Marxism as the 'extreme contender', the radical challenge. Some Marxists might claim that this is a plot of the establishment, because post-modernism is ultimately reactionary and thus it was a nice move for the establishment to get rid of the really dangerous challenge, Marxism, and be hospitable to an ultimately undangerous new challenger, post-modernism. Post-modernists will emphasise how their criticism of logo-centric, Western, essentialist theories punches Marxism at least as hard as it does the establishment, and therefore criticism has become more radical as they took over. Watching with the task of writing the history of the discipline, it can just be noticed that the role of Marxism as contender in great debates clearly has waned. There is still – maybe increasingly – important work from Marxists that contributes significantly in IPE, in foreign policy theory and not least in macro-historical reflection on the emergence and evolution of the modern state. In the debates which the discipline uses to orient itself, the position which used to be occupied by Marxists was in the mid and late 1980s taken over by post-modernists.

The rationalist–reflectivist axis was not the only but the biggest axis in the 1980s. In a sense it was supplemented by a perpendicular but shorter one: the debate over absolute and relative gains (debate 4b in Table 7.3).[15] The remaining short distance between neo-realism and neo-liberalism is being argued out in this debate, which clearly echoes old realist–liberalist debates, but in its form is very post-third debate like: 'this is not the inter-paradigm debate' (as Keohane said in a panel on the relative/absolute gains debate at the APSA meeting in 1992; cf. also Keohane, 1993a, pp. 291ff), this is not about incommensurable paradigms. We agree on 90 per cent and the remainder is essentially an empirical question.[16] The proportions of how much state action is driven by relative and how much by absolute gains and under what conditions, that is a researchable matter wonderfully suited for the rationalist, neo-neo research programme. And actually this has become a cottage industry for the most mathematical modellers in the discipline. Not many of those who originally formulated the IR theory issues behind this can follow the Snidals and the Powells into their equations, but this is logically the apex of the neo-neo programme. One might even speculate that causality runs the opposite way: this business boomed exactly because it was so modelable – finally International Relations could make

Table 7.3 *Comparing the third and the fourth debate*

	3rd debate (Inter- Paradigm Debate)	Debate 4a (Reflectivist– Rationalist)	Debate 4b (absolute-relative gains)
Form of relationship among debaters	Incommensurability	War	Differences within a research programme
Theme (or substance) of disagreement	World View	Philosophy	Empirical question to be settled
Combatants	The Three paradigms	Neo-Neo synthesis against post-modernists	Neo-Realists versus Neo-Liberal Institutionalists

it into the *American Political Science Review* with articles full of equations. Most important is, however, to notice that the absolute/relative gains debate is not just any debate, but a very well structured debate among participants who have been striving to set up a joint framework. Therefore it was possible to conduct such a disciplined debate, with so much agreement, and lessons about how well organised it has been, logically should not be used to tell others how to discuss (for instance: use game theory), because this well-organised debate was only possible because it was located in a very particular place: within the neo-neo aspiration for agreement.

Thus, it should be clear, that the fourth debate is not the third, the inter-paradigm debate. Table 7.3 sums up how on all three defining dimentions, it has changed. Not only has this move taken us beyond the inter-paradigm debate; now we are probably *after* the fourth debate (Wæver, 1994).

In the 1990s there have been tendencies towards opening up a middle ground on the rationalist/reflectivist axis. After the clear polarisation between rationalists and reflectivists which was at times a rather tough struggle not least in the USA in the 1980s, we have in the 1990s witnessed increasing signs of *rapprochement* between the two. Among leading rationalists there have been signs of increasing boredom in relation to the rational choice extremes and on the side of the reflectivists we can see what could be called *post-radical reflectivism*, a move away from the self-marginalising guerrilla approaches towards attempts to contribute to conceptualisations and handling of various issues. Discussions on 'sovereignty' have been one meeting point, where rationalists have admitted the existence of 'deep conventions' and thereby moved towards acknowledging the role of constitutive principles like sovereignty, very close to writings of some reflectivists (Wendt and Duvall, 1989; Keohane, 1993a). Along the axis of debate of the 1980s – rationalist/reflectivist – we thus see an increasing marginalisation of extreme rationalists (rational choice) and of extreme anti-IR approaches (deconstructivists), and the emergence of a middle ground where neo-institutionalists from the rationalist side meet constructivists arriving from the reflectivist side (Figure 7.4). More 'philosophical' issues are increasingly welcome in the mainstream.

At the rationalist end, we have witnessed a certain emptying of the energy of the neo-neo programme. Joseph Nye has pointed out that neo-realism in the 1980s was often wedded to rational actor approaches, to rational choice theories and expected utility models. These are not really theories, they lack questions to play with, and these they could get from neo-realism (and one could add: often in comparative tests of neo-liberal and neo-realists hypotheses).

> Rational-choice theories can be parsimonious and powerful, but as research strategies, they run risks that are reinforced by the sparse structure of neorealism. (. . .) The benefit of marrying rational choice with neorealist approaches is a double parsimony. The danger is that each already has a negative heuristic that directs attention away from preference formation and transnational interactions. (Nye, 1988, p. 248)

Stated differently: Keohane and others have in the 1980s – especially around the journal *International Organization* – conducted for the discipline a surprisingly consistent and systematic attempt to create cumulative research from a few theoretical questions (the consequences of anarchy, of polarity and of institutionalisation). This has naturally pushed in the direction of not too philosophical articles but often sophisticated methods for testing. This has been useful and successful. But boring. This project cannot keep its hold on one's attention. A few continue along with testing and modelling central variables. There is, for example, a resurgence of writings on the importance of bi- versus multi-polarity, which is partly triggered by the political situation (end of the Cold War), but partly by the fact that this is the dimension Waltz's theory points out as that to be analysed. A structural shift in world politics according to Waltz *has* to be a change at level 3, i.e. of polarity. And then it seems so wonderfully measurable.

But what if we approach this slightly more reflectively? Isn't it possible that we watch a change at some other level? Maybe the second Waltzian level? Are we approaching neo-medieval or post-modern political structures? This can be analysed through a Waltzian/Ruggian conception

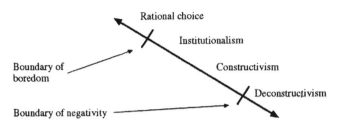

Figure 7.4 The 1990s

of structure as a possible second tier change possibly combined with a study of the constant reformulation of principles in a praxis/structure cycle inspired by Giddens, Luhmann or post-structuralism (cf. Ruggie, 1983, 1993; Wæver, 1991; forthcoming a). This is just one example of interesting developments that are of interest to the rationalists but somehow better articulated from the reflectivist side (or at least by giving the rationalist theory a socially constructed status). Some of the semi-philosophical question asks for at least English school reflections but probably also more refined analysis of the discursively constructed meta-institutions of the system. The issue of *sovereignty* especially has pushed the rationalists out of their own garden. Sovereignty is clearly not an 'institution' in the narrow rationalist sense, but rather a 'thick' social phenomenon with historicity. And it is hard to avoid the centrality of the concept and possible changes in it for our present situation.

From the opposite direction we see the beginnings of 'post-radical reflectivism' – reflectivists not sticking to the post-structuralist guerrilla war against the 'system', but also conducting concrete analysis in dialogue with the establishment.[17] An important feature of post-radical reflectivism is that it does not continue to ghettoise itself, as post-structuralism partly did in the 1980s. In a situation where the rationalist corner has reached the point where realists and liberalists agree more than 90 per cent, only discuss details and these details are tested with much mathematics, it can hardly surprise that moderate reflectivists like Ruggie and even Wendt are met with considerable openness.

Recent years have witnessed an increasing interest in the so-called English school. This would seem to fit nicely into the scheme. The English school is a respectable, traditional approach which includes quasi-philosophical and historical reflection, and especially it interrogates deep institutions in the system. Thus, it can relatively easily be linked to more or less post-modernist notions, an emphasis on the cultural colouring of international systems and especially the general 'radical' interest in thinking the basic categories of the international system instead of taking them as mechanical givens. At the same time, the classics of the English school, especially Bull's *Anarchical Society* is a comprehensible, seemingly straightforward discussion of the actual system with relatively clear, operational concepts. Thus, the American mainstream can find a moderate way to extend its institutionalism in a not too dangerous way by using Bull (and reading him almost as a regime theorist or neo-liberal institutionalist).[18] The new wave of English School enthusiasm thus ties in with the attempted *rapprochement* between reflectivists and rationalists, with the deradicalisation of reflectivism and the rephilosophisation of the rationalists.

What's wrong with the inter-paradigm debate?

This implies actually two questions:

1 Is it true? Is the triangle of incommensurable paradigms the final, inevitable pattern? Can we rise above incommensurability, or is this 'relativist' argument actually impossible to deal with, because one's own argument will always remain one of the positions in this world of self-reaffirming positions who can't establish a joint language? (cf. Cox, 1981; Neufeld, 1993; Rengger, 1988, 1989, 1992).

2 What's wrong with keeping this as an image of the discipline, using it as a handy way of introducing the discipline to students, and as a map when discussing broadly the development of the discipline? Is it so important to argue over whether we are in the inter-paradigm debate or not?

A post-modern solution to the problem of incommensurability

It has often been assumed that post-structuralists should love the argument of incommensurability. These post-modernists allegedly argue the impossibility of communication (or rather the impossibility of actual communication approximating our ideal of communication as the transmittance of messages meaning the same to sender and receiver; of course, 'communication' as a social phenomenon takes place all the time). And here comes a surprising reinforcement from (defectors?) among the Anglo-Saxon philosophers of ordinary language and of theory of science. Thus, post-structuralists should be the most radical supporters of incommensurability, the arguers of 'radical incommensurability' (Rengger, 1989). I will argue the opposite: the quandary of incommensurability – which most commonsensical Anglo-Saxon minded social scientists find unacceptable but difficult to rebut – can be dealt with most fundamentally from a post-structuralist perspective.

The first step is to notice that the concept of incommensurability is not the problem, the problem is the concept of commensurability. The *argument* about incommensurability rests on a dichotomy, between on the one hand radical incommensurability (and ultimate incommunicability) *among* paradigms and on the other hand radical commensurability and communicability *within* paradigms. A post-structuralist immediately reacts against the latter: total understanding *never* happens. No communication (in the phenomenological sense) is ever communication (in the ideal sense). But communication takes place all the time, so obviously human beings experience that it makes sufficient sense for us (or most of us) to go on. (Some even make a living of it, for instance as IR scholars and teachers.) We do not have total incommunicability all over. But this does not mean that we should lean on the image of transparent meaning transference, where the parties argue with concepts that have been given an ultimate definition. Post-structuralists argue that all meaning systems are open-ended systems of signs referring to signs referring to signs.[19] No concept can therefore have an ultimate, unequivocal meaning. The image of closed paradigms or any other closed culture assumes that a closed sign system has been achieved which gives a stable and ultimate meaning to its participants. This would be possible within French *structuralism*, but exactly not in *post*-structuralism, the main difference between the two being that structuralism is a theory of signs, post-structuralism a critique of the sign; structuralism investigates how social phenomena can be explained by stable and pervasive meaning systems, post-structuralism shows how all meaning systems are precarious, self-defeating and only *strive* for closure without ever succeeding.

The image of paradigms internally communicating, externally only interacting, closely resembles late eighteenth–early nineteenth-century *romanticism*. Romanticism is a belief in closed cultures. Meaning rests with the community. Cultures are the carriers of meaning systems, and can only be understood from within, by the participants who share these cultures as complete persons, aesthetically, linguistically and sometimes even ethnically or historically. Especially in romantic nationalism it is clear how one assumes total understanding within (the complete, gratifying *understanding* in the warm embrace of the nation) and the total lack of understanding between cultures.

Incommensurability is only a meaningful term if combined with romanticising the warmth of community (as we see in its replay today in US multi-culturalism). Incommensurability as concept derives its meaning from a distinction, the distinction between incommensurability and commensurability – a deeply problematic distinction, as it becomes most clear by investigating the concept of commensurability. Anglo-Saxon criticisers have attacked 'the myth of the framework' (Popper, 1970) or 'the very idea of a conceptual scheme' (Davidson, 1974). They focus on the exaggeration of *limits* to communication. A solution to the problem of incommensurability is to be found in an investigation of the exaggeration of *unlimited* communication.[20]

It could seem surprising that the theme of incommensurability arose from within Anglo-Saxon philosophy – why not the allegedly more relativist French? (The seeming parallelism of Kuhn and 'the French' has tempted IR authors to link Kuhn, Foucault, Wittgenstein and Gadamer (Rengger, 1988, 1989; George and Campbell, 1990).) It is, however, not at all surprising that incommensurability arose out of Anglo-Saxon philosophy of science. Actually it is a logical question to arise out of their problematique – only to those who have believed in complete communication can walls of incommunicability and incommensurability appear. (As often noticed, logical positivism was in many ways a rerun of at least aspects of Enlightenment ideals, including the belief in a rational, universal language and transparent communication. It ended in many of the same problems – and generated thus a similar romanticist/culturalist counter-movement.)[21]

When we have deconstructed this image of walls encircling crowds who are forced to communicate meaningfully only within their throng, and replaced it by a general image of difficult, incomplete, partial 'communication' which might exhibit variations in density and thus patterns or groupings, but no fixed, ultimate distinctions of an inside/outside nature, there is no reason to assume (radical) incommensurability (specifically) among paradigms. There is, however, one remaining argument which is often made for incommensurability: these paradigms are really political groupings. The three 'paradigms' are obviously the three classical political main orientations: conservative, liberal and radical. Therefore, they can never be brought to agree. Not because of cognitive filters or the closedness of sign systems, but because their world views are tied with different *normative* programmes (Krasner, 1989, pp. 425f; Little and Smith, 1991). This argument, however, ought to lead to a *general* relativism or perspectivism. It can hardly sustain a picture of e.g. three paradigms. Even if there are these three grand ideologies, political struggles do not consistently form themselves in such triangles. Why does this discipline then? Paradigms have to be applied first of all as sociological concepts for discipline internal developments.

Do international relationists today still use 'incommensurability' as implicit guide? No, we have seen the neo-neo synthesis which strives for a classical shared methodology, and even among the theories that do not vie for such close merger, there is a changed attitude. The trend of the last decade has exactly been for all the more dominant theories also to establish more self-knowledge and a better understanding of their limits, inner logic and their couplings to other kinds of theory. Thus, the mode of relating schools in the 1990s is not incommensurability but a kind of 'division of labour'. What the theory of science rationale of this attitude can be is a little less clear.

Based on realist premises (i.e. that all theories are ultimately talking about the same reality out there), a division of labour can have evolved because the different explanatory sources are placed in different areas. Each theory carves out its own explanatory mechanisms and sources in ways that do not overlap. In the end they partly explain the same object, but they do not compete for this, and should not be tested against each other. They should be articulated, since they base themselves in separate parts of the system. Or as Ruggie has recently put it:

Clearly, different bodies of contemporary international relations theory are better equipped to elucidate different domains of contemporary change and continuity. (. . .) Each, therefore, can become a 'grand theory' only by discounting or ignoring altogether the integrity of those domains of social life that its premises do not encompass. Nor are the various bodies of extant theory in any sense additive, so that we could arrive at a grand theory by steps. (1993, p. 169)

There is no overarching logic *of* the different stories. They each have unfolded from their own inner logic, constructing a coherent story which has, however, in the last decade zoomed in on specific, partial levels, with the effect that the theories can be treated as complementary sources of negative predictions.

The theories do not modify each other – they have each their separate area: domestic, international political structure, systemic pressure, political action and interaction. They are each absolute demands. The theoretician has to accept the inner logic of Waltzianism when he enters an analysis in terms of international political structure. The same for the other places. They each have their inner logics, but they have managed to carve out complementary sections and they have made linkages that allow for a mutual serviceability.

This implicit emerging attitude, however well it functions as social ideal in the discipline, comes to rest on some heroic assumptions if it stays on realist ground (realist in theory of science sense). The different theories have moved in the direction of different fields/levels, but still they do have a lot of shared references (state, interest, politics, etc.) that are given different meaning in the different theories. To a realist, it then becomes problematic to combine the theories. This new attitude *could* then be reformulated as a more radical constructivism in which the objects are seen as constructed by the separate theories.

Therefore these do not compete for explaining 'the same'. They each do different jobs. The theories can only be linked externally, when one theory reaches out on its own terms for another theory to exploit it, which it can then only do by grasping the inner logic of this other theory and its material. This self-referentiality of the theories in no way prevents researchers from entering several of these – the limitations are not in our heads but in the logic of the theories and their ensuing 'realities'. Grand 'synthesis' and (literal) co-operation (simultaneous running) of several theories (that might in some abstract sense be logically incompatible), thus becomes possible if the meta-theory is adjusted towards constructivism (Luhmann, 1990a, 1990b; Wæver, 1994). This in a sense is to play *with* incommensurability, but against the cognitivist idea of different 'lenses' that create different pictures of 'the same'.

A strategic approach to 'IR debates'

The second question is the famous *and so what?* Does the inter-paradigm debate idea harm anyone? Yes, there is a tendency in it to produce straw men, not least of the realists (cf. Buzan's chapter in this volume; Wæver, 1992, ch. 3). But more importantly these debates and the ideas about the debates are part of the self-reflection and thus self-management of the discipline. Thus, there are dangerous effects of counting wrongly.

My argument in terms of four debates is unconventional. According to established wisdom there is no fourth debate. We are still in or after the third, and now I even claim that we are leaving the fourth. The disagreement stems from the peculiar way of counting in International Relations: 1st debate, 2nd debate, 3rd debate, 3rd debate. Three is a magic number – three paradigms, three debates. In academic debates, there always have to be three positions, three options, three scenarios.[22] As argued (above, and Wæver, 1994), I am convinced that there are (at least) four major debates. To ignore this enumeration error is problematic because it means to assimilate the fourth into the third. Hereby the third debate is prolonged. Self-reflection in International Relations of the 1980s and 1990s is blocked if presented with the choice of either using the triangle as scheme or abstaining from pictures of its own development. We need new metaphors and depictions to foster self-reflection in the discipline.

This implies that a sub-theme of this article has been the uses and abuses of 'schools'. Danger arises especially when one model of schools gets fixed, such as the timeless triangle, and projected backwards as well as forwards, as the map of all possible positions. On the other hand, images of the internal battlelines do exist and they have effects. Thus, it is worth taking seriously how they function, what they are, and what could possibly be achieved by trying to reshape them. The 'debates' operate as a dialectic between implicit pictures and articulate self-representations of the discipline. The debates are partly constructed and artificially imposed on much more diverse activities, partly they are implicit operators in actual academic practice, they are distinctions involved in the work of the discipline. Academic work is always guided by a picture of the discipline itself as the immediate social context. Each of the debates first emerged as constellation, as implicit picture – the picture is not totally consistent from person to person, but since debate in a discipline is an inter-subjective and interactive phenomenon, there will be a certain convergence. Then in a second step, this constellation is *labelled*, which reinforces the constellation, but also guides the phase of moving beyond it, because the next phase will be defined in relation to this picture of the discipline.

Probably, 'the inter-paradigm debate' should be retained as a very informative metaphor for telling discipline history about the 1970s–early 1980s. To grasp the later 1980s and 1990s we need new images, possibly like the neo-neo merger and the pincer movement of the radicalists and then later the two-sided exclusion beyond the boundaries of boredom and boundaries of negativity resulting in a new middle-ground which is not just any middle-ground ('let's meet'), but a specific one because it has grown out of the self-conceived positions and battle-lines of the preceding period. So again: even the 'after the fourth debate' of the 1990s will be misunderstood if read as a *rapprochement* among the positions of the third debate (the inter-paradigm debate) when actually it takes place among the contestants of the fourth debate (rationalists and reflectivists). There is a difference between being after the fourth debate and after the third debate. Especially if one wants to be prepared for the fifth debate, which will inevitably come. The discipline seems to organise itself through a constant oscillation between grand debates and periods in-between where the previous contestants meet. One of these debates was the inter-paradigm debate. None of these debates lasts forever. Even if they could all be constructed as nice typologies – exhaustive and exclusive – they would still become misleading at a point when the practitioners had organised themselves along different lines, arguing the next debate.

NOTES

I would like to thank Barry Buzan, Richard Little, Jaap de Wilde, Lene Hansen and Wojchiech Kostecki as well as participants in the Aberystwyth conference for helpful comments on earlier drafts.

1 Keohane and Nye, for instance, in the most famous book of the period, *Power and Independence*, solved the problem through what was in part a dualist approach: realism got what was realism's (conflictual politics among not too civilised states), while an alternative model of 'complex interdependence' was deemed more relevant to politics among the developed, democratic states. This complementarist approach was not easily absorbed by the academic world (Suhr, 1995) – complementarity was not much reflected on, while *Power and Independence* (like other contemporary books) was taken as 'a new, alternative paradigm' (which was probably not totally against the intentions of its authors).

2 Kuhn's *The Structure of Scientific Revolutions* appeared in 1962, but gained much wider circulation in the social sciences after the publication of Lakatos and Musgrave (1970).

3 Incommensurability does not – as often wrongly suggested – imply the impossibility of dialogue, in which case the term 'inter-paradigm debate' would be a contradiction in terms. It means first of all, that no neutral language is available into which the competing theories can be translated and then compared (Kuhn, 1970c). It might be possible to translate one theory into the language of another, and this is in a sense what we are all asked to strive for (Kuhn, 1970c; Bernstein, 1991, pp. 65ff), but we still have to recognise that this is not the same as to understand the other theory as that which is to itself, in its own language, nor does it supply any measure outside the competing theories by which to judge them and choose the better one.

4 It is, however, possible to make a distinction between the terms pluralism and liberalism, cf. Richard Little's chapter in this volume.

5 The most obvious adjustment to make – especially in the British context – would be to merge the tri-partition of the inter-paradigm debate with another equally famous tri-partition, that of Martin Wight (realist, rationalist, revolutionist or Machiavelli, Grotius and Kant); cf. Meyers, 1990; Buzan, this volume. Most obviously Wight's Grotian/rationalist position is absent in the inter-paradigm debate, although it is possible either to interpret realism in a very statesman-diplomacy-international law manner and thus include a lot of the rationalist position (McKinlay and Little, 1986) or to see Grotianism as a brand of liberalism. Wight himself makes to some extent the Grotian position a compromise position between the other two and thus creates more of a continuum than a triangle. How to read the *nature* of Wight's 'debate' in contrast to the other contrived debates in IR self-presentation, I have addressed briefly towards the end of Wæver (1994). How to place the revival of the 'English school' as such in the – more or less triangular – map of IR theory, is briefly dealt with below.

6 Also in the case of the first and second debates, the major explicit *debates* and characterisations appeared after the alleged occurrence of 'the debate'. The first debate is normally presented as occurring in the 1930s and sometimes

1940s, but the major works defining a debate appeared from 1939 to the early 1950s. The second debate is normally said to have taken place in the 1950s and 1960s; the major debate that gave words to this took place from 1966 (Bull, 1966; Kaplan, 1966) and was collected in Knorr and Rosenau (1969). The third debate as a pattern and an often implicit attitude to other schools could be seen to emerge during the 1970s, but got its name(s) around 1980–5.

7 'Ontology' as the issue of 'what is' has become a fashionable label for that which was discussed in the third debate (the inter-paradigm debate): basic images of international relations, for instance state-centric versus pluralist. More seriously, the term ontology should refer to more basic questions about what 'stuff' the world is made up of: relations, processes, action, units (self-conscious, present to themselves and relating to other units each given in and of themselves), consciousness, the march of the world spirit, or power? Cf. Patomäki (1992) and Ringmar (1995).

This devaluation of 'ontology' can have confusing effects regarding the conception of debates. Real 'philosophical' ontology was not discussed until the fourth debate, whereas the watered-out version of ontology can be applied to that which was discussed in the third debate (then without the term).

8 This is probably spelled out most clearly in the articles by Michael Banks (1984, 1985, 1986). Also Rosenau was in the late 1970s and early 1980s very clear about linking substantive premises and methodological impulses into closed paradigms and emphasising that they were all equally closed: 'Openness to new data supporting alternative approaches and resulting readiness to change approaches (. . .) Virtually nil' (1982, p. 3). The 'inter-paradigm' terminology has then been employed in a number of articles and studies on various specific issues which are related to each of the 'paradigms', cf. e.g. Hoffman (1987).

9 Stefano Guzzini a bit speculatively links the inter-paradigm debate to the second debate. The attacks of behaviouralism had weakened the *boundaries* of the discipline, the distinctiveness of international relations, and the inter-paradigm debate was a reaction to this. Thus, he reads the further debate as a search for a new delineation of 'the international unknown' (1992, pp. 136 and 145f).

10 This is at least true for *The Structure of Scientific Revolutions*. Kuhn's later development is a complicated issue (excellently investigated by Hoyningen-Huene, 1993). He partly followed the same track as the international relationists (from sociology to world meanings). Kuhn, however, is uncompromising in avoiding an individual focus and instead concentrating on the similarity/difference relations shared by a field's practitioners that binds their community together. Kuhn's second trend of movement has been from assuming that one encountered the world through *seeing* it, to encountering it through *language* (Hoyningen-Huene, 1993, pp. 100ff; Kuhn, 1993).

11 For some reason, this optimistic, evolutionary interpretation of Kuhn – emphasising normal science as an ideal rather than the incommensurability as pluralism – came to dominate more consistently the self-reflection of the

sub-discipline of Comparative Foreign Policy and to some extent the wider Foreign Policy Analysis; cf. Hermann and Peacock (1987).

12 John Herz, for example, wrote in 1950 'Whether man is by nature peaceful and cooperative, or domineering and aggressive, is not the question. The condition that concerns us here is not a biological or anthropological but a social one' (1950, p. 157). Kenneth Waltz's book *Man, the State and War* (1959) was organised around the argument in favour of 'third image' explanations of war, i.e. causation from the structure of the international system in contrast to the first image (human nature and psychological mechanisms) and second image (the nature of the state). The distance to Niebuhrian realism was explicit in Waltz's contention with the first image.

13 Classical realism was a full and whole philosophy or ideology with expressions like: 'The statesman is therefore like one of the heroes in classical drama who has had a vision of the future but cannot transmit it directly to his fellow-men and who cannot validate its "truth". Nations learn only by experience; they "know" only when it is too late to act. But statesmen must act as *if* their intuition were already experience, as if their aspiration were truth' (Kissinger, 1957, p. 329).

14 This formulation might lead some to emphasise in their interpretation of the rationalist–reflectivist debate, that the reflectivists are interested in the *perceptions* and *motives* of the actors, which would be incredibly un-post-structuralist, and *de facto* leave the reflectivist position for hermeneutics. This, however, was not the main gist of Keohane's argument. He focused rightly on the fact, that the rationalists start out from actors and construct institutions from the preferences and rationality of the actors (even if *liberal* rationalists are very interested in feed-back that shape in turn the preferences of the actors). The reflectivists see 'institutions' in a wider and deeper sociological sense as shaping the identities and meaning spaces for the actors. (This is important to stress, because this is where the rationalists in the late 1980s and 1990s increasingly found resonance in the establishment, cf. below.)

15 Grieco (1988, 1990), Keohane (1989, pp. 10, 14 and 18). Baldwin (1993) has recently collected most of the main interventions in the debate.

16 David A. Baldwin in the preface to *Neorealism and Neoliberalism* compares the book to its predecessor from 1986, *Neorealism and its Critics*, but claims that 'Unlike that volume, however, the contributors to this one share many fundamental assumptions about the nature and purpose of social inquiry. This allows them to engage one another's arguments directly and results in a more focused and productive debate' (Baldwin, 1993, p. 3). Actually, figures like Waltz, Keohane and Gilpin of the previous book also 'share many fundamental assumptions about the nature and purpose of social inquiry', the differences between the two books are (a) that the reflectivists (Ashley, Cox) participated in the 1986 book, not in 1992, and (b) that there is a growing awareness of being 'beyond the inter-paradigm debate', of no longer rehearsing debates among positions that are not allowed to merge because they allegedly have different positions in a fundamental debate among incommensurable schools. Waltz at times reaffirms this image by insisting on

'pure' realism without any interest in accommodation, and thus the Baldwin remark was probably as much directed at him as at the reflectivists.

17 More eccentric are attempts at 'post-structural rationalism', which is a possibility since post-structuralist (and even more structuralist) linguistics open up the possibility of quite formalised treatments of the movements and patterns of discourse (Suganami, 1990; Wæver et al., forthcoming).

18 Note the increasing number of references in Keohane's articles to Bull and recently also to Wight (1993b). Buzan's English school article (1993) is in this context interesting, (a) for the fact that the article is published in International Organization, (b) for the explicit argument made about the usefulness of the English school for the Americans. See also the explicit articles on regime theory and English school: Hurrell (1993), Evans and Wilson (1992), Knudsen (1994). On how to save the English school from the Americans, see Wæver (forthcoming).

19 The general concept of the sign is probably most clearly presented in Derrida (1978 [1967]), the consequences in relation to the image of 'communication' in Derrida (1977 [1972]). Laclau and Mouffe (1985) is a theory of politics generated from the constant but ultimately impossible attempts to create closed and stable systems of meaning.

20 A different argument against incommensurability which ultimately stems from the same problem has been nicely put by Stefano Guzzini: that one cannot give conclusive arguments for incommensurability since this would presuppose a common framework of meaning which is exactly what the incommensurability thesis denies (Guzzini in Guzzini, Patomäki and Walker, 1995). Thus, the incommensurability thesis can by definition not have proven itself beyond doubt.

21 This raises the more general question how wise it is to lump together (as 'the new') mixtures of 'French' post-structuralism, 'German' hermeneutics and 'Anglo-Saxon' late analytical philosophy and post-Popperian theory of science (as is done for instance by Rengger, 1988, 1989, who admits that this is an 'unholy alliance'; George and Campbell, 1990). These different 'critical' philosophies actually build on very different conceptions of basic philosophical issues. It is certainly possible and often valuable to engage these traditions in debates (cf. e.g. Bernstein, 1991), but for the purpose of an almost 'derived' debate like that in IR, it seems advisable to be more clear about premises and to take a more distinctly defined philosophical starting point.

Here I would suggest that one can by now rule that post-structuralism has become the most significant and sustained (!) voice in the 'radical' corner. The Hoffman–Rengger debate in 1988 had Hoffman suggesting that critical theory was (German) Frankfurt school critical theory and Rengger advocating openness as to the possibility that (French) post-structuralism might equally well become a critical force (and to let at least the flowers bloom – with the tone that either it would be unsettled or Habermas would win). By now, very little has come out of the Habermas-inspired 'German' branch of critical theory in IR, whereas the 'French' brand has led to a network of writings at various levels of abstraction, from philosophical engagements with general IR theory to specific readings of texts in international relations practice (cf. Wæver, 1992, ch. 9). Another important critical newcomer to IR is feminism, but also here the post-structuralist inspiration seems to be very important among the more theoretically inclined writers. The 1994 launching of a German journal of International Relations Theory (*ZIB, Zeitschrift für Internationale Beziehungen*) might change this by getting more Habermasian IR in circuit (cf. Schaber and Ulbert, 1994). Also the 1995 introduction of a *European Journal of International Relations*, could have this effect.

22 The basic superstitial origin has been strengthened by features of modern bureaucracy and academia: a civil servant who has to present some options for a decision maker's choice will often come up with three suggestions: one which is unrealistic because it is too extreme in one direction, another which is impossibly far in the opposite direction and then the third in-between which the politician is supposed to pick. And in academic debates, an author will often present the discipline in terms of three positions: the two existing views who discuss with each other but are actually both faulted – the superior alternative is a third approach, mine. On this operation, see elegantly: Arendt (1972, p. 12).

REFERENCES

Alker, Hayward R. and Biersteker, Thomas J. (1984), 'The Dialectics of World Order: Notes for a Future Archaeologist of International Savoir Faire', *International Studies Quarterly*, 28 (2), pp. 121–42.

Arendt, Hannah (1972), 'Lying in Politics: Reflections on the Pentagon Papers', in *Crisis of the Republic* (San Diego, New York, London: Harvest/HBJ).

Ashley, Richard (1984), 'The Poverty of Neo-realism', *International Organization*, 38 (2), pp. 225–86.

Baldwin, David (ed.) (1993), *Neorealism and Neoliberalism: The Contemporary Debate* (New York: Columbia University Press).

Banks, Michael (1984), 'The Evolution of International Relations Theory', in Michael Banks (ed.), *Conflict in World Society: A New Perspective on International Relations* (Harvester), pp. 1–21.

(1985), 'The Inter-Paradigm Debate', in M. Light and A. J. R. Groom (eds.), *International Relations: A Handbook of Current Theory* (London: Pinter), pp. 7–26.

(1986), 'The International Relations Discipline: Asset or Liability for Conflict Resolution', in E. A. Azar and J. W. Burton (eds.), *International Conflict Resolution: Theory and Practice* (Sussex: Wheatsheaf), pp. 5–27.

Bernstein, Richard J. (1991), *The New Constellation: The Ethical–Political Horizons of Modernity/Postmodernity* (Cambridge: Polity Press).

Biersteker, Thomas J. (1989), 'Critical Reflections on Post-Positivism in International Relations', *International Studies Quarterly*, 33 (3), pp. 263–7.

Brown, Chris (1992), *International Relations Theory: New Normative Approaches* (Harvester Wheatsheaf).

Bull, Hedley (1966 [1969]), 'International Theory: The Case for a Classical Approach', in K. Knorr and J. Rosenau (eds.), *Contending Approaches to International Politics* (Princeton: Princeton University Press), pp. 20–38.

Buzan, Barry (1993), 'From International System to International Society: Structural Realism and Regime Theory meet the English School', *International Organization*, 47 (3), pp. 327–52.

Buzan, Barry, Little, Richard and Jones, Charles (1993), *The Logic of Anarchy: Neorealism to Structural Realism* (New York: Columbia University Press).

Cox, R. (1981), 'Social Forces, States and World Orders: Beyond International Relations Theory', *Millennium*, 10 (2), pp. 126–55.

Davidson, Donald (1974), 'The Very idea of a Conceptual Scheme', *Proceedings and Addresses of the American Philosophical Association*, 47, pp. 5–20.

Der Derian, James (1987), *On Diplomacy: A Genealogy of Western Estrangement* (Oxford: Blackwell).

Derrida, Jacques (1977 [1972]), 'Signature Event Context', *Glyph*, 1, pp. 172–97.

(1978 [1967]), *Writing and Difference* (Chicago: University of Chicago Press).

Evans, Tony and Wilson, Peter (1992), 'Regime Theory and the English School of International Relations: A Comparison', *Millennium*, 21 (3), pp. 329–52.

Feyerabend, Paul (1975), *Against Method* (London: Verso).

(1978), *Science in a Free Society* (London: Verso).

George, Jim and Campbell, David (1990), 'Patterns of Dissent and the Celebration of Difference: Critical Social Theory and International Relations', *International Studies Quarterly*, 34 (3), pp. 269–94.

Gilpin, Robert (1981), *War and Change in World Politics* (New York: Cambridge University Press).

(1987), *The Political Economy of International Relations* (Princeton: Princeton University Press).

Grieco, Joseph M. (1988), 'Anarchy and the Limits of Cooperation: A Realist Critique of the Newest Liberal Institutionalism', *International Organization*, 42 (3), pp. 485–508.

(1990), *Cooperation among Nations: Europe, America, and Non-tariff Barriers to Trade* (Ithaca and London: Cornell University Press).

Groom, A. J. R. (1988), 'Paradigms in Conflict: The Strategist, the Conflict Researcher and the Peace Researcher', *Review of International Studies*, 14 (2), pp. 97–115.

Guzzini, Stefano (1988), *T. S. Kuhn and International Relations: International Political Economy and the Inter-Paradigm Debate*, London School of Economics and Political Science: unpublished MA thesis.

(1992), *The Continuing Story of a Death Foretold: Realism in International Relations/International Political Economy* (Florence: European University Institute *Working Paper* SPS 92/20; revised version forthcoming at Routledge).

Guzzini, Stefano, Patomäki, Heikki and Walker, R. B. J. (1995), 'A Concluding Trialogue', in Patomäki (ed.), *Peaceful Changes in World Politics* (Tampere: TAPRI).

Hermann, Charles F. and Peacock, Gregory (1987), 'The Evolution and Future of Theoretical Research in the Comparative Study of Foreign Policy', in Charles F. Hermann, Charles W. Kegley and James N. Rosenau (eds.), *New Directions in the Study of Foreign Policy* (Boston: Allen & Unwin), pp. 13–32.

Herz, John H. (1950), 'Idealist Internationalism and the Security Dilemma', *World Politics*, 2 (2), pp. 157–80.

Hoffman, Mark (1987), 'Critical Theory and the Inter-Paradigm Debate', *Millennium*, 16 (2), pp. 231–49.

Hoffmann, Stanley (1977), 'An American School Science: International Relations', *Dædalus*, 106 (3), pp. 41–60.

Holsti, K. J. (1985), *The Dividing Discipline – Hegemony and Diversity in International Theory* (Boston: Allen & Unwin).

—— (1986), 'The Horsemen of the Apocalypse: At the Gate, Detoured, or Retreating?', *International Studies Quarterly*, 30 (4), pp. 355–71.

—— (1988 [1967]), *International Politics: A Framework for Analysis*, 5th edition (Englewood Cliffs, NJ: Prentice Hall).

—— (1993), 'International Relations at the End of the Millennium', *Review of International Studies*, 19 (4), pp. 401–8.

Hoyningen-Huene, Paul (1993), *Reconstructing Scientific Revolutions: Thomas S. Kuhn's Philosophy of Science* (Chicago: University of Chicago Press).

Hurrell, Andrew (1993), 'International Society and the Study of Regimes: A Reflective Approach' in Volker Rittberger (ed.), *Regime Theory and International Relations* (Oxford: Clarendon Press), pp. 49–72.

Janis, Irving and Mann, Leon (1977), *Decision Making: A Psychological Analysis of Conflict, Choice and Commitment* (New York: Free Press).

Jervis, Robert (1970), *The Logic of Images in International Relations* (Princeton: Princeton University Press).

—— (1976), *Perception and Misperception in International Politics* (Princeton: Princeton University Press).

Kaplan, Morton A. (1966), 'The Great Debate: Traditionalism vs. Science in International Relations', *World Politics*, 19 (1).

Kauppi, Mark V. and Viotti, Paul R. (1992), *The Global Philosophers: World Politics in Western Thought* (New York: Lexington Books).

Keohane, Robert (1989), *International Institutions and State Power: Essays in International Relations Theory* (Boulder, CO: Westview Press).

—— (1993a), 'Institutionalist Theory and the Realist Challenge: After the Cold War', in David Baldwin (ed.), *Neorealism and Neoliberalism: The Contemporary Debate* (New York: Columbia University Press).

—— (1993b), *Hobbes's Dilemma and Institutional Change in World Politics: Sovereignty in International Society*, Paper presented at the Conference on Economic and Security Cooperation in the Asia-Pacific: Agendas for the 1990s, Canberra, 28–30 July.

Keohane, Robert O. and Nye, J. (1977), *Power and Interdependence: World Politics in Transition* (Boston: Little Brown).

Kissinger, Henry A. (1957), *A World Restored: Castlereagh, Metternich and the Restoration of Peace, 1812–1822* (Boston and London: Scott, Foresman & Co.).

Knorr, Klaus and Rosenau, James N. (eds.) (1969), *Contending Approaches to International Politics* (Princeton: Princeton University Press).

Knudsen, Tonny Brems (1994), *Det Nye Europa: Orden eller Kaos?*, University of Aarhus: MA thesis.

Krasner, Stephen D. (1989), 'Fortune, Virtue, and Systematic versus Scientific Inquiry', in Joseph Mruzel and James N. Rosenau (eds.), *Journeys through World Politics: Autobiographical Reflections of Thirty-four Academic Travellers* (Lexington, MA: Lexington Books), pp. 417–27.

Kratochwil, F. and Ruggie, John G. (1986), 'International Organization: A State of the Art of an Art of the State', *International Organization*, 40 (4), pp. 753–75.

Kuhn, Thomas S. (1970a [1962]), *The Structure of Scientific Revolutions*, 2nd edition enlarged (Chicago:University of Chicago Press).

(1970b), 'Logic of Discovery or Psychology of Research', in Imre Lakatos and Alan Musgrave (eds.), *Criticism and the Growth of Knowledge* (Cambridge: Cambridge University Press), pp. 1–23.

(1970c), 'Reflections on my Critics', in Imre Lakatos and Alan Musgrave (eds.), *Criticism and the Growth of Knowledge* (Cambridge: Cambridge University Press).

(1993), 'Foreword' to Paul Hoyningen-Huene, *Reconstructing Scientific Revolutions: Thomas S. Kuhn's Philosophy of Science* (Chicago: University of Chicago Press).

Laclau, Ernesto and Mouffe, Chantal (1985), *Hegemony and Socialist Strategy: Towards a Radical Democracy* (London: Verso).

Lakatos, Imre and Musgrave, Alan (eds.) (1970), *Criticism and the Growth of Knowledge* (Cambridge: Cambridge University Press).

Lapid, Yosef (1989), 'The Third Debate: on the Prospects of International Theory in a Post-positivist Era', *International Studies Quarterly*, 33 (3), pp. 235–54.

Lenin, V. I. (1916 [1966]), *Imperialism: The Highest Stage of Capitalism*, in *Collected Works* (Moscow: Progress Publishers).

Little, Richard *et al.* (eds.) (1981), *Perspectives on World Politics* (London: Croom Helm).

Little, Richard and Smith, Michael (1991), *Perspectives on World Politics*, 2nd edition (London: Routledge & Kegan Paul).

Luhmann, Niklas (1990a), *Die Wissenschaft der Gesellschaft* (Frankfurt/M: Suhrkamp).

(1990b), *Soziologische Aufklärung 5: Konstruktivistische Perspektiven* (Opladen: Westdeutscher Verlag).

Maghrori, Ray and Ramberg (eds.) (1982), *Globalism Versus Realism: International Relations' Third Debate?* (Boulder, CO: Westview Press).

Mansbach, Richard W. and Vasquez, John A. (1981), *In Search of Theory – A New Paradigm for Global Politics* (New York: Columbia University Press).

Masterman, Margaret (1970), 'The Nature of a Paradigm', in Imre Lakatos and Alan Musgrave (eds.), *Criticism and the Growth of Knowledge* (Cambridge: Cambridge University Press), pp. 59–89.

McKinlay, R. and Little, Richard (1986), *Global Problems in World Order* (London: Pinter).

Meyers, Reinhard (1990), 'Metatheoretische und methodologische Betrachtungen zur Theorie der internationalen Beziehungen', in *Politiche Vierteljahresschrift* (special issue on theories of international relations; ed. Volker Rittberger), Sonderheft 21/1990, pp. 48–68.

Neufeld, Mark (1993), 'Reflexivity and International Relations Theory', *Millennium*, 22 (1) (Spring), pp. 53–76.

Nye, Joseph (1988), 'Neorealism and Neoliberalism', *World Politics*, 40 (2), pp. 235–51.

Patomäki, Heikki (1992), 'What is it that Changed with the End of the Cold War? An Analysis of the Problem of Identifying and Explaining Change', in Pierre Allan and Kjell Goldmann (eds.), *The End of the Cold War: Evaluating Theories of International Relations* (Dordrecht: Martinus Nijhoff Publishers), pp. 179–225.

Popper, Karl (1970), 'Normal Science and its Dangers', in Imre Lakatos and Alan Musgrave (eds.), *Criticism and the Growth of Knowledge* (Cambridge: Cambridge University Press), pp. 51–8.

Rengger, N. J. (1988), 'Going Critical? A Response to Hoffman', *Millennium*, 17 (1), pp. 81–9.

   (1989), 'Incommensurability, International Theory and the Fragmentation of Western Political Culture', in John R. Gibbins (ed.), *Contemporary Political Culture: Politics in a Postmodern Age* (London: Sage/ECPR), pp. 237–50.

   (1992), 'A City which Sustains all Things? Communitarianism and the Foundations of International Society', *Millennium*, 21 (3), pp. 353–69.

Ringmar, Erik (1995), 'Alexander Wendt – a Scientist Struggling with History', in Iver B. Neumann and Ole Wæver (eds.), *The Future of International Relations: Masters in the Making?* (London: Routledge & Kegan Paul).

Rittberger, Volker and Wolf, Klaus-Dieter (1988), 'Problemfelder internationaler Beziehungen aus politologischer Sicht', *Tübinger Arbeitspapiere*, no. 5.

Rosenau, James N. (1982), *The Scientific Study of Foreign Policy*, revised and enlarged edition (London/New York: Frances Pinter/Nichols).

Rothstein, R. (1972), *Planning, Prediction, and Policymaking in Foreign Affairs – Theory and Practice* (Boston: Little, Brown).

Ruggie, John G. (1983), 'Continuity and Transformation in the World Polity: Toward a Neo-Realist Synthesis', *World Politics*, 36 (2), pp. 261–85.

   (1993), 'Territoriality and Beyond: Problematizing Modernity in International Relations', *International Organization*, 47 (1), pp. 139–74.

Schaber, Thomas and Ulbert, Cornelia (1994), 'Reflexivität in den Internationalen Beziehungen: Literaturbericht zum Beitrag kognitiver, reflexiver und interpretativer Ansätze zur dritten Theoriedebatte', *Zeitschrift für Internationale Beziehungen* 1 (1), pp. 139–69.

Smith, Steve (1987), 'Paradigm Dominance in International Relations: The Development of International Relations as a Social Science', *Millennium*, 16 (2), pp. 189–206.

Snyder, G. H. and Diesing, P. (1977), *Conflict Among Nations: Bargaining, Decisionmaking and System Structure in International Crisis* (Princeton: Princeton University Press).

Suganami, Hidemi (1990), 'Bringing Order to the Causes of War Debates', *Millennium*, 19 (1), pp. 19–35.

Suhr, Michael (1996), 'Robert Keohane – a Contemporary Classic', in Iver B. Neumann and Ole Wæver (eds.), *Masters in the Making: Eleven International Relations Theorists Assessed* (London: Routledge & Kegan Paul).

Viotti, Paul R. and Kauppi, Mark V (1993 [1987]), *International Relations Theory: Kauppi (1990) International Relations Theory: Realism, Pluralism, Globalism* (New York: Macmillan).

Waltz, Kenneth (1959), *Man, the State and War* (New York: Columbia University Press).

(1979), *Theory of International Politics* (New York: Random House).

(1986), 'Reflections on *Theory of International Politics*: A Response to My Critics', in Robert Keohane (ed.), *Neorealism and its Critics* (New York: Columbia University Press).

(1990), 'Realist Thought and Neo-Realist Theory', *Journal of International Affairs*, 44 (1), pp. 21–37.

Wendt, Alexander (1992), 'Anarchy is What States Make of it: The Social Construction of Power Politics', *International Organization*, 46 (2), pp. 391–426.

Wendt, Alexander and Duvall, Raymond (1989), 'Institutions and International Order', in Ernst-Otto Cziempel and James N. Rosenau (eds.), *Global Changes and Theoretical Challenges: Approaches to World Politics for the 1990s* (Lexington: Lexington Books), pp. 51–76.

Wæver, Ole (1991), 'Territory, Authority and Identity: The Late 20th Century Emergence of Neo-medieval Political Structures in Europe', paper presented at the inaugural EUPRA conference in Florence, November 1991.

(1992), *Introducktion til Studiet af International Politik* (Copenhagen: Forlaget Politiske Studier).

(1994), 'After the Fourth Debate – Patterns of International Relations Theory in the 1990s', manuscript.

(forthcoming a), 'Transformation and Institutionalization: With Ruggie across IR Paradigms', in Iver B. Neumann and Ole Wæver (eds.), *The Future of International Relations: Masters in the Making?* (London: Routledge & Kegan Paul).

(forthcoming b), 'Europe's Three Empires: A Watsonian Interpretation of Post-wall European Security', forthcoming in Fawn, Larkins and Newman (eds.), *International Society After the Cold War* (Millennium and Macmillan).

Wæver, Ole, Holm, Ulla and Larsen, Henrik (forthcoming), *The Struggle for 'Europe': French and German Concepts of State, Nation and European Union*.

Wilde, Jaap de (1991), *Saved From Oblivion: Interdependence Theory in the First Half of the 20th Century. A Study on the Causality Between War and Complex Interdependence* (Dartmouth: Aldershot).

8 Margins, silences and bottom rungs: how to overcome the underestimation of power in the study of international relations

Cynthia Enloe

When I think about what it is that seems so unrealistic (yes, that loaded term) in most formal analyses of international politics, what strikes me is how far their authors are willing to go in *under*estimating the amounts and varieties of power it takes to form and sustain any given set of relationships between states. This conclusion, of course, rings oddly. So many analysts, after all, profess to be interested chiefly in power – who has it, how they got it, what they try to do with it. Their profession notwithstanding, I believe that by concentrating so single-mindedly on what is referred to euphemistically as the 'centre', scores of analysts have produced a naive portrait of how international politics really (there's that tricky concept again) work.

No individual or social group finds themselves on the 'margins' of any web of relationships – a football league, an industry, an empire, a military alliance, a state – without some other individual or group having accumulated enough power to create the 'centre' somewhere else. Beyond its creation, too, there is the yearly and daily business of maintaining the margin where it currently is and the centre where it now is. It is harder for those at the alleged centre to hear the hopes, fears and explanations of those on the margins, not because of physical distance – the margin may be two blocks from the White House, four stops on the Paris metro from the Quai d'Orsay – but because it takes resources and access to be 'heard' when and where it matters. Consequently, those who reside at the margins tend to be those deemed 'silent'. They are imagined either to have voices that simply cannot be heard from so far away, or they are portrayed as lacking language and articulateness altogether: the taciturn Indian, the deferential peasant, the shy woman.

None of this amounts to an earth-shattering revelation, but let's continue. Travelling from the centre to the margins is not traversing a horizontal plane, even if one does move horizontally from Djakarta to East Timor or from London to Aberystwyth. It is making a journey along a vertical relationship, from the top of a political pyramid down to its base. Those apparently silent on the margins are actually those at the bottom of the pyramid of power. Thus it is that East Timorese have more in common politically with African Americans living in row houses a stone's throw from the White House than they do with the ethnic Javanese military commander whose headquarters is uncomfortably close by. Thus too it is on another continent that today's manager of Dole Corporation's hacienda in the south of Chile is more likely to have his (no pronoun is casually employed) needs taken seriously in that country's centre of power than is the maid who lives a mere lung-clogging half-hour bus ride away from La Moreda, Chile's once-besieged presidential palace.

Margins, silences and bottom rungs – they express different qualities, but they have as their common denominators lacking public power and being the object of other people's power.

Fine. That isn't too hard to accept. But one might still argue that that does not mean that those people lacking significant public leverage, living on the margins, whose voices are hard to hear at the centre are inherently interesting. Perhaps socialist scholars in Britain's History Workshop interviewing East London garment workers or African feminist oral historians working in the Western Cape will devote scarce time and recording tape to the powerless. But that is because they apparently are committed to a democratic sort of scholarly practice that presumes value in human experience for its own sake: if a person has dwelt on this planet, they are worthy of being recorded; to be recorded assigns dignity; all humans, because of their humanity, possess dignity, or should.

This is a woefully incomplete sketch of both socialist and feminist scholarly motivation, but my guess is that it is one widely held.

Such a humanitarian, populist approach, whatever motivates it, is still not, it is argued, what a formal analysis of international politics is all about. Or, rather, most international relations analysts feel ambivalent towards human dignity's and democracy's relevance to their own intellectual enterprise. They derive from the tradition of the European Enlightenment a belief in the human capacity to reason, and with that reason, the possibility of uncovering untainted universal truths. This is the same conviction that has permitted so many people to imagine that democratic forms of governance are within human grasp – at least for those, the Enlightenment's inheritors would caution, who have realised their human potential for reason, that is men who have been thoroughly assimilated into the culture of Western Europe (Harding, 1993; Hartsock, 1994). Still, as practised, this same Enlightenment-derived faith espouses a scientific pursuit 'free' of the burdens of identity and space. So few mainstream academic international relations analysts would admit that they are designing their research self-consciously to accord with democratic values of either the socialist or feminist sort. The *raison d'être* for studying international politics, instead, is *explanation*. One is on the trail of cause and effect. And when sorting out cause and effect, one has to be economical, discriminating. Everything is not the cause of some one thing. Likewise, something does not cause every single thing. For an explanation to be useful, a great deal of human dignity has to be left on the cutting room floor.

By definition, people on the margins, those who are silenced, those perched on the bottom rung are precisely those who, for whatever reason – and the reasons may be grossly unjust – lack what it takes to have a meaningful impact on the course of those particular events that together cause certain regional or world patterns to take the shape they do. Silenced marginalised people hovering on the lower rungs of any international hierarchy may be able to find the voice to sing while doing their laundry, may be able to affect the local patterns of inter-marriage, may even be able to create micro-pyramids of inequality. Not everyone at the bottom rung has a zinc roof; some only have thatched. Not everyone at the bottom carries equal weight when the decision is made whether to use a condom in bed at night. Yet none of these distinctions is of a potency that can be decisive in determining flows of weapons trade, patterns of investment, rules for inter-state peace.

Thank goodness, then, for the anthropologists. Let *them* listen to the laundry lyrics, let them meticulously chart those mind-boggling kinship patterns and the distribution of zinc roofs. They can afford to be open to the sort of populist values imported by socialists and feminists. None of them has to shoulder the heavy responsibility of finding economical explanations for the workings of entire international systems.

To study the powerful is not autocratic. It is simply reasonable.

Really?

There is, I think, a serious flaw in this analytical economy, and in the research strategy that flows from it. It presumes *a priori* that margins, silences and bottom rungs are so naturally marginal, silent and far from power that exactly how they are *kept* there could not possibly be of interest to the reasoning, reasonable explainer. A consequence of this presumption is that the actual amount and the amazing variety of power that are required to keep the voices on the margins from having the right language and enough volume to be heard at the centre in ways that might send shivers up and down the ladder are never fully tallied. Power, of course, is a relationship. So omitting a myriad strands of power amounts to exaggerating the simplicity of the entire political system. Today's conventional portrait of international politics thus too often ends up looking like a Superman comic strip, whereas it probably should resemble a Jackson Pollock.

A second consequence of this presumption – that margins stay marginal, the silent stay voiceless, and ladders are never turned upside down – is that many orthodox analysts of international politics are caught by surprise. If one imagines that unequal power relationships – the ones that allow the analyst the luxury of focusing only on the people at the top, the decision-makers with foreign policy portfolios – are natural (well, almost natural, so firmly anchored in place that they might as well be natural), then one is very likely to be uncomfortably jolted by any tremors that jeopardise those unequal power relationships.

Let's take the Mayan Indians of Chiapas. Here may be one of the groups that an efficient international politics realist could quint-essentially afford to leave to the anthropologists – or to the socialists or the feminists. No explanatory risks here. Keep your hotel reservations restricted capital. Fly down (one is unlikely to be flying up) to Mexico City with a stop over in Tijuana or Juarez perhaps. Macquiladora managers (Mexican, American and Japanese) have become too vocal and visible to be defined as inhabiting the margins, even if geographically that is precisely where they reside. Rent a Hertz car in the capital and drive up to talk to some of the bankers in Monterrey for a couple of days if necessary.

Chiapas fits all the criteria of a classically marginal political space. Mexico City seems a world away from the farms, villages and (disappearing) forests of Chiapas, Mexico's southern state bordering Guatemala. To border on Guatemala certainly is different than to border on the United States. The latter bordering existence magnifies political voice, the former muffles it. As poor peasants, many of whom are ethnic Indians from a multiplicity of distinct communities too easily labelled 'Mayan', in a society which accords influence to agribusiness entre-preneurs, joint venture industrialists and senior state technocrats with ties to the ruling Institutional Revolutionary Party, the PRI, the majority of Chiapas residents rarely have had their voices heard in the rooms where national decisions were being made. Indian motifs may decorate Diego Riviera's heroic murals, but being painted on a public wall does not amount to a voice in Mexican affairs. Octavio Paz, Mexico's Nobel Laureate, knew what he was talking about when he said that the Spanish conquistadors and their bourgeois mestizo successors each adopted the Aztec pyramid as their model for a political order (Paz, 1972). No one has been more unarguably shoved to the twentieth-century's Mexican pyramid's base than poor Indian-dialect speaking rural Chiapans.

So it made little sense for international relations specialists to devote any thought to Chiapas when they were seeking to explain why the North American Free Trade Agreement (NAFTA) was being negotiated when it was and in the fashion that it was. Not paying any attention to the Mohawks and Cree of Canada hadn't cost analysts anything when trying to explain the origins and outcome of NAFTA's precursor, the US–Canada Free Trade Agreement, had it? No more than not wondering whether the French-speaking Quebecois women who provided the swing vote in the earlier Quebec separatist referendum would do so again when the vote was retaken in 1995. No more than had neglecting Asian Canadian women sewing in garment factories along Toronto's Spadina Avenue (Cohen, 1987).

'Mexico' never negotiated with 'the United States', anymore than four years earlier 'Canada' had negotiated with 'the United States'. Particular officials of particular ruling regimes conducted these complex negotiations under the more or less credible pretence that the states they spoke for were functioning and durable. Even though we all know this, we frequently slip into using these misleading lazy shorthands. They may save breath, but they disguise the artifice that is the ultimate foundation of every state. In disciplinary terms, international relations analysts rest too heavily on the presumptions derived from their comparative politics colleagues without examining them very closely. Maybe international relations specialists need to do more of their own homework. Maybe they need to make their own assessments about the modes of power it is taking at any time to keep these fictions – 'Mexico', or 'Canada' or 'the United States' – glued together. By leaving it all to their friends in comparative politics – who in turn typically leave too much to the anthropologists – international relations analysts: (1) underestimate the amount and varieties of power operating in any inter-state relationship and (2) mistakenly assume that the narrative's 'plot' is far more simple and unidirectional than it may in truth be. Taking seriously the experiences and responses – even explanatory theories – of people living voiceless out on the margins, down at the bottom, is one of the most efficient ways I know of accurately estimating just how fragile that artifice is, just how far off the mark it is to describe 'Mexico' as negotiating NAFTA with 'the United States'.

Actually, scholarly commentators specialising in Mexico have been trying for several decades, especially since the capital city massacre of 1968, to alert their colleagues to the fragility of the artifice that is the Mexican state (Hellman, 1983). They have tried to reveal just how much power and of what sorts it has taken not just to keep the Institutional Revolutionary Party, better known as the PRI, in control of the state since 1929, but what consequences this has had for Mexican state evolution. Until 1994, the skill and dexterity poured into this state construction and maintenance enterprise matched those of Japan's Liberal Democrats and Italy's Christian Democrats. This year Mexico's statist artisans stand alone. Nervously.

Rosario Castellanos gave us a finely drawn portrait of Chiapas political subtleties in her famous novel *The Nine Guardians* (Castellanos, 1992). Castellanos herself grew up in the 1930s as a child of cattle ranching, coffee growing hacienda owners. Writing in the 1950s, she looked back at this decade in the political evolution of the Mexican *Priista* state, believing that inspection of intimate routines and tensions woven into the lives of Chiapas Indians and their hispanicised local *patrons* could expose the gendered and racialised contradictions running through that state system even then, even at the moment in the 1930s that commentators typically point to as the moment when the current Mexican state system was successfully consolidated. It has been the decades-long perpetuation of this particular statist formula – with regular infusions of pragmatic refinements always far short of radical change – crafted by the PRI under populist president Lazaro Cardenas that made the NAFTA negotiations possible in the early 1990s. Assuming that this formula remains fundamentally unassailable led the post-Cold War analysts to imagining that neglecting marginalised Chiapas seemed reasonable.

Castellanos introduces us to 1930s Chiapas politics by putting us in the shoes of a white young Mexican girl who feels closer to her Mayan nanny than to her privileged mother and father.

I go to the kitchen where Nana is heating coffee . . . I sniff in the larder. I like to see the colour of the butter and to touch the bloom of the fruit, and peel the onion skins . . .

'Just look what they've done to me.'

Pulling up her *tzec*, Nana shows me a soft reddish wound disfiguring her knee . . .

'Why do they hurt you?'

'Because I was brought up in your house. Because I love your parents, and Mario, and you.'

'Is it wicked to love us?'

'It's wicked to love those that give orders and have possessions. That's what the law says . . . '

I go away, sad because of what I've just heard. My father dismisses the Indians with a gesture, and lies on in the hammock reading. I see him now for the first time. He's the one who gives the orders and owns things. (Castellanos, 1992, p. 19)

Rosario Castellanos is describing a racialised political economy that is being challenged both by a new generation of Mayans who have travelled outside Chiapas and have learned Spanish, the patrons' language, and by

PRI president Cardenas, who is fashioning a new populist mantel for his party, a mantel he hopes will end the peasants' revolution, yet domesticate the generals and keep the loyalty of both the new commercial class and the old land-owning rural elite. For Cardenas and the emergent state elite the stakes are not merely national; they are continental, even hemispheric. Woodrow Wilson's American military incursion is still fresh in Mexicans' minds. Only if the PRI's strategy for state consolidation succeeds, at least minimally, can the statist boundaries within the hemisphere gel along lines that will keep American imperialism at bay (Kaplan and Pease, 1993). It will take more than the taming of bandits and the nationalising of foreign-owned oil companies; it will require co-opting the patrons, channelling the resentments of their Indian employees. Listening to women of any class? Perhaps this will not be necessary at this juncture in the hemisphere's statist stabilisation, so long as husbands and fathers can keep them confined to the margins of public affairs.

Nana, herself ambivalent, nonetheless has aided the Cardenas state-building hemispherically transformative enterprise. She has caused a little white girl to see her own father with new racially conscious eyes. Still, Castellanos's fictional father is confident he can play his own *patron*'s shell game. Few states are so powerful that policies issued at the centre can be assured faithful implementation on the margins, especially if the state itself depends on the continuing support of these very people, people with privilege derived from accumulating the resources on the margins, it is calling upon to sacrifice a good portion of their income and their sense of class honour.

'Go on, Jaime, you almost scared me. When I saw you arrive with that hang-dog look I thought there really had been some disaster. But this (the government's new requirement that hacienda owners build and staff schools for their Indian employees) isn't important. You remember when they fixed the minimum salary? Our hearts went into our boots. It was the end of everything. And what happened? We're slippery lizards and they can't catch us as easily as all that. We discovered a ruse by which we didn't have to pay.'

'No Indian's worth seventy-five *centavos* a day. Nor even a month.'

'Besides, I ask you, what would they do with the money. Only get drunk.' (Castellanos, 1992, p. 46)

And, of course, the hierarchical relationships that undergirded the region's political system and thus the contradiction-ridden state itself are not based on cattle and coffee alone. Not even on language. There's always the politics of sexuality.

Castellanos, raised in a privileged Spanish-speaking, land-owning white family, but learning the local Mayan language by listening to her nanny, employed a feminist imagination to create credible renditions of Mayan Indians' political discussions. She did not lump all Chiapas Indians together in a single ungendered literary stew; she refrained from authorily putting political thoughts into the minds and mouths of Indian men alone; nor did she turn all her Indian women characters into activist popular heroes, as if they were unfettered by the oppressive interplay of Mayan and hispanicised patriarchal expectations. It had taken not just racialised class hierarchies, but also daily reinforcement of complementary notions about ranchers' wives and peasants' wives to sustain the political systems of Chiapas, and thus of Mexico, for generations. To ignore those political structures, Rosario Castellano implied, would be to present a far too naive analysis of the chances of Lazaro Cardenas's success (Ahern, 1988).

> Felipe rocked with laughter. His wife watched him terrified, thinking he'd gone off his head.
> 'I'm remembering what I saw in Tapachula. There are whites so poor they beg and drop with fever on the streets.'
> The rest hardened their eyes unbelieving.
> 'It was in Tapachula that they gave me the paper to read, and it speaks well, I understood what it says: that we're equal to white men . . . On the oath of the President of the Republic . . . '
> Felipe's wife slipped silently to the door. She couldn't go on listening . . .
> Juana had borne no children . . . In vain she pounded the herbs the women recommended . . . Shame had fallen upon her. But in spite of everything, Felipe did not want to leave her. Whenever he went away – for he seemed to be a rolling stone – she stayed sitting with clasped hands as if she had said goodbye to him for ever. Yet Felipe always returned. But this time, coming back from Tapachula, he wasn't the same any more. His mouth was full of disrespectful words and bold opinions. She, being humble and still full of gratitude to him, did not repudiate him in front of the rest but kept her thoughts silent and secret. She feared this man whom the lands of the seacoast had thrown her back, bitter and harsh as salt, a trouble-maker . . . She longed for him to be off once again. Far, far away. And that he'd never come back. (Castellanos, 1992, pp. 99–100, 105)

Hierarchies are multiple, because forms of political power are diverse. But the several hierarchies do not sit on the social landscape like tuna, egg and cheese sandwiches sitting on an icy cafeteria counter, diversely multiple but unconnected. They relate to each other, sometimes in ways that subvert one another, sometimes in ways that provide each with their respective resiliency. The bedroom's hierarchy is not unconnected to the hierarchies of the international coffee exchange or of the foreign ministry. The questions to pose, then, are: when and how exactly are these hierarchies connected? With what consequences for the lives lived in bedrooms, on trading floors and around diplomatic tables?

For instance, a male rancher's ability to bargain with central state officials over land reform and tariff proposals depends in no small part on his confidence – and the credibility in the eyes of the state official – in his ability to control his ranch employees, his confidence that they won't be able to bargain with that same official behind his back, his confidence that they, or at least most of them, wouldn't even imagine that bargaining independently with the state was in their own interests. Part of that confidence, and thus part of the male rancher's political arsenal, derives from his on-going sexual access to the women among his employees and their families. Part of the weakening of his employees' sense of their own agency in dealings with state officials comes from the humiliation or even confusion that such masculinised access sows. The male state official, for his part, is likely to accept the rancher's confident political stance – and thus be more receptive to his arguments about land politics and their implications for international trade negotiations – precisely because he shares the rancher's masculinised version of how race and class hierarchies are effectively sustained. The official sees those unequal sexual encounters as so natural that he never even imagines they require discussing, except perhaps as a basis for common masculine bonding to create mutual comfort between the two men before the 'real' political bargaining begins.

Castellanos had spent years eavesdropping on masculinised conversations among the white Mexican men who dominated Chiapas.

Cesar and Ernesto went down the steps from the veranda to the farmyard. They mounted, and at a slow trot put the house behind them . . . The women, kneeling on the ground to pound the grain, stopped their tasks and sat quietly with arms rigid, as if rooted into the stone of their mortars, their slack breasts hanging loose in their blouses. They watched the two men pass . . .

'There are the Indian women to do your bidding, Ernesto. We'll be looking out for one of these brats to turn up with your complexion . . . Beggars can't be choosers. I'm talking from experience.'

'You?'

'Why so surprised? Yes, me. Like everyone I've a sprinkling of children among them.'

It was doing them a favor, really, because after that the Indian women were more sought after and could marry where they liked. The Indian always recognized this virtue in his woman, that the *patron* had found pleasure in her. And the children among those that hung about the big house and served there faithfully. (Castellanos, 1992, p. 127)

Unless, that is, the state could expand its civil service broadly enough to absorb some of those offspring, especially the sons, the 'godsons'. In the 1930s, the post-revolutionary Mexican state was indeed expanding. The ruling party, the party that Cardenas was attempting to provide with lasting access to this state was (and is) called the *Institutional Revolutionary Party*.

'Don't you recognize me, Don Cesar?'
Cesar scrutinized him. The swart face and bushy eyebrows awakened no memory.
'I'm Gonzalo Utrilla, son of Georgia that was.'
'You? But why did no one tell me? Look, Zoraida, it's my godson . . . And now you're a fine strapping man.'
'All thanks to your care, Godfather.'
Cesar decided to ignore the irony in this . . .
'I work for the Government . . . '
All enemies are big ones, Cesar thought. If only he'd been kinder to this Gonzalo when he was a bit of an Indian lad! . . .
'What exactly is your work?'
'I'm an agrarian inspector.' (Castellanos, 1992, pp. 128–9)

Even this unfair excerpting of Castellanos's richly textured novel offers up a variety of forms of power that is quite mind-boggling. Bureaucratic co-optation, racial intimidation, exclusive access to the language of the state, marital pressures, elite connections, land proprietorship, denial of access to schooling, sexual imposition, ownership of models for sexual emulation, employment patronage. And this list still omits the distribution of formal voting rights to some (men), while withholding it to others (women would not manage to win the vote until 1953, almost four decades after the Mexican revolution, during which anti-clerical revolutionary men argued that women would use their votes to support the Church). The list also still omits access to private armies' force and to federal police and military force. When was the last time one saw an analysis of an international trade negotiation – and its implications – that gave serious attention to landowners' private armies (called *mapaches* in 1930s Chiapas, *guardias blancas* in 1990s Chiapas)? (Nigh, 1994, p. 10). What is the equivalent omission in the study of the European Union, of the emergence of Asian NIC 'tigers'?

The Chiapas peasant rebellion launched in January 1994, was led by an unknown organisation whose members called themselves the Zapatista National Liberation Army (ZNLA). Officials of the PRI-dominated government of President Carlos Salinas initially tried to portray the ZNLA as urban intellectuals, Communist agitators, out-siders, hiding under bandanas and ski masks while opportunistically exploiting the still-potent legend of peasant revolutionary hero Emiliano Zapata. This portrayal soon had to be abandoned. It was too clear that the majority of the rebels were poor peasants, many identifying them-selves as Mayan Indians, though this is a many-sided and fluid identity, especially given the immigration of thousands of Indians in the 1980s trying to escape the civil war in Guatemala. The Zapatistas and their less organised supporters were the economically, culturally and politically disenfranchised of Chiapas, people who remembered the unfulfilled revolution-legitimising promises of 1910 and the unfulfilled *Priista* state-legitimising promises of the 1930s (Earle, 1994).

Their selection of January 1994, as a moment for direct confrontation with the Chiapas PRI-rancher alliance, the federal military and the regime of President Carlos Salinas, apparently was based in part on their assessment of diminishing local alternatives. Their selection of early 1994, however, also seemed to stem from their monitoring of the government's half-hearted electoral reforms in preparation for the crucial August 1994 nation-wide election of Salinas's presidential successor as well as their accounting of the NAFTA negotiations, its winners and losers. These peasant farmers of Chiapas were doing what so many international relations commentators were not: tracing causal connections between local political economies, state system contradictions and emergent inter-state relationships. They connected the Mexican state's bowing to the US state's pressure to the lowering and eventual abandoning of state corn price subsidies and to the fall in international oil prices, on which many male Indians had come to depend as part-time petroleum workers. They connected those trends to the escalating violence wielded by *guardias blancas* hired by wealthy Chiapas landowners who thought that by driving Indians off land carved out of the rainforest they could attract US investors into joint cattle raising NAFTA-fuelled ventures. In their sophisticated international analysis, the Zapatistas went still further: they contended that none of these moves would have been possible were not the PRI able to control the national political system through an electoral process that insured that poor peasants' voices could not have an impact on state decision-making (Nigh, 1994, p. 10).

In their formal communique, the ZNLA leadership spoke a great deal about the structural conditions for having a 'voice':

To the People of Mexico:
To the Peoples and Governments of the World:
To the national and international Press:
Brothers:
. . . When the EZLN was only a shadow, creeping through the mist and darkness of the jungle, when the words 'justice,' 'liberty' and democracy' were only that: words; barely a dream that the elders of our communities, true guardians of our dead ancestors, had given us in the moment when day gives way to night, when hatred and fear began to grow in our hearts, when there was nothing but desperation; when times repeated themselves, with no way out, with no door, no tomorrow, when all was injustice, as it was, the true men spoke,

the faceless ones, the ones who go by night, the ones who are jungle, and they said:

. . . Let not the voices of the few be silenced, but let them remain in their place, waiting until the thoughts and hearts become one in what is the will of the many and opinion from within and no outside force can break them nor divert their steps to other paths.

Our path was always that the will of the many be in the hearts of the men and women who command . . . Thus was born our strength in the jungle, he who leads obeys if he is true, and he who follows leads through the common heart of true men and women. Another word came from afar so that this government was named and this work gave the name 'democracy' to our way that was from before words travelled.

. . . We see that it is the few now who command, and they command without obeying, they lead commanding. And among the few they pass the power of command among themselves, without hearing the many . . . the word comes from afar says they lead without democracy, without the command of the people, and we see that this unreason of those who lead commanding, directs the road of our sorrows and feeds the pain of our dead.

. . . We are despised, we are small, our word is muffled, silence has inhabited our houses for a long time, the time has come to speak for our hearts, for the hearts of others, from the night and from the earth our dead should come, the faceless ones, who are the jungle, who dress with war so their voice will be heard, that their word later falls silent and they return once again to the night and to the earth, that other men and women may speak, who walk other lands, whose words carry truth, who do not become lost in lies. (Zapatista National Liberation Army, 1994a, p. 12)

The rebellion surprised everyone – almost: not the local human rights monitors, not the liberation theology priests working in this southernmost state, not those farmers imprisoned for petitioning the PRI governor for access to arable land, instead of to the dregs that usually were handed out in the state's sporadic land title distributions. Their voices had not been heard, or if heard, not taken seriously, not heard as if what they had to say mattered in the larger scheme of Mexican state affairs, not heard as if their messages mattered for the evolution of continental politics, as if they mattered for understanding the tendencies in the fluid post-Cold War international system. Instead, virtually all the commentators who had been recording the successes of *Salinismo*, the current president's own brand of state refinement was credited with not only warding off serious electoral challenges but with navigating the ship of state through the shoals of unequal continentalism and into the safe post-Cold War harbour of NAFTA (Harvey, 1994).

What had been underestimated by most analysts, most of those following the making of the new international system in which trade apparently was replacing nuclear targeting as the medium of state security and inter-state stability, was that the Mexican state system was in a condition of creeping crisis. While much attention had been focused, with good reason, on President Carlos Salinas's deft refurbishing of the PRI's famous patronage machine, too little attention had been paid to the state's reliance on repression. Mexican human rights groups had been documenting the uses of coercion – state and para-state – yet these documents rarely were deemed relevant to international relations analysis (Americas Watch, 1990). Human rights reports opened a window into the ways in which Chiapas large landowners, the grandsons (not the grandgodsons), had managed to weather the Cardenas' state building innovations of the 1930s without surrendering much of their power. Human rights documents, when read along with Rosario Castellanos's novel, provided ample clues that the 'Mexico' that was represented at the NAFTA bargaining table in the early 1990s had earned those inverted commas.

The Grupo Rosario Castellanos is one of the new civil organisations that has provided the means for achieving such a surprising level of political mobilisation in Chiapas (Lovera, 1994). It is one of several groups that women have organised to assess the relationships between patriarchal male practices, the *Priista* state formula, Chiapas political economy and NAFTA. It is no more adequate in the 1990s to analyse international politics from the margins as if those politics were ungendered than it was in the decade when Rosario Castellanos was absorbing her early lessons about how political power is constituted. The Cold War was created and sustained by the flows of gendered forms of power; so too now are its endings – at the centres, on the margins, along the borders. And as in the previous international system, of 1946–89, so too today, those forms of power are not always easy to see, their contestations not always easy to delineate.

Via electronic mail, the Zapatista National Liberation Army distributed a document entitled 'Women's Revolutionary Law'. It declares that women 'regardless about their race, creed, color or political affiliation', may be incorporated into the revolutionary struggle, so long as they 'meet the demands of the exploited people'. Among the ZNLA's principles spelled out in this document, are women's 'right to work and receive a just salary'; women's right to 'decide the number of children they have and care for'; women's right 'to be free of violence from both relatives and strangers. Rape will be severely punished'; women's right 'to occupy positions of leadership in the organization and hold military ranks in the revolutionary armed forces' (Zapatista National Liberation Army, 1994b).

Precisely who wrote this and out of what process and with whose commitment of support is not yet clear. Early and sketchy reports suggest that the drafting of the 'Women's Revolutionary Law' was begun months before the open revolt in January. These same reports describe a woman member of the ZNLA's co-ordinating body, the Indigenous Revolutionary Clandestine Committee (CCRI), who goes only by the name 'Susana', as developing women's demands by 'making the rounds of dozens of communities, speaking with groups of women to pull their ideas together' ('Mexico', 1994, p. 16).

Mayan communities are described by outside anthropologists as being infused with a democratic culture, though they are also sustained in their present forms by patriarchal practices. Sometimes impressed by the former, a visitor can overlook the latter. Thus a visiting *New York Times* reporter, trying to understand why so many Mayan peasants who did not take part in the 1994 uprising nonetheless voice support for the ZNLA's objectives, spent time in El Carrizal, an Indian village whose members had been trying for over a decade to find a way to make the government respond to their legal land claims.

'In the afternoon, after the men return from the fields and the women are busy preparing the evening meal, a kind of assembly occurs in El Carrizal', the American observed (De Palma, 1994). Has the reporter prepared for his visit by reading Rosario Castellanos? Will he listen for who does not speak?

> The men sit on two benches made from tree trunks. These people do not vote in regular elections (it costs 50 cents to take the bus into town and it is just not worth it they say) but here all decisions are made democratically.
> This day they discussed the land conflict, again . . . Those who want to speak leave the bench and sit on a rough white rock at the other end of the parallel rows, their hats at their feet.
> One old man in a ragged knit shirt placed his hat on the ground. 'All of the newspapers all say that Mexico is at peace, that everyone now is happy because the fighting is over, they are wrong,' he said. 'Companions, it is true that in Mexico we are almost all equal. But what is equality here? It is that nobody has anything . . . ' (De Palma, 1994).

Maybe 'Susana' managed to get the village men to share a seat on the white rock with their wives and daughters when she came to formulate the Zapatistas' demands.

Looking at NAFTA from Chiapas, giving Mayan Indian women and men voices and visibility in an analysis of this major post-Cold War political construction, is not a matter of simply choosing post-positivist 'Roshomon' over Enlightenment-inspired 'Dragnet'. *Roshomon* was the highly acclaimed Japanese film that told the story of a highway robbery and abduction not just from the omnipotent – 'true' – perspective of the film-maker, but from the multiple – perhaps all 'true' – perspectives of several of the characters. *Dragnet* was one of American television's most popular shows in the era of the small black and white screen. Joe Friday, the series' male protagonist, was a laconic police detective. His style was persistent and deadpan. Taking Chiapas' landless peasants seriously does more than open questions about detective hero Joe Friday's 'Just the facts, M'am' approach to international politics, though it certainly does do that. It does indeed appear to make far more sense to adopt a 'Roshomon' posture, to assume that people playing different roles in any international phenomenon will understand its causes and its meanings differently. For instance, Benedict Kerkvliet and Resil Mojares have revealed how, by looking at the 'February Revolution' that overthrew Philippines' autocrat Ferdinand Marcos in 1986 not just from Manila and not just from the vantage point of Marcos and his chief elite allies and opponents, but from the multiple perspectives of provincial elites and ordinary citizens throughout the archipelago, we can gain a much clearer sense of exactly what cost the Marcos regime its legitimacy (Kerkvliet and Mojares, 1992). For students of international relations this 'Roshomon' approach improves one's clarity of vision. One can more fully explain how the fall of Marcos led to the US military being forced to give up Subic Bay naval base, an installation constructed as pivotal to the American government's hegemony in the Pacific.

Similarly, if we take seriously the interplays of power in Chiapas when we explore post-Cold War attempts to integrate three North American political economies we will, I think, comprehend the meanings of that complex process more fully. But this is only half the story. I believe that the 1994 Chiapas rebellion and its ripples now spreading throughout the Mexican political system – to press reporters' relations with the state, to the opposition parties' relations with electoral officials, to citizens' sense of their political capacities – reveal that those 'facts' that are relevant to explaining any given international phenomenon are buried far deeper down in any political system than is typically imagined by academia's 'Dragnet' afficionados. It is only by delving deeper into any political system, listening more attentively at its margins, that one can accurately estimate the powers it has taken to provide the state with the apparent stability that has permitted its elite to presume to speak on behalf of a coherent whole. Only with this explicit political accounting can we explain why the evolving international system takes the turns it does today.

This effort is likely to reveal that there is much more power and many more forms of power in operation in international relations than is conventionally assumed. What has it taken to keep Mayan women off the white rocks? The answer to that question is pertinent to explaining the international politics of beef and coffee, and thus to explaining the intra-state politics of the PRI and *Salinismo*, and therefore to making sense of the continental politics of NAFTA and consequently the politics of the post-Cold War world.

Sound far-fetched? I don't think so. As students of international politics we need to become less parochial, more energetic, more curious. Joe Friday, the Enlightenment's policeman, may have gotten his man, but he probably underestimated the crime.

REFERENCES

Ahern, Maureen (ed.) (1988), *A Rosario Castellanos Reader* (Austin: University of Texas Press).

Americas Watch (1990), *Human Rights in Mexico: A Policy of Impunity* (New York: Human Rights Watch).

Castellanos, Rosario (1992), *The Nine Guardians* (London: Readers International).

Cohen, Marjorie Griffin (1987), *Free Trade and the Future of Women's Work* (Toronto: Garamond Press).

DePalma, Anthony (1994), 'Rage Builds in Chiapas Village Where Land is Life', *New York Times*, 27 February.

Earle, Duncan (1994), 'Indigenous Identity at the Margin: Zapatismo and Nationalism', *Cultural Survival Quarterly*, 18 (1), pp. 26–30.

Harding, Sandra (ed.) (1993), *The 'Racial' Economy of Science* (Bloomington: Indiana University Press).

Hartsock, Nancy C. M. (1994), 'Theoretical Bases for Coalition Building: An Assessment of Postmodernism', unpublished paper, Seattle, Department of Women's Studies, University of Washington.

Harvey, Neil (1994), *Rebellion in Chiapas* (La Jolla, CA: Center for US–Mexican Studies, University of California at San Diego).

Hellman, Judith Adler (1983), *Crisis in Mexico* (New York and London: Holmes and Meier Publishers).

Kaplan, Amy and Pease, Donald E. (eds.) (1993), *Cultures of United States Imperialism* (Durham and London: Duke University Press).

Kerkvliet, Benedict J. and Mojares, Resil B. (eds.) (1992), *From Marcos to Aquino: Local Perspectives on Political Transition in the Philippines* (Honolulu: University of Hawaii Press).

Lovera, Sara (1994), 'Se Constituye el Grupo Rosario Castellanos "23 de Marzo"', *DobleJornada*, 7 February, p. 5.

'Mexico' (1994), *MS*, 4 (6), May/June, p. 16.

Nigh, Ronald (1994), 'Zapata Rose in 1994', *Cultural Survival Quarterly*, 18 (1), pp. 9–11.

Paz, Octavio (1972), *The Other Mexico: Critique of the Pyramid* (New York: Grove Press).

Zapatista National Liberation Army (1994a), 'Communiqué from the Clandestine Indigenous Revolutionary High Command of the Zapatista National Liberation Army (CCRI-CF del EZLN)', first published in *La Jornada*, 27 February 1994, reprinted in a translation by Ronald Nigh in *Cultural Survival Quarterly*, 18, p. 12.

(1994b), 'Women's Revolutionary Law', trans. Mat Miscreant, Love and Rage New York News Bureau, 1nr@blythe.org.

9   Is there a classical international theory?

Robert Jackson

Martin Wight on international theory

In the 1960s Martin Wight (1966) provocatively argued that there is no international political theory worthy of the name – if we compare it to domestic political theory which is a foundational subject of long-standing. Very few classical theorists devoted their talents and energies to international relations and those who did – such as Kant or Machiavelli or Burke – are not famous for that part of their contribution. There is no classical masterpiece of international political theory except, perhaps, Thucydides' history of the Peloponnesian war (Warner, 1972). International relations is 'at the margin' of the greatest political theorists' curiosity or concern.

By 'political theory' Wight is of course not referring to 'scientific' or positivist theory of politics, which he considered to be a deeply flawed enterprise resting on an erroneous conception of human beings and their relations. Nor is he referring to anti-foundational theory, such as the theories of certain continental European philosophers of his day, to which I have found no reference in his published writings. Nor, again, is Wight referring exclusively to academic theories. He would see departments of international relations as merely the current home of theorising about international relations most of which has been carried out historically in other places, such as monasteries, foreign embassies, chancery offices, military quarters, prisons, the studies of private scholars and other such places. Theoretical reflection on the political world beyond one's own community is as old as the Western intellectual tradition. The academic study of the subject is merely an innovation of the twentieth century.

Wight is referring to the traditional kind of political theory which considers international relations to be a sphere of human relations and not something apart – such as a system of autonomous social forces or a purely technical subject of policy-making by experts. Classical political theorists seek to comprehend the human condition and the values fundamental to it – such as order, freedom and justice – as well as the political arrangements and public policies necessary for their realisation or augmentation. International studies is on that view a broadly humanistic subject which involves the scholar in a philosophical, historical, jurisprudential or sociological approach: it is not and could never be a strictly scientific or narrowly technical subject.

The poverty of international theory is explained by Wight according to its distinctive subject: the fundamental problem of international politics is that of survival, which is a question of effective means rather than of rival ends or values. Domestic political theory is basically a theory of the good life and thus a theory of values, but international theory is merely a second-order and largely derivative theory of security: a conservative theory rather than a progressive theory. Here we catch a glimpse of Martin Wight the arch-realist. He is not alone in drawing a nearly water-tight distinction between international politics and domestic politics. Arnold Wolfers (1965) and Kenneth Waltz (1979), among other leading realist theorists, do much the same.

But to regard domestic politics as a sphere of permanent peace and progress and international politics as a sphere of recurrent disorder and war clearly is not only to exaggerate but also to misread the historical evidence. Civil wars are a commonplace and peace can be international as well as domestic: in the past half century there have been far more internal conflicts than international conflicts. Building the state is a more urgent problem in many parts of the world at the present time than building the society of states which in recent decades has developed enormously in terms of organisation.

International politics is thus subject to both change and development. It is strongly affected and even shaped by human innovation – such as scientific and technological advances – which have been provoked as much by international circumstances as any others. One need only glance at the profound relationship between war and technology – not only in the present century but also in previous centuries. The distinction between domestic politics and international politics is of course an important one which theorists should take note of. But the distinction should not be pressed too far: international political theory and domestic political theory diverge at certain points but they are two branches of one overall political theory which is fundamentally pre-occupied with the conditions, arrangements, and values of organised political life on the planet Earth.

There is no denying Wight's observation that the works of the greatest political thinkers pay limited attention to international relations – as compared to relations between the state and the citizen or between different groups within the state. But it is nevertheless a fact that human relations across the boundaries of distinctive and often separate political communities have for more than two millennia provoked theoretical reflections – by philosophers, theologians, lawyers, politicians, administrators, revolutionaries, diplomatists, publicists, historians, and social scientists – among others.

Although Wight had a deep understanding of international relations, based on exceptional historical learning, I think he was mistaken in his above-noted claim about the classical approach to international relations. His account really applies only to realism – and an exceedingly narrow and instrumental realism at that to which few classical realists subscribe except, perhaps, Machiavelli. Was he being deliberately provocative in denying the existence of international theory? His principal publications on the subject prompt the question because they are written in the idiom of the history of political ideas. The title of a posthumous book (Wight, 1991) which contains his famous lectures on international theory delivered at the London School of Economics in the 1950s is *International Theory: The Three Traditions*. Viewed from the perspective of his own contribution, his assertion that there is no international political theory worthy of the name seems perverse. I wonder if there is not more than a hint of irony in his argument?

I shall argue that the classical approach is alive and well today and that it will continue to thrive tomorrow, because it speaks to some perennial problems of human relations usually in non-technical language which ordinary people can understand. This chapter addresses four main issues: whether a classical approach to international theory can be said to exist, if so what sort of theorising and theories does it encompass, what is its relationship to social science theories, and what does it have to say to the theoretical concerns of the late twentieth century?

The classical approach

Hedley Bull (1966) once summed up the classical approach: 'What I have in mind [is] . . . the approach to theorizing that derives from philosophy, history, and law, and is characterized above all by explicit reliance upon the exercise of judgement.' Locating judgement at the heart of international theory serves to emphasise the fundamentally normative character of the subject which at its core involves difficult moral problems, such as nuclear weapons or armed intervention, from which neither politicians nor diplomats nor anyone else who is involved can escape. That is because the development and deployment of power in human relations always has to be justified and can thus never be divorced completely from normative considerations.

As indicated, classical theorists view international relations as posing a distinctive set of human problems which grow out of the inescapable social fact of men and women living side by side, often cheek-to-jowl, and thus coming into social contact – not only as individuals but also as groups – in relations that exhibit amity and enmity, co-operation as well as conflict, power and wealth alongside weakness and poverty, differences as well as similarities of civilisation, culture, language, physical geography, ecology and so forth. The most important of such groups historically are states the independence of which defines a basic 'anarchical' condition of international relations (Bull, 1977) upon which so much theory of a classical kind focuses our attention. The age-old inquiry, first, of making sense of the relations of human groups and particularly independent states and, second, of hopefully resolving – if only for the time being – the social problems which arise in that human setting has left a rich legacy of international relations theories that reaches back to antiquity.

The classical tradition embodies a literature (Williams, 1992; Williams, Wright and Evans, 1993) consisting of famous texts handed down from past generations. One way to access that tradition is of course to study the writings of Aristotle, Augustine, Aquinas, Machiavelli, Grotius, Hobbes, Rousseau, Kant, Hegel, Bentham, Clausewitz, Mill, Marx, Carr, Morgenthau, Walzer and other celebrated thinkers. Anybody who hopes to understand the normative heart of international relations would have to be conversant with at least some of their thought on the subject.

But even more important than the literature is the language and in particular the various idioms through which international theory is expressed. The classical tradition consists of several interwoven discourses each of which discloses significant differences in its approach and emphasis. E. H. Carr (1964) differentiates the sceptical approach – realist theory – from the 'wish-dreams' of utopian theorists – idealist theory. Martin Wight (1991) identifies realism or the Machiavellian tradition of power politics, rationalism or the Grotian tradition of natural and international law, and revolutionism or the Kantian tradition of the community of humankind. Wight regarded each of these voices as an authentic moral position which deserves our respect. Hedley Bull (1977) employs the same basic distinctions. Michael Donelan (1990) adds two further voices: historicism and fideism. Chris Brown (1992) divides international political theory into two fundamental voices: cosmo-politanism and communitarianism. One could go on. But perhaps this will suffice to identify some of the main strands in the classical tradition.

The tradition thus embodies several voices which communicate with each other like conversationalists or debaters. In other words, the theorists are engaging in political argument usually concerning fundamental normative issues in international relations. That clearly suggests that the several classical voices are mutually intelligible and represent not separate cosmologies or worldviews but, rather, distinctive normative positions in a dialogue. Theorists may hold fundamentally different and even contradictory views of international ethics yet still speak a common language – in the same way that Burke understood Rousseau while disagreeing fundamentally with just about everything he wrote.

The three 'r's' identified by Martin Wight (1991) – realism, rationalism, revolutionism – should therefore be understood in terms of a mutually interactive process of thought. That process is evident not only between theorists – such as a realist Rousseau, a rationalist Burke, and a revolutionist Kant – but usually also within the thought of classical thinkers of the first rank. Grotius makes provision for the duties of individuals imposed by natural law. But he also pays heed to the rights of sovereigns established by positive law. International relations cannot be comprehended if either individuals or sovereigns are ignored as bearers of rights and duties. Hobbes makes provision for a conception of international relations as an anarchical sphere with an ever-present potential for war. But he also recognises that sovereigns can contract legal relationships with each other. International relations cannot be comprehended if either military power or legal authority are ignored. Kant makes provision for humanity as the most fundamental community to which men and women necessarily belong. But he also acknowledges the definite limits to human justice imposed by particular national communities, or states. International relations cannot be comprehended if either humans or states are ignored.

It is thus risky to pigeon-hole the complex thought of classical theorists – as rationalists or realists or revolutionists or anything else – because their theories, even if they do have a definite tendency in one direction or another, are rarely one-dimensional. That is what makes them fascinating as well as enlightening. How could any one-dimensional theory, no matter what human dimension it singles out to theorise, capture at all adequately the obvious complexity and notorious contrariness of human beings and their relations? The fashion of attempting to force international relations theories of leading thinkers into static classification schemes ought to be recognised for what it is: a pedagogical device which may be useful in sorting out some preliminaries but is unlikely to hold up as a paradigmatic distinction.

To sum up thus far it may be worth emphasising this last point: an adequate theoretical understanding of international relations cannot be achieved by any one tradition alone: it can only be achieved by all traditions taken together and thus by an analysis of the debates they jointly provoke (Nardin and Mapel, 1992). Even realism – however important it may be – is only one voice among several in the classical approach to international relations. It should be understood in relation to other important voices which together make up the classical tradition. I think that represents Wight's and Bull's position on the issue; it certainly represents my own.

The classical approach and modern social science

The classical tradition is an inclusive rather than an exclusive approach which is not fundamentally at odds with social science theories of international relations. It accommodates humanist social science and only excludes strictly positivist social science – which really excludes itself by disavowing normative theory.

As far as social science positivism is concerned, the classical approach sees it as resting on a category mistake. The specific mistake in question is that of treating human relations as an external phenomenon in the same general category as nature so that the theorist stands *outside* the subject – like an anatomist dissecting a cadaver. According to the classical approach, the theorist of human affairs is a human being who can never divorce himself or herself completely from human relations: he or she is always *inside* the subject (Hollis and Smith, 1990). Being part of the subject is in fact the principal source of insight into human relations (Collingwood, 1956), including that branch we refer to as international relations.

Thus the classical approach fully accommodates what Max Weber (1968) refers to as a *verstehen* or interpretative orientation to social science which focuses on social action. This he defines as any human action which is inherently meaningful to the actor and which takes account of the actions of other humans. That means that ideas, interests, concerns, intentions, ambitions, calculations, miscalculations, desires, beliefs, values, hopes, fears, confidence, doubt, uncertainty and similar human dispositions and orientations must be at the centre of analysis. It also means that international theory can only be – as Hedley Bull (1966) once put it – 'a scientifically imperfect procedure of perception and intuition' which has at best a 'tentative and inclusive status'. Any theorist who aspires to achieve more than that is unduly optimistic if not slightly naive.

International relations, like all other human relations, is a historical and thus a changing subject. I think that would be a fundamental assumption of the classical approach. Very little in human relations is permanently fixed: very much is in flux. That does not mean that there are not features of human relations which disclose themselves over vast temporal and spatial distances: intelligence, stupidity, affection, hatred, co-operation, discord, trust, suspicion, respect, contempt, are but a few. Nor does it mean that the societies that men and women produce by their actions cannot stand virtually still for long periods. But any social mould can be broken: that is because humans can be discontented as well as content with the world in which they live; they can imagine a different and better life on earth, they can look back to the past, they can come up with new ideas and techniques about how to live together or apart, they can borrow from their neighbours, and they can endeavour, with greater or lesser success, to put those innovations or borrowings into effect at certain times or places. About all they cannot do is escape from their humanity.

In short, people are free within the constraints of their own limitations and whatever circumstances they find themselves to decide whether or not to retain, modify or abandon current practices, institutions, laws, rules, treaties, agreements, decisions, policies or any other social arrangements they come up with. That imaginative and innovative and imitative faculty of men and women, and also their well-known fickleness, produces changing political worlds and thus a continually unfolding, recurrently surprising, and never fully predictable human history. International relations, like all other human relations, is socially constructed and can thus have different shapes and substances at different times and places. That means, for example, that there could be human relations without the idea – or the institutions which express the idea – of sovereign statehood as we have known it for the past three and a half centuries. Arguably the feudal society of medieval Europe is an instance: whether or not we are entering a new medievalism (Bull, 1977) is a controversial issue at the present time. Even the international realm as we have known it in recent centuries could become far less prominent and perhaps disappear – if human relations around the globe take on a decidedly different shape in which independent political communities become far less important.

Today there are of course theorists who believe that is happening: their beliefs are fully consistent with the classical tradition which has always contained thinkers of the first rank who discerned before almost anyone else the outlines of the new world to come. Machiavelli, Grotius, Hobbes, Rousseau and Marx are only the most outstanding cases in point. Thus, the classical tradition could accommodate, for example, contemporary liberal theorists who see the emergence at the present time of a far more interdependent and unified world than any that has previously existed. I return to this point in the final section.

That international relations is socially constructed also means that just as each generation of political practitioners – such as the state-leaders of an era – will by their actions help to generate the political history of their own time with its distinctive possibilities and problems, so, too, will each generation of political commentators have something fresh to say about those activities – or any other activities to which they give their attention. Contemporary theorists working in the classical tradition are not confined merely to reiterating or recycling the thought of past thinkers. They are perfectly free to engage in their own independent thinking and try to make their own theoretical contributions.

Of course there will always be some theorists – but only a select few – who stand head and shoulders above the crowd: their theories speak to us from across the centuries. Thus we return time and again to Thucydides or Augustine or Machiavelli or Grotius or Hegel or Kant for insight into the problems of international relations not only in their time but also in our time. Yet even the greatest theorists can never have the final word on international relations or, indeed, on any other subject of human relations. There is always something more to be said. That is evident in the flourishing international relations theories of our own time a few of which will in centuries to come probably be studied as classics. I think that is already happening in the case of Michael Walzer's (1983, 1992) pluralist theory.

But the classical approach, certainly as understood by Wight and Bull, rests on a fundamental conviction: that there is more to be learned from the long history of speculation on international relations and from the many theorists who have contributed to that tradition than can be learned from any single generation alone – including the latest thought of the social science theorists of the past thirty years. International studies is not a strict scientific discipline in which new discoveries allow us to discard old theories at no cost to our knowledge.

Rather, each generation of thinkers must struggle anew with the problem of understanding human relations in the international sphere, learning what they can from past generations, paying close attention to the workings of the world in which they live, noticing how it is changing if it is changing at all, and from that analysis trying to add something to our inherited stock of knowledge. Because international theory in the classical manner is basically derived from history and experience no theory will ever have the final word, because changing historical circumstances and different human experiences will always provoke new theoretical understanding.

Realism and the 'English School'

Among the three traditions of international thought singled out for special attention by Martin Wight (1991) one has dominated international relations theory since the end of the Second World War: realism. He was of course referring to classical realism which is a normative theory that focuses primarily on states as moral communities and on the conduct of state leaders. Unquestionably, that is the theory against which all others must define themselves and stake out their position. It is of course far older than the 'classical' realism of the postwar era and dates back not only to Rousseau or Hobbes or Machiavelli but ultimately to Thucydides. Classical realists emphasise the fundamental human values of security and survival which are at stake in international politics; they also emphasise the intelligent and responsible employment of the instrumentalities of power in the pursuit of those values. The ethics of statecraft is at the heart of realist ethics.

Since the decisions and actions of national leaders and other important international actors are always made in concrete circumstances of time and of place, scholars who seek to understand the ethics of statecraft usually feel obliged to adopt some version of situational ethics. The distinctive ethics involved has been aptly characterised by Arnold Wolfers (1965) and Stanley Hoffmann (1981) – two twentieth-century realists writing in the classical tradition – as 'nonperfectionist ethics'. This is the morality of the best choice in the circumstances, or perhaps the least damaging choice if in the circumstances prevailing at the time all choices are lamentable to some degree – which is characteristic of moral responsibility in extreme international situations, such as war. That is the decision that we feel bound to make, however reluctantly, after canvassing the options available, taking into account as best we can their foreseeable consequences, taking stock of our responsibilities as we understand them, and being honest with ourselves and forthright with others. At this point classical realism is almost indistinguishable from the just war tradition – Thucydides merges with Augustine.

In classical realism, politics and morality are never divorced but are always combined in an understanding of international relations as an enlightened – if definitely limited – sphere of human conduct. This is perhaps most clearly evident in the realism of E. H. Carr (1964) who emphasises the intimate dialogue of power and morality and condemns, equally, those who would divorce these two elements and focus either on the one or the other. To focus on morality alone is as fatal a mistake as it is to focus on power alone: 'The utopian who dreams that it is possible to eliminate self-assertion from politics and to base a political system on morality alone is just as wide of the mark as the realist who believes that altruism is an illusion and that all political action is based on self-seeking' (Carr, 1964, p. 97). Unqualified moral idealism in international theory lost most of its credibility not least because of the withering assault of Carr and other influential realist commentators writing in the classical vein.

However, the same cannot be said of amoral realism and its mainly American successor, positivist social science realism. That is perhaps most evident in the wide reception accorded to Kenneth Waltz's (1979) theory of international politics. Waltz's realism is fully in the spirit of social science positivism: the first part of the book explicitly sets out, right from the start, the requirements of 'theory' in the scientific meaning of the word. For Waltz, there is no explicit place for morality or ethics in international relations theory. Indeed, to introduce ethical theory would defeat the scientific nature of the theoretical enterprise. There are of course unstated ethical assumptions in Waltz's text – such as the assumption that states are worth fighting for which suggests that they must embody genuine value for their populations. But these assumptions sadly remain inarticulate: Waltz provides no guide for evaluating let alone making international moral choices. The realism of Waltz thus differs significantly if not profoundly from the realism of Carr in which morality – if only the morality of safety and prudence in an uncertain and dangerous world – is an integral and explicit element.

Stanley Hoffmann (1990) has commented, in connection with Bull's (1966) critique of behaviouralism, that Waltz's (1979) book would be 'a prime example of the very approach which Hedley Bull had condemned'. I believe Hoffmann hits the nail on the head and I think it is worth quoting him at greater length on this point:

Waltz . . . begins by laying down a very interesting and rigorous notion of theory, and then, by applying it to international relations, manages to leave most of the substance of the field outside the straitjacket . . . Bull started with . . . questions about society and culture, about the place of war and conceptions of it . . . about the nature of the state . . . [and] the right of states to intervene in each other's affairs . . . To begin with such questions is to realize . . . that they can only be understood by reference to the works of the political philosophers who have discussed and sharpened them. (Hoffmann, 1990, p. 17)

This fundamental difference of approach between Waltz and Bull is emblematic of the difference between contemporary positivist realism and classical humanist realism. It is perhaps also emblematic of the different emphases between American and British international relations theory during the past three decades – the latter has arguably stayed closer to classical realism and its normative concerns.

Among the latter realists we find a conscious effort to steer clear of normative questions and a very awkward ability to deal with such questions when they cannot be avoided. If contemporary positivist realism has one fundamental defect, in my view it is its handicap in addressing normative questions many of which are of enormous practical importance in international relations at the present time. Positivist realism pays a high price in social relevance for cutting itself off from such questions. Among the latter realists we find a moral theory based on a view of human beings which underlines their limited generosity and fellow-feeling. As indicated, this view (Butterfield, 1953) is reminiscent of the non-pacifist branch of traditional Christian ethics and specifically the just war tradition which makes ample provision for human imperfection. Classical realism occupies a central place in the international relations theory of the 'English School' and particularly that of E. H. Carr (1964), Herbert Butterfield (1953), the earlier Martin Wight (1979) and the younger Hedley Bull (1961). But in the later writings of both Wight and Bull it does not occupy an exclusive place. For there are the revolutionists and the rationalists whose theories are also taken into account: for both Wight and Bull the study of international theory involves exploring all three traditions.

To sum up: the 'English School' as represented by Carr or Butterfield could be understood as a version of classical realism – in the case of Carr (1964) a secular version, in the case of Butterfield (1953) a Christian version. But as represented by Wight (1991) and Bull (1977), the 'English School' is a more comprehensive academic enterprise which emphasises the interactive relationship between all three of these basic human inclinations in international relations. Rationalism or 'Grotianism' is, of course, at the heart of that relationship.

The classical tradition and post-positivist theories

There may be those who believe that the classical tradition has run its course, is no longer relevant even if it once might have been, and can be safely ignored. We could perhaps believe that if we thought social science positivism had triumphed and international relations could be explained without putting normative questions at the forefront of analysis. Or, like some post-modernist thinkers, we could perhaps believe it if we thought human reason and the associated idea of the autonomous human agent were illusory. But if anyone believes that international relations is a special sphere of human conduct in which honesty, honour, fidelity, judgement, responsibility, prudence, compassion and similar normative considerations have a centrally important place then he or she will find it difficult to believe anything but that the classical tradition continues to grasp the human fundamentals of international relations.

Like all traditions, academic or otherwise, classical international theory is living and evolving. In principle, there is nothing to prevent any approach which acknowledges the humanistic and thus fundamentally normative character of international relations from being taken up and incorporated into the classical tradition. Whether in the future any contemporary theory of international relations will become a fixture of the classical tradition it is of course impossible to say for sure. But it is not impossible to speculate. I think it is almost bound to happen in the case of those theories which are drawing our attention to significant features of the human condition in international relations which are emerging at the present time or have been overlooked, or neglected, in the past.

Classical international theory can of course be defined in various ways. But one way is to suggest that it is preoccupied with normative claims in international affairs which cannot be ignored. There are theories concerning who must be taken into account and who can be left out of account by moral accounting; there is also changing historical practice on the question. Undoubtedly the most fundamental traditional claimants are, firstly, political communities or states (communitarianism) and, secondly, human beings (cosmopolitanism). But however fundamental those categories may be, they scarcely exhaust the moral universe of international relations which is constantly in flux. That is because men and women have the faculty of identifying themselves and organising themselves in diverse ways which they then proceed to employ as a basis of moral justification.

Ancient Greek commentators noted the basic normative standing of the *polis* (city state) and its exclusively male and Greek members – but were blind to the moral claims of women, slaves and foreigners or barbarians. Medieval thinkers conceived of a complex hierarchy of status relationships: the great chain of moral being which extended from God down to the lowest serf. It was by no means clear what foreign relations were and who could legitimately engage in them. The exclusive jurisdiction of the territorial state was not yet a reality and international relations – if we can even use the expression – involved a variety of different actors: kings, bishops, nobles, merchants, etc. Early modern theorists of the sixteenth and seventeenth centuries acknowledged the normative autonomy of princely rulers and the subject status of the people they managed to rule; sovereignty became the monopoly of kings. Enlightenment theorists of the seventeenth and eighteenth centuries identified not only generic humans but also citizens as claimants; romantic theorists of the eighteenth and nineteenth centuries identified not only the state but also the nation as moral communities. This is of course only a crude summary of a complex historical subject.

Contemporary theorists have likewise been calling our attention to other normative categories and I think it is accurate to say that the moral universe of international relations is expanding. Marxism – of a humanist rather than a positivist strain – draws attention to the previously marginalised category of class and particularly the working class. Globalists focus attention on the profound international economic inequalities between North and South and the claims of the Third World on global wealth. Critical theory takes notice of 'the other' which could be any social category whose members suffer from exclusion at the hands of insiders (Linklater, 1990). Feminism and ethnicity theory also call attention to previously silent or marginalised categories – such as gender and national or ethnic minorities. Environmentalist theorists do the same for non-human species and ecological systems. One could go on but perhaps this will suffice to make the point: that the definition of normative claimants in international relations is continually changing as men and women find new ways of arranging and rearranging their joint lives.

Whether any of the new theories discussed in this book become important additions to international theory – or turn out merely to be temporary fashions – only time will tell. Here I merely suggest that the history of international political theory, like any other intellectual history, is open to new ideas most of which will prove to have little historical staying power but a few of which are perhaps destined for a permanent place in the pantheon of classical international theories alongside enduring theoretical voices of the past. In that way the classical approach is continually renewed and enriched.

However, this thesis should not be pressed too far. There are limits to the accommodation of new international theories by the classical tradition. I suppose the basic limit is determined by the intelligibility of a theory and its communication with other classical theories. When I try to read some of the most self-consciously scientific theories of contemporary international relations I feel rather like a visitor to another planet: as if I had entered a remote place whose inhabitants speak an arcane language and seem preoccupied with theoretical concerns entirely unconnected with those of history or ordinary human experience. That same feeling also occurs when I try to make sense of post-modern theories of an anti-foundational kind which deny the possibility of universal human reason and a historical conversation among human beings. In short, I cannot see how the classical approach could possibly accommodate theories which explicitly repudiate the classical tradition itself.

Another limit would be theories of extreme cultural relativism in which virtual silence is postulated between civilisations and cultures making dialogue impossible. Such theories should of course be distinguished from pluralist theories which notice the limits of cosmopolitanism in international relations and give the moral claims of nations and other political communities their due but which do not deny the possibility of a moral conversation of humankind. Michael Walzer's (1992) international theory and Isaiah Berlin's (1992) political theory, while different in other respects, can each be associated with that view.

There is yet another limit which perhaps has not been made as explicit as it should now be: the classical tradition takes human experience as a starting point – even though theorists disagree about what part of that experience is important. The heart of the tradition is reflection on experience, our own experience and that of others. The so-called 'real world' of organised human life is what captures the attention of classical thinkers, whether they want to preserve it or tear it down and replace it with something else. Some theorists – Aristotle and Burke, for example – lay heavy emphasis on judgement and common sense. Some theorists – Plato and Kant – place equally heavy emphasis on imagination and intellect. Both tendencies can be accommodated. But I very much doubt that the classical tradition could take anti-experience or anti-reason as a valid starting point. That would again seem to exclude at least some post-modernists.

There is a final point that should also be made in this context: the classical approach to international theory operates on the assumption that international theories – if they wish to be pertinent – should always take their cue from human relations in that sphere. In other words, they should be 'indigenous' to their subject. Contemporary international theorists have been more inclined to look outside political science and sometimes even outside the human sciences – for example, to mathematics or the natural sciences – for theoretical inspiration. There is a penchant for innovation – rather than cultivation and improvement – which often seems to amount to little more than borrowing for borrowing's sake. As a result contemporary international relations theory tends to be a mixed bag of unrelated approaches which usually are not in dialogue. I would borrow less from unrelated disciplines and make better use of the abundant traditional resources which are available for theorising contemporary problems of international relations seeking thereby to add to our accumulated historical stock of theoretical knowledge. That process of cultivation and augmentation is how I understand the classical approach.

NOTE

I wish to acknowledge the financial support of the Social Sciences and Humanities Research Council of Canada.

REFERENCES

Berlin, Isaiah (1992), *The Crooked Timber of Humanity* (New York: Vintage Books).
Brown, Chris (1992), *International Relations Theory: New Normative Approaches* (New York: Wheatsheaf).
Bull, Hedley (1961), *The Control of the Arms Race* (London: Weidenfeld & Nicolson).
  (1966 [1969]), 'International Theory: The Case for a Classical Approach', in K. Knorr and J. Rosenau (eds.), *Contending Approaches to International Politics* (Princeton: Princeton University Press), pp. 20–38.
  (1977), *The Anarchical Society* (London: Macmillan).
Butterfield, Herbert (1953), *Christianity, Diplomacy and War* (London: Epworth).
Carr, E. H. (1964), *The Twenty Years' Crisis* (New York: Harper).
Collingwood, R. G. (1956), *The Idea of History* (New York: Oxford University Press).
Donelan, Michael (1990), *Elements of International Political Theory* (Oxford: Clarendon Press).
Gallie, W. B. (1978), *Philosophers of Peace and War* (Cambridge: Cambridge University Press).
Hoffmann, Stanley (1981), *Duties Beyond Borders* (Syracuse, New York: Syracuse University Press).
  (1990), 'International Society', in J. D. B. Miller and R. J. Vincent (eds.), *Order and Violence: Hedley Bull and International Relations* (Oxford: Clarendon Press).
Hollis, Martin and Smith, Steve (1990), *Explaining and Understanding International Relations* (Oxford: Clarendon Press).
Linklater, Andrew (1990), *Men and Citizens in the Theory of International Relations*, 2nd edition (London: Macmillan).
Nardin, Terry and Mapel, David (eds.) (1992), *Traditions of International Ethics* (Cambridge: Cambridge University Press).
Waltz, Kenneth N. (1979), *Theory of International Politics* (New York: McGraw-Hill).

218   *Robert Jackson*

Walzer, Michael (1983), *Spheres of Justice: A Defense of Pluralism and Equality* (New York: Basic Books).

(1992), *Just and Unjust Wars*, 2nd edition (New York: Basic Books).

Warner, R. (tr.) (1972), *Thucydides: History of the Peloponnesian War* (Harmondsworth: Penguin Books).

Weber, Max (1968), *Economy and Society* (New York: Bedminster Press).

Wight, M. (1966), 'Why is There No International Theory?', in H. Butterfield and M. Wight (eds.), *Diplomatic Investigations* (London: Allen and Unwin), pp. 12–33.

(1979), *Power Politics* (Harmondsworth: Penguin Books).

(1991), *International Theory: The Three Traditions* (Leicester: Leicester University Press).

Williams, Howard (1992), *International Relations in Political Theory* (Milton Keynes: Open University Press).

Williams, Howard, Wright, Moorhead and Evans, Tony (eds.) (1993), *A Reader in International Relations and Political Theory* (Buckingham: Open University Press).

Wolfers, A. (1965), *Discord and Collaboration* (Baltimore: Johns Hopkins University Press).

IV

Openings

10 Authoritarian and liberal militarism: a contribution from comparative and historical sociology

Michael Mann

Introduction

I have been asked to write on the theoretical contribution that historical sociology has made to International Relations (IR). This puts me in a quandary. I am not an admirer of what passes for theory among academics, all those abstract -isms and -ologies. I have no stamina for those in my own academic specialism, sociology, let alone for those in International Relations. I am more a consumer than a producer of international relations research, one of those 'general readers' on whom the sales of IR books depend. Thus what I need from IR specialists is not the positivist, pluralist, realist, structuralist (classical, neo- and post-) scholastic games of schoolmen (and women), but *substantive* theory about real-world international relations. More precisely, what we outsiders *really* want from IR is substantive theory on its most important issue of all: the question of war and peace. So in the same spirit I do not offer here yet another school or -ology – historical sociology. Instead I offer a modest substantive theory, from the point of view of a comparative and historical sociologist, on the centrality of ferocious militarism to our own Western society. I will build upon one of comparative and historical sociology's favourite themes – the contrast between authoritarian and liberal-democratic movements and regimes. I draw out its implications for the IR issue, the matter of war and peace. These movements and regimes generated two major and ferocious forms of militarism, central to Western civilisation, but often neglected by IR theory. I shall call these 'nation-statist' and 'civil society' militarism.

I first offer three general orienting principles derived from the practices of comparative and historical sociologists. First, we are resolutely empirical, not to say empiricist. Sociology had its own -ism and -ology wars in the 1960s and 1970s, including all of IR's (save post-structuralism not then invented, and with realism being an epistemological position rather than a statement of how states behave), plus some others of which I sincerely hope IR remains entirely innocent. Though not entirely unproductive, these produced the customary consequences of major wars – exhaustion, the waste of a generation and a cry of 'never again'. But they left the more productive scholars adhering to a kind of 'as if positivism', recognising the insecure epistemological bases of social science, recognising that theory and data are inescapably entwined, but continuing pragmatically to do research, generating theoretical conclusions challengeable and challenged by others and then discussed and evaluated within what is a very diverse profession. Since sociologists then immediately faced insurgent feminist and ethnic and other minority challenges to many of their theoretical presuppositions, 'as if positivism' proved an especially fertile strategy for generating radical new research and theory. I hate to think what might have happened if feminists or minorities had seriously pursued the strategies of some of the armies of the -ism and -ology wars, which had claimed (almost always spuriously) to challenge the *epistemological* bases of sociology.

This leads me to pronounce my dissatisfaction with the contents of much of this book. Too many of its chapters discuss theoretical paradigms with disturbingly little reference to the empirical world and with disturbingly little interest in 'test cases' with which to evaluate rival theories. It is interesting that the three most empirical chapters of this book (by myself, Immanuel Wallerstein and Cynthia Enloe) are all by persons with sociological training. Wallerstein and I have elsewhere produced what amount to rival general empirical theories of international relations. His, argued briefly in this volume, explains the modern world in terms of the logic of a single system, that of the capitalist world-economy. Mine, expounded in the two published volumes of my *The Sources of Social Power* (1986, 1993), explains it in terms of the entwinings of four logics, four 'sources of social power': ideological, economic, military and political. Both theories are argued with great empirical detail, and both of us accept that the judgements of our readers and colleagues will be based primarily on our ability to explain the facts as they see and organise them. That is all that matters.

My second orienting principle is that comparative and historical sociologists contrast societies scattered through time and space, acutely aware of the diverse and curious ways human beings have regulated their affairs. We tend to relativise, not reify social institutions. Thus we treat states as only one possible form of political and military organisation. For most of history centralised states had little salience for most social actors. States might be essentially the possession of certain lineages or clans, oligarchies or ruling classes. Questions of war and peace might be largely their private concerns, having little to do with 'whole societies'.

Conversely, questions of peace or war might be partially or mainly the private concerns of civil society members, even in modern societies (as I shall argue here). All political institutions, including states, have their particularities. To understand them we must study their variable relations with other social institutions.

This should be borne especially in mind by IR specialists who do sometimes reify modern states, crediting them with a solidity, cohesion, autonomy and power in society that they rarely have (especially realists do this). IR can continue to produce research assuming that war and peace are exclusively the prerogatives of autonomous and analogous sovereign states. It can continue to generate correlations between wars and state-centred variables of about 0.25, thus explaining about 5–10 per cent of the total variance. But to go further, to explain a more significant proportion of the variance, would involve relaxing the assumption of state sovereignty in order to analyse the multiple social pressures operating on international relations, whether or not these influences go through states. I recently attempted such an analysis with regard to the Great Power relations which culminated in the First World War (1993, esp. chapters 8 and 21). Here I do likewise in analysing modern militarisms.

Yet not all the fault lies in IR. Some IR practitioners have been examining the impact of social relations on geopolitics for well over a decade. Sociologists did not respond as helpfully as we might. It was over a decade ago that some sociologists became aware that our specialism was neglecting the impact of geopolitics on social relations. We first borrowed precisely the traditional form of realism from which many IR practitioners were then fleeing (as Barry Buzan notes in his chapter). We passed each other in the night.

Indeed, sociological and IR blinkers have tended to reinforce one another. Since Max Weber, sociologists have defined 'the modern state' as the institution monopolising the (legitimate) use of violence in society. Modern times have been supposed to have fused military and political power on one agency, the state. IR specialists sometimes quote approvingly sociologists' definitions of the modern state. But they don't need to, since it corresponds exactly to their own traditional orthodoxy, that 'sovereignty' over matters of war and peace lies with the state.

I will contest this shared orthodoxy. My own model of social power analytically distinguishes military from political power. In this chapter I will separate them in modern Western societies. I will argue that the most ferocious forms of modern militarism have not been monopolised by the state, and so they have been neglected.

This brings me to the third orienting principle: awareness of historical and social development (which Wallerstein also stresses in this volume). I will argue that relations of war and peace have changed considerably across the modern centuries – within the so-called 'Westphalian period' – as social development has enhanced the role of popular mobilisation projects. Only some of these projects have centred on the state. We must not reify the state or the nation-state. Beware the old-fashioned sociological notion that 'society' consists only of those social relations contained within the boundaries of a state. The nation-state has been quite rare in history. Even in modern times it only 'contains' a part of social life. Thus only some of modern militarism has centred on the nation-state, while some has diffused through broader continental, religious or racial networks of interaction. To allow for this possibility we must define militarism in a way that makes it at least potentially separable from states. *Militarism is the persistent use of organised military violence in pursuit of social goals.*

Constitutional and absolutist states

I will argue that the two most ferocious forms of modern militarism arose historically out of two contrasting forms of European regime, liberal-democratic and authoritarian. Much of comparative and historical sociology has focused on the growth of these two over the last six or so centuries. It asked why two such different regimes could emerge in a single continent. It noted that medieval Europe already possessed embryo elements of both. On the one hand, most rulers were princes and most centralised states (to the extent that they existed) actually *belonged* to princes. On the other hand (as Weber remarked), conceptions of local 'rights' were more developed than in most other parts of the world at the time. Christianity conferred a minimal equality on all (or at least on all men). Custom and contract guaranteed individual legal rights. Collectivities based on villages, towns, corporations and estates possessed both legal rights and active deliberative assemblies (emphasised by Downing, 1993). These rights were both locally and transnationally entrenched. Thus monarchical, centralised, authoritative states and decentred, diffuse 'civil societies' both already existed within European Christian civilisation.

There have been two schools of thought as to why two different lineages can be traced out of this dual but common ancestry. The first has been a Marxian 'social' and materialist school led by Barrington Moore (1969), Perry Anderson (1979) and Robert Brenner (1987). Their account has seen different state forms as essentially produced by different modes of economic production and class relations. Thus, they argue, constitutional government arose in countries where two powerful classes emerged: urban and trading bourgeoisies, and peasants possessing individual or collective control over the land. Only the strength of these classes *vis-à-vis* the landholding aristocracy and the monarchy could preserve constitutional rule. Thus absolutism emerged in the opposite situation: where there flourished a landholding aristocracy able to use dependent peasant labour. These writers disagree a little among themselves. Moore stresses the bourgeoisie, Brenner the peasantry. Moore and Anderson also acknowledge that the monarch had certain autonomous powers: Moore wrote of an *alliance* between a 'strong state' and the aristocracy, while Anderson stressed empirically (though not theoretically) the significance of state militarism in the emergence of absolutism.

Such observations move centre-stage for the second school, a more 'military-political' one, classically associated with Weber and Hintze, more recently with Theda Skocpol (1979), Charles Tilly (1990), Brian Downing (1993) and myself (1986). First, they argue that most of what states actually did was geared to militarism rather than to the regulation of class relations. Second, therefore, the growth of central state powers was more closely related to the rhythms of inter-state war than to those of capitalist development. Third, the absolutist project arose from the need to extract taxes to fight wars without the consent of the mass of subjects. Thus if a state could pay for war without taxing its own subjects heavily, or if it could find military projects for which powerful subjects would willingly help pay, then it did not need an absolutist project. Fourth, different types of warfare had different implications. Since navies cannot sail on dry land, naval powers are poorer at domestic repression and coercive tax extraction than army powers. Naval powers were the more likely to develop constitutional government.

It is not easy to separate the causes stressed by the two schools. They were entwined and most outcomes were 'over-determined'. Most constitutional regimes had stronger bourgeoisies and peasantries than most absolutist ones; but they also tended to be naval rather than land powers and to finance their wars either from profitable foreign trade or by taxing foreigners; while the connection between strong bourgeoisies, profitable foreign trade and naval power was almost a necessary one in the early modern period. And while the original balance of power between peasants and landlords may have been relatively uncontaminated by warfare, this deeply affected the relations between bourgeoisies and monarchs. There are also deviant class cases. English landlords surely did have sufficient powers over their labour to assist an absolutist project. It was primarily for military–geopolitical–fiscal reasons that this failed: an island position meant that standing armies were weakly developed and once naval power brought colonial and trading rewards, coercive taxation became less necessary. Swedish landlords (especially in the more populated south) seem to have had some of the economic power Moore and Brenner would expect to lead to absolutism. Yet the proto-absolutist seventeenth-century Swedish monarchy paid for its imperialism by taxing Germans rather than Swedes. After this burst of imperialism failed there were no more serious wars in Scandinavia to encourage an absolutist project.

Thus *both* economic and political-military causes were important. To establish *how* important would require further empirical research – including a comparative analysis of the whole of Europe, systematically collecting all available regional and country statistics of land tenure, taxation and warfare and correlating them with surges towards absolutism and constitutional government. But my concern here is not with the regimes themselves, but with the forms of militarism they encouraged. It is often argued that their successor states of the nineteenth and twentieth centuries differed greatly in their militarism. Constitutional or 'liberal' regimes have been considered more pacific than absolutist or authoritarian ones. Sometimes it is only argued that liberal regimes are less likely to go to war with each other. Indeed, Doyle (1983) notes that liberal twentieth-century regimes have been *more* likely to aggress against non-European powers.

I intend to make a sociological contribution to this debate by identifying the different forms of militarism associated with liberal and authoritarian regimes and to identify the changes wrought upon them by modern social development across the West, especially by rival projects of popular mobilisation.

Varieties of successor states and militarism

By 1900 we can identify four main types of 'European' state, one descended from absolutism, the others from constitutional regimes.
1 Five Great Powers were essentially authoritarian: Austria-Hungary, Prussia/Germany and Russia, plus the Ottoman Empire and Spain as declining outliers. As might be predicted by materialist theory, in these countries dominant classes retained more direct control of the state than in more 'liberal' states. But, as political-military theory would predict, they were also essentially land-based powers – Austria, Prussia and Russia traditionally so, the Ottomans and Spain more recently turning inward as their naval imperialism became blocked by greater powers. Both entwined causes generated a very visible

militarism, since their large military forces were stationed within the country. Their garrisons and conscription systems were available for domestic class repression, their striking-forces and defences were geared against their immediate neighbours (except for Spain). So I term this *militarism of the neighbourhood*, deployed domestically and across the borders.

Yet until 1914 militarism of the neighbourhood remained quite restrained and ritualised. Since the state possessed a combination of overwhelming force and considerable traditional legitimation, the dissatisfied (especially lower classes) did not often oppose it. When they did resist, a ritualised 'show of force' rather than brutal slaughter usually sufficed to clear them. Across the borders their militarism was also rather rule-governed, since it was staffed by upper classes who were often kinsmen.

2 The representative Great Power was typified in Europe by Britain and France. As social-materialist theory emphasises, these had also been the most developed economies with the largest bourgeois, commercial farmer and working classes, and less significant landed upper classes actually controlling agriculture. Yet they were also essentially naval and colonial powers – though France was a borderline case because also a great land power. So for both entwined reasons, their neighbourhood militarism was weak, since their massive militarism was mostly stationed abroad – much of it far away – and it was globally oriented. Yet their military resources were considerable, no less than authoritarianism's. They were as 'militaristic', though in a rather different way.

I call their militarism *militarism of the globe*, rather than of the neighbourhood. This is only a difference of degree rather than of kind, since the British and French also had garrison troops – which the British used routinely in Ireland, more occasionally on the mainland, and which the French deployed around their borders and in civil disturbances. Nonetheless, it was a real difference.

3 The Minor Powers in Europe, mostly around the northern and western seaboards, were constitutional (Portugal being a borderline case) and relatively pacific since small and protected by the Great Powers. Yet they also had important trade and sometimes colonies abroad, and so some had a *scaled-down militarism of the globe*.

4 Finally come the settler states mainly composed of Europeans: Britain's former colonies, the United States, Canada, Australia, New Zealand. They were the most constitutional states in the world, partly because of their British heritage, partly because of their ability to win (male) democracy from Britain. Unthreatened by other powers, they

also had relatively unmilitaristic states. Though this was not true of the USA during the Civil War, and though the USA did enter into a lesser global militarism from 1899, these four *states* were the most fully 'liberal' and the least militaristic of all the states of the Europeans.

Modern Western militarism: 1. Nation-statism

So far I have discussed militarism as a product of state policy – as in orthodox views. But these states of the Europeans were also caught up in massive social development occurring across the seventeenth to the twentieth centuries. The commercialisation of agriculture, industrialisation, larger-scale warfare, popular literacy and notions of popular political representation all made 'the people' far more relevant to macro-power relations and all generated projects of mass popular mobilisation. These occurred both in Europe and outside of it. European development saw mass emigration and colonial settlements soon escaped control by the European mother states. Thus we can distinguish different popular mobilisation projects, leading to different militarisms which did not necessarily depend on the state.

The absolutist powers, covering central, eastern and much of southern Europe, attempted modernisation and some national mobilisation from above. Before 1914 they remained uncomfortable with the nationalism they were helping foment. Their religion, their kin networks and monarchy itself was European-wide, not nationally confined. But their collapse in the First World War furthered the spread of what I term 'authoritarian nation-statism' in the many successor states of the region. By 1938 the entire eastern and southern bloc of the continent (with the exception of Czechoslovakia) had authoritarian regimes: from the southern Baltic shoreline, then across the south of the Danish–German border, then east along the borders of the Low Countries, then east and south along the borders of France and Switzerland, running finally into the Atlantic at the Spanish border. This half of Europe was ruled by sixteen authoritarian regimes basing their legitimacy on a supposed ability to mobilise the nation through a para-militarised mass movement and a strong and explicitly militaristic state.

Thus these regimes had retained the neighbourhood militarism of their absolutist ancestors, repressing domestic enemies and deploying for cross-border actions. Yet they were also greatly changed by the upsurge in national mobilisation. The nation-state, that is a nation and a state whose vanguard was a single mass party was now the bearer of a collective moral project, to be imposed on dissidents within and unfriendly neighbours without. This might be termed a *nation-statist militarism.* Of course, these countries and movements combined the nation and the state in variable ways. Fascists stressed the nation more and mobilised a more mass party and mass para-militaries to take over the state. More conservative regimes which centred on monarchies, militaries, churches and dominant classes mobilised less and relied on the state more. But the boundaries between fascists and conservatives became blurred: to seize and hold power fascists needed deals with conservatives, while conservatives generated single mass regime parties and para-militaries in imitation of fascism.

Such movements were popular in the sense that large numbers of peoples were mobilised for marches, violence and atrocities. Just how popular the movements were is hotly debated and sometimes difficult to judge. Thousands would normally risk limb and perhaps life by activism, hundreds of thousands (in the bigger countries) offered more passive and verbal support, millions (in the bigger countries) voted for them. Though the movements all claimed to be truly 'national', their mass base was always more particular. Militants were overwhelmingly young males, so that this seemed both a generational and a masculinist project. Both fascist and non-fascist militant groups bore the marks of the adolescent male gang. 'Male bonding' was important (in the Nazi SA so was homosexuality). Nonetheless – especially where churches offered support – women formed enthusiastic support groups and (where we have information) they voted for fascists just as often as men did (slightly more so in Germany, slightly less so in Austria). In this sense authoritarians offered a reactionary form of patriarchy attractive to many men *and* women. The class base of such authoritarian movements varied: the more conservative ones usually received disproportionate support from upper and middle classes; fascist movements had no single class base (Italian fascism was somewhat bourgeois, German fascism was not significantly related to class, Hungarian and Romanian fascisms were somewhat proletarian). Regions and religions which were considered to be the core of the nation, or with strong historic relations to the state, or threatened by local irredentism, were highly over-represented (like German Protestantism, Spanish Catholicism, or Romanian Orthodoxy; or like Castile, North-Central Italy, and Yugoslav border areas, and Western Transylvania). Even more over-represented were men involved in the military and civil institutions of the state: ex-soldiers (especially ex-front line troops), serving soldiers and civil servants (though often covertly), public sector manual workers, and students and (to a lesser extent) professors and graduates of public universities. There was, unsurprisingly, a 'nation-statist' social base within civil society for 'nation-statist militarism'.[1]

Its ideology stressed the importance of combating enemies. Along with the authoritarian socialism of the inter-war period, it had a highly developed sense of the enemy within. The authoritarian nation-statist movements of all sixteen countries argued that socialists, anarchists, liberals and regional and religious minorities were 'traitors' to the nation since they favoured internationalism and fomented divisive conflict. Leftists were almost always referred to as 'Bolsheviks' (i.e. influenced by foreign ideas), liberals as French- or British-inspired, religious minorities were more obviously foreign-influenced, regionalists more obviously divisive. A 'purer' or more 'integral' nation must be ruled by a more 'organic' state than the corrupt, chaotic liberal democracy composed of warring interests and parties; while corporate structures could transcend class conflict. Order, discipline and hierarchy – obvious military virtues – could eventually remedy this chaos. But, in the short-term, organised violence would be mobilised to defeat present enemies.

Only the Nazis went as far as mass slaughter of those they claimed could not be assimilated into the nation – Jews, Slavs, gypsies, homo-sexuals and the mentally defective (though their wartime collaborators in several countries became equal partners in the slaughter). But apart from their racism Germany and Austria were not unusual. With a few exceptions (perhaps Pilsudski in Poland, Pats in Estonia) authoritarian nation-statists legitimised suppression and selective killing of their domestic opponents by denying them membership in the nation. In the Spanish Civil War, for example, the rightists styled themselves as 'Nationalists'; and their various factions as 'Nationalcatholic', 'National-syndicalist' etc. They killed thousands of Republican prisoners, during and after the war, in the name of 'Spain' against 'anti-Spain' – though Republicans sometimes responded with appeals to 'the people' or 'the popular forces' (Aguilar, 1995; Juliá, 1990). Everywhere mass killings and intimidations were perpetrated by a variety of entwined military and para-military forces. In Germany the early atrocities were almost entirely the responsibility of Nazi para-militaries – though in 1934 Hitler used the army to purge the SA. In Italy some army units were implicated in what was nonetheless essentially a fascist *squadristi* project of destroying the socialist movement. Hungarian and Romanian atrocities were committed (often against each other) by criss-crossing organisations of serving soldiers, veterans and political para-militaries, including fascist ones. In Spain the agencies of rightist repression during the 1920s were both the army and the para-military *sindicatos libres*. The 1936 Spanish insurrection was the work of regular army units, but the worst Nationalist atrocities were later committed by volunteer Carlist and Falange (fascist) units. In Austria the 'Austro-fascists' para-military

Heimwehr operated alongside the regular army in repressing the socialists and the Nazis in 1934; while in 1938 the Austrian Nazis took their revenge on Austro-fascism alongside the German army. In these and other cases militarism was both nationalist – rooted in a civil society movement – and statist – wielded by the state.

There were also foreign enemies. The ideologies claimed national superiority over foreigners. From Aryan supremacy to Italian 'proletarian nationalism' to 'Hungarism' (Magyars being the only nation to blend Asian and European virtues) to *Hispanidad* (Spain's historic world-civilising role), each movement claimed to have a 'mission' to the world and to its region in particular, reducing the sense of a broad 'European' or 'Christian' civilisation. Where Christianity was harnessed to the new ideologies, it became nationalist: Spain was 'the Most Christian Nation', the Romanian Orthodox Church alone could express true 'mysticism of the soul'. The European or Christian bounds of civil society were giving way to national bounds.

State elites appeared more in control of foreign policy. Most diplomatic negotiations were calculated and circumspect – as realists would expect. Not those of Germany or Italy, of course. But most nation-statist regimes went into the Second World War for what they believed was pragmatism (Hitler and Mussolini would win, so join the winning side). Franco and Salazar stayed out altogether, though Franco almost went in. But some of these states' soldiers then behaved with great barbarity against their neighbours. Even in the First World War many *entente* stories of German atrocities against French and Belgian soldiers and civilians had turned out to be true – and were not matched by their constitutional opponents. Germans also behaved ruthlessly in the west towards the French, Belgians, Dutch, Danes and Norwegians in the Second World War.

But the major German Second World War atrocities were directed eastward against Jews and Slavs, when militarism of the neighbourhood became more than nation-statist – it became 'nation-racist'. But, again, the worst atrocities were committed not by the main agencies of the central state, but by an autonomous agency with considerably grassroots support based on a social movement: 'the SS state'. This militarism was not merely the property of a sovereign state; it was also deeply embedded in a section of national civil society.

Jews and gypsies were methodically 'eliminated' by the SS state, probably over 70 per cent of the Jews of the areas involved, perhaps over 80 per cent of gypsies. But the German army on the Eastern Front also let die 58 per cent of its Soviet POWs, whom it considered *Untermenschen*. The Soviets reciprocated in kind: perhaps 36 per cent of

German POWs died in their prison camps (though the Soviets claimed this figure was exaggerated). Only 4 per cent of Germany's Anglo-American prisoners perished, since German racism of the neighbourhood allowed the distant Anglo-Saxons membership in the Aryan race (Bartov, 1985, pp. 153–6). Austrians, Hungarians, Romanians, Russians, Ukrainians and the Baltic nations also transgressed against the Jews – not only in terms of race, but also because Jews were 'internationalists', supposedly fomenting both foreign 'Bolshevism' and big capitalism. Jews were the greatest defilers and traitors of the nation.

Austrians were especially anti-semitic, even occasionally horrifying German SS officers by the spontaneous ferocity of their attacks on the Jews they were escorting to the camps. There were also atrocities committed between the remaining imperial regimes and subordinate minorities and neighbours – Russians versus Poles and Ukrainians, Serbs versus Croats. We might add a non-European case: Japanese authoritarian nation-statism also perpetrated atrocities against its conquered neighbours. In these cases nations were often conceptualised as races.[2] In the most extreme case, Nazi racism against Jews and gypsies, there was an unusual omission from the normal catalogue of atrocities: rape. Nazis feared the pollution that rape would bring. Jewish and gypsy women were gassed, but were far less vulnerable to rape than were the victims of all the other atrocities listed in this essay.

The atrocities of nation-statist militarism have been subsequently considered by the liberal world to be extraordinary, a bizarre blight on European civilisation. Considered merely within the continent of Europe, they were indeed historically unparalleled. Neighbourhood militarism was pushed to its worst excesses as state absolutism turned into authoritarian nation-statism, then national-racism, murdering millions of its own subjects and neighbours. Luckily these nation- and race-states were comprehensively defeated in war and banished from Europe in 1945.[3] In the wake of the collapse of the Soviet Union they stir again in the south-east of the continent.

Modern Western militarism: 2. Civil society militarism

This was in stark contrast to the milder national sentiments found further west. There popular mobilisation deepened representative government into (white) manhood suffrage. The liberal democracies did not glorify state power, order, discipline or hierarchy. Within Europe they also believed diversity, conflict and compromise conferred strength, not weakness. They retained a broader sense of Europe and of

Christianity. Though nationalism grew, it was much milder. Where it proclaimed the superiority of the nation, this was far less racial and usually claimed the nation embodied rather pacific virtues. Dominant classes within liberal regimes found democratic ways of compromising with their domestic opponents, especially proletarian and peasant movements. Apart from scattered 'Red Scares' they did not deny them full membership in the nation. Nor did they start the wars. They stayed neutral or moved reluctantly into them and committed few war time atrocities.[4] Liberal regimes have largely eschewed militarism in their European neighbourhood. Indeed, European Minor Powers without colonies have been almost totally pacific. By the mid-nineteenth century the Nordic countries from Iceland to Sweden,[5] plus Switzerland and Luxemburg, conformed more or less to the liberal pacific stereotype.

However, this does not exhaust the question of their militarism. Within liberalism not the nation and the state but the individual and the civil society have been viewed as the bearers of the moral developmental project. Thus the liberal 'civilizing mission' was decentred and diffuse, rooted equally in a democratic polity, in 'free' economic markets and in the decency of the ordinary Christian. The geographic bounds of liberal 'civil society' remained unclear – as had long been so in Europe – since the polity, the capitalist economy and Christianity all had different boundaries.

The two great representative states, Britain and France, the Minor Powers possessing colonies and the ex-colonies had all inherited militarism of the globe. This was now intensified by social mobilisation of communities based on these competing terrains. Since they were more economically advanced, mobilisation had begun much earlier, in the eighteenth century. The more economically advanced – which were also the more successful colonial-naval imperialists – were the earliest states to be pressured by their subjects towards full representative government and therefore towards a degree of popular nationalism. While France was still a great land power these pressures emerged during the Revolution as a distinctive 'citizen militarism', spread to other combatant democracies in the US Civil War and the two World Wars. This militarism was formidable but, in the twentieth century, proved essentially defensive. This co-existed with – and after 1945 gave way to – 'spectator-sport militarism' in the nation (see Mann, 1987). Here global wars became rather like a football match. The citizens cheer on the sidelines, but their commitment is only skin deep and they are asked for no real sacrifices. Ruling regimes know they have some national support for global militarism, though their diplomacy may be cautious since citizens rarely have the stomach for the real sacrifices a major war would bring. Thus the national militarism of liberal regimes has remained muted – when compared to that exhibited by modern authoritarian regimes.

Yet mobilisation was especially precocious in the colonies, whose citizens enjoyed a real independence from the mother-state, soon converted into political self-rule. They no longer thought of themselves as British; yet to consider themselves as 'American' or 'Australian' was problematic since the indigenous peoples might share that identity and they were enormously different and 'inferior'. The most plausible ideological self-identity (which could cope with the increasing diversity of their origins) was 'European'. But they were also tempted towards other plausible terms. 'Christian' was appropriate, except that the Churches kept on converting the natives. 'White' perhaps did best, since regardless of the real complexity of skin pigmentation the difference between settlers and natives was usually recognisable from sight alone. Later, 'Western' became less a term of strict geography than a cultural statement of similarity between all white peoples. But with the exception of 'Christian', these terms all more or less reinforced each other in a 'continental–civilisational' identity.

As representation was conceded to Europeans in the colonies, their collective sense of their difference from colonial 'natives' intensified. As competition for land grew, so did their racism. This differed from the much later racism appearing within Central Europe, since it was substantially independent from both the nation and the state. It focused not on national but continental–civilisational identity, on a very real power preponderance enjoyed by 'White' Europeans or 'Westerners'. Indeed, the Spanish, Portuguese and British states, as well as their official Churches, behaved with more restraint towards the natives than did the local settlers. Colonial racism was located deep in civil society, amid ordinary Europeans who had secured citizenship and universalism among themselves.

Thus colonial militarism did not occur in single acts of policy centred on state or para-state agencies like the Nazi Holocaust. Not that states remained on the sidelines. The US army was used throughout the nineteenth century in ruthless Indian-clearance projects, while the elimination of native Tasmanians was a planned operation. Several governments also proclaimed the legal doctrine of *terra nullis*. Land occupied by native peoples was declared 'empty', without property or settlement rights, especially if the natives were hunter-gatherers who had not 'improved' the land. But most atrocities were committed in a series of irregular, decentralised waves organised in para-military forms by vigilante or volunteer units of the local population itself, with states turning a blind eye or with its local agents complicit because they too belonged to 'White' civil society. They were also intermingled with the more devastating but usually unintended effects of disease and destruction of the natural habitat. Perhaps those studying these events have used the word 'Holocaust' a little too freely. The word means 'total slaughter' and this was rarely practised by a single organised group at one point in time. On the other hand the Caribs were completely wiped out and most of the other native peoples of the Americas and Australasia were reduced to 10 per cent of their numbers at the first point of contact.[6] Such persistent, organised violence for social purposes eventually petered out – when it had achieved the almost total annihilation of the indigenous peoples. This was horrendous militarism, sufficiently independent of states to be given the label of *civil society militarism*.

Thus the association of liberalism, constitutionalism or democracy with pacifism is a complete and utter fabrication. Here I am not referring to the minor sleights-of-hand of a writer like Doyle in defining terms and choosing periods to exclude the aggression of the first French Republic, the War of 1812 or the American Civil War. Nor am I referring to the great but primarily defensive 'citizen militarism' of democracies engaged in modern mass-mobilisation warfare. Nor am I referring to the excited but shallow 'spectator-sport militarism' of contemporary liberal democracies. Rather I refer to the wilful exclusion of 'civil society militarism', state-supported but not state-led, directed against peoples who were often stateless – though they had political institutions. At this kind of militarism the citizens of liberal regimes were the undisputed world leaders for two centuries.

Indeed, and most disconcertingly, the more domestically liberal the regime, the nastier the record. A regime which does not regard its subjects as equal citizens may be less likely to espouse racism to justify expropriation and violence. And it was European racism that encouraged the worst atrocities. Thus the Spanish and Portuguese colonies saw fewer atrocities than the British, while the democratic American, Canadian, Australian and New Zealand ex-colonies perpetrated more than had their former colonial masters.

This form of militarism was very widely diffused across the settler population. However, just like nation-statist militarism, it presumably had more particular social bases of core support and militancy, just as milder liberal or religious beliefs had their social bases. There were many humanitarian militants in the settler realms, from Las Casas to the abolitionists to white revolutionaries and Communists. Since I am unfamiliar with the literature in this area, I do not know what these rival social bases were. However, one very broad characteristic suggests itself.

As the actual perpetrators of the atrocities were overwhelmingly male, we may be tempted to ascribe to them a 'masculinist' project. Supporting evidence comes from a colonial sexual aggression so ubiquitous, so institutionalised, that it rarely needed violence to enforce. It was also seemingly perpetrated almost entirely by European men against native women. In this volume Cynthia Enloe quotes a casual conversation suggesting how normal this was for Spanish-American men. 'Masculinism' would receive further support if we follow the argument of various historians that in the colonies and in the American South rule in the household, mostly supervised by European women, was more lenient than rule 'in the fields', supervised by men. However, sexual practices apart, and even if few women carried guns, the collective interests of women were as great as were the men's in the settler project, including clearing away the native population. It is also striking that all the earliest cases of female suffrage, those occurring in the late nineteenth century in western states of the US and in New Zealand, were in zones of native clearances. Thus liberal atrocities, except for sexual ones, may not have been essentially masculinist but more broadly diffused.

The record was not as bad in colonies with fewer Europeans. They did not need to grab all native land. Where they employed native labour, they also had an incentive to keep it alive, housed and fed. Thus the colonies which remained under direct British Crown rule into the twentieth century, along with the other European colonies – of France, Belgium, Holland, Denmark, Spain and Portugal – usually had milder regimes. However, they still expropriated productive resources, imposed subsistence wages, sexually molested and responded to resistance with military force. Since their numbers were smaller, their militarism relied more heavily on the state – though private armies, also mentioned by Enloe in Mexico, were an alternative for the richest Europeans. As societies and states they were dual, their duality best typified by what is usually taken to be an extraordinary case, South Africa. Here an impeccably liberal society and democratic state for whites coexisted with authoritarian and militaristic rule over blacks.

For liberal countries there is no single horrific case like the Nazi Holocaust marring a record which would otherwise be merely a normal story of human exploitation. Such was the militarism of absolutism and authoritarianism until the inter-war period. But 'liberal' civil society contained a systemic tendency lasting through the entire modern period towards committing genocide when seeking *Lebensraum* and towards cruel coercion when merely employing labour. These two tendencies have an unmistakable resemblance to those of the SS state.

Conclusion

I have tried to show that the course of peace and war has been decisively influenced in modern times by varying relations between states and societies. This would also be true of other times and places – though these interrelations would take rather different forms. The question of war and peace cannot be understood anywhere in the recent or contemporary world without studying, in addition to states, the overlapping networks of social interaction, the competing approximations to a 'society' offered by nations, continental civilisations, religions and self-styled races.

Both of the two most ferocious kinds of modern militarism – 'nation-statist' and 'civil society' militarism – have been neglected by most IR practitioners and historical sociologists alike. That is because neither militarism was wielded only or (in the latter case) even principally by the state. Military and political power have not been fused in all modern states.

Gentleman scholars of the London and Eastern Establishments can continue to chronicle the exchanges of gentleman diplomats. They can continue aggregating their actions into statistical data-sets. State-centric research can continue in both IR and sociology. Liberals can continue to deplore the atrocities of their historic opponents. But all this would leave out three things. First, it would omit the massive social pressures emanating from competing 'societies' – from the nation and from the European, capitalist, Christian and Western bases of our civilisation. These pressures got larger in modern times with the growth of popular mobilisation projects. Second, it would leave out the popular brutality of both forms of modern militarism these have generated. Third, it would leave out the essential part that two different kinds of racism, 'national' and 'European' or 'Western', have played in modern international relations.

This is the most disturbing omission of all. That the great modern ideologies, of nationalism, of liberalism and – including the Soviet experience – of socialism, should have committed such systematic near-genocidal atrocities exactly as they were achieving their greatest successes seems more than bad luck. Their great mobilising drives, their universalistic and inclusionary drives towards the nation, towards Europeans or towards the proletariat were all associated with the emergence of a great, evil, sub-human Other – traitors to the nation or the class and 'coloured' or 'heathen' peoples. Universalism and comradeship within, militarism and near-genocide without. Is this the essential paradox of Western civilisation? And if a more pacific liberalism may be at last triumphing over the West, is this mainly because it violently defeated its nation-statist and socialist rivals, annihilated its own Other in the settler colonies, and retreated from its own Other in the remaining colonies? I fear the answers are positive. As I remarked at the beginning, sociologists tend to relativism. I have been here driven to reject the benign, liberal view of itself which Western civilisation has enjoyed since at least the Enlightenment. All civilisations juxtapose good and evil, though some, like ours – or like the Aztecs or the Apache – do it more starkly than others.

NOTES

1 Since all movements had their particularities, none of these generalisations apply perfectly right across Europe. There is no up-to-date source synthesising the massive literature on the social correlates of fascism and conservative authoritarianism across the countries of Europe. Linz (1976) gave a sensitive account of material then available; the authors in Mühlberger (1987) produced more variable accounts. On German Nazism, by far the best-researched case, important recent studies are those of Mühlberger (1991) and Falter (1991; his findings have been briefly summarised in English by Hamilton, 1993). All the research will be critically reviewed in vol. III of my *Sources of Social Power*, currently underway.

2 Though never in a totally unqualified way. Thus the Germans were not the only members of the Aryan race, while Koreans and Chinese could – if cleansed of all their native culture – be admitted as equals to the Japanese Empire.

3 I have not discussed the Soviet Union here, though it perhaps offered a leftist version of neighbourhood militarism. Its mass mobilisation was more of class than nation, and so its main atrocities during the 1930s were legitimated in terms of supposed class rather than national treason. During the Second World War national mobilisation modified this somewhat. In my 1987 essay I described the Soviet post-war system as one of 'militarised socialism'.

4 I am excluding from the category of 'atrocity' the callous technocratic military decisions taken by both sides, like mass bombing of civilian areas.

5 Finland remained an exceptional case, still part of the Russian Empire until 1917, then fighting a bloody civil war and a fierce war against neighbouring Russia.

6 The one alleged case which does not bear much close scrutiny is the so-called Afro-American 'Holocaust', the 'total slaughter' of Africans transported to America. Here there was no real European motivation towards 'elimination' – these Africans occupied no desired territory and their labour was too useful to be 'eliminated' – and the allegations of the numbers of deaths seem enormously exaggerated. On the other hand violence against them also tended towards para-military and para-legal forms: the KKK, organised lynchings etc.

REFERENCES

Aguilar, P. (1995), 'Guerra civil (1936–1939) y nacionalismo', in A. de Blas et al. (eds.), Diccionario sobre Nacionalismo (Madrid: Technos).

Anderson, P. (1979), Lineages of the Absolutist State (London: Verso).

Bartov, O. (1985), The Eastern Front, 1941–45. German Troops and the Barbarization of Warfare (London: Macmillan).

Brenner, R. (1987), 'The Agrarian Roots of European Capitalism', in T. Aston and C. Philpin (eds.), The Brenner Debate (Cambridge: Cambridge University Press), pp. 213–327.

Downing, B. (1993), The Military Revolution and Political Change: Origins of Democracy and Autocracy in Early Modern Europe (Princeton, NJ: Princeton University Press).

Doyle, M. (1983), 'Kant, Liberal Legacies and Foreign Affairs', Parts 1 and 2, Philosophy and Public Affairs, Part 1, 12 (3), pp. 205–35, Part 2, 12 (4), pp. 323–53.

Falter, J. (1991), Hitler's Wähler (Munich: Beck).

Hamilton, R. (1993), 'Hitler's Voters', Contemporary Sociology, 22 (4), pp. 543–6.

Juliá, S. (1990), 'Guerra civil como guerra social', in La Iglesia Católica y La Guerra Civil Española (Madrid: Fundación Friedrich Ebert).

Linz, J. (1976), 'Some Notes Toward a Comparative Study of Fascism in Sociological Historical Perspective', in W. Laqueur (ed.), Fascism: A Reader's Guide (Berkeley: University of California Press), pp. 3–121.

Mann, M. (1986), The Sources of Social Power, Vol. i: A History of Power from the Beginning to 1760 AD (Cambridge: Cambridge University Press).

(1987), 'The Roots and Contradictions of Modern Militarism', New Left Review, no. 162, reprinted in Mann, States, War and Capitalism (Oxford: Blackwell, 1988).

(1993), The Sources of Social Power, Vol. ii: The Rise of Classes and Nation-States, 1760–1914 (Cambridge: Cambridge University Press).

Moore, B. Jr. (1969), Social Origins of Dictatorship and Democracy (Harmondsworth: Penguin).

Mühlberger, D. (ed.) (1987), The Social Basis of European Fascist Movements (London: Croom Helm).

(1991), Hitler's Followers (London: Routledge).

Skocpol, T. (1979), States and Social Revolutions (Cambridge: Cambridge University Press).

Tilly, C. (1990), Coercion, Capital and European States, AD 990–1990 (Oxford: Blackwell).

11   The achievements of post-structuralism

Richard Ashley

A single sentence, interjected by a colleague into one of my more rambling attempts to make a point in the course of a discussion a few months back: 'You *boys* in IR,' my colleague exclaimed, arching her eyebrows chidingly upon inflecting the second of these words, 'you boys always talk as if you're out there on the plains somewhere, on horseback, galloping alone.' The comment, accompanied by my colleague's pantomiming of a rider gripping reins and by her own sound effects suggestive of racing hoofbeats, might have been immediately prompted by my own conversational turns. It was clear, though, that she was having her fun, not just with my words, but with the entire field of international relations. My colleague was conveying some sense of amusement at, if not exasperation with, the tendency of conversations among 'the IR boys' to hightail it across the surfaces of historical experience, a stranger to every place, seldom pausing to dismount and explore any locale, eschewing all commitments, always moving as if chasing some fast-retreating end or fleeing just ahead of the grasp of some relentless pursuer.

The very language of 'the IR boys'' conversation, I learned from my colleague, seemed to her to be preoccupied with questions of strategy. Yet it also seemed to her to be especially austere and abstract, as if designed both to dispense with the encumbering weight of historically sedimented meanings and to permit the most rapid redeployment of available terms to new circumstances. Ours, she seemed to be suggesting, might be a strategic language fitted out for the battlefield, but it is precisely not a language that commits us to pitched battles, to trench warfare, indeed, to any sort of strategy in which we might have to depend upon lines of supply linking our endeavours to some fixed historical sources of the powers we would deploy. Ours is a language that enables us to shift and manoeuvre, outflank and charge, turn tail and run, retreat into historical ambiguity, commandeer resources where we find them, shed one uniform and don another, and then return to fight another day – all the while working to create an impression that our forces have always been wholly mobilised, fully armed, ever prepared to advance from anywhere, to seize command at any time.

I do not dispute this appraisal of the way in which we 'IR boys' talk and write (nor am I inclined to quarrel with my colleague's sense that this way of talking is male-marked). At the same time, though, I have to note that this appraisal of the discursive habits of international relations, so enabling of a sort of hypermobility of subject 'positions', seems puzzlingly out of kilter with an at least equally familiar disposition of the 'IR boys': the persistent, almost ritualistic affirmation of the sovereign territoriality of agents of thought and action. If ever there was a field of discourse whose parties' every performance presupposes the necessity of thinking, acting and narrating political life in the service of some sovereign centre of decision that can at once represent and derive its powers from a familiar territory of its exclusionary being, international relations is surely it.

This, to be sure, is not to deny that international relations discourse comes in many varieties, and it is certainly not to neglect the fact that many if not most parties would jealously resist the claim that they, in their work, identify with and ascribe an absolute being to one or another historical instance of the modern sovereign state. The state is a fiction, most would remind us, and many would hasten to add that the question of the problematic constitution of the territorial state is one that they insistently pose.

Still, despite the pluralism of the international relations field, and even regarding those who would want to make a question of every historical rendition of the modern sovereign state, just this can be said: parties to the field know that their every instance of interpretation and conduct will be held to proceed from a standpoint, a position, a subjective perspective that enables them to justify what they say and do, impose interpretive limitations, and then, so limited, decide the meanings of events. Parties know that they will be called upon to show that their practices represent and derive their powers from one or another coherent, bounded paradigm, tradition, model, or community of interpretation that has its own code and categories, that has its recognised loyalists, that can be named, and that can be implicated in the major conflicts of the field, including the spectacular summitry of the field's great debates. Where do you stand? What position do you take? To what side do you belong? What tradition, perspective or community do your labours faithfully represent? These are questions that we ask one another from the first moment of our entry into the field. These are questions, we are given to know from the start, to which we must have our already prepared replies.

How, though, can this be? How can this insistence upon the sovereign, territorial positionality of speaking, writing, and acting be sustained if, as my colleague reminds me, the discourse that would sustain it is always fleeting across the surfaces of life, honouring no boundaries, estranged from every place and position, never quite alighting upon any ground? I shall want to keep this paradox in mind. More than that, I shall want to trace this paradox's long career in international relations, to explore its workings, to consider its effects within and beyond the field. I shall want to contend that just this paradox – so austere, so mobile – is, in itself, the subjective posture at the very centre of the field, the discipline, or, as I shall say, the 'meta-discipline' of International Relations. I shall want to maintain that this paradoxical posture regulates the field's discourse and limits its possibilities, at once inciting its parties to action in reply to problems and channelling the ways in which problems may be understood. But why?

Why busy myself with this paradoxical posture in a paper whose assigned task, after all, is not to assay the field but to consider the accomplishments, if accomplishments there be, of post-structuralist works of thought? My answer requires four premises, several of which advance an interpretation of the circumstances in which I reply to this assignment.

First, this task, though perhaps only recently placed before me, is hardly one that can be taken up afresh, as if a conversation on just this topic were not already well underway. Many, in fact, might say that the conversation on post-structuralist contributions to the field has already been fully played out, already grown stale, already reached a phase in which the parties are content to recite now tired positions or to rehearse long-practised, situationally workable rhetorics.

Second, insofar as the conversation remains interesting, it is primarily in those aspects that have made it their business to interrogate, comment upon, and in some measure judge post-structuralist interventions as instances of theoretical labours that would be critical, that is, as works of thought that would make it possible to question and resist the practices of power by which limits are imposed and prevailing modes of subjectivity, objectivity and conduct are effected in global political life. If I am to be responsive to the conversation already underway, I shall need to intersect it in just this aspect, in the exploration of post-structuralist works as *critical* labours.

Third, even here, in regard to post-structuralist theory as a critical labour of thought, the conversation today approaches an impasse. Those who comment upon post-structuralist interventions more or less regularly recur to a model of critical activity as a kind of standard in terms of which these interventions can be found wanting. Specifically, commentators regularly recur to a model that heralds a subject-in-estrangement – a subject estranged from the familiar subjectivity of an order of domination, a subject whose voice is repressed or silenced by that order, a subject who, thanks to the very fact of its oppression, is positioned to clearly represent that order and its place in relation to it, to decide what must be made of that order and of itself. They invoke this subject-in-estrangement as the heroic figure central to the undertaking, the self-narration, and the regulation of any enterprise that would be authentically critical. Then, speaking as if in defence of one or another variant of such a heroic subject-in-estrangement, critical commentators regard post-structuralist writings as either lacking, for their failure to represent such a decisive figure, or threatening, for their supposed determination to dissolve the grounds upon which any such a figure might undertake critical, emancipatory, transformative action. Thus, post-structuralist interventions are frequently decried as but a canonical series of negations addressed to key elements of a model of critical activity – most especially as a denial of the subject of theory who would also be the subject of emancipatory practice. Thus also, with nearly equal frequency, post-structuralist writings are themselves subjected to a theatre of demystification – a theatre in which these writings are dramatically exposed, for example, as instances of a conservative (or neo-conservative) ideology that would at once universalise and immunise from criticism the political pacification and repression strategies of the late-modern bourgeoisie. Such judgements, which cast post-structuralism as a negativity opposed to the positivity of a critical subject-in-estrangement, are today surely well known. No doubt, many of my colleagues are well-practised in delivering judgements such as these.

Of course, one cannot speak of an impasse simply because such verdicts are now so widely issued. What warrants my mentioning of an impasse is the short-circuiting of conversation upon which such judgements surely depend. For in fact, writings that we might associate with the name post-structuralism have not been posed or offered in the manner of a negativity. They have simply not said no to the model of criticism I have been discussing or to the ideal of a coherent subject-in-estrangement heralded by this model. They have not asserted the untruth of this model. They have not prohibited all enactments of the idealised subject upon which this model turns.

Yes, post-structuralist writings have rigorously explored the dangers, the difficulties, the enclosures of possibility that result when it is maintained that this model, and this alone, can fully capture and express the creative potentials of human activity. Yes, they have explored the practical–critical possibilities exceeding this model's limits. And yes, above all, they have shown, and shown quite unmistakably, that the question of this model's invoking is not one that can be decided yes or no, for or against, once and for all. But to demonstrate the undecidability of this model's claim to sovereignty in thought and action is not to lay down an injunction against its deployment, to decide for one and all that it is outlawed, to say that anywhere and everywhere it is banned. In a word, it is not to propose the model's negation.

To demonstrate the undecidability of sovereignty claims on behalf of this model is instead to show that the imposition of this model or any variant of it is just that, an imposition, an effect, indeed, an effect that might not happen, an effect that is resisted and undone in and through the actions that produce it, an effect that can claim no justification beyond the effect itself. It is to show that such an imposition is in effect of a hazardous, arbitrary play of actions upon actions – actions that are not attributable to any ultimate source; actions that are not directed towards any certain end; actions that do not necessarily obey any mono-logic of necessity; actions that are never finally containable within the limits of the effects they produce; actions, then, whose workings will ever exceed and never finally submit to the supposed power, interpretive code, or determinate logic of whatever figuration of a heroic subjectivity might happen to be imposed here or there. It is to show, in sum, that however inescapable may be one's recurrence to this model whenever one purports to offer a unique, monological representation of life-making and its possibilities, one cannot assume, for this reason alone, that the reality of human struggles to make life go on will finally and necessarily give proof to any rendition of this model, any series of such renditions, any dialectical unfolding of renditions negating their negations. Will this model be put to work? Can it be? Should it be? To these questions there are no timeless, universal, already prepared answers. There is only the reality of actions working upon actions across all those varied localities where people struggle amidst difficulties, dangers and ambiguities to somehow make life go on.

How, then, can I claim justification for my third premise, which speaks of an impasse in the current conversation on post-structuralist interventions? The premise is warranted, I can say, because contemporary commentators on post-structuralist interventions, in order to sustain their judgements to the effect that these interventions amount to works of negation, must somehow refuse to hear and take seriously the better part of post-structuralist writings bearing upon the model they invoke as a standard. They must refuse to understand that these writings, far from pronouncing a stern no to this model, have in fact been content to

exemplify a respect for the contingency, the historicity, the utter para-
doxicality of every attempt to bend actions and events to assertions of its
absolute hegemony.

Fourth, it follows that in performing my assigned task, in taking up the
question of post-structuralist accomplishments, what at first would seem
to be the most likely approach is in fact among the least likely to avoid
this impasse. This 'most likely' approach is to offer a straightforward
inventory of post-structuralist accomplishments or contributions to the
field. Any such inventory would almost certainly include:

- the discovery of the centrality of the problem and paradox of representation to modern political life;
- the posing of questions of the visible and the articulable, vision and
  language;
- the sensitisation of theory to the importance and functions of paradox
  and ambiguity in political life;
- the problematisation of the subject;
- new ways of thinking the questions of agency, power and resistance;
- invitations to radical rethinkings of questions of the political functions
  of knowledge, memory, history;
- novel approaches to relations of time and space, pace and place,
  boundaries and transgressions;
- the introduction of distinctive interpretations of relations between
  parts and wholes, localities and totalities, individualisation and social
  institutionalisation;
- demonstrations of the importance and possibility of taking seriously
  the manifold subaltern voices of modern political life, coupled with
  painstaking attention to the difficulties, dangers, and paradoxes
  involved in any attempt to theorise and speak a radical alterity;
- openings to modalities of excessive politics, never quite containable
  within the institutional categories of the social;
- openings to modalities of the politics of marginal movements, never
  quite graspable according to a logic of state-oriented politics;
- explorations of the dependence of modern statecraft upon practices
  that work to tame resistances, domesticate or exteriorise excess, and
  constitute some semblance of an exclusionary space of subjectivity that
  the state can be claimed to represent;
- interpretations of practices of international organisation and diplomacy, not as a field of action among states regarding happenings
  overflowing or exterior to their boundaries, but as ways of globally
  regimenting the fixing of what will count as exterior dangers, thus
  to enable the conductorless orchestration of practically effective,
  mutually recognisable boundaries beyond which certain activities and

happenings can be excluded without calling into question the supposed simple presence of bounded, representable national communities;

- the implication of constructs of race, gender, ethnicity, nativity, exile, needs, rights, and more in practices of statecraft so interpreted;
- explorations of the complicity of the scholarship in the practices of statecraft;
- explorations of possible (re)articulations of time-honoured constructs such as community, pluralism, democracy, citizenship, civility, ethics, and, one might add, scholarship and the university;
- the innovation and elaboration of deconstructive, genealogical, interpretive-analytic and other 'methods' that, though problematising the very notion of methodology, nevertheless enable an engaged, rigorous, criticism-conscious exploration of events and activities at once imposing and transgressing limits of social possibility;
- experiments with distinctive styles and strategies of reading, of writing, of theoretical practice in general, attentive to their effects;
- demonstrations of the possibilities of modes of research that are transdisciplinary in the real sense that they put the very effecting of disciplinary boundaries in question;
- the exemplification of theoretical postures that, while surely serious, are more experimental, more sensitive to their imbrications in localities of real political struggles, more oriented to the tasks of listening and relaying across localities, more 'dialogical' or even 'heterological' in orientation, and less preoccupied with the *deadly* serious business of differentiating, authenticating, empowering, and deflecting every threat to the institutional figure of the Theorist, secure in his cultural space, powers, and socially-ascribed right to decide what events beneath his gaze must mean.

On this most likely approach, I might take each of these and many other contributions down from the shelf, briefly describe it, and then set it once more among the others, there to await the appreciation of passers-by.

Again, though, this approach would be unlikely to avoid the impasse that troubles me. This is so because this most straightforward of approaches would involve a kind of performance that would actually affirm the adequacy and appropriateness of the model of critical activity that commentators are disposed to invoke in rendering post-structuralist writings as labours of negativity. In particular, it would involve a performance of *attribution* in which a whole series of supposed accomplishments are arrayed, not as interesting activities in themselves, not as activities whose discursive entanglements might be pursued across all manner of boundaries, but as products of a source, an origin, another subjectivity-in-estrangement that can be no less coherent, no less well-bounded, no less self-assured of its simple presence, no less capable of deciding what does and does not belong to it than any other. It would thus presuppose a paradigmatic subjectivity-in-estrangement of the very sort idealised in the model of critical activity I have been taking up, a subjectivity that is simply there, waiting to be named as the wellspring of all the novelties attributed to it. Having engaged in this performance, having framed the conversational stage just so, having enacted this idealisation of subjectivity at its centre, how could I possibly expect that others, joining me in conversation, would not feel warranted in imposing the very model that I might seem to have made my own?

These, in sum, are my premises, which together provide a rendering of my present situation:

1 In taking up my appointed task, in considering post-structuralist interventions in the field, I am entering a conversation already long underway.

2 I am entering a conversation whose most interesting aspect relates to post-structuralist interventions as critical activities; it is in this aspect that I want to intersect the conversation.

3 In just this respect, however, the conversation threatens to move towards an impasse insofar as commentators, relying upon a model of critical activity as a standard, refuse to take seriously those strains of post-structuralist argumentation bearing upon the undecidability of claims to sovereignty on this model's behalf.

4 Under these circumstances, what would seem to be my most likely course, that of conducting a stocktaking of 'poststructuralist accomplishments', holds little promise of avoiding this impasse; as a performance in its own right, it would seem to summon this model of critical activity, inviting the very sort of brutal dismissives to which post-structuralist writings have so often been subjected.

And to these four premises I might add just one more. Under these circumstances, it can make little sense to rehearse all those strains of argument that have explored the limitations of the model of critical activity I have been discussing – this in the hope that I might thereby open up a conversation that seems so disposed to closure. Call them post-structuralist or call them what you will, these, once more, are strains of argument that have rigorously demonstrated how very paradoxical is every attempt to cling fast to this model of criticism in the face of all manner of excessive happenings that transgress or overflow the limits of every rendition of it; how much every such attempt depends upon stratagems for disciplining excess whose arbitrariness, whose violence, is right there on the surface for all to see; how much, therefore, every such attempt must rely upon effecting a blindness to its own stratagems, an amnesia with respect to the violences of its own emergence; and how readily, thanks to all of this, these attempts can be drawn into a complicity (though not a secret complicity) with those very practices that would arrest ambiguity, discipline the proliferation of possibilities, tame resistances, and sustain structures of domination ostensibly opposed.

Anything but unfamiliar, these strains of argument have by now repeatedly appeared, albeit with inflections as varied as the circumstances, in every niche of every discipline of the human sciences, including international relations. Despite their rigour and despite their repetition, however, these strains have evidently given commentators little reason to question their commitment to this model of critical activity in their responses to post-structuralist interventions. To these strains of argument, as I say, commentators have evidently developed effective means of turning a deaf ear. What possible reason is there to think that one more paltry recitation of these arguments on my part, just here, would somehow induce a readiness to hear among those who have repeatedly shown themselves so proficient at doing what it takes not to hear, not to take these strains seriously, not to follow their implications through? I confess that I can summon little optimism in reply.

All in all, these premises sketch out what is, to say the least, a rather complex, difficult situation for anyone who would want to open up a serious conversation bearing upon post-structuralist interventions as critical activities in international relations. Somehow, in order to avoid stumbling into one more instance of the conversational impasse I have been discussing, I must elicit a certain doubt regarding the hegemony of a model of critical activity that heralds a subject-in-estrangement as the necessary, central figure of any labour that would have critical, emancipatory, transformative potentials. So long as this model is hegemonic – so long as my possible partners in conversation are disposed to presume the absoluteness of its power – this impasse is a foregone conclusion. And yet, as I have just said, a repetition of direct, critical arguments regarding the limits of this model is unlikely to elicit this doubt. Sustaining a practised deafness to these strains of argument, my conversational counterparts are likely not only to hold fast to the model, understanding themselves and their critical activities in its terms, but also to wield this model as a standard in terms of which post-structuralist interventions must be understood as works of negativity.

It is in reply to just these difficulties that I return to the paradoxical posture, so characteristic of parties to the discourses of international relations, with which I began: the posture that we may imagine in terms of a figure on horseback who gallops across the plains of global political life, a figure who is a stranger to every place, but a figure who, just the same, seems relentlessly committed in every word and deed to the ideal of a fixed territoriality of being that he may represent as the deep source of his powers, the intimately familiar basis for his every sovereign word. True enough, in gesturing to this figure and in focusing on the place and functions of this paradoxical posture in the field, I may seem at first to be departing from my assigned task. I may even seem to be neglecting the difficulties I have been discussing – the difficulties posed by the hegemony a certain model of critical activity. In fact, however, what I am trying to do is make way for a serious, appreciative consideration of post-structuralist interventions by showing why we might reasonably have our doubts regarding this model of critical activity, especially as it bears upon the conversations of international relations. I am trying to do so, not by rehearsing genealogical or deconstructive analyses of that model's limitations – not, in other words, by way of recitations of strains of argument to which so many have turned a deaf ear – but by making it possible to see how remarkably *misplaced* is this model just here, in the cultural space of international relations.

This model is misplaced, I shall want to say, not because it does not properly belong to the field of international relations, but precisely because, as a model of critical activity that celebrates a subject-in-estrangement, this model affirms a mode of subjectivity that is not at all strange to this field. It clings to a mode of subjectivity that effects no critical distance from this field, whose way of experiencing estrangement is too much at home here. It holds fast to a mode of subjectivity whose dispositions are too readily assimilated to the practices that prevail here, whose orientations are too readily bent to the tasks that the subjects of this cultural space take as their own. The cultural field of international relations, populated by subjects who are disciplined and discipline one another to sustain the paradoxical posture that my colleague so eagerly pantomimed, is already a field of strangers, already a field of subjects-in-estrangement. As such, it is a field of activity in which the model of critical activity I have been discussing simply cannot do what it claims: it cannot effect a critical break from a prevailing subjectivity ever disposed complacently to affirm the self-evidence of its familiar, taken-for-granted existence, and it cannot because the subjectivity that prevails in inter-national relations has already effected this break, has already become a stranger to every interpretation of self and setting, has already constituted for itself a task remarkably similar to the critical theorist's own.

I can imagine that there are those who will find in these suggestions a note of pessimism, a readiness to throw in the towel on behalf of all those movements that would sustain a critical attitude with respect to global political life. Is not estrangement a condition of possibility of critical, emancipatory action? If I am saying that the cultural field of international relations is already a field of strangers, a field already populated by subjects-in-estrangement, am I not suggesting that global political life is somehow and necessarily *immune* to the force of critical thought and action? And am I not thereby urging resignation in the face of all the wounds inflicted here, all the indignities suffered here, all the inequities so regularly generated here, all the ways in which human beings are deprived of capacities to make life go on?

I am, I must say, very tempted to surge forth with answers to these questions. But then, I do not think that I can answer them – not now, not yet. For my replying would presume the possibility of a conversation for which, I believe, I have not yet made way. I need first to move beyond remembrances of a chat with a colleague. I need to consider somewhat more carefully than I have so far a paradoxical posture, an attitude, an orientation towards the problematisation of self and selves in global life. I need to take up the characteristic posture of the subjects of the cultural field of international relations.

The intrinsic nomadism of political thought and practice, the necessary sovereign territoriality of agents of political thought and practice – in the joining of these commitments, it might be held, one encounters a logical lapse of sorts. As I want to suggest, however, this paradox does not amount to an incidental defect or transitory problem that the discourses of international relations might be expected someday to resolve or over- come. In this very paradox, on the contrary, one encounters what is, in fact, the characteristic attitude, style, orientation – let us call it the subjective *posture* – of parties to the field, the conversation, the conver- sational battlefield of international relations. One encounters a posture of *estrangement*: a characteristic attitude towards the event of estrangement, a way of problematising one's self and circumstances in relation to that event, a strategic orientation towards the difficulties and dangers involved in working one's way through it. One encounters a mobile strategic posture that virtually constitutes the field of international relations in all its varieties: its subjects, its objects of thought and conduct, its characteristic modes of practice, and the principal prob- lematic, the problem of sovereignty, to which it recurs. And, it may be pointed out, one encounters a posture that is in fact very old. It is indeed the sort of practical orientation that might have been packed in the saddlebags of that proverbial man on horseback, the itinerate *condottiere* of late Renaissance and Early Modern Europe.

The figure of the itinerate *condottiere* – this figure will in fact be my way of imagining, and configuring important features of, the paradoxical strategic posture that I understand to be constitutive of the field of international relations. The posture and strategic orientation of international relations, I want to say, is the posture and orientation of this uprooted, estranged, nomadic figure, who is never far from engagement in battle but who, in his engagements, is committed to nothing other than an abstract and mobile will to territorialise, to make some sort of sovereign territorialisation of life work, wherever he might be.

The itinerate *condottiere* or, if you will, the IC, is a figure who travels light. Representing no thing and no place, he wears the most austere dress, bears no flag, carries no seal, commands no enduring loyalties, fields only those soldiers whom he is able immediately to reward, and has sure access to no treasury that would enable him reliably to reward them. The IC lives the life of a vagabond, for he is a stranger to every place and faith, knowing that he can never be at home among the people who dwell there, knowing that no place or faith can secure his life and assuredly serve his will, knowing that he is always in jeopardy of being forcefully evicted therefrom. But this nomadic figure is also one who gallops across the surfaces of life in search of some locality, any locality, where a strategic art can be performed; where the hazardous forces in play can be bent to a will; where an intention to territorialise can be made historically effective; where people can be domesticated as faithful subjects who will freely and reliably participate in the empowerment of a territorialising will, at once submitting to the rule of a word and forgetting the ways in which this vagabond and violent political art exceeds the limits of whatever word it enforces; where people can be made often enough to understand these violent excesses as glorious ventures undertaken in the service of their will, their desire to defend themselves and the place they call home; where people can even be made to value these violent excesses as a kind of trial, an ordeal and a test of faith, that defines who they are and gives proof to the IC's claim to rule.

To say the least, this figure of the itinerate *condottiere* is paradoxical. As described, the IC is one who presumes his necessary vagabondage, his own lack of territories of meaning and being that are metaphysically given, that he might call his own, and that might be reliably called upon to lend authority to his actions or to serve his will. The IC presumes the lack of any already accomplished bounding and channelling of the hazardous play of power, any mobilisation and focusing of power so that power might be reliably summonable on his behalf. If, therefore, the IC does not presume his indebtedness to any place or space, neither can he presume that he is already credited with any powers to be wielded as his own. Yet the IC, despite his intrinsic nomadism, despite his utter lack of power, is nevertheless possessed of a will to territorialise, a disposition somehow to discipline and constitute a bounded place that he may claim to represent. Despite his unmistakable sense of his utter lightness, he is disposed to constitute what may be made to work as a reliable source of power, a source of a weighty power that seems always already to be in the service of a word that even now he prepared to project. A disposition to territorialise and concentrate the play of power, making a disciplined territory function as power's necessary source and constituting a sovereign voice of rule whose word alone can represent this territory and determine power's necessary source; yet a disposition that struggles to find its footing in a precarious, unrepresentable extra-territoriality where contingency seems to displace every pronounced necessity and the play of power is dispersed, undisciplined, exceeding and undoing the bounds of every imaginable territorial domain – this is the strange situation. Or, rather, this is the estranged unsituatedness of the itinerate *condottiere* and his will to rule, so oriented to the constitution and empowerment of a familiar situatedness of a sovereign voice of rule.

To speak of the IC, then, is not just to speak of a subjective posture; it is to speak also of a problem or, better, of a characteristic way of problematising self and selves under conditions of estrangement – under conditions where the subject does not relate to self and circumstances in a relation of unquestioning familiarity but, instead, as a task, a project, an effect, or a work of art, if you will, in which one's own participation is required. For the itinerate *condottiere*, I would say, the mode of prob-lematisation is that of sovereignty, a point that needs some elaboration.

To say that the IC is oriented to relate to the reality of estrangement in terms of a problematisation of sovereignty is to say, first of all, that he is not disposed to comprehend his estrangement simply as it is, as the reality of a life in which every attempt to speak is rendered paradoxical, as an opening that enables the traversal of once taken-for-granted institutional limits and the exploration of hitherto closed-off connec-tions. While the IC might be ready to exploit these opportunities, his primary attitude towards the event of estrangement is a negative one. He relates to it as a lack to be feared. And he so relates to it because, even as he is estranged, he holds fast to an ideal, an ideal that he privileges, an ideal that he identifies with and equates with life itself. This is the ideal of a self-identical institutional subject contentedly at home with an institutional order whose limitations are self-evidently given and at one with whatever word of authority is spoken. This is the ideal of inhabiting a securely bounded territory of truth and transparent meaning beyond doubt, a place given as if by some author beyond time, a place where it is possible to appeal to the word in order to decide what things mean and to justify one's self and one's conduct beyond doubt, a place where the unruly can be reliably named and tamed and the person of unquestioning faith in the word can be secure. This is the ideal of being at one with a word that can never lack for power, that can never fail to prevail, because its claims to represent the ultimate source of power can never be doubted.

The IC, while holding fast to this ideal, does not deny the reality of a condition of estrangement, retreating into abstract affirmations of a now rarefied ideal. Instead, and this is the second point, the failure of his reality to make good on the privileged ideal constitutes for him a definite, if abstract, will or desire: a will to compensate for the lack by effecting here or there whatever can be made effectively to *count* as a territory of self-evident being – an already domesticated source of truth and power that excludes all doubt, that his word might be claimed to represent, and that he might claim as his own, his home, his source of powers. It constitutes for him a will to territorialise, a territorialising intentionality, in the making of self and selves.

And yet, and this is the third point, even as the IC works to compensate for the lack, even as he struggles to constitute some substitute conditions in which people will willingly submit to a centre of rule whose word would decide the meaning of things, he is never mesmerised by the works he creates, never trapped within the territories he would inscribe, never given to mistake his renditions for earthly realisations of the ideal. Even from his own most beautiful accomplishments he is estranged, knowing that they can never be more than contingent effects, ever threatening to come undone. One may say, in other words, that the IC conducts himself 'virtu-ally', that is, according to a general ethos or art of life in which one endlessly struggles amidst contingency and chance to somehow make it possible to live an inherently virtuous ideal *in effect*. One may also say that the work he performs, though it be a work of territorialisation, is never fixed to any territory, ever nomadic, ever ready to move on in search, not of a destination, not of an end, but of whatever localities might be made the object of a strategy, an art of life, a way of problematising self and selves.

12   The contributions of feminist theory to international relations

Christine Sylvester

'What big teeth you have.'
'The better to eat you with.'   (from Little Red Riding Hood)

There are many texts encrusted in this simple dialogue, having to do with violence about to happen and the breakdown of security; having to do, as well, with sex, cross-species relations, gender relations, cross-dressing boundary practices, and aesthetics. Perfect for an era of feminist international relations.

Drawn together by the prospect of considering 'our' field at a momentous time – the seventy-fifth anniversary of official recognition, and the near turn of the century to a new millennium – 'we' are suddenly confronted with feminist theoretical international relations. This presence, so pleasing to some and so much the affront to others, would not have been contemplated in such a gathering ten years ago. Earnestly, 'we' would then have dug around realism and its neos and its world systems and its trade relations and would not have sought to understand 'how we think or do not think or avoid thinking about gender' (Flax, 1987, p. 622) when we think about topics near and dear to us. Now the challenge to do so is on, forced to the fore by the only theoretical orientation in international relations that takes gender as its starting point (although not necessarily as its end point) and by a field's rather abysmal record of taking gender seriously on its own.

To think about gender has come to mean thinking more now about women and men in international relations and in the texts that purport to nail it all down. But with feminist theory in our immediate memory banks, we can also study the construction of masculinity and femininity in the field – indeed, the gendering of whole arenas of substantive practice, of entire texts. We can also confidently re-pose the question Simone de Beauvoir (1952, p. xv) raised on the eve of the ladylike 1950s: 'Are there women, really?' That is, we can ask whether 'women', even 'gender' is not a bit hackneyed, a bit too modern for a post-modern era of hyphenated identities and smashed subject statuses. We can advocate. We can equivocate. We can limn. We can flash teeth.

So can the other side. There have been four answers to feminist interventions into the field of International Relations, and they can be summarised by thinking of a bell-shaped curve. At one extreme there are the fanged responses, the tooth-flashing dismissals and refusals of feminist international relations by some scholars, some departments, and some professional journals: the *International Studies Quarterly* is notoriously big-toothed on this issue. Moving closer to the mean, one finds tooth-picking advocates at the ready to tell feminists what we should do for an always already pre-given field of International Relations. Thus, Robert Keohane (1989) admonishes feminists to put our minds to the research agendas at hand, particularly to his agenda of neo-liberal institutionalism. Thomas Biersteker (1989, p. 266) says: 'I would like to contrast a feminist construction of international security with a neo-realist one.' Read: Security is a settled issue; what is your angle on it? Read from Keohane: The field of international relations has established a research agenda; what do you propose to contribute to *it*?

Still near the mean, the third group of respondees equivocates. With-it and politically correct, this group knows it is terribly uncool to not-notice feminism in this day and age. So they shield their teeth and tip their pens to us in lengthy footnotes. But they do not actually use feminist international relations in their analyses (e.g., Vasquez, 1995; Ferguson and Mansbach, 1991). On the other side of the fanged response are those who have developed a bit of a sweet tooth for feminist analysis. These daring souls not only cite feminists in international relations, they incorporate some of our ideas into their work (e.g., Goldstein, 1994; Walker, 1992; Halliday, 1988; George, 1994, 1995; Brown, 1994). Are they turncoats or prophets making straight crooked paths to feminist-inspired IR, to what Emery Roe (1994, p. 100) refers to as a complexity discourse, in which all sides simultaneously limn the 'complex, simple, immediate and mediating?'

'Progress'. But still a long row to hoe. When I speak about feminist international relations in the USA, UK and Australia, the efforts I make to theorise international relations differently can be lost in such 'burning' audience questions as: 'What do you think of Anita Hill (or Margaret Thatcher)?' 'Do you approve of Hillary Clinton?' This line of questioning demonstrates fascination with women who are out of line, out of place, out of their minds. It is also a departure from the usual standards of evidence and analysis in its celebration of outliers, residuals, and cases beyond one or two standard deviations. Transparently dismissive of feminism as a complex specialist field with depth beyond analysis of individual women, it presumes the formulaic and simple. As ignorance bears down, however, circling into lagers and setting teeth and a *trou-de-loup* for feminists, I keep seeing feminism birthed and rebirthed in international relations by the prodigious performance of the masculine.

Feminists theorise

The matter of feminist responses to International Relations is what I really mean to focus on in this chapter. And, like the responses of International Relations to feminism, the matter is decidedly complex.

There is, first, the issue of feminist theory. Judith Butler and Joan Scott (1992, p. xiii) correctly point out that theory is a contested notion among feminists. Perennially we ask:

what qualifies as 'theory'? Who is the author of 'theory'? Is it singular? Is it defined in opposition to something which is atheoretical, pretheoretical, or post-theoretical? What are the implications of using 'theory' for feminist analysis, considering that some of what appears under the sign of 'theory' has marked masculinist and Eurocentric roots? Is 'theory' distinct from politics? Is 'theory' an insidious form of politics?

The iterated questioning reflects concerns to refuse knowledge syndromes that privilege certain people, experiences, and texts while evacuating others from the history of ideas and actions. It reflects angst over a period of theorising in feminism when we replicated these syndromes as we wrote – quite earnestly and with good intentions and some good results – about women's oppression and plausible routes to emancipation: liberal feminism sought to make liberal rights of men applicable to women without querying what the men had built and bequeathed and would still manage for us; Marxist feminism put women in the workplace, where social relations of production would activate a worker consciousness, without dealing with patriarchy in the workplace and women (and men) who, for various reasons, work at home; radical feminism lambasted patriarchy and then reified its notions of women by lumping all such biologically determined people together as keepers of a mysterious submerged wisdom; socialist feminism sought to assault capitalism and patriarchy through progressive cross-cultural alliances; but, as with radical feminism, 'a universal female experience was necessary in order to ground [it]' (J. Grant, 1993, p. 45).

The pitfalls in this type of theorising – Eurocentrism and disregard for countervailing experiences – have led feminist theorists to take a more epistemological turn of late, asking what it means to know, who may know, where knowers are located, and what the differences among them mean for the knowledges that result. We do not want to tyrannise some people while emancipating others. We do not want to notice and announce and analyse some activities relevant to international relations and fail to consider the salience of others. Feminists have long concerned ourselves with the politics of our theories, but now the politics of *theorising* women and men and the locations of gender assume primary importance.

Theorising is a more nebulous activity than theory building exercises aimed at constructing law-like statements or prescribing systems of norms. Nevertheless, feminist theorising has these general signposts: it critically probes social theories for marks of gender that have gone unnoticed, and reveals distortions, biases, exclusions, inequalities, and denied identity politics in such theories; it traces how it has come to be that gendered theories seem neutral and universal and without gender; it transgresses the boundaries of supposedly true theories by posing gender experiences or narratives that counter or deepen our knowledge, or that reveal another side, a different puzzle, perhaps a different story than gender; it looks in 'strange' places for the people, stories, or even data (we are not necessarily anti-empirical) to fill out or rewrite, sometimes with unusual linguistic moves, what we think we know. Such theorising may or may not result in universal statements, may or may not be parsimonious (usually not), and may or may not establish new gender boundaries as it transverses those in existence.

There are many ways to order the results of such theorising. Sandra Harding (1986) talks about empiricism, standpoint, and post-modernism, to which others add post-modern feminism (Sylvester, 1994a; Fraser and Nicholson, 1990; Hirschmann, 1992). Jane Flax (1987) maintains that all feminisms reflect the post-modern tradition of philosophy (or post-positivism, says Peterson (1992a)). Elshtain (1993, pp. 101–2) places feminist and other theories in two categories – 'grand narratives of closure' and 'perspectives that, more modestly and sure-footedly, give us insight, even insistencies robustly defended'. Kathy Ferguson (1993) outlines praxis, cosmic, and linguistic feminisms and the mobile subjectivities that can enable us to be in more than one of them at a time. Catharine MacKinnon (1983) says that feminism is radical . . . period. Chandra Mohanty (1991) thinks that feminism all too often projects white women on to a host of others.

Rather than throw up one's hands at the disorder, feminists increasingly work with the controversies and debates our theorising elicits, embracing tensions and contradictions. Yet, with contestation a hallmark of feminist theorising in general, where is feminist International

Relations located? Having written an overview of feminist contributions to the field (Sylvester, 1992b), I will not repeat all the topics, issues and people of feminist International Relations here. Rather, I want to address these questions along a circuitous route, first following others to lands of personal reminiscence of gender in International Relations and then to moments of everyday and sceptical feminist theorisings about security, anarchy, war and peace and development.

Genealogical beholdings of gender in International Relations

The International Studies Association has initiated a study on the status of women in the field. My contribution consists of interviewing women about their experiences doing or not doing or avoiding International Relations.[1] The ghost behind the story-gathering exercise is not science – someone else will send out a machine-codable questionnaire. Rather, the narratives are vehicles of genealogy and interpretation. They enable us to listen in on discoveries of and responses to gender in international relations, remembering the feminist adage that the so-called personal is a realm of the political. They expose the ways feminist theorising begins to manifest itself and make contributions before we begin to know it as theory. As we traipse through the woods to grandmother's house, though, the reader must bear in mind that none of what follows is necessarily 'true'. Controversies abound and big teeth glimmer on all sides.

Here is what I have heard:

'All of the mentoring in my life has been by men. But I guess that's because there are only men out there. I don't know any senior women in International Relations. I don't know if that's a comment on me, on them, or just on the structure of IR.'

'I was thinking of political actors, and the whole state system and the bi-polar world, and I realised I just didn't fit. And there were no women on the faculty.'

'I've learned to talk over the end of men's sentences, because otherwise you don't get recognised. Some of the difficulty tends to be generational. I think it's just harder because they don't know quite what to make of you, because you really ought to be a secretary probably. But they can't say that anymore. Sexism is more subtle these days than it used to be.'

'I hear from a lot of women the question "Are we the ones doing all the work? And ultimately who will have the power?" '

'The style of argumentation and oral presentation at the conferences is so macho: "I make myself look good by making you look bad." It's not a collective endeavour: "Let's think about this problem." Comments tend to be destructive rather than constructive. I think all of that is gender related.'

'IR has managed to control a lot of women by saying: "First of all the rule is you don't make political statements, and feminism is political." But how silly, given that most IR has such obvious liberal politics.'

Feminist theoretical International Relations does not come out of the air, any more than other theories do, despite conventions of disembodied rationalism which encourage theorists to transcend particularistic experiences. These oral histories are very grounded in material reality. To come to see that a field is not recognising the gender it takes on, to know we avoid the subject of gender when we think about a variety of topics, is to recognise a theoretical vacuum and a politics of exclusion that requires exposure and rectification. Personal experience can tell a mighty story about such realisations, and much writing by feminists in International Relations echoes comments recorded in the ISA study, unabashedly politicising the personal rather than attempting to transcend it. Explicitly drawing attention to the social identity of the investigator, it questions objectivity and challenges the aesthetics of proper scholarship.

I remember plowing through many abstruse exercises. In one whose significance eluded me altogether, the outbreak of the First World War, having been reduced to a finite number of variables, got transformed into a model for computer simulation. Would the 'outcome' be the 'same'? Who cares? I thought – the war's nine million soldiers will stay buried. But evidently I was supposed to marvel at the conclusion that, if the statesmen at the time had the knowledge available to them of what the outcome was going to be, they might have acted differently! (Jean Bethke Elshtain, 1987, p. 89)

Despite the presence of large Asian-American, Chicano, and African-American communities just outside the university gates – in Berkeley and Oakland, in the nearby farming valleys, and across the Bay – the University of California was itself in the mid-1960s a largely white institution. There were few tenure-track women professors (none among the fifty in political science). It was news when the first woman was chosen to be Head Teaching Assistant. *Feminism* was not yet in the Berkeley lexicon, and neither I nor most of my friends noticed that the word *woman* scarcely ever crossed the lips of political science lecturers. What was on our minds was nationalism. (Cynthia Enloe, 1993, p. 228)

My memories from the late 1970s:

We were trained at the graduate level to build on and add to the knowledge established by numerous forefathers. We contributed to theories that, at best, sought to 'link' women-occupied phenomena across levels of analysis instead of questioning why the occlusions and the levels were there. We were party to a professional contract – lucky to be among the chosen for IR – and saw no gender in our studies; rarely did anyone else, except only sometimes in the study of elite attitudes on foreign policy (Holsti and Rosenau, 1981). We controlled for the sex of respondents in certain studies, thinking of 'women' as 'females' and 'men' as 'males', as though biological and social identities were the same thing. Not knowing much feminist theory, we asked whether there was a difference when we controlled for sex that could be explained *post hoc* in terms of the IR theory we were testing. Usually we missed our feminist cues altogether; for instance, there were no females-women in the deliberations constituting the Cuban missile crisis and we did not query the meaning of that glaring social skew for the outcome of the crisis. We trained to be empiricists, not feminist empiricists; or we became traditionalists, not feminist reformulators of tradition. (Sylvester, 1994a, p. 133)

Those experiencing the surreality of academic training learned that there can be meaningful life, insight, and knowledge where there is glaring inability to fit the shoe that appeals to an international relations prince.

I've become too aware now of the ways in which men have used nationalism to silence women, too conscious of how nationalist ideologies, strategies, and structures have served to update and so perpetuate the privileging of masculinity. In recent years I've come to see how nationalism – not inevitably, perhaps, but with notable regularity – can grease the wheels of militarization, a process that ultimately marginalizes women. At the same time . . . critics rarely couple their critiques of nationalism with a call for the dismantling of patriarchy or pay attention to feminist analyses of masculinity inside nationalist movements. (Enloe, 1993, p. 229)

As we contemplate rewriting IR methods, feminists remember that we cannot be banished for our sins. We are, after all, already among the homeless in the field. Our task is to seek out more positions of homelessness as well as to inter-face between the masks all of us wear, thrusting out to crack them (Anzaldua, 1990, pp. xv–xvi) with the unexpected flair that is denied those routinely culled from a herd. (Sylvester, 1994a, p. 139)

Genealogical moments in feminist International Relations reveal the pervasiveness of gender power in a field that denies it has anything whatsoever to do with gender. We can now notice Hedley Bull's (1966, p. 26) 'clever' rejoinder to the scientists of IR, who were beginning to crowd the turf of traditionalism in the 1960s: 'they are committing themselves to a course . . . that keeps them (or would keep them if they really adhered to it) as remote from the substance of international politics as the inmates of a Victorian nunnery were from the study of sex'. What big teeth! Twenty years later, Hidemi Suganami (1989) writes about the domestic analogy in International Relations and we notice that he does not notice the realm of domesticity routinely familiar, through assignment, to many people called women; nor, obviously, does he see its relevance to the usual analogy.

Many such 'indiscretions' in the master texts (and sometimes in alternative texts) are now disallowed from resting content. Those noticing are not Little or Red, nor are they Hooded handmaids. 'Outed' feminist professionals tell tales of International Relations in their own ways. Thus, contribution number one of feminist theorising: Even before feminist International Relations is theorised in earnest, revelations of disciplinary practices that instantiate a politics of gendered knowledge and power surface and survive and begin to alter our perceptions of what the field is up to and how it should be studied. No small achievement.

Trail blazers have been required for further changes to occur. From the ISA study on the status of women:

'When I got my first job at a research university in the northeast [USA], I was the only woman on the political science faculty. Now they have six.'

'As a graduate student, my experience beyond the classroom has been with the International Studies Association, which has been the most beneficial or, at least, the conference that I enjoy the most. There's a really supportive group of women that I've met there. I understand it wasn't always that way.'

'We're lucky here. We have someone who teaches feminist IR. The men in the class are defensive, but then, slowly, the light bulb over their head comes on. This is how it should be in the other classes, but never is. There simply isn't a critical focus in most classes, just a bunch of yeah, yeah for the canon.'

'The first thing that struck me about the ISA was how male it seemed to be. That was before the feminist theory and gender studies section was organised. It was when women had a very marginal place in the organisation. I remember that I gave my first paper as a graduate student and the room was almost completely men. Now I give papers and the audience is women, and women are citing women. Men certainly don't do that.'

Genealogical achievement number two: the cages of professional International Relations rattle, pull apart, and lose some of their wheels as feminist trail blazing roots. Feminist courses pop up in the USA and Australia, perhaps most consistently in the UK (Krause, 1993). Some textbooks now offer feminist theory as the key framework for analysing the field (Tickner, 1992; Peterson and Runyan, 1993; Beckman and D'Amico, 1994). Writers of other texts heed the accomplishments of feminism (R. Pettman, 1992; Rosenau, 1993; Goldstein, 1994; Rourke, 1995). Anthologies appear on gender and/in International Relations (Grant and Newland, 1991; Harris and King, 1989; Peterson, 1992; Zalewski and Parpart, forthcoming), and a range of single-authored treatises poke into the light like fresh spring crops (Mies, 1986; Elshtain,

1987; Enloe, 1989, 1993; Stiehm, 1989; Sylvester, 1994a; Whitworth, 1994). Scholarly collections on subjects other than feminist International Relations now incorporate our chapters (Booth and Smith, 1995; Light and Groom, 1994; Rosow, Inayatullah and Rupert, 1994; Ringrose and Lerner, 1993; Bowker and Brown, 1993; Murphy and Tooze, 1991; Forcey, 1989; Smith, Collins, Hopkins and Muhammed, 1988; Moghadam, 1994; Glenn, Chang and Forcey, 1994; Pirages and Sylvester, 1990). Feminism takes over journal issues (*Millennium*, 1988; *Alternatives*, 1993; *Fletcher Forum*, 1993) and spices up the pages of 'normal' numbers (Cohn, 1987; Jaquette, 1982; Sylvester, 1987, 1994c; Peterson, 1992a; Runyan and Peterson, 1991). A new and enlarged cast of feminists warms the climate of professional meetings. The changes are monumental.

From awareness to theorising

To give the debates in feminism their due, however, I cannot refuse the problems in what I have just implicitly argued. 'Experience,' Joan Scott (1992, p. 37) reminds us, 'is at once always already an interpretation *and* is in need of interpretation.' To draw the conclusion that the experiences of women in international relations have nudged the field in new directions would be to ignore the question of how we should interpret those interpretations against the backdrop of other politics at work in a post-modern, late-modern era. Moreover, a few women I interviewed were perplexed by a study on the status of women in International Relations, claiming not to have noticed themselves as women in the field. Is gender awareness the mark of people who have learned to rehearse an identity that is a social construction without teeth? Does gender awareness (over)politicise minor human differences? Is it 'the discovery of truth (conceived as the reflection of a prediscursive reality)' (Scott, 1992, p. 35), the discovery of a pregiven woman or man? Or does it simply enable 'the substitution of one interpretation for another' (Scott, 1992, p. 35), one set of questions about International Relations for another? How one answers these questions depends on where one perches in feminist theorising.

Several typologies can fit feminist analyses of international relations. I have observed, however, that two major, albeit overlapping, manifestations of feminist theorising perch there, the one removed from the other only, but importantly, in relative emphasis. What I call 'everyday forms of feminist theorising' – pirating James Scott's (1985) notion of everyday forms of resistance and struggle – issue from activities of average people, as interpreted by feminist analysts. This form *outlines* women, power and international politics where this gender triangle was not presumed to exist. It is an alternative form of realism that seeks to get the real right. A second, radically sceptical approach, *inlines* identity in international politics with respect to shapes that surround men and women in theories and in practices, 'leaving behind, in the middle so to speak', shadows of gender and boundaries of gender transgressed.[2]

Everyday forms of feminist theorising and issues of security

Telling tales in the ISA study and reflecting on revelatory moments in one's turn towards feminist analysis can be thought of as writing theory at the cusp of IR and feminism. Ordinary women who leave trails of engagement with the bananas, beaches and bases of international relations also write feminist international relations. These are everyday forms of theorising that recuperate women and their experiences of power and agency from the kitchens of diplomatic services, from marketing logos, secretarial pools, solitary places in graduate schools, and from between-the-lines narratives of disciplinary texts.

Although she does not use the term 'everyday feminist theorising', Enloe is the chief proponent of this approach. She (1989, p. 201) says: 'We don't need to wait for a "feminist Henry Kissinger" before we can start articulating a fresh, more realistic approach to international politics. Every time a woman explains how her government is trying to control her fears, her hopes and her labor such a theory is being made.' The exposure of gender exclusions, controls, and labour for international relations corrects the historical and contemporary record concerning the identity of actors of note for the discipline. It also – and this is terribly important – changes 'our presumptions about just what "international politics" is' (Enloe, 1989, p. 196). In short, it changes the outlines of what we see and how we see.

There is distinctive method to everyday forms of feminist theorising. Elshtain (1987, p. xi) talks about following people and events rather than imposing a pre-formed framework on them. She follows famous and not so famous narrators of war and peace to see where they have gone with issues of gender, interspersing Plato, Aristotle, Hegel, Clausewitz and Augustine with such unheralded experts on the subject as Clausewitz's wife and Jean herself in adolescence. She finds that much of the conventional wisdom, which is subsumed in International Relations discussions, has it that Just Warriors fight and Beautiful Souls 'woman' the homefront. But this truth is given lie by gender-mingled activities and sentiments exhibited by everyday public-sphere combatants and everyday private homefronters, who confuse their places by 'womaning' the front and 'manning' peace (see discussions in Sylvester, 1994c, 1993b, 1993c, 1989).

To follow, we must locate the people of international politics in their places of action, which are apt to be far less heroic and insufficiently abstract to qualify for usual attention in the field. Such places are lower than 'low politics', being households, factories, farms, remote rural areas, and international immigration posts in lesser as well as great power settings. To suggest bringing such people into international relations is earthshaking for a field that admits only official decision-makers, soldiers, statesmen, terrorists, kings, and the occasional 'crazed' religious group to the fold. Yet to follow what people in these very subaltern places relate is easier said than done. A growing literature argues that when we (finally) give marginalised people voice, we really give ourselves microphones through which to broadcast Western subject-centred egoism (Spivak, 1988; Ong, 1988; Mohanty, 1991; Williams and Chrisman, 1993).

Devotees of feminist International Relations have endeavoured, nonetheless, to follow women to their locations of international politics, such as to peace camps in England and the USA, where women chain themselves to base fences, women dance on missile silos, women affix diapers and tea sets to military fences, women willy-nilly jump onto convoy jeeps as they pass by. Here women challenge the usual painted landscapes of realist defence and defy 'the belief, widely held in the United States and throughout the world by men and women, that military and foreign policy are arenas of policy-making least appropriate for women' (Tickner, 1992, p. 3; also see McGlen and Sarkees, 1993). International Relations, meanwhile, does not take any peace camp corner of international relations very seriously. Gaggles of women doing non-violent things. Nothing of substance here.

A close following of Greenham's anti-oxymoronic embrace of the profoundly mundane reveals an international politics that refuses the canons of International Relations knowledge in several overlapping areas. First, there is the refusal to stay out of sight in one's protected place far from anything resembling the international relations of states (tying yellow ribbons around every hometown tree in sight is one thing; putting potatoes up exhaust pipes of military vehicles is out of place). Second, once the camp becomes operational, participants seem disinclined to develop policy strategies that mime 'our' favourite decision-making models in International Relations:

The meeting started out with hard-line opposing views and consensus seemed unlikely. But acting on the suggestion of a participant to break into smaller circles of like opinion, including a middle-ground group, and create a circle within a circle, each group taking its turn, the discussion proceeded. Without fear of judgement now, because speaking with those with whom we felt most at ease – while the others listened in. And so speaking more deeply than before. When we formed one large circle again, the talk was no longer strained . . . And consensus to the astonishment of all, I think, was reached easily. (Linton, 1989, p. 243)

Third, in setting up governanceless communities, the camps illustrate, at least heuristically, the possibility that certain anarchies can cultivate high levels of co-operation without full co-ordination, without concern over freedom of movement or suboptimal outcomes, without satisficing, without relying on hidden hands of the market, international donors or other forms of bureaucratic politics (although there can be 'defections' (Schwartz-Shea and Burrington, 1990)).

Here is an international politics that challenges core concerns of IR – the nature of anarchy and security, the location of the international, approaches to decision making. The key actor of international relations, the state, hounds women's peace camps and issues notices to vacate, in effect, new Common-based 'homes' in international relations for the homeless lives back 'home'. Meanwhile, the state is undertheorised in international relations (Peterson, 1992c; Harrington, 1992). Meanwhile, the usual authorities on the international system do not recognise the anarchy-defying, gender-ruled barricades they erect against 'women' in International Relations (Sylvester, 1994a). They lock themselves into a regime of co-operative autonomy from women, and then fail to include that regime among those deemed relevant to International Relations (Sylvester, 1993a).

But of course. The problem is that none of this is important. Peace camps do not lead us to the edge of war. They do not stockpile weapons and hurtle us into arms races. They do not have significant trade patterns with the world. They do not sit at the UN. They do not matter. Gender regimes do not matter either. The everyday is insignificant – something for women's magazines to chronicle and for daytime television to parody.

But consider Enloe's important (everyday) feminist theorisation of militarisation. Using what are considered unimportant sources, like Rambo films and interviews with US government-sanctioned prostitutes at military bases, as well as the usual 'important' data – the Persian Gulf war – Enloe (1993, p. 253) finds that governments and societies wield a variety of tools to militarise gender so that men will be ready to defend 'the' national interest and women will be readied for deployment as Beautiful Souls:

Today, as yesterday, militarism cannot be perpetuated merely by drawing on raw civilian masculinity; it has always required drill sergeants . . . Militarism couldn't get along with just men's willingness to earn their manhood credentials by soldiering; it required women to accept particular assumptions about mothering, marriage, and unskilled work . . . [as well as] policies to ensure certain sorts of sexual relations: male bonding that stopped short of sexuality; men's sexual liaisons with foreign women that stopped short of the affection that might reduce militarized racism; misogyny that stopped short of a domestic violence that might undermine discipline and morale . . .

She also outlines women's efforts to challenge aspects of militarised international relations, recounting the story, for example, of American women soldiers who reported sexual assaults by fellow soldiers and thereby attempted to outline themselves as warriors rather than as hand-maids to the 'real' soldiers. She finds women organising against their country's pro-US, anti-Communist government, linking it with violence against women:

Many Brazilian women who organized against their country's anti-Communist military government in the 1970s and 1980s came to the conclusion that militarized anti-Communism and domestic violence against women needed to be critiqued in the same breath, for the construction of the worldview that placed danger at its core relied on gendered danger as well. Male bonding among policymakers privy to state secrets, recruiting military 'manpower', and keeping checks on women-led social reform movements – all were part of a web woven to perpetuate the Cold War, each thread of which required women to relate to danger in a markedly different way than was required of men. (Enloe, 1993, p. 16)

From such mundane stories we learn that supports and challenges to *war* – a core concern in International Relations – can be framed in gender terms, and that certain wars-within-wars may maintain the combat readiness of militarised masculinity and femininity.

There are other lessons in the literature. We can see women within state-centric security dilemmas and can ponder the economic, and even environmental, dimensions of such gendered dilemmas (Tickner, 1992). We learn that as women soldiers increase in numbers as resources for the state, other realist states do not notice and, therefore, do not gang up to prevent a power surge, as they might were more men added to conventional forces of a strong state (Sylvester, 1992a). We find that the scope, location and tools of the Cold War become candidates for gender analysis, and that concepts such as 'freedom fighting' and 'space terrorism', already controversial in international relations, need an infusion of controversial gender awareness to 'get real' (Morgan, 1989).

Outlining everyday people in everyday places helps us think of international politics existing in places International Relations by-passes through fealty to the relations of only a few international actors of 'importance' – great (state) powers and their regimes, decision-makers, economic zones. Moreover, it challenges the field to examine untheorised theories submerged by efforts to describe, explain and predict the abstracted phenomenon of the 'out there', to which the theorist is only loosely, if at all, connected. Helen Longino (1993, p. 111) argues that there are 'puzzles introduced by the theory-laden nature of observation and the dependence of evidential relations on background assumptions'. Everyday forms of feminist theorising reveal those puzzles, assumptions and observations while challenging the practices of authority that determine the events to CREON, the CORRELATES to code, the regimes to study.

Very centrally, IR learns from everyday feminist theorising 'how the conduct of international politics has *depended* on men's control of women' (Enloe, 1989, p. 4), on gender mechanisms of power, and on women as unheralded resources for men and their institutions (see Sylvester, 1992a; Tickner, 1992; Mies, 1986). Here, real women and real men turn the levers of international politics while the field of International Relations gathers in planetariums to look for the important actors 'out there'. Because everydayness has been such a neglected focus, we have much to learn, such as about the many women who strolled through the Berlin Wall in November of 1989 and helped change the face of post-Second World War international relations. Xenophobic male 'skinheads' fascinate more than relations-changing womenandchildren (Enloe, 1991) at the walls of international politics. How odd.

Finally, feminist analysts who do everyday feminist theorising send the message that those who do International Relations must take gender seriously as an organising framework of world politics in order to do their work properly (as do Windsor, 1988; Halliday, 1988). They must get over the sense that international relations is exclusively about states, war, trade and official decision-makers, and consider politics unfolding in everyday places and around activities that can have more than everyday consequences. Women are part of the everyday. It is their assigned place. Fixed on the over-stuffed, gout-ridden or bullet splattered grandiose, we merely fool ourselves into thinking that there is no everyday realm to international relations.[3]

Sceptical inlining and the borders of development

Whereas everyday forms of feminist theorising privilege a logic of gender identity that highlights women's experiences as sources of knowledge, inliners ask: Can we know 'women' so easily? Can we be so sure that their experiences are authentic sources of knowledge? What about

268   *Christine Sylvester*

borderlands of experience and knowledge? What about hyphenated lives that turn 'women' and 'men' into shadowy moments of identity, none of which can be outlined in black? We are talking about a shift in aesthetics from the realist landscape that plants women where we did not see them before to a pointillist style of fixed perspective refused, paint all tangled up and jumbled, shapes changing depending on where one stands to view them.

Kathy Ferguson (1993, p. 322) writes about the 'important tension within feminist theory . . . between articulating women's voice and deconstructing gender'. 'Woman' trips so easily off the tongue because we think we know women when we see them: Enloe (1989, 1993) sights women everywhere in international politics; Tickner (1992, p. xi) speaks of women students thinking International Relations is not 'their subject'; Jane Jaquette (1982) reviews women and modernisation. But do we know women? Judith Butler (1990, 1993) talks about the performativity of sex and gender. Monique Wittig (1989) questions whether lesbians can be thought of as 'women' given the conventions of a conventional term. Queer theory has us thinking about borderlands of sexuality and even about homosexuality as a vampiric subversion of all categories reproducing sex/gender (Case, 1991). If we cannot always be certain that we are sighting a women when we sight someone who looks like (our notions of) one, how can we outline her so confidently?

Everyday feminist theorisers say women are a real absence in International Relations. Some outliners bear down heavily on identity by positing a special knowledge of peace immanent in women's bodies and/or in their usual activities of caretaking (Caldicott, 1984; Ruddick, 1983; Reardon, 1985; Brock-Utne, 1985; overview in Forcey, 1994). This supposedly demarcating experience forecloses mediations on 'women' involving factors of race, class, generation, age, sexual style, and other locational and situational identities. It assumes that 'a' meaning of 'women' is already present and ready to be exhumed, recorded, counted and correlated. When not essentialist and ethnocentric, it can reify, and simply turn topsy, the patriarchal assignments bestowed on us. It can bundle women into one monolithic (usually 'White') group that carries its social mores wherever it goes. It can parody positivist dichotomies even as it seriously critiques ways of knowing that shut out alternatives.

An inliner query: Who engages in decision-making at women's peace camps? Who are the Brazilian women of whom Enloe speaks? How is the agency of subjects, their lines, 'created through situations and statuses conferred on them' (Scott, 1992, p. 34)? Gender is not always something obvious, universal, and readily delimited from other political and cultural subject statuses. Nor is it easy to say which of many identities determines one's behaviour. After all: 'What qualifies as "reality," "experience" and "agency . . . " and indeed, of "politics" ' (Butler and Scott, 1992, p. xiv)?

Because feminist inlining has difficulty with the boundaries drawn by outlines, their analyses often embrace the contradictions and multiplicities and shadows around them. Linda Rennie Forcey (1994, p. 372), for example, refuses the lines feminist typologies typically draw between standpoint and post-modernist epistemologies. She says: '[f]eminist peace researchers . . . must be both radical doubters *and* believers'. By this, she means that

the argument that women, because their nurturing capacities, are essentially different from, and perhaps on some levels better at peacemaking than, men should be neither dismissed out of hand nor embraced as the *truth*. Rather . . . a more complex picture . . . sees the essentialists and their poststructural critics as part of the whole picture – part of the changing social construction of gender.

Peterson (1992a, p. 197), speaking more generally, tells us that feminism is always about transdisciplinary orientations: 'Less bounded by any narrow disciplinary lens, feminists examine insights from diverse locations, situate them in larger transdisciplinary contexts, and weave new understandings out of these multiple threads.' Not surprisingly, I find the inlines of a transdisciplinary International Relations – a more complex picture – etched in the ISA study on the status of women:

'There has been a disincentive for a person to be an area specialist. I think IR would be greatly improved if everyone in it had some kind of grounding in one particular part of the world besides the United States.'

'Before I entered a doctoral program in IR, I had assumed that it was an interdisciplinary field, and that was part of its attraction to me, having spent a lot of time in various countries, and having a broad background disciplinarily, I was interested in continuing that breadth. And so it's been some disappointment for me to discover the narrowness of the discipline and its failure to be either aware of or appreciative of interdisciplinary scholarship.'

'The last thing I would do as a feminist is look a woman of color in the eye and tell her that that's not my problem in the way that IR tells feminists that gender is not its problem.'

Implicit in these comments is an admonition to International Relations: develop boundary capacities, interdisciplinary potential, and intermethodological skills. That is, instead of developing everyone and everything 'out there', develop insight 'in here'.

Develop. Marianne Marchand (1994, p. 127) argues that '[v]ery few new ideas about "development" have emerged during the last ten years'. We are stuck, it seems, with dependency theory and neo-conservative economic experiments of the modernisation mode. At the same time, she says, 'the meaning of *development* is now more than ever at issue . . . [in no small measure because] the boundaries between "domestic" and "foreign" have become blurred' (pp. 128–9). Even as we in International Relations learn about a capitalist order of hierarchically arranged economic zones, which is fuelled by the circulation of commodities and enforced by statist military power, we also learn that it is alive with racist and sexist logics that roost in local places (Smith, Collins, Hopkins and Muhammed, 1988). Maria Mies (1986) finds that the consumer-housewife, working in micro-locales around the world system, is the optimal labour force for capital everywhere. Meanwhile, 'women' subjected to the swirling wake of anti-Keynesian development theories (Marchand, 1994) need less and not more integration (Rathgeber, 1990; Mbilinyi, 1992).

What we need is to develop the capacity to see and theorise the domestic-international shadowlands around us. US border dwellers, like Chicana feminist Gloria Anzaldua (1987, p. 87), tell us that 'Chicago, *indio*, American Indian, *mojado*, *mexicano*, immigrant Latino, Anglo in power, working class Anglo, Black, Asian – our psyches resemble the bordertowns and are populated by the same people.' Norma Alarcon (1990, p. 364) argues that borderland dwellers live 'in multiple registers of existence'. Rudo Gaidzanwa (1993) tells of average Zimbabwean women who regularly cross back and forth into South Africa and Botswana and into and out of an import–export world of business, as they become itinerant traders who confound geospatial, gender, class, and occupational lines. Maria Nzomo (1993) writes about Kenyan women who travelled, in effect, to the international spotlight when they held a hunger strike in 1992 for the release of political prisoners held by the Moi government. Marjorie Mbilinyi (1992, pp. 47–8) writes disapprovingly about the ways that Western liberal approaches to development nestle into African donor consciousness: 'WID [women and development] is no longer a "Western" or "European"/"White" phenomenon; most WID experts in Africa are indigenous women, although "Northern"-based women still monopolise the greater share of global funding and resources such as publications and consultancy work' (also Parpart, 1993; Goetz, 1991). I write about women's co-operatives in Zimbabwe becoming entangled in identity-shifting negotiations with international donors: people who have no canonical right to narrate issues of international co-operation do so anyway and funds are dispensed to 'co-operatives' that would be 'families' (Sylvester, 1994a, 1994b).

In not outlining a traditional set of geospatial puzzles for analysis, these feminists, and others who write on borderlands in the Middle East (Sharoni, 1993), the 'new' Germany (Fischer and Munske, 1993;

Fiedler, 1993), Australia (J. Pettman, 1992), and about inter- and transnational organisations (Whitworth, 1994), serve notice that *their* sense of relations international is not what *our* international relations studies. Insubordinately, these feminists refuse to save, caretake, or even, in many cases, to address a boundary-forcing field in a direct way. Their theory is the practice of ignoring irrelevant lines and the 'arrogant perception' (Gunning, 1991–2; Frye, 1983) that sees the lines and marks their edges with heavy ink.

Insubordinate border dwellers dwell in methods and spaces that Maria Lugones (1990) has termed 'world-travelling'. They find it productive, substantively and intellectually, to be 'in different "worlds" and ourselves in them' (Lugones, 1990, p. 396). That is, instead of sighting one path to grandmother's house, they see via their travels that the 'house' is plural instead of singular and that the paths to 'it' are multiple – to say nothing of grandmothers as multi-identified, unfixed moments of identity. They find their subjectivities shifting and hyphenating with the worlds they encounter in a multi-cultural world, until inconsistencies, contradictions and incommensurabilities elude assimilation.

World-travelling feminisms develop from emulating the challenge of being many things at once in many places that international relations, trying to colour within the lines, does not see. Through empathetically co-operative world-travelling, we become subjects moving in, through and around subject statuses of self and other. 'We' develop ourselves, our research skills, our capacities to see with less arrogance, by negotiating knowledge at and across experiences, theories, locations, and worlds of insight and relationships (Sylvester, 1995, 1994c, 1994a, 1993b, 1993c).

To be sure, sceptical inlining draws on substantive everydayness as a time and site of knowledge, much as does everyday feminist theorising. It understands experience, however, as mobile, indeterminate, hyphenated, homeless, and, through negotiation and mediation, homesteading of steadfast, rigid lines between 'us' – the ones to study in international relations – and the rest. It challenges the field to develop sufficiently to see the spectrum of developments in places once ignored – to join the world and its relations on a 'ground that belongs to no one, not even the creator' (Trinh, 1990, p. 374).

There is no Eureka at the end . . .

At the end of the day, Eureka! is not in sight. I cannot solve the question of feminist theoretical contributions to International Relations, cannot say who has the teeth now in the field. Our enterprises of theorising go beyond International Relations as presently constituted, correcting a field whose subject matter is the absence of that which its title advertises – neither very worldly in its sense of the international nor very attuned to the range of relations that are often involuntary connections of identities and locales.

The point is not to wrestle a fortress ignominiously to the ground. After all, wolves can be cross-dressed as grandmothers. The point is to take on everyday people and their international politics, and sceptics who hole-up in a nearly peopleless (though not genderless) International Relations, as partners in a 'political conversation oriented towards diversity and the common, towards world rather than self' (W. Brown, 1991, p. 81). As we move toward situations that do not toothfully devour some for the supposed good of all, we remember that something called Little Red Riding Hood, rescued from the belly of the beast, lives on in the end.

NOTES

Thanks to the editors of this volume, colleagues at the Aberystwyth conference, and friends at The Australian National University and the universities of Sydney, Darwin, and Adelaide for comments on this paper.

1 The Status of Women study is a three-year, four-part exploration of the locations and experiences of women in academic International Relations and in the International Studies Association (ISA). I am the chair of that study and am responsible for collecting narratives from women professionals about the history of their involvements in the field, including experiences that affected them particularly negatively or positively. As of the summer of 1994, I have taped fifteen long interviews with women of all ranks and a variety of institutional and geographical locations in the field. The study will culminate in a report to the membership of the ISA in 1996–7.

I have no personal reminiscences of men in IR at my disposal to offer as a counterweight. But all of us have the many, many texts of IR men to pore over. The canon, debated and also insouciantly rehearsed, lies before all of us as a collection by knowers who usually refrain from discussing how being mostly 'white professional men' may affect what one writes about International Relations, and the ways non-men and non-whites socialise into 'the' field.

2 Emery Roe (1994, p. 96) summarises Fred Riggs's concept of outlining and inlining using the metaphor of a ship: 'Say I have before me a sketch of a ship. The ship could be outlined as well as inlined. In the former, the shape was drawn as a ship; in the latter, a number of surrounding shapes were drawn leaving behind, in the middle so to speak, the shape of a ship.'

3 James Rosenau (1990) talks about everyday people and their skills for influencing the world. He is not attentive, however, to the gender dimensions of this issue and does not tell us how much the skills of certain types of people (men) have increased relative to other types of people (women), or how sovereignty-free regimes may sovereignly render women and their well-known skills invisible, to international politics. Thus, for example, secretaries in the

UN never get promoted into the practice or the theories of international relations, even though their skills keep the organisation going. We must ask what types of skills qualify as salient skills and which ones we keep overlooking (Sylvester, 1994a, 1992a).

REFERENCES

Alarcon, Norma (1990), 'The Theoretical Subject(s) of *This Bridge Called My Back* and Anglo-American Feminism', in Gloria Anzaldua (ed.), *Making Face, Making Soul – Haciendo Caras: Creative and Critical Perspectives by Women of Color* (San Francisco: Aunt Lute), pp. 356–69.

Alternatives (1993), Christine Sylvester (ed.). Special issue, 18 (1): 'Feminists Write International Relations'.

Anzaldua, Gloria (1987), *Borderlands/La Frontera* (San Francisco: Spinsters/Aunt Lute).

(1990), 'Haciendo Caras, una entrada', in Gloria Anzaldua (ed.), *Making Face, Making Soul – Haciendo Caras: Creative Perspectives by Women of Color* (San Francisco: Aunt Lute), pp. xx–xxviii.

Beckman, Peter and Francine, D'Amico (eds.) (1994), *Women, Gender and World Politics: Perspectives, Policies and Prospects* (Westport, CT: Resgin and Garvey).

Biersteker, Thomas (1989), 'Critical Reflections on Post-Positivism in International Relations', *International Studies Quarterly*, 33 (3), pp. 263–8.

Booth, Ken and Smith, Steve (eds.) 1995, *International Relations Theory Today* (University Park, PA: University of Pennsylvania Press).

Bowker, M. and Brown, R. (ed.) (1993), *From Cold War to Collapse: Theory and World Politics in the 1980s* (Cambridge: Cambridge University Press).

Brock-Utne, Birgit (1985), *Educating for Peace: A Feminist Perspective* (New York: Pergamon Press).

Brown, Chris (1994), 'Turtles All The Way Down: Anti-Foundationalism, Critical Theory and International Relations', *Millennium*, 23(2), pp. 213–35.

Brown, Wendy (1991), 'Feminist Hesitations, Postmodern Exposures', *Differences*, 3 (1), pp. 63–84.

Bull, Hedley (1966 [1969]), 'International Theory: The Case for a Classical Approach', in Klaus Knorr and James Rosenau (eds.), *Contending Approaches to International Politics* (Princeton: Princeton University Press), pp. 20–38.

Butler, Judith (1990), *Gender Trouble: Feminism and the Subversion of Identity* (New York: Routledge).

(1993), *Bodies That Matter: On the Discursive Limits of 'Sex'* (New York: Routledge).

Butler, Judith and Scott, Joan W. (eds.) (1992), *Feminists Theorize the Political* (New York: Routledge).

Caldicott, Helen (1984), *Missile Envy: The Arms Race and Nuclear War* (New York: William Morrow).

Case, Sue-Ellen (1991), 'Tracking the Vampire', *Differences*, 3 (2), pp. 1–20.

Cohn, Carol (1987), 'Sex and Death in the Rational World of Defense Intellectuals', *Signs*, 14 (4), pp. 687–718.

de Beauvoir, Simone (1952), *The Second Sex*, trans. H. M. Parshley (New York: Vintage Books).

Elshtain, Jean Bethke (1987), *Women and War* (New York: Basic Books).

(1993), 'Bringing It All Back Home, Again', in James Rosenau (ed.), *Global Voices: Dialogues in International Relations* (Boulder: Westview), pp. 97–116.

Enloe, Cynthia (1989), *Bananas, Bases, and Beaches: Making Feminist Sense of International Relations* (London: Pandora).

(1991), 'Womenandchildren: Making Feminist Sense of the Persian Gulf Crisis', *Village Voice*, 25 Sept. 1990.

(1993), *The Morning After: Sexual Politics in the Post-Cold War Era* (New York: Routledge).

Ferguson, Kathy (1993), *The Man Question: Visions of Subjectivity in Feminist Theory* (Berkeley: University of California Press).

Ferguson, Yale and Mansbach, Richard (1991), 'Between Celebration and Despair: Constructive Suggestions for Future International Theory', *International Studies Quarterly*, 35 (4), pp. 363–86.

Fiedler, Soja (1993), 'And the Walls Come Tumbling Down? A Feminist View from East Berlin', *Alternatives*, 18 (1), pp. 97–108.

Fischer, Martina and Munske, Barbara (1993), 'Women and the German Merger: Views from West Berlin', *Alternatives*, 18 (1), pp. 75–96.

Flax, Jane (1987), 'Postmodernism and Gender Relations in Feminist Theory', *Signs*, 12 (4), pp. 621–43.

Fletcher Forum of World Affairs (1993), Kimberly Silver and Eric Giordano (eds.), Special issue, 17 (2): 'Gender in International Relations'.

Forcey, Linda Rennie (1989), *Peace: Meanings, Politics, Strategies* (New York: Praeger).

(1994), 'Feminist Perspectives on Mothering and Peace', in Evelyn Nakano Glenn, Grace Chang and Linda Rennie Forcey (eds.), *Mothering: Ideology, Experience, and Agency* (New York: Routledge).

Fraser, Nancy and Nicholson, Linda (eds.) (1990), *Feminism/Postmodernism* (New York: Routledge).

Frye, Marilyn (1983), 'In and Out of Harm's Way', in Marilyn Frye (ed.), *The Politics of Reality: Essays in Feminist Theory* (Trumansburg, NY: Crossing Press), pp. 52–83.

Gaidzanwa, Rudo (1993), 'Citizenship, Nationality, Gender, and Class in Southern Africa', *Alternatives*, 18 (1), pp. 39–59.

George, Jim (1994), *Discourses of Global Politics: A Critical (Re)Introduction to International Relations* (Boulder: Lynne Rienner).

(1995), 'Realist "Ethics", International Relations and Post-modernist Thinking beyond the Egoism – Anarchy Thematic', *Millennium*, 24(2), pp. 195–213.

Glenn, Evelyn Nakano, Chang, Grace and Forcey, Linda Rennie (eds.) (1994), *Mothering, Ideology, Experience, and Agency* (New York: Routledge).

Goetz, Ann Marie (1991), 'Feminism and the Claim to Know: Contradictions in Feminist Approaches to Women in Development', in Rebecca Grant and

Kathleen Newland (eds.), *Gender and International Relations* (Bloomington: Indiana University Press), pp. 133–57.

Goldstein, Joshua (1994), *International Relations* (New York: Harper Collins).

Grant, Judith (1993), *Fundamental Feminism: Contesting the Core Concepts of Feminist Theory* (New York: Routledge).

Grant, Rebecca and Newland, Kathleen (1991), *Gender and International Relations* (Bloomington: Indiana University Press).

Gunning, Isabella (1991–2), 'Arrogant Perception, World-Travelling and Multicultural Feminism: The Case of Female Genital Surgeries', *Columbia Human Rights Law Review*, 23 (2), pp. 189–248.

Halliday, Fred (1988), 'Hidden from International Relations: Women and the International Arena', *Millennium*, 17 (3), pp. 419–28.

Harding, Sandra (1986), *The Science Question in Feminism* (Ithaca: Cornell University Press).

Harrington, Mona (1992), 'What Exactly is Wrong with the Liberal State as an Agent of Change?', in V. Spike Peterson (ed.), *Gendered States: Feminist (Re)Visions of International Relations Theory* (Boulder: Lynne Rienner), pp. 65–82.

Harris, Adrienne and King, Ynestra (eds.) (1989), *Rocking the Ship of State: Toward a Feminist Peace Politics* (Boulder: Westview).

Hirschmann, Nancy (1992), *Rethinking Obligation: A Feminist Method for Political Theory* (Ithaca: Cornell University Press).

Holsti, Ole and Rosenau, James (1981), 'The Foreign Policy Beliefs of Women in Leadership Positions', *Journal of Politics*, 43 (May), pp. 326–47.

Jaquette, Jane (1982), 'Women and Modernization: A Decade of Feminist Criticism', *World Politics*, 34 (January), pp. 267–84.

Keohane, Robert (1989), 'International Relations Theory: Contributions of a Feminist Standpoint', *Millennium*, 18 (2), pp. 245–54.

Krause, Jill (1993), *Gender and International Relations: A Survey of Teaching and Research in the UK*. Occasional Paper in Politics and International Relations (Nottingham: The Nottingham Trent University).

Light, M. and Groom, J. (eds.) (1994), *Contemporary International Relations: A Survey of Theory* (London: Frances Pinter).

Linton, Rhoda (1989), 'Seneca Women's Peace Camp: Shapes of Things to Come', in Adrienne Harris and Ynestra Kind (eds.), *Rocking the Ship of State: Toward a Feminist Peace Politics* (Boulder: Westview), pp. 239–62.

Longino, Helen (1993), 'Subjects, Power and Knowledge: Description and Prescription in Feminist Philosophies of Science', in Linda Alcoff and Elizabeth Potter (eds.), *Feminist Epistemologies* (New York: Routledge), pp. 101–20.

Lugones, Maria (1990), '"Playfulness," "World-Travelling," and Loving Perception', in Gloria Anzaldua (ed.), *Making Face, Making Soul – Haciendo Caras: Creative and Critical Perspectives by Women of Color* (San Francisco: Aunt Lute), pp. 390–402.

MacKinnon, Catherine (1983), 'Feminism, Marxism, Method, and the State: Toward Feminist Jurisprudence', *Signs*, 14 (5), in Katharine Bartlett and Roseanne Kennedy (eds.), *Feminist Legal Theory: Readings in Law and Gender* (Boulder: Westview), pp. 181–200.

276   *Christine Sylvester*

Marchand, Marianne (1994), 'Latin American Voices of Resistance: Women's Movements and Development Debates', in Stephen Rosow, Naeem Inayatullah and Mark Rupert (eds.), *The Global Economy as Political Space* (Boulder: Lynne Rienner), pp. 127–46.

Mbilinyi, Marjorie (1992), 'Research Methodologies in Gender Issues', in Ruth Meena (ed.), *Gender in Southern Africa: Conceptual and Theoretical Issues* (Harare: SAPES Books), pp. 31–70.

McGlen, Nancy and Sarkees Meredith (1993), *Women in Foreign Policy: The Insiders* (New York: Routledge).

Mies, Maria (1986), *Patriarchy and Accumulation on a World Scale: Women in the International Division of Labour* (London: Zed).

Millennium (1988), Rebecca Grant and David Long (eds.). Special issue, 17 (3): 'Women and International Relations'.

Moghadam, Valentine (1994), *Identity Politics and Women: Cultural Reassertions and Feminisms in International Perspective* (Boulder: Westview).

Mohanty, Chandra (1991), 'Cartographies of Struggle: Third World Women and the Politics of Feminism', in Chandra Mohanty, Ann Russo and Lourdes Torres (eds.), *Third World Women and the Politics of Feminism* (Bloomington: Indiana University Press), pp. 1–47.

Morgan, Robin (1989), *The Demon Lover: On the Sexuality of Terrorism* (London: Methuen).

Murphy, Craig and Tooze, Roger (eds.) (1991), *The New International Political Economy* (Boulder: Lynne Rienner).

Nzomo, Maria (1993), 'The Gender Dimension of Democratization in Kenya: Some International Linkages', *Alternatives*, 18 (1), pp. 61–73.

Ong, Aihwa (1988), 'Colonialism and Modernity: Feminist Representations of Women in Non-Western Societies', *Inscriptions*, 3/4 (October), pp. 79–93.

Parpart, Jane (1993), 'Who is the "Other"? A Postmodern Feminist Critique of Women and Development Theory and Practice', *Development and Change*, 24, pp. 439–64.

Peterson, V. Spike (1992a), 'Transgressing Boundaries: Theories of Knowledge, Gender and International Relations', *Millennium*, 21 (2), pp. 183–206.

(ed.) (1992b), *Gendered States: Feminist (Re)Visions of International Relations Theory* (Boulder: Lynne Rienner).

(1992c), 'Security and Sovereign States: What is at Stake in Taking Feminism Seriously?', in V. Spike Peterson (ed.), *Gendered States: Feminist (Re)Visions of International Relations Theory* (Boulder: Lynne Rienner), pp. 31–64.

Peterson, V. Spike and Runyan, Ann Sisson (1993), *Global Gender Issues* (Boulder: Westview).

Pettman, Jan (1992), *Living in the Margins: Racism, Sexism and Feminism in Australia* (Sydney: Allen and Unwin).

Pettman, Ralph (1991), *International Politics: Balance of Power, Balance of Productivity, Balance of Ideologies* (Boulder: Lynne Rienner).

Pirages, Dennis and Sylvester, Christine (eds.) (1990), *Transformations in the World Political Economy* (London: Macmillan).

Rathgeber, Eva (1990), 'WID, WAD, GAD: Trends in Research and Practice', *Journal of Developing Areas*, 24, pp. 489–502.

Reardon, Betty (1985), *Sex and the War System* (New York: Teacher's College, Columbia University).

Ringrose, Marjorie and Lerner, Adam (eds.) (1993), *Reimagining the Nation* (London: Open University Press).

Roe, Emery (1994), 'Against Power: For the Politics of Complexity', *Transition*, 62, pp. 90–104.

Rosenau, James (1900), *Turbulence in World Politics: A Theory of Change and Continuity* (Princeton: Princeton University Press).

Rosenau, James (ed.) (1993), *Global Voices: Dialogues in International Relations* (Boulder: Westview).

Rosow, Stephen, Inayatullah, Naeem and Rupert, Mark (eds.) (1994), *The Global Economy as Political Space* (Boulder: Lynne Rienner).

Rourke, John (1995), *International Politics on the World Stage*, 5th edn., (Guildford, CT: Pushkin Publishing Group).

Ruddick, Sara (1983), 'Pacifying the Forces: Drafting Women in the Interests of Peace', *Signs*, 8 (3), pp. 471–89.

Runyan, Anne Sisson and Peterson, V. Spike (1991), 'The Radical Future of Realism: Feminist Subversions of IR Theory', *Alternatives*, 16, pp. 67–106.

Schwartz-Shea, Peregrine and Burrington, Debra (1990), 'Free Riding, Alternative Organization, and Cultural Feminism: The Case of Seneca Women's Peace Camp', *Women and Politics*, 10, pp. 1–37.

Scott, James C. (1985), *Weapons of the Weak: Everyday Forms of Peasant Resistance* (New Haven: Yale University Press).

Scott, Joan (1992), 'Experience', in Judith Butler and Joan Scott (eds.), *Feminists Theorize the Political* (New York: Routledge), pp. 22–40.

Sharoni, Simona (1993), 'Middle East Politics Through Feminist Lenses: Toward Theorizing International Relations from Women's Struggles', *Alternatives*, 18 (1), pp. 5–18.

Smith, Joan, Collins, J., Hopkins, T. and Muhammed, H. (eds.) (1988), *Racism, Sexism, and the World-System* (New York: Greenwood).

Spivak, Gayatri Chakravorty (1988), 'Can the Subaltern Speak?', in Cary Nelson and Lawrence Grossberg (eds.), *Marxism and the Interpretation of Culture* (Urbana: University of Illinois Press), pp. 271–313.

Stiehm, Judith (1989), *Arms and the Enlisted Woman* (Philadelphia: Temple University Press).

Suganami, Hidemi (1989), *The Domestic Analogy and World Order Proposals* (Cambridge: Cambridge University Press).

Sylvester, Christine (1987), 'Some Dangers in Merging Feminist and Peace Projects', *Alternatives*, 12 (4), pp. 493–509.

(1989), 'Patriarchy, Peace, and Women Warriors', in Linda Rennie Forcey (ed.), *Peace: Meanings, Politics, Strategies* (New York: Praeger), pp. 97–112.

(1992a), 'Realists and Feminists Look at Autonomy and Obligation in International Relations', in V. Spike Peterson (ed.), *Gendered States: Feminist (Re)Visions of International Relations Theory* (Boulder: Lynne Rienner), pp. 155–78.

(1992b), 'Feminist Theory and Gender Studies in International Relations', *International Studies Notes*, 17(1), pp. 32–8.

(1993a), 'Homeless in International Relations? Women's Place in Canonical Texts and in Feminist Reimaginings', in Marjorie Ringrose and Adam Lerner (eds.), *Reimagining the Nation* (London: Open University Press).

(1993b), 'Reconstituting a Gender-Eclipsed Dialogue', in James Rosenau (ed.), *Global Voices: Dialogues in International Relations* (Boulder: Westview), pp. 27–53.

(1993c), 'Riding the Hyphens of Feminism, Peace, and Place in Four- (Or More) Part Cacophony', *Alternatives*, 18 (1), pp. 109–18.

(1994a), *Feminist Theory and International Relations in a Postmodern Era* (Cambridge: Cambridge University Press).

(1994b), 'Reginas in International Relations: Occlusions, Cooperations, and Zimbabwean Cooperatives', in Stephen Rosow, Naeem Inayatullah and Mark Rupert (eds.), *The Global Economy as Political Space* (Boulder: Lynne Rienner), pp. 109–26.

(1994c), 'Empathetic Cooperation: A Feminist Method for IR', *Millennium*, 23(2), pp. 315–34.

(forthcoming), 'Western and African Feminisms: World-Travelling the Possibilities', *Signs*.

Tickner, J. Ann (1992), *Gender in International Relations: Feminist Perspectives on Security* (New York: Columbia University Press).

Trinh, Minh-ha (1990), 'Not You/Like You: Post-Colonial Women and the Interlocking Questions of Identity and Difference', in Gloria Anzaldua (ed.), *Making Face, Making Soul – Haciendo Caras: Creative and Critical Perspectives by Women of Color* (San Francisco: Aunt Lute), pp. 371–5.

Vasquez, John (1995), 'The Post-Positivism Debate: Reconstructing Scientific Enquiry and International Relations Theory After Enlightenment's Fall', in Ken Booth and Steve Smith (eds.), *International Relations Theory Today* (University Park, PA: Pennsylvania State University Press), pp. 217–40.

Walker, Rob (1992), 'Gender and Critique in the Theory of International Relations', in V. Spike Peterson (ed.), *Gendered States: Feminist (Re)Visions of International Relations theory* (Boulder: Lynne Rienner), pp. 179–202.

Whitworth, Sandra (1994), *Feminism and International Relations: Towards a Political Economy of Gender in Interstate and Non-governmental Organizations* (London: Macmillan).

Williams, Patrick and Chrisman, Laura (eds.) (1993), *Colonial Discourse and Post-Colonial Theory: A Reader* (London: Harvester Wheatsheaf).

Windsor, Philip (1988), 'Women and International Relations: What's the Problem?', *Millennium*, 17 (3), pp. 451–60.

Wittig, Monique (1989), 'The Straight Mind', *Feminist Issues*, 1 (1), pp. 103–11.

Zalewski, Marysia and Parpart, Jane (eds.) (forthcoming), *Feminisms, Masculinity and Power in International Relations: Theory and Practice* (New York: Routledge).

13   The achievements of critical theory

Andrew Linklater

Over the past ten years Marxian-inspired critical social theory has exercised significant influence upon international theory and has emerged as a serious alternative to orthodox approaches to the field. Critical theory has enlarged the parameters of the discipline by showing how efforts to reconstruct historical materialism offer direction to International Relations in the post-positivist phase. The position covered in this chapter, Marxian-inspired critical theory, should be distinguished from post-modern critical theory which displays considerable scepticism towards the emancipatory project associated with Marxism. The relationship between these perspectives is a matter to come back to later. The main aim of this chapter is to consider the achievements of the Marxian branch of critical theory, discuss some of the criticisms which have been levelled against it and suggest areas for further research.

As a strand of social theory and as an approach to international relations, critical theory has four main achievements. First, critical theory takes issue with positivism by arguing that knowledge does not arise from the subject's neutral engagement with an objective reality but reflects pre-existing social purposes and interests. Critical theory invites observers to reflect upon the social construction and effects of knowledge and to consider how claims about neutrality can conceal the role knowledge plays in reproducing unsatisfactory social arrangements. In International Relations, these themes have been crucial elements in the critique of neo-realism and in the gradual recovery of a project of enlightenment and emancipation reworked to escape the familiar pitfalls of idealism.

Second, critical theory stands opposed to empirical claims about the social world which assume that existing structures are immutable. The central objection to these claims is that notions of immutability support structured inequalities of power and wealth which are in principle alterable. Critical theory investigates the prospects for new forms of community in which individuals and groups can achieve higher levels of freedom. Its orientation towards existing constraints is shaped by the Marxian assumption that all that is solid eventually melts into air, and by the belief that human beings can make more of their history under conditions of their own choosing. It rejects the utopian assumption that there is an unchanging universal ethical yardstick for judging social arrangements, recognises the constraints upon radical change stressed by perspectives such as neo-realism but avoids the latter's advocacy of resignation to international political fate. Having overcome the flawed dichotomy between realism and idealism which has lent a peculiar structure to so much debate within the field, critical theory examines the prospects for greater freedom immanent within existing social relations.

Third, critical theory learns from and overcomes the weaknesses inherent in Marxism. The project of reconstructing historical material-ism associated with the writings of Habermas is especially significant in this regard. This project denies that class power is the fundamental form of social exclusion or that production is the key determinant of society and history. Post-Marxist critical theory extends conventional Marxist analysis by considering axes of exclusion other than class and by analysing the variety of forces, including production, which shape the contours of human history. Particular emphasis is placed upon the forms of social learning. Recent analysis stresses how human beings learn to include some within, and exclude others from, their bounded com-munities and also how they can develop the capacity to engage all others in open and potentially universal discourse. The analysis of boundedness opens up new possibilities for constructing an historical sociology with an emancipatory purpose.

Fourth, critical theory judges social arrangements by their capacity to embrace open dialogue with all others and envisages new forms of political community which break with unjustified exclusion. Realist and neo-realist arguments that communities must deal with one another in the currency of military power is rejected by critical theory which envisages the use of unconstrained discourse to determine the moral significance of national boundaries and to examine the possibility of post-sovereign forms of political life. The theme of dialogue is one area where different strands of post-positivist theory can converge to chart future possibilities for the study of international relations and to envisage forms of political community which overcome the limitations of the bounded sovereign state.

The remainder of this chapter is in four parts. Sections one and two consider the first two achievements in more detail. Since these achieve-ments are now firmly embedded in the literature this paper pays more attention to the reconstruction of historical materialism and to the relationship between discourse ethics and international politics. These themes are considered in sections three and four.

Subject and object

In an oft-quoted article Cox (1981) made the important observation that knowledge is always for someone and some purpose. Problem-solving knowledge is geared to making the international system function more smoothly on the understanding that fundamental change is either impossible or improbable. Critical-theoretical knowledge searches for evidence of change on the assumption that present structures are unlikely to be reproduced indefinitely. If change is not imminent it might seem wise to ensure that existing arrangements operate as smoothly as possible but critical theory rejects this conclusion since those who belong to the same political order are not treated equally or fairly by it. If international order works to the advantage of the most privileged groups then the well-meaning aim of managing an existing order has the unpalatable political effect of neglecting marginal groups and subordinate interests. Observers who analyse the prospects for the smoother functioning of the existing system may claim value-neutrality for their inquiry but they fail to understand that intellectual projects have important moral implications for the national and international distribution of wealth and power. Any assumption that critical theory starts from normative and inevitably subjective preferences whereas problem-solving theory avoids moral commitments in order to grapple with basic truths objectively is therefore untenable.

Critical theory collapses the subject/object distinction and emphasises the human needs and purposes which determine what counts as valuable knowledge. As already noted Cox identified two interests. Following the publication of Ashley (1981) it is now widely known that Habermas (1972) identified three: the technical interest in understanding how to extend control over nature and society, the practical interest in understanding how to create and maintain orderly communities and the emancipatory interest in identifying and eradicating unnecessary social confinements and constraints. From the critical-theoretical perspective these three interests constitute knowledge, frame the subject's mode of analysis and reveal that serious difficulties attend the claim that knowledge is value-free. Critical theory argues that knowledge about society is incomplete if it lacks the emancipatory purpose.

Critique of the immutability thesis

Claims that the social world is immutable illustrate these points. Critical theorists are inevitably troubled by the immutability thesis given their assumption that human beings make their own history and can in principle make it differently. According to this thesis social structures or forms of human action are natural and unchangeable rather than contingent and renegotiable. Critical theory aims to subvert immutability claims and to identify and channel countervailing tendencies immanent within social frameworks.

Three examples may suffice to explain how critical theory endeavours to undermine perspectives which naturalise what is essentially social and historical. The first is Marx's critique of bourgeois political economy which supposed the institution of private property was natural. The second is Hegel's critique of the Indian caste-system which contended that nature decreed that human beings be arranged into sharply divided social categories. The third is the feminist critique of the patriarchal claim that the nature of womanhood precludes full involvement in the political realm. For Marx, private property is not a natural institution but an historical product to be overcome within Communist society. For Hegel, caste distinctions are not given in nature but arise within a particular ensemble of social relations in which spirit has yet to release itself from nature. For feminism, nothing in the nature of womanhood precludes full involvement in a public realm which can be reconstituted in the post-patriarchal state. In each case, the critical-theoretical response is to oppose claims that structures cannot be transformed because they are securely grounded in human nature or in a condition (like anarchy) which human beings are deemed powerless to alter. Critical theory therefore takes issue with accounts of reality which underestimate the human capacity to problematise and transform inherited, and apparently natural, social conventions. It rejects systems-determinism and affirms the capacity of human agents to act collectively to free themselves from structural constraints.

Critical theory is sharply opposed to neo-realism and its variant of the immutability thesis. The immutability thesis here is that political communities cannot escape the logic of power inherent in the condition of anarchy. The thesis fails to provide an adequate account of the relationship between agency and structure (Wendt, 1987; Hollis and Smith, 1990). For example, Waltz (1979) recognises that units have the capacity to influence the operation of the international system but strongly argues that in the main causality flows in the opposite direction with the result that units are forced into similar responses to the constraints inherent in the anarchic system. However, Waltz's observation that the study of international relations is primarily concerned with relations between the great powers recognises that although they are forced to act in the context of anarchy (and may be powerless to transform it) they enjoy a capacity to determine the functioning of the system which lesser powers do not possess. To adopt Wendt (1992) to a large extent anarchy is what the great powers make it. The incidence of war and the prospects for peace depend not on the anarchic nature of the international system, *per se*, but upon the ambitions of the great powers, the principles of foreign policy to which they are committed and the effectiveness of international norms as constraints upon their behaviour (Linklater, 1994). The logic of conflict and competition cannot be regarded as unalterable.

Not that it can be easily swept aside either, and one of the virtues of the neo-realist stress on long-standing international constraints is that it usefully counterbalances voluntarism in international relations. Even so, the immutability thesis sanctifies historically specific configurations of power which the weak may resent and which the strong are not powerless to change. Contingent political arrangements are placed outside the ambit of legitimate efforts to secure political reform. Knowledge is confined to the problem-solving mode and performs the ideological function of perpetuating the international status quo. Not only does the language of immutability convert humanly produced circumstances into quasi-natural forces – it also contributes to the production of political subjects who accept that relations between political communities must be as they are. Immutability claims help construct political subjects who accept sharp and politically stultifying distinctions between utopia and reality (Ashley, 1984).

For Horkheimer (1978) critical theory was contrasted with traditional theory or positivism which sought to explain social laws and regularities. Critical theory regards the analysis of social regularities as useful for understanding the constraints upon political change but it transcends positivism by analysing logics which may bring about the transformation of social systems. To illustrate, whereas neo-realism aims to account for the reproduction of the system of states critical theory endeavours to highlight the existence of counter-hegemonic or countervailing tendencies which are invariably present within all social and political structures. The sceptical retort that countervailing forces may be ineffectual, even short-lived, is not a decisive objection to this project because critical theory endeavours to identify the sources of potentially far-reaching change so that human subjects can grasp the possibility of alternative paths of historical development which can be explored through collective political action. It need only suppose that what is not at present a principal determinant of society and history could become so in future. In contrast, neo-realism privileges structure over agency, provides legitimation for the status quo and assumes that the threat and use of force are an essential part of international anarchy. It obscures the crucial point that the reform of the international system should begin with the transformation of the idea of the state as a moral community, with the alteration of past assumptions about the rights and duties of bounded communities (Linklater, 1990a, pp. 26–32).

The reconstruction of historical materialism: from production to discourse ethics

The first and second achievements of critical theory imported critical tools fashioned by Marx and Marxism into International Relations in order to challenge orthodox approaches such as realism and neo-realism. The third and fourth achievements criticise Marxism in order to develop a more adequate account of social evolution and an improved normative standpoint. The crucial theme here is the transition in critical social theory from the paradigm of production to the paradigm of communication in the writings of Habermas which has immense significance for the development of post-realist international relations theory.

The limitations of the paradigm of production are well-known. The emphasis of historical materialism fell too heavily on modes of production and class conflict while the historical importance of race, nation, gender, state-building and war was relatively unexplored. Three criticisms of the paradigm of production stem from these observations. In the first place, Marxism pondered the conceptual issue of what it would mean to be free from capitalist exploitation but failed to define freedom in relation to forms of oppression anchored in state power, patriarchy, nationalism or racism. In the second place, Marxism lacked an adequate historical sociology. Too much emphasis was placed on production, and too little importance was attached to state-building, war, morality and culture. In the third place, Marxism produced a clear but limited political vision which defended the abolition of class relations, private property and commodity production but offered no clear vision of the social order which was required to secure freedom outside the sphere of production. Recent critical theory has endeavoured to solve these problems by developing the idea of undistorted communication, creating a more complex historical sociology which is based on the idea of social learning and envisaging the democratisation of politics, domestic and international. These important developments rework the

Marxian analysis of the historical development of species-capacities and construct an account of human emancipation which is concerned with enlarging the meaning and scope of discourse rather than with elaborating the relationship between the species and nature (Habermas, 1979).

To begin with social learning, the essence of Habermas's critique of Marx is that Marx assumed that progress in learning how to master nature would create the context in which freedom could be realised. Marx overlooked the danger that the expansion of technological control would enable new forms of domination to develop. For these reasons Habermas (1979) argues that technical-instrumental learning which enables humans to increase their collective control over nature should be distinguished from moral-practical learning in which human beings learn to create more consensual social relations. Habermas introduces a third type of learning, strategic learning, in which human beings learn how to manipulate and control others. These distinctions are designed to support an analysis of freedom and history which overcomes the problems inherent within earlier Marxist analysis. Social evolution is explained by focusing on diverse learning-processes involving species-wide competences and capacities.

Having separated the spheres of technical-instrumental and moral-practical learning Habermas analyses the species-capacities which develop in this second and independent realm. Learning in this sphere does not have any particular kind of technical-instrumental learning as its prerequisite; the preconditions of freedom include moral and cultural factors which cannot be reduced to material circumstances and which can undergo separate logics of change. Moral-practical learning refers to the ways in which human beings learn how to conduct social relations consensually so transcending strategic considerations of power. Habermas (1979) draws upon Kohlberg's analysis of stages of individual cognitive development and suggests that there are homologies between individual and social development. Three forms of morality are identified. Pre-conventional morality exists when actors obey norms because they fear that non-compliance will be sanctioned by a higher authority; conventional morality exists when norms are observed because actors are loyal to a specific social group; post-conventional morality exists when actors stand back from authority structures and group membership and ask whether they are complying with principles which have universal applicability.

The development of various species-powers is evident within the post-conventional stage which is for Habermas the highest form of morality. Post-conventionalism demonstrates a capacity for ethical reflectiveness in which agents recognise that moral codes are malleable social products rather than immutable conventions to which they must submit. It reveals a capacity for de-centredness in which agents recognise that moral standpoints are diverse and that none has *prima facie* validity across time and place. It demonstrates a capacity for universality in which human agents move away from efforts to resolve age-old disputes about the universalisable good life and seek to define universal procedures for dealing with moral and political disputes.

Discourse ethics affirms that the validity of principles must be established through a mode of dialogue in which human beings strive to reach an agreement. No person and no moral position can be excluded in advance. True dialogue exists when moral agents accept that there is no *a priori* certainty about who will learn from whom and when they are willing to engage in a process of reciprocal critique (Habermas, 1990, p. 26). Dialogue makes it easier for agents to understand how their moral choices and preferences reflect personal biases and local cultural influences which others may not share. Discourse ethics is therefore regarded as overcoming the weaknesses inherent in monologic reasoning such as that employed by Rawlsian contractors choosing political principles behind a veil of ignorance without any form of communication with one another (Habermas, 1990, p. 36). Participants aim to be guided by nothing other than the force of the better argument (Habermas, 1990, pp. 66, 89) and agree that norms cannot be valid unless they command the consent of everyone who stands to be affected by them (Habermas, 1989, pp. 82ff). The objective is unconstrained communication although this is an ideal which may never be realised completely because agents could not be sure that they had reached a stage of social development in which there are no further constraints for them to discover.

Extending this further, moral-practical learning involves, *inter alia*, a willingness to question all social and political boundaries and all systems of inclusion and exclusion. Systems of exclusion have been problematised in most parts of the world and the critique of the systematic exclusion of women, national minorities, racial and religious minorities is a fundamental dimension of the politics of most societies. What Marx took to be the fundamental form of struggle against exclusion (the struggle between social classes) proved to be an instance of the broader phenomenon of resistance to 'the closure of social relationships and the monopolisation of opportunities' (Kalberg, 1994, pp. 120ff) in all its forms. The contention that the human species constructs complex systems of inclusion and exclusion in the course of its development is a better starting point for critical theory.

In particular, human beings learn how the social bond which unites them in one community simultaneously divides them from outsiders. They learn subtle distinctions between insiders and outsiders, but they can also unlearn them and move to new principles of organisation in the light of changing normative commitments. Discourse ethics reflects a particular stage in moral development in which human beings question inherited systems of inclusion and exclusion and ask whether the boundaries between insiders and outsiders can be justified by principles which are agreeable to all. The attempt to move beyond Marxism as critical theory is a response to these themes, and specifically to the diverse ways in which boundaries are contested in modern political life (Linklater, 1992).

In the contemporary world of international relations critical theory is inevitably concerned with the ways in which bounded communities include and exclude. The focus is on the state although the significance of other political actors is not overlooked. Two main approaches to the state have appeared within critical-theoretical writing in recent years (George, 1994). One approach, developed by Robert Cox (1981, 1983, 1989) emphasises the revolt of Third World states and political movements against the effects of the globalisation of relations of production and the linkage of elites in core and periphery on the distribution of the world's wealth. The main emphasis falls upon counter-hegemonic states and social movements and their ability to pool their political resources to transform the world economy. A second approach, closer to Habermasian critical theory, emphasises the changes affecting the social bond which unites members of the sovereign state and separates them from the outside world. The main emphasis falls upon the tensions within, and the challenges to, the sovereign state which are evident not just in peripheral areas but in varying degrees throughout the world. The second approach is explicitly concerned with the nature and future of the state as a bounded moral and political community.

To illustrate what is significant from this point of view, it is useful to recall that the social bond which simultaneously unites and divides has been problematical from the beginning of the modern states-system. Great difficulties have arisen in trying to understand the relationship between duties to fellow-citizens and duties to the rest of humankind (Linklater, 1990a; Habermas, 1979). These difficulties are evident in many areas of international political life including the theory and practice of the law of war, human rights and social justice. Quite what the bond which unites the members of the state means for the rights of those living outside the state – exactly what its moral significance should be – is a matter of continuing debate, as is the sociological question of whether the social bond is weakening as new patterns of economic and social interaction (usefully captured by the term globalisation) entangle nation-states.

Much recent literature has focused upon the developments which are weakening the bond between the citizen and the state and undermining tightly bound communities in many parts of the world (Linklater, 1995). They are discussed here not in order to reach any definite conclusion about the future of the sovereign state but to outline some important sociological questions from a critical-theoretical point of view. The obsolescence of force between the major industrial powers is one development, possibly a temporary one, with implications for the bond between citizens and the state. Given the role that war has played in the creation of national communities it is unsurprising that the pacification of the Western or Western-inclined regions of the world-system has been accompanied by calls for greater political representation and voice from national minorities and migrant organisations which feel marginalised by dominant conceptions of the community and its purpose. Globalisation and pacification are interconnected in important respects as Rosecrance (1986) observes in the analysis of the rise of the trading state. If the conquest of territory is no longer necessary for economic growth but is detrimental to it then the cult of violence is less likely to feature strongly in the self-image and behaviour of the great powers and centrifugal forces are, in consequence, freer to develop.

Centripetal forces are also more able to emerge. Globalisation fragments national cultures as some groups embrace what Bull and Watson (1984) described as 'the cosmopolitan culture of modernity' but others rebel against the intrusion of predominantly Western symbols and images. The social bond which unites citizens and divides them from other societies is further weakened by the challenge to a dominant theme in the ideology of state-building, namely national-assimilationism. Sub-national groups and indigenous peoples spearhead the politics of identity in which dominant conceptions of national community are challenged and the recognition of group rights is demanded. For these reactions the immanent possibility of new forms of political community has become apparent – a possibility which neo-realism blinkered by the immutability thesis cannot explore. New conceptions of citizenship, community and sovereignty are invited by these changes, and new constructions of community are beginning to appear (Connolly, 1993; Held, 1993; Kymlicka, 1989; Linklater, 1990a; Walker, 1993).

One function of this brief analysis of the forces currently affecting nation-states is to raise several questions which can be asked of bounded communities at any stage in the development of the human race. These questions are not concerned with the traditional question in

International Relations of how bounded communities interact with one another but with the much-neglected issue of how boundedness is constituted in the first place (Devetak, 1995). The main questions are these:

1 What unifies insiders as members of a bounded community? What is their shared identity? Who is 'the other' within the community and how does otherness within the community help define common identity (Habermas, 1989, p. 400; Foucault, 1979)?

2 What level of social and political homogeneity within the bounded community is demanded of insiders, and what level of heterogeneity is permitted?

3 How do members of the bounded community understand their separateness from other communities? What are the principles of separability (Ruggie, 1983) to which they are committed?

4 How closed is the community to outsiders? Does the bounded community allow outsiders to become members? What level of inter-nationalisation is possible between bounded communities? Which areas of social and political life are most subject to internationalisation (Nelson, 1971, 1973)?

5 To what extent is the moral significance of boundaries open to question? How far does the boundary between inside and outside include or exclude the forms of moral-practical learning noted above: namely ethical reflectiveness, the decentring of world-views and open dialogue with outsiders to decide the moral significance of political boundaries and to determine the principles of social interaction?

Some of these questions about bounded communities have been central to Marxist critical theory (Linklater, 1990b). Marx's social theory aimed to show how capitalist social relations were being transformed in ways which would both deepen and widen communities: deepen them by enabling subordinate classes to enjoy the material wealth of a community previously constructed to advance the project of the dominant class; widen them by lowering the barriers between the national community and the species in general. But, as already noted, Marx overemphasised the role of the class struggle in his account of political resistance to systematic exclusion and obscured wider logics of change within the moral-practical domain. Arguably, the logic of Marx's project invites problematising all forms of social exclusion but Marx neither articulated this claim precisely nor argued that principles of inclusion and exclusion required the authority of dialogue. Later Marxist writings on nationalism and imperialism asked how the national bond might be reconstituted and how community might come to be shaped by the principles of socialist internationalism, but the paradigm of production meant that the possibilities inherent in the analysis were not realised. The reconstruction of historical materialism, as it is understood here, takes some of the questions which Marxism raised in connection with modes of production, extends them and applies them to a larger domain.

Coming at this from another angle, one of the main sociological critiques of Marxism over the past ten years points to its simplistic single-logic account of human history. Multi-logic analysis has been emphasised in the analysis of the nature of social power (Mann, 1986, 1993) and in accounts of the state and violence (Giddens, 1985; Tilly, 1990) but there has been no similar account of how boundedness arises from the interaction between multiple logics. Boundedness arises as a sociological question in the writings of Mauss and Durkheim (Nelson, 1971) and in an important essay by Benjamin Nelson (1973) but hardly ever as a theme in International Relations. Closer co-operation between Sociology and International Relations is required to develop sophisticated analyses of bounded communities (Scholte, 1993; Rosenberg, 1994).

Discourse ethics: implications for politics

The preceding section set out the main themes of discourse ethics, explained how it renders boundaries problematical and suggested some issues for historical sociology. This section considers the relationship between discourse ethics and practical politics. It begins with the criticism that the universalistic dimension of critical theory generates its own form of exclusion and proceeds to the claim that discourse ethics fails to offer guidance on substantive moral issues. Neither claim is wholly convincing.

Deep concerns about the exclusionary character of Western universalistic reasoning have been raised by many post-modernist writers. Foucault claimed that 'the search for a form of morality acceptable by everyone in the sense that everyone would have to submit to it, seems catastrophic to me' (Hoy, 1986, p. 119). However, as McCarthy (1990) has argued, Foucault and Habermas were agreed that the politics of speech was preferable to the politics of force. The gulf between Habermas and Foucault's thought is not as great as it is sometimes thought to be, as recent comments by the leading post-modernist thinker, Lyotard, reveal. Lyotard (1993, pp. 140–1) claims that the right to speak, and the right of the different not to be excluded from the speech community, are fundamental rights. He argues that it is possible 'to extend interlocution to any human individual whatsoever, regardless of national or natural idiom' (p. 139). Through speech, human beings 'can come to an agreement, after reasoning and debate, and then establish their community by contract' (p. 138). Stressing the universalistic theme which has long been central to critical social theory, Lyotard (p. 139) concludes that 'civility may become universal in fact as it promises to do by right'.

Although Habermas (1985, pp. 94–6) defends a 'pluralism of life forms' and adds that a 'fully transparent . . . homogenised and unified society' is not a political ideal his claim that the aim of dialogue is to determine which interests are generalisable seems to imply the search for a universal consensus (Benhabib, 1992, p. 9). Feminist theorists have argued that ethical universalism is an exclusionary and masculinist ethic. In her critique of Kohlberg, Gilligan (1993) argues that the public domain which is largely populated by men is regulated by general principles which apply to everyone irrespective of personal character- istics. Gilligan argues that the belief that the higher forms of moral reasoning are concerned with creating abstract principles of justice devalues the moral skills present in the ethic of care and responsibility which is concerned with the particular needs of concrete persons. The belief that the most advanced moral perspectives are specifically con- cerned with universal principles devalues the moral skills displayed most typically by women within the family.

Young (1991) refers to the need for a communicative ethic which does not permit the search for universalisable principles to overshadow efforts to respond to the specific needs of particular human beings. Some theorists such as Benhabib (1992), Gilligan (1993) and O'Neill (1989) argue that the moral agent needs to balance the two moralities which deal with the generalised and the concrete other. Remarking on Gilligan's critique of Kohlberg, Habermas argues that discourse ethics requires the hermeneutic skills which are evident in the ethic of care and responsi- bility. Discourse ethics is not a form of 'moral rigorism' which applies universalisable principles in a mechanical fashion with no regard for personal need and social context. The hermeneutic skill of reflecting on the relationship between moral principle, social context and the concrete needs of particular individuals is central to discourse ethics (Habermas, 1990, pp. 176–80).

However, the contention that the moralities of justice and care complement one another has more profound implications which concern the meaning of true dialogue. True dialogue is not exhausted by the quest for generalisable principles governing similar persons in similar circumstances: it requires genuine engagement with the different and possibly alien standpoint taken by the 'other'. In her argument for 'post- conventional contextualism' Benhabib (1992, pp. 151, 163–4) makes the crucial point that knowledge of the concrete other is essential before deciding the extent to which the circumstances of others are alike and therefore capable of being regulated by generalisable principles. Frazer and Lacey (1993, pp. 203–12) in their recent defence of the 'critical feminist enterprise' argue for 'dialogic communitarianism' which recognises the role of community in the constitution of the self and the value which particular groups have in the lives of individuals. From this point of view open dialogue recognises the significance of 'unassimilated otherness' and renounces any commitment to a 'unified public' or stultifying social consensus (Frazer and Lacey, 1993, p. 204). These feminist approaches are not opposed to universalism in all its forms but take issue with a universalism which opposes or attaches little significance to difference (Young, 1991, p. 105). Their effect is to imagine a strong universalism in which dialogue encounters difference and is open to what White (1991) has called 'responsibility to otherness'.

No doubt debate will continue over whether or not this construction of discourse ethics retains too much emphasis on a universalistic ethic which undervalues and threatens cultural difference. It should be noted, however, that discourse ethics defends procedural universalism and does not claim that any one conception of the good life should be universalised. The contention that critical theory is committed to modes of thought and action which would subsume difference within one totalising identity is increasingly widespread in the literature (George, 1994, ch. 7) but totally false. The error is to suppose that reaching an agreement is the same as arriving at a total consensus (Benhabib 1992, p. 9).

To develop this further it is useful to identify four forms of understanding. The first is anthropological understanding which has the aim of comprehending difference for its own sake. The second is strategic understanding which has the aim of understanding the other's aspirations, interests and intentions in order to control the other's behaviour or to outwit and outmanoeuvre the other conceived as adversary. The third is socratic understanding in which actors suspend their truth claims and enter into dialogue with others to seek the truth. The fourth is political understanding which has two dimensions: the attempt to understand the plurality of moral views in order to reach agreement about the principles of inclusion and exclusion, and the attempt to understand the rules of coexistence which agents could accept where they fail to reach consensus.

Three of these forms of understanding are relevant for the emancipatory project. Anthropological understanding is relevant because it requires the empathetic skill of appreciating what is unique or different about the other. Socratic understanding is relevant since actors can only arrive at principles which are true for all by first embracing the moment of Cartesian doubt and succumbing to a process of reciprocal critique. Political understanding is relevant since it maintains that principles of inclusion and exclusion and rules of co-existence can only acquire universal validity through open dialogue embracing all points of view. Strategic understanding alone clashes with the emancipatory project since it is geared towards controlling others and belongs therefore to the sphere of strategic as opposed to moral-practical learning. The accusation that critical theory is driven towards the cancellation of difference misreads the nature of its commitment to 'the goal of coming to an understanding' (Habermas, 1979, p. 3). Coming to an understanding may not culminate in a moral consensus. But it is reaching an understanding which captures the most important respect in which critical theory, post-modernism, feminism and also philosophical hermeneutics (Shapcott, 1994) are involved in a common project.

One further criticism accuses discourse ethics of formalism. There is some truth in this charge. Discourse ethics sets out the procedures to be followed so that individuals are equally free to express their moral differences and able to resolve them, if this is possible, through the force of the better argument. Discourse ethics is not an attempt to predict or pre-empt the likely result of dialogue; it does not provide putative solutions to substantive moral debates, envisage end-points or circulate blue-prints. But it is not wholly lacking in content. The gulf between actual social practices and discourse ethics provides an immediate rationale for political critique. In addition to setting out the formal conditions which have to be satisfied before open dialogue can exist, discourse ethics invites the critique of structures and beliefs which obstruct open dialogue. On this basis critical theory develops a normative vision which is often missing from, although it is not necessarily inconsistent with, elements of post-modernism. Ashley and Walker (1990, pp. 391, 394–5) take issue with claims 'to stand heroically upon some exclusionary ground' and challenge obstacles to dialogue across the 'institutional limitations that separate nations, classes, occupational categories, genders and races'. This concern with advancing an 'ethic of freedom' (Ashley and Walker 1990, p. 391) is the starting point for critical social theory.

Illustrating this theme, Cohen (1990, pp. 71, 100) argues that discourse ethics is critical of 'forms of life based on domination, violence and systematic inequality' which prevent full participation and therefore supportive of moves to equalise power. Cohen stresses the achievements of liberal-democratic society in this regard without losing sight of its imperfections and without assuming that Western liberal democracy is the model of government which should apply universally. Discourse ethics can be institutionalised in structures of participation the precise character of which varies from place to place.

It is important to take this point further by noting that discourse ethics cannot be completed by a number of separate experiments in democratic participation within independent sovereign states. Discourse ethics clashes with the idea of sovereignty which restricts the capacity of outsiders to participate in discourse to consider issues which concern them. The important point that such discourse needs to be embodied transnationally is captured in recent writings on cosmopolitan democracy (Held, 1993). The logic of discourse ethics is that moral agents should be willing to problematise all boundaries and bounded communities.

Discourse ethics therefore invites the questioning of traditional notions of sovereignty and the reconsideration of citizenship. Rethinking citizenship is crucial since this concept is central to the bond which unites the members of the sovereign state and separates them from other communities. Part of the recent challenge to citizenship concentrates upon the denial or inadequate consideration of the rights of members of other communities. Notions of cosmopolitan democracy imagine communities in which insiders and outsiders participate on equal terms. An additional critique of the modern idea of citizenship raises issues about the supposition that citizens must share the same identity or have exactly the same rights. Criticisms of this belief argue that particular groups within the sovereign state (such as indigenous peoples) reject the dominant understandings of community and desire the recognition of particular cultural rights. This critique argues that traditional ideas of citizenship possess an assimilationist logic which indigenous peoples and sub-national groups increasingly reject (Kymlicka, 1989). Not only might one imagine communities in which outsiders have greater representation and voice; one might imagine communities which recognise the claims of the culturally marginal within their boundaries and promote their representation within international institutions authorised to implement principles of transnational democracy. Discourse ethics questions the social bond between the citizen and the state which perpetuates the sovereign state as a system of exclusion.

Finally, some observations about the earlier theme of the relationship between universalism and difference in the light of these comments on sovereignty. An account of the prospects for increasing dialogue across bounded communities might note the following developments. Post-nationalist claims and identities are developing in two ways: through the universalisation of moral ideas such as the rights of women or the need to care for the environment, and through regionalism. Each move generates fears. The first raises the fear that universalisation will incorporate the other within an essentially Western framework. According to this view, the process of universalisation might therefore result in the triumph of a world-view in which there is no strongly felt need for dialogue with others. For its part, regionalism raises the fear that new boundaries will be drawn between the regional community and outsiders. Each of these fears recognises how the rise of post-nationalist frameworks might pose threats to difference or reinstate problematical boundaries.

A further pronounced development in the modern world – the politics of cultural identity in which groups react against perceived threats to their values – may produce several different responses: first, that such responses should encourage those in the dominant culture of the West to question the universal significance of their world-view in the light of its rejection by groups in other parts of the world; second, that expressions of difference can be as unwelcome as the form of universalisation mentioned above – unwelcome because some racist and nationalist expressions threaten the existence of different communities; third, that claims to defend culture invite basic questions about who claims to represent the culture and who may be excluded from the more vocal representation of its values and traditions. Discourse ethics is an approach to the dangers mentioned above. Discourse ethics encourages open dialogue between the diversity of moral views and facilitates the expansion of the range of moral and political points of view. Open dialogue is a check against the dangers of domination inherent in some claims about cultural difference (such as arguments in defence of racial superiority). It seeks to ensure that only those norms which meet with the approval of all who are affected acquire universality. Discourse ethics therefore encourages efforts to strike the right balance between unprecedented levels of diversity and universality. Achieving the aims of critical theory requires the reconstruction of the state as a bounded community and the introduction of post-nationalist conceptions of citizenship (Linklater, 1995). This is the meaning of an earlier claim that the reform of international relations has to begin with the transformation of the state as a bounded moral community.

Conclusion

Four main achievements of critical theory have been discussed in this paper: one, its critique of the supposition that subjects can be engaged in the politically neutral analysis of an external reality and its stress on the role which knowledge can play in the reproduction of problematical social arrangements; two, its critique of the immutability thesis and its argument for the analysis of immanent tendencies towards greater human freedom; three, its critique of Marxism and its argument for a more complex account of social learning and discourse ethics; four, its critique of barriers to open dialogue and support for post-sovereign communities in which new levels of universality and difference become possible. Critical theory maintains its faith in the enlightenment project and defends universalism in its ideal of open dialogue not only between fellow-citizens but, more radically, between all members of the human race.

REFERENCES

Ashley, R. K. (1981), 'Political Realism and Human Interests', *International Studies Quarterly*, 25, pp. 204–46.
    (1984), 'The Poverty of Neo-Realism', *International Organization*, 38, pp. 225–86.
Ashley, R. K. and Walker, R. B. J. (1990), 'Reading Dissidence/Writing the Discipline: Crisis and the Question of Sovereignty in International Studies', *International Studies Quarterly*, 34, pp. 337–426.
Benhabib, S. (1992), *Situating the Self: Gender, Community and Postmodernism in Contemporary Ethics* (Cambridge: Polity).
Bull, H. and Watson, A. (eds.) (1984), *The Expansion of International Society* (Oxford: Oxford University Press).
Cohen, J. (1990), 'Discourse Ethics and Civil Society', in D. Rasmussen (ed.), *Universalism vs Communitarianism* (Cambridge, MA: MIT Press), pp. 83–105.
Connolly, W. (1993), 'Democracy and Territoriality', in M. Ringrose and A. J. Lerner (eds.), *Reimagining the Nation* (Buckingham: Open University Press), pp. 49–75.
Cox, R. W. (1981), Social Forces, States and World Orders: Beyond International Relations Theory', *Millennium*, 10, pp. 126–55.
    (1983), 'Gramsci, Hegemony and International Relations: An Essay in Method', *Millennium*, 12, pp. 162–75.
    (1989), 'Production, the State and Change in World Order', in E.-O. Czempiel and J. Rosenau (eds.), *Global Change and Theoretical Challenges: Approaches to World Politics* (Lexington: Lexington Books), pp. 37–50.
Devetak, R. (1995), 'Incomplete States: The Theory and Practice of State-craft', in J. MacMillan and A. Linklater (eds.), *Boundaries in Question: New Directions in International Relations* (London: Frances Pinter), pp. 19–39.
Foucault, M. (1979), *Discipline and Punish: The Birth of the Prison* (Harmondsworth: Penguin).
Frazer, E. and Lacey, N. (1993), *The Politics of Community: A Feminist Critique of the Liberal-Communitarian Debate* (Hemel Hempstead: Harvester).

George, J. (1994), *Discourses of Global Politics: A Critical (Re)Introduction to International Relations* (Boulder, CO: Lynne Rienner).

Giddens, A. (1985), *The Nation-State and Violence* (Cambridge: Polity).

Gilligan, C. (1993), *In a Different Voice*, 2nd edition, (Cambridge, MA: Harvard University Press).

Habermas, J. (1972), *Knowledge and Human Interests* (Boston: Beacon Press).

(1979), *Communication and the Evolution of Society* (London: Heinemann).

(1985), 'A Philosophical-Political Profile', *New Left Review*, 151, pp. 75–105.

(1989), *The Theory of Communicative Action, vol. 2: The Critique of Functionalist Reason* (Cambridge: Polity).

(1990), *Moral Consciousness and Communicative Action* (Cambridge: Polity).

Held, D. (1993), 'Democracy: From City States to a Cosmopolitan Order', in D. Held (ed.), *Prospects for Democracy: North, South, East, West* (Cambridge: Polity), pp. 13–52.

Hollis, M. and Smith, S. (1990), *Explaining and Understanding International Relations* (Oxford: Clarendon Press).

Horkheimer, M. (1978), 'Traditional and Critical Theory', in P. Connerton (ed.), *Critical Sociology: Selected Readings* (Harmondsworth: Penguin), pp. 206–24.

Hoy, D. C. (1986), *Foucault: A Critical Reader* (Oxford: Blackwell).

Kalberg, S. (1994), *Max Weber's Comparative Historical Sociology* (Cambridge: Polity).

Kymlicka, W. (1989), *Liberalism, Community and Culture* (Oxford: Oxford University Press).

Linklater, A. (1990a), *Men and Citizens in the Theory of International Relations* (London: Macmillan).

(1990b), *Beyond Realism and Marxism: Critical Theory and International Relations* (London: Macmillan).

(1992), 'The Question of the Next Stage: A Critical-Theoretical Point of View', *Millennium*, 21, pp. 77–98.

(1994), 'Neo-Realism in Theory and Practice', in Ken Booth and Steve Smith (eds.), *International Political Theory Today* (Cambridge: Polity), pp. 241–62.

(1995), 'Political Community', in A. Danchev (ed.), *Fin De Siècle: The Meaning of the Twentieth Century* (London: Tauris Academic Publishing).

Lyotard, J. F. (1993), 'The Other's Rights', in S. Shute and S. Hurley (eds.), *On Human Rights: The Oxford Amnesty Lectures* (New York: Oxford University Press), pp. 135–47.

Mann, M. (1985, 1986), *The Sources of Social Power*, 2 vols. (Cambridge: Cambridge University Press).

McCarthy, T. (1990), 'The Critique of Impure Reason: Foucault and the Frankfurt School', *Political Theory*, 18, pp. 437–69.

Nelson, B. (1971), 'Note on the Notion of Civilisation by Emile Durkheim and Marcel Mauss', *Social Research*, 38, pp. 808–13.

(1973), 'Civilisational Complexes and Inter-Civilisational Relations', *Sociological Analysis*, 74, pp. 79–105.

O'Neill, O. (1989), 'Justice, Gender and International Boundaries', *British Journal of Political Science*, 20, pp. 439–59.

Rosecrance, R. (1986), *The Rise of the Trading State: Commerce and Conquest in the Modern World* (New York: Basic Books).

Rosenberg, J. (1994), 'The International Imagination: IR Theory and Classic Social Analysis', *Millennium*, 23, pp. 85–108.

Ruggie, J. (1983), 'Continuity and Transformation in the World Polity: Towards a Neo-Realist Synthesis', *World Politics*, 35, pp. 261–85.

Scholte, J. A. (1993), *International Relations of Social Change* (Buckingham: Open University Press).

Shapcott, R. (1994), 'Conversation and Coexistence: Gadamer and the Interpretation of International Society', *Millennium*, 23, pp. 57–83.

Tilly, C. (1990), *Coercion, Capital and European States: AD 990–1990* (Oxford: Blackwell).

Todorov, T. (1984), *The Conquest of America* (New York: Harper and Row).

(1993), *On Human Diversity: Nationalism, Racism and Exoticism in French Thought* (Cambridge, MA: Harvard University Press).

Walker, R. B. J. (1993), *Inside/Outside: International Relations as Political Theory* (Cambridge: Cambridge University Press).

Waltz, K. N. (1979), *Theory of International Politics* (Reading, MA: Addison Wesley).

Wendt, A. (1987), 'The Agent-Structure Problem in International Relations Theory', *International Organization*, 41, pp. 335–70.

(1992), 'Anarchy is What States Make of it: The Social Construction of Power Politics', *International Organization*, 46, pp. 391–425.

White, S. K. (1991), *Political Theory and Post-Modernism* (Cambridge: Cambridge University Press).

Young, I. M. (1991), *Justice and the Politics of Difference* (Princeton: Princeton University Press).

V

Directions

14 The last post?

Martin Hollis

> *Reason* is the *pace*; increase of *science* the *way*, and the benefit of
> mankind the *end*.   Thomas Hobbes (*Leviathan.* ch. V)

These words make a fine inscription for the gateway at the start of the
Enlightenment trail. They promise mastery and control of nature, to be
gained, Hobbes believed, by applying Reason to the discovery of causal
forces, laws and mechanisms throughout the natural realm. Since human
beings belong to the order of nature, this same method would illuminate
the social world also. It would reveal the art of creating and maintaining
commonwealths, thus resolving the problem of social order at home and
abroad. By applying Reason to nature we were first to see why there is a
problem of order, then to learn to solve it by constructing a Leviathan
armed with the power of the sword to keep all in awe and sanctified with
the artificial virtue of justice. Increase of science would bring peace, a
prospect of commodious living and a restless kind of felicity.

Had Reason set as firm a pace as Hobbes hoped, our conference would
not have been held. The Enlightenment trail started splendidly with
increase of science in mathematics, physics and biology. Light was soon
cast on the secrets of nature to great practical effect and, whatever one's
post-modern doubts about Reason, there is no denying the illumination
gained. Think, for instance, how human life has been transformed by the
lightbulb, the horseless carriage, the atomic bomb, the laser gun and
the formula for Coca-Cola. Although such examples may challenge
Hobbes's faith in the benefit of mankind, they demonstrate his case for
the power of Reason to control nature.

Hobbes is plainly an Enlightenment figure. Is he also a 'positivist'? The
question matters, despite its seeming anachronism, because critics
who take positivism to be exploded need to be clear what exactly they
are rejecting. Are 'post-positivists' thereby also post-modern, post-
Enlightenment, post-empiricist and post-philosophical? Or is the moral
only that a false turn has been taken on a trail which may yet lead to
increase of science and the improvement of the human condition? In

what follows I shall first sketch four themes in 'positivist' thinking which are possible targets of post-modern doubts. Then I shall focus on naturalism as the one likeliest to divide the house and ask whether, in embracing hermeneutics, we are rejecting an Enlightenment unity of natural and social worlds or natural and social sciences.

When Steve Smith and I were writing *Explaining and Understanding International Relations* (1990), we soon found that usages differ instructively. Positivism in International Relations circles has senses both narrower and broader than a philosopher expects. At the narrow end, it sometimes refers to a hard-nosed behaviourism which insists on quantitative data and statistical techniques suited to physics or engineering, to the exclusion of all namby-pamby attempts to ask what is going on in the actors' minds. At the broad end, Comte, Marx, Durkheim and Weber have all been called positivists, and it is a very broad church which can embrace them all. Well, perhaps there is one. All four evangelists believed in the possibility of objective knowledge acquired by increase of science, and even this is currently disputed by post-modernists. All four were also naturalists, although in different ways, and post-modernists are often sceptical on this score too. I shall say more about objectivity and naturalism in a moment.

Meanwhile, none of the four was a behaviourist, if that means disclaiming interest in the social world as the actors take it to be. Nor, for that matter, was Hobbes, even if he did hold that 'life is but a motion of the limbs' and that 'the act of understanding is nothing really but motion in the substance of the head'. Although his human beings were ultimately physical machines, their immediate dispositions were richly psychological: aggression and a readiness to quarrel prompted by competition, distrust of their fellows and a thirst for glory (or what we might now term status). The main Enlightenment line for the social sciences has always regarded social actors as subjects as well as objects, thus refusing the apparent behaviourist by-pass round the notorious paradoxes which beset the interplay between subject and object in all its forms.

There are thus at least four doctrines which might be rejected in discarding positivism. They range from a broad *objectivism* to a narrow *behaviourism*, with *naturalism* and *empiricism* in between. These last two will strike philosophers as the more characteristically positivist, although neither exclusively so, and I shall next say a word about each.

Naturalism stakes its principal claims in ontology and methodology. Ontologically, human beings and societies belong squarely to the natural order, even if they are among its complexities. This theme was memorably captured in *L'Homme machine* (1747, p. 56):

Man is not fashioned out of a more precious clay. Nature has used only one and the same dough, in which she has merely varied the leaven.

Methodologically, therefore, there will be a single method for all sciences, presumably the one which has guided the natural sciences so triumphantly. This presumption, admittedly, needs to be chewed twice before it is swallowed. Firstly, there has long been radical disagreement among naturalists about the character of the unitary scientific method. Disputes in epistemology have generated fierce argument about the role of theory in natural science and, on many fronts, realists quarrel deeply with anti-realists of several kinds. Secondly, when they turn to the social sciences, naturalists often start by suspending their naturalism so as to allow an initial hermeneutic exercise in exploring the social world from within. Only then do they proceed to explain it from without or after the manner of the natural sciences. Their opponents can then retort that, with hermeneutics doing so much work, the unity of scientific method is a mere shibboleth. Despite these complications, however, we can safely say that all positivists are naturalists, even if the converse does not hold.

The other doctrine which philosophers deem typically positivist is empiricism, subscribed to by all versions of positive science and deployed most ruthlessly in logical positivism. Empiricism is an epistemological doctrine to the effect that claims to knowledge of the world, including the social world, can be justified only by final reference to observation. Traditionally empiricism has relied on there being moments of truth, gained by pure observation and prior to all interpretation, so that science can rest on a bedrock of what Quine has elegantly termed 'unvarnished news'. To secure this bedrock, observation is treated as subjective experience, typified by the momentary, private sense-datum which attends my seeing what seems to me a red patch here and now. On this slender foundation rests the whole scientific edifice, with the solid, public world an inferential construct, confirmed (or at least not refuted) by testing whether generalisations hold in particular instances. The sole test of theories is the success or failure of prediction, as in Milton Friedman's seminal (1953) essay on 'The Methodology of Positive Economics'.

It is worth noting that empiricism, thus construed, is the enemy of behaviourism, and not, as some have carelessly supposed, its friend. The reason has to do with realism – another term with different uses in philosophy and International Relations. In its philosophical sense, realism asserts that the world is independent of human beliefs and knowledge of it. That makes empiricist theories of knowledge and science anti-realist at bottom, even though they try to finesse their way to speaking of an independent world. This independent world is a construct, perhaps hypothetico-deductive, perhaps grandly transcendental, but nevertheless a construct made by extracting a consistent story from experiences which are nevertheless subjective. Here lies a fertile source of paradox and a ready invitation to 'post-empiricism', which pragmatists in particular are quick to exploit.

Yet paradox is not easily removed. If everything that experience tells us is a matter of interpretation and consensus, as many post-moderns maintain, what underwrites our preferred rules of interpretation and consensus? Pragmatists argue that they are a matter of choice and of convention, with alternative ways of weaving the web of belief always open to us in principle. It is hard to see how empiricists can block this fashionable thought but equally hard to stop it leading to an insidious relativism.

In summary so far, there are four Enlightenment doctrines which 'post-positivists' might wish to reject. In order of decreasing generality, they are:

1 Objectivism: objective knowledge of the world is possible, whether or not this knowledge is grounded in subjective experience.
2 Naturalism: human beings and societies belong to a single natural order, which yields its secrets to a single scientific method.
3 Empiricism: claims to knowledge of the world can be justified finally only by experience.
4 Behaviourism: 'life is but a motion of the limbs', at any rate for purposes of social science.

I suspect that all present will want to reject behaviourism; but so will thoughtful positivists. What about the other three?

The doctrine likeliest to cause the most heart-searching is, I think, naturalism. The idea that nature has used only one and the same dough can seem essential to the claim of the social sciences to be scientific. Indeed, reject it and there can seem to be no hope of any objective knowledge in general or of any kind of objectivity in social science in particular. If we are led to contrast nature with culture, and natural objects with human subjects, then what we thought external becomes internal, truth yields to meaning, meta-narratives yield to narratives, knowledge yields to discourses, and value-neutrality yields to ideology. Although we enjoy flirting with these excitements, we probably flirt in the spirit of St Augustine's prayer: 'Lord, make me good; but not yet.'

Yet I do not accept that naturalism is finally compulsory, on pain of relativism. In what follows I shall argue the contrary case.

No speaker at our conference doubted that the first step in analysing international relations is to view events from within. Whatever theory one espouses in the end, the first move is to reconstruct the interplay of social actions on the international scene. So let us start from the opening chapter of *Economy and Society* (1922), where Max Weber declared that 'the science of society attempts the interpretative understanding of social action'. In 'action' he included 'all social action, when and in so far as the acting individual attaches subjective meaning to it'; by 'social action' he meant action 'which takes account of the behaviour of others and is thereby oriented in its course'. I stress that this is only a starting point. We need not agree that the ultimate aim is interpretative understanding, if that is finally an alternative to scientific explanation. Nor need we agree that an approach which begins with individual actions need thereby commit us to a final individualism.

But this starting point does commit us to finding out what the actors on the international stage think they are doing, their intentions and motives, what their actions mean. For instance, the British foreign secretary proposes new rules of veto by member states over EC legislation. What are his intentions and what do other foreign ministers intend in opposing him? Although these are questions about meaning, they do not imply the primacy of *subjective* meaning. The British foreign secretary speaks from a social position and not, one hopes, off the top of his head. He speaks for the British government, which claims in turn to speak for Britain. He does so on the advice of the Foreign Office, tempered by advice from other departments and influenced by other sources. His talk of rules of veto on legislation presupposes a framework of laws, directives and a host of less formal conventions which constitute and regulate the European Community. The foreign secretary speaks intentionally, even personally; but one can still maintain that, even for intentions, the inter-subjective is presupposed in the subjective.

Intentions are connected with motives, but not always simply. It may be that Britain's proposal is a bargaining device, whose real motive is to extract a concession as the price of withdrawing it. Or it may be that the motive is domestic, being to do with splits over Europe in the ruling party at home. I suggest that we think of intentional actions as moves in a game, which need to be understood by reference to the rules of the game. They are distinct from motives, some of which are internal to the game and some of which are not. For example, if challenged to justify the proposed veto, the foreign secretary may reply that it is needed to protect the sovereignty of member states – a motive within the game, which clarifies the intention; or may reply, although only, so to speak, in private, that the right wing of the party back home demands it. That is a motive external to the European game, internal to the domestic game of party politics and intriguingly ambiguous for the British national game of advancing British interests in high-minded terms which suit the ruling party only *per accidens*.

The initial idea that social action must first be understood from within thus leads swiftly to the fertile thought that national role-players and individuals play games; and hence that the meanings central to the science of society are inter-subjective. But this thought is only a first step and it leads in three directions, which may or may not be exclusive. The first direction, as just hinted, is that there are games within games. If this is taken to be the crucial pointer, then I recommend a Wittgensteinian gloss on the notion of a game. Here intentions are to be construed as moves made in accordance with meaning-rules which constitute the identity of action and motives as reasons for interpreting the rules in a particular way. Rules are not fully definite in advance of what is done in their name and interpretation injects a useful fluidity into an approach which would otherwise turn the actors into cultural dopes. Interpretative understanding is achieved when we have traced the 'form of life' encompassing the set of games within games: 'What has to be accepted, the given, is – so one could say – *forms of life*' (Wittgenstein, 1953, p. 226).

I offer Wittgenstein as an analytical voice for post-modernists who want to converse with English-speaking philosophers. He suggests with force and clarity that social facts are as they are inter-subjectively taken to be, thus implying that to change the rules of the game is to change the reality of the social world. This line of thought might appeal, for instance, to feminists who argue that International Relations theory has obscured the significance of gender in international politics and hence mis-described the games which nations play. Moreover, in considering whether they are right, notice that International Relations theorising is itself a game. If the players can be persuaded to take gender seriously as a relevant category for understanding action, then feminism is thereby vindicated by its very success. Similarly, in the first-order games of social life itself, gender has whatever significance the players come to give it. Whatever is taken seriously is thereby serious.

This immensely fertile line of thought, however, poses stark problems about truth and objectivity, to say nothing of questions raised about the status of claims made by feminists and others in the name of morality and justice. We seem led to a view typified by Richard Rorty when he contrasts philosophers and poets, sides with the poets and commends what he terms 'edifying philosophy' in contrast to the scientific kind. With all meta-narratives dethroned, there apparently remains only 'the conversation of mankind', where 'the point of edifying philosophy is to keep the conversation going rather than to find objective truth' (Rorty,

1979, p. 377). The threat of a relativism in which power defines reality by dictating discourse is palpable and one which feminists will be especially wary of. One might try to stop the rot by claiming that some meta-narratives are better than others, or by trying to define the conditions of ideal conversation where whatever emerges is true, good and just. That is no doubt why some worried post-modernists are hastily buying shares in Kant. But, as said, the threat of a poetic relativism is palpable.

Hence the other two directions have to do with dropping anchor outside the games of social action. One starts by insisting that we are indeed subjects as well as cultural embodiments. Foreign secretaries are not simply interchangeable. Each is a particular person leading a particular life, influenced by inter-subjective relations of meaning no doubt but not merely their walking artefact. This points to some sort of individualism. In the most familiar version, we are dealing with the individuals of rational choice theory, playing games of a sort defined not by Wittgenstein but as in game theory. In similar vein, we might want to think of nations as individuals in the international world, rather as firms are individuals in the marketplace. This way of dropping anchor outside systems of meaning by restoring our individuality has the blessing of the best worked out of the social sciences, neo-classical economics.

Yet there are notorious snags in trying to think of ourselves as individuals motivated by self-interest or, more accurately, by a disposition to maximise our expected utility. Perhaps they are not crippling and I do not have space to rehearse them here. Meanwhile, there may be other more human or sociable accounts of what a person is, which are more defensible philosophically and leave us a truer individuality, more in keeping with a liberal tradition than a market-minded libertarianism can offer.

The other way to anchor a floating social construct or 'form of life' is in the realities of structure and function. That means rejecting empiricism, I fancy, so as to make objective knowledge of external mechanisms possible. Yet it seems too late for that. The case for thinking of social structures as webs of normative expectations, rather than as invisible systems of forces, has been too well made of late. On the other hand, social science is not a serious undertaking unless there is more to the games of social life than the players themselves know; and it can be argued that some notion of social function is indispensable.

These brief remarks are intended to put naturalism on the spot. International Relations starts by identifying the games nations play. It recognises both senses of 'game' used here. The actions of states and of their representatives have the kinds of meaning which Wittgenstein bids us explore. Equally, states and their representatives make strategic choices in pursuit of their interests, as any game theorist will be pleased to demonstrate. And if interests seem to stand outside the games which nations play, just try asking whether the real interests of a fundamentalist Islamic state are material or cultural, as a preface to asking the same question about all real interests. So far, it looks as if post-positivists must dispense with empiricism and naturalism, thus leaving a terrible headache about objectivism.

Yet surely there is more to it than the games we play, in both senses of 'game'. Real life is full of pain and hunger, love and laughter. Power over minds may be cultural but it grows out of the barrel of guns which deal death. Institutions may be artificial but they are real in their conse-quences, some of them spreading light, virtue and justice, while others deal in distrust, hatred and oppression. Hobbes wrote *Leviathan* in the aftermath of a bloody civil war, whose weapons of destruction, national and international, were as nothing to our own. He did so to show how peace could be achieved in a world of scarcity and quarrels, and that is still as real a problem as any to focus on. All this is predicated on a given human nature ensconced in a given natural order, with cultural artifices doomed to fail unless they obey the natural laws of reason.

So must naturalism have the last word? No, it follows only that the games we play are for real. Whether their reality sets a divide between nature and culture and hence between the methods proper to natural and social sciences is another matter altogether.

REFERENCES

Friedman, M. (1953), 'The Methodology of Positive Economics', in *Essays in Positive Economics* (Chicago: University of Chicago Press).
Hobbes, T. (1651), *Leviathan*, ed. J. Plamenatz (London: Fontana, 1962); ed. R. Tuck (Cambridge: Cambridge University Press, 1991).
Hollis, M. and Smith, S. (1990), *Explaining and Understanding International Relations* (Oxford: Clarendon Press).
La Mettrie, J. O. de (1747), *L'Homme machine*, trans. G. A. Bussey, as *Man a Machine* (La Salle: Open Court, 1912).
Rorty, R. (1979), *Philosophy and the Mirror of Nature* (Princeton: Princeton University Press).
Weber, M. (1922), *Economy and Society: An Outline of Interpretative Sociology* (Berkeley: University of California Press, 1978).
Wittgenstein, L. (1953), *Philosophical Investigations* (Oxford: Basil Blackwell).

15   Probing puzzles persistently: a desirable but improbable future for IR theory

James Rosenau

It is sheer craziness to dare to understand world affairs. There are so many collective actors – states, international organisations, transnational associations, social movements and sub-national groups – and billions of individuals, each with different histories, capabilities and goals. And they all interact with innumerable others, thus creating still more historical patterns that are at all times susceptible to change. Put more simply, world affairs are pervaded with endless details, far more than one can hope to comprehend in their entirety.

And if the myriad details comprising the international scene seem overwhelming during relatively stable periods, they seem that much more confounding at those times when dynamism and change become predominant. Such is the case as the twentieth century draws to a close. In all parts of the world long-established traditions and relationships are undergoing profound and bewildering transformations. Indeed, the pace of change has been so rapid, with the collapse of the Soviet Union following so soon after the end of the Cold War – to mention only the most dramatic of the changes that have cascaded across the global landscape – that it becomes reasonable to assert that change is the only constant in world affairs!

And we dare to think we can make sense of this complex, swift-moving world, with its welter of details, intricate relationships, mush-rooming conflicts, and moments of co-operation! How nervy! How utterly absurd! What sheer craziness!

But the alternatives to seeking comprehension are too noxious to contemplate, ranging as they do from resorting to simplistic and ideological interpretations to being propelled by forces we can neither discern nor influence. So dare we must! However far-fetched and arrogant it may seem, we have no choice as concerned persons but to seek to fathom the meaning and implications of the events and stunning changes that are presently bombarding us from every corner of the world.

Happily there are at least two handy mechanisms available for easing the task. One involves a sense of humility and puzzlement. If we can remain in awe of the complexities and changes at work in the world, ever ready to concede confusion and always reminding ourselves that our conclusions must perforce be tentative, then it should be possible to avoid excessive simplicity and intellectual paralysis. Secondly, and no less important, we can self-consciously rely on the core practices of theory to assist us in bringing a measure of order out of the seeming chaos that confronts us. For it is through theorising that we can hope to tease meaningful patterns out of the endless details and inordinate complexities that pervade world politics.

Puzzlement

One would think, given the startling and rapid developments that have recently marked the course of events, that humility and a sense of awe might have reached new heights among students of world affairs. So much is new and unfamiliar, how can one not pause and wonder what it all means? So much is surprising and unprecedented, how is it possible not to feel undermined and to question the possibility that one's approach to the subject is in need of repair, if not replacement? So much no longer seems relevant, how can one not return to the theoretical drawing board and give free rein to a combination of one's humility and creativity in order to explore new ways of describing and explaining what is transpiring on the world stage?

For all three questions, the answer would appear to be, 'easily!' Analysts appear to have had no hesitation in acknowledging their surprise over the turn of events in recent years, but their surprise has not turned to humility and puzzlement. Rather, collectively we seem to have picked up where we left off, as if on second thought the old formulas seem to fit, allowing us to stay the course and proceed as we always have. A bit chastened perhaps, but not to the point of yielding to puzzlement as to whether there may be new underlying forces at work in the world.

If this is so, if analysts have not been given pause, if they have not seen enough to be in awe of the gap between the dynamics of world affairs and their tools for explaining what has happened and anticipating what may lie ahead, why have they remained so immune to the sheer craziness of their undertaking? A number of reasons can be offered – ranging from the felt professional need to protect one's standing in the field to a conviction that this is a time for discipline rather than awe – but I suggest the primary reason is that the virtues of puzzlement over the continuing and complex changes have never been extolled and championed. Such is the purpose here: to make the case for remaining in awe of the enormity

– the utter absurdity – of the task we face in trying to explain world affairs.

It should be made clear at the outset that by puzzlement is not meant simply a relentless capacity to ask questions. Nor does puzzlement consist merely of awe over the complexity of the global system. As conceived here, puzzlement is more disciplined, more focused, than sheer curiosity and bewilderment. The discipline derives from two criteria: first, one needs to be puzzled by observable outcomes for which existing explanations seem insufficient or erroneous and, second, one needs to be puzzled by huge outcomes, by events or patterns that encompass most of humankind and that appear to spring from some-where in the core of human affairs. If these two criteria are met when pos-ing a problem, one has what I call a genuine puzzle (Rosenau, 1976), the kind that is not easily answered but that is sufficiently engaging to linger, agitate or otherwise sustain motivation in the face of continuous frustrations over the elusiveness of the answer. To probe puzzles persistently, in other words, is neither a license to investigate trivial questions, the answers to which are relevant only to a narrowly defined set of phenomena, nor is it latitude to ask endlessly open-ended questions that cannot be fully and satisfactorily resolved because they allow for a multitude of diverse answers.

Genuine puzzles can be generated by either anomalies or recurring patterns. If a single development is so startling as to deviate dramatically from the usual routine, or if a less immediately startling event keeps recurring when logically it should return to a prior, long-established routine, the analytic antennae of analysts open to puzzlement get activated. The anomaly seems too consequential to ignore and the recurring pattern seems too unrelenting to dismiss.

Good illustrations of genuine puzzles provoked by both anomalies and recurrent patterns can be found in the work of the Santa Fe Institute, where economists, biologists, demographers and computer scientists (among others) acknowledged their puzzlement and converged around massive conundra that, through collaboration, began to yield to new understandings (Waldrop, 1992). Among the puzzles they probed persistently, for example, was the question of what are the origins of life, a query that is a genuine puzzle inasmuch as it specifies an outcome (life) and is huge in the sense of seeking an answer that is relevant to everyone.

Precursors to theory

Before undertaking the task of identifying genuine puzzles about world politics, it is useful to clarify the relationship between the fashioning of theory and the framing of puzzles. The two are not the same. To have a theory is to think you know how things work; to be puzzled is to wonder why and how they culminate as they do. Sound theories allow for their own negation and thus perceptive theorists are ever ready to acknowledge they may be wrong. But to be prepared to be proven wrong does not involve anywhere near the uncertainty that attaches to puzzles. Until a theory is demonstrated to be unmistakably false, theorists have every reason to continue to believe they understand the dynamics at work and what the outcomes are likely to be. If they did not have such confidence, they could hardly seek to perfect the fine points of their theories. To be genuinely puzzled, on the other hand, is to be confused as well as curious about the combination of factors that produce the outcomes that seem so inexplicable. There is no certainty and thus there is not likely to be great confidence that the puzzle can eventually be solved.

Other things being equal, therefore, it follows that in times of rapid change one is well advised to go through the puzzle stage before returning to the theoretical drawing board. Why? Because, if one doesn't, if one starts at the theory stage, one is likely to cling to the updated or revised theory, to frame *ad hoc* hypotheses that account for deviations from the theory, to treat deviations as explicable rather than as hints that one should be more bewildered and stand in awe of the fact that seemingly inexplicable outcomes occur.

Desirable as it may be to allow for the intrusion of some perplexity in our work, however, the probabilities of this occurring seem very bleak indeed. We do not know how to be puzzled, how to tolerate ambiguity for a while, how to suspend interpretations until after we have experienced awe in the regularity of recurrent patterns or the challenge of singular anomalies. Accordingly, IR theory is unlikely to flourish in the future. Practitioners are not, for example, in awe of how social and political systems get from Friday to Monday and Monday to Tuesday, from August to September, from 1990 to 1991, from the 1980s to the 1990s, from the twentieth century to the twenty-first century. They take such continuities for granted. It does not puzzle them that patterns hold and systems endure across long stretches of time. Hence they are surprised when a system – such as the Soviet Union – does not get from a Friday to the following Monday, or from August to September, or through 1991, or into the twenty-first century.

But, the question arises, if puzzlement is treated as a precursor to theory, how does one resist the temptation to rush to theoretical judgement? What can one do to avoid hastily reacting to an anomaly or pattern by stretching to find a niche for it in the comfort of one's paradigm? The answer may seem trite, but it lies in retaining a sense of awe over the extraordinary complexity of world affairs and then elevating it to a feeling of pride that one somehow has the audacity to treat the complexity as susceptible to systematic comprehension.

In addition to the blockage that derives from ego involvement in one's prior accomplishments, several other obstacles to proceeding audaciously can usefully be noted. One concerns the confidence analysts have in their training and the paradigms they have since evolved. For some it is not a matter of arrogance, but simply an unshakable commitment that hinders the generation or maintenance of awe and puzzlement. Having developed a hard-won perspective, they are reluctant to concede confusion, ambiguity or ambivalence. For other analysts surprising outcomes foster defensiveness. Rather than conceding surprise that derives from faulty reasoning, such analysts rationalise that their failure to allow for major outcomes stemmed from the fact that their inquiries focus on different problems and that therefore their theories were not at fault (e.g. Hopf, 1993).

Another obstacle to the generation or retention of awe may be an undue preoccupation with methodology. Instead of focusing prime attention upon the substance of world politics and/or criticising each other for their conceptions of how the system functions and changes, all too many analysts drift into a preoccupation with what constitutes the proper route to understanding and/or faulting each other for their methodological premises. There is, of course, a close and intricate connection between what we know and how we go about knowing it, but these connections follow from ontological presumptions which set the substantive framework within which issues of methodology are confronted and resolved. If some analysts allow their methods to narrow their substantive horizons – as surely does happen – why be concerned? That is their business and their problem; sure, they make good targets for playful ribbing and righteous analytic indignation, but their activities are essentially irrelevant to our theoretical concerns.

A good example of the needless diversions to which methodological concerns can lead is provided by Gaddis's extensive assessment (1992–3) of the failure of IR theory to anticipate the end of the Cold War. His otherwise trenchant criticisms of why the behavioural, structural and evolutionary lines of theory lacked the basis for anticipating the most startling and significant set of developments of our time consist, unfortunately, more of methodological evaluation and less of substantive appraisal. Indeed, it is this form of evaluation that drives his analysis: as he sees it, the fact that three dominant approaches failed to predict the end of the Cold War 'ought to raise questions about the *methods* we have developed for trying to understand world politics' (Gaddis, 1992–3,

p. 6, italics added). At a later point Gaddis briefly acknowledges that ontological premises precede methodological ones by praising a behaviouralist (Karl Deutsch) for departing from quantitative analysis when it became clear that 'subject determined methods' (Gaddis, 1992–3, p. 26), but the basic thrust of his assessment is that IR theory suffered a setback because of its methodological perspectives. In effect, he is puzzled more by the conduct of theorists than by the conduct of actors who brought an end to the Cold War.

(It might be argued that Gaddis was not seeking to explain the end of the Cold War, that rather he was perplexed by the failure of theorists in this regard, and that thus he did have a puzzle. Yes, such was his perplexity, but by the criteria employed here Gaddis was not provoked by a genuine puzzle: he did focus on a recurrent outcome – the failure of theorists – but surely this is not a huge outcome, one that touches on the lives of large numbers of people.)

Much the same criticism can be levelled at the organisers of the conference for which this chapter was prepared. The organising document is pervaded with a concern for the virtues and weaknesses of 'positivism' and the ways in which mainstream methodologies have made it difficult for alternative approaches to be heard. What seems to be missing from this framework is an attention to the underlying continuities and transformations through which the world gets from one moment in time to the next. Again, the puzzlement concerns the activities of theorists rather than of global actors. Perhaps the 100th anniversary of the Aberystwyth Department of International Relations can be organised around an effort to enumerate the phenomena of world politics that are so genuinely puzzling that they ought to be probed persistently.

One way to avoid methodological preoccupations and ensure puzzlement is to engage in analysis that makes no mention of other approaches and does not use the work of others as a backboard against which to evolve ideas of one's own. Try it! Try writing up some observations, thoughts, puzzles, propositions or conclusions that make no reference whatever to what others have said! Or, if this exercise is too difficult, try discerning the underlying puzzles that mark the work of others. Try teasing out their puzzlement and then assessing whether they have the makings of genuine puzzles that might foster new and creative perspectives and concepts.

Of course, there is no guarantee that proceeding this way or treating methodology as ancillary to substantive preoccupations will allow for the awe out of which creative theory can evolve. Some substantive approaches preclude puzzlement by proceeding from presumptions that either exclude consideration of a wide range of variables or do not allow for wide variation in the variables that are considered central. Rational-actor models are a case in point. The more analysts presume rationality, the less are they likely to evolve an awe towards the field. Why? Because such a presumption leads not to a search for the patterns that rational actions may form, but to a concern for whether the rational actor can outwit his competitors – an interesting question, to be sure, but one that is unlikely to provoke attention to awesome patterns. To be concerned with rational actors is to ignore the bases of authority and legitimacy, the links between systems and their sub-systems, the processes through which publics are socialised, integrated, mobilised and fragmented, the channels and mechanisms whereby ideas pulsate or otherwise circulate through communications systems, the underpinnings of culture and belief systems, and the ways in which major societal institutions evolve, solidify, change and atrophy. In effect, a rational-actor focus takes our eyes away from some of the more truly puzzling dimensions of human affairs.

Some routes to puzzlement

Having suggested the desirability of allowing ourselves to be awed by world affairs, and having noted some of the obstacles to yielding to a sense of bewilderment, let us turn briefly to identifying substantive areas that are loaded down with puzzles (or at least they are for me). I would argue that the behaviour of macro systems – be they states, societies, ethnic groups or any impersonal organisation – offers an especially fertile field for experiencing awe and puzzlement. All such systems are highly complex, highly dependent on extensive co-ordination, and highly con-ditioned by the ways in which their micro and macro parts shape each other (Rosenau, 1990, pp. 141–77). Hence their functioning is not easily grasped and their outcomes can be variable and, thus, startling. As previously noted, there is no assurance that organisations can adapt effectively, and thereby get from Monday to Tuesday without mishap, and the fact that most do is, for me, awesome in the extreme. Consider, for example, the awe one (or at least this author) experiences in pondering the following account of a small organisation, an aircraft carrier, that requires error-free operations all the time:

imagine that it's a busy day, and you shrink San Francisco Airport to only one short runway and one ramp and one gate. Make planes take off and land at the same time, at half the present time interval, rock the runway from side to side, and require that everyone who leaves in the morning returns that same day. Make sure the equipment is so close to the edge of the envelope that it's fragile. Then turn off the radar to avoid detection, impose strict controls on radios, fuel the aircraft in place with their engines running, put an enemy in the air, and scatter live bombs and rockets around. Now wet the whole thing down with sea water and oil, and man it with 20-year olds, half of whom have never seen an airplane close-up. Oh and by the way, try not to kill anyone. (Weick and Roberts, 1993, p. 357)

This account is both awesome and puzzling because 'even though carriers have been depicted as "a million accidents waiting to happen," almost none of them do' (Weick and Roberts, 1993, p. 358). How to explain such error-free functioning in a complex organisation? Why is it that the personnel of aircraft carriers are able to co-ordinate their tasks so thoroughly that they almost invariably get the planes off and back on the deck without untoward results? Profoundly puzzled by such questions, the authors found a cogent answer that is provocative if not accurate; no less important, their awe accomplishes what is here argued constitutes the hidden agenda of puzzlement: it led them to open up what would appear to be a whole new line of theory about the behaviour of macro organisations. The theory, which involves an elaborate conception of how and when the 'collective mind' concentrates exclusively on a single goal, may well be applicable to a number of puzzles in IR. For example, I have long remained stunned by the fact that on a particular day and hour in late May 1989, more than one million people gathered in the same place, Tiananmen Square, *without any prior organisation*. My effort to cope with this puzzle (Rosenau, 1992) turns out to be consistent with the collective-mind theory that seems to account so amply for the concerting of action that occurs on aircraft carriers. Indeed, if the collective mind is treated as a continuum, it would not be difficult to locate different types and forms of political organisation along it, with most falling near the opposite extreme where individuals are moved by a multiplicity of diverse goals.

The conditions under which leaders do or do not change direction may be another fertile field for puzzlement. More accurately, the occasions on which they reverse course 180 degrees can be a source of numerous puzzles about the interplay of forces that eventuate in such behaviour. Recall the reversal of Mikhail Gorbachev and the puzzlement that attached to his leadership when he was the major figure in turning around the Soviet Union and ultimately precipitating its demise. Remember the reversal of Anwar Sadat and the astonishment that accompanied his seemingly sudden decision to accept an invitation to give a speech to the Israeli Knesset. Or consider the puzzle posed by Adam Michnik, a leading Polish dissident who is now editor-in-chief of a leading Warsaw daily: 'That is the paradox: the same people who proclaimed martial law in 1981 allowed Poles to put communism behind them, without bloodshed, without barricades, and without the gallows' (Michnik, 1994, p. 28). Reversals such as these do not occur often, but their occurrence can be arresting precisely because they are so infrequent. What larger forces, if any, produce them? Or are they exclusively a function of personal drives? And if several such arresting reversals occur within a decade, do they form a pattern that is worth probing persistently? Surely such puzzles give cause as to what causal interplay may be at work. And if they give pause, surely they are likely to be theory-evocative.

In sum, we need to view all continuities as problematic, all theories as tentative, all events as potentially hiding unrecognised patterns, all breakdowns of human systems as complex and significant messages, all patterns as tending towards both order and collapse, all human endeavour as awesome and all co-ordinated human endeavour as especially awesome. Virtually an impossible requirement, to be sure, but surely a goal that can be approached if one pauses to ponder the fragility of human relationships and the delicacies that hold collectivities together.

REFERENCES

Gaddis, John Lewis (1992–3), 'International Relations Theory and the End of the Cold War', *International Security*, 17 (Winter), pp. 5–58.

Hopf, Ted (1993), 'Getting the End of the Cold War Wrong', *International Security*, 18 (Fall), pp. 202–15.

Michnik, Adam (1994), ' "More Humility, Fewer Illusions" – A Talk Between Adam Michnik and Jurgen Habermas', *The New York Review of Books*, 41 (24 March).

Rosenau, James N. (1976), 'Puzzlement in Foreign Policy', *The Jerusalem Journal of International Relations*, 1 (Summer), pp. 1–10.

(1990), *Turbulence in World Politics: A Theory of Change and Continuity* (Princeton: Princeton University Press).

(1992), 'The Relocation of Authority in a Shrinking World: From Tiananmen Square in Beijing to the Soccer Stadium in Soweto via Parliament Square in Budapest and Wenceslas Square in Prague', *Comparative Politics*, 24 (April), pp. 253–72.

Waldrop, M. Mitchell (1992), *Complexity: The Emerging Science at the Edge of Order and Chaos* (New York: Simon & Schuster).

Weick, Karl E. and Roberts, Karlene H. (1993), 'Collective Minds in Organizations: Heedful Interrelating on Flight Decks', *Administrative Science Quarterly*, 38 (September), pp. 357–81.

16 The future of international relations: fears and hopes

Fred Halliday

Three-quarters of a century of IR: a balance-sheet

No crisis, no academic discipline. As E. H. Carr himself stressed, IR like all academic subjects emerged as a distinct *academic* discipline because of a particular crisis in modern society, in this case that of relations between states (Carr, 1981, pp. 8–9). If there had been no need for a distinct discipline during the period of the long peace between great powers of the nineteenth century, there was certainly one from August 1914 onwards: IR responded, as much as did economics, sociology or geography to particular contemporary needs. This did not mean that 'international relations', as reality or as a set of ideas, originated with the First World War, but rather that it was at that historical point that a particular kind of reflection upon it was institutionalised: the subsequent development of theory and the use of history, be it that of inter-state relations or of ideas about such relations, have served to illuminate present concerns.

Set against this backdrop, the discipline of International Relations finds itself, three-quarters of a century after the founding of the Aberystwyth chair, in a situation marked by both great opportunity and some danger. The opportunities arise from the achievements of the discipline and the particular, intellectual and historical, context in which the subject now finds itself. On the one hand, it is a well established academic discipline, with an institutional emplacement and a substantial specialist, theoretical and analytic, literature; on the other hand, it represents an area of considerable intellectual attraction, be it at the level of student demand, or that of broader interest within the social sciences. This interest has, in several ways, been stimulated by processes accompanying, or following from, the end of the Cold War. The result is that, in the 1990s, there is unprecedented interest, political and intellectual, in the subject matter of International Relations.

Yet this success has to be set against a number of weaknesses that afflict the subject. In the first place, widespread public and intellectual interest in matters 'international', be it in the university or elsewhere, is not matched by any remotely comparable awareness of the distinctive conceptual framework with which the discipline operates or, indeed, of the possibility of examining international questions in a comparative and theoretical vein. Those who are aware, with at least some vague recognition, of the theoretical fields of economics, law or sociology are rarely conscious of any such body of work pertaining to the international. At the same time, the increased awareness of matters international in other social sciences, notably geography, history and sociology, has paid little attention to the work of IR specialists. The result is that, in the broader intellectual culture of the times, IR remains largely an invisible discipline, its subject-matter considered as inherently atheoretical, and open to everyone to assert of it what they will. That the most widely read books on matters international pay scant attention to the IR literature serves only to compound this.[1]

These external constraints have been to a considerable degree compounded by academic practitioners of IR itself. Here three forms of distortion have been particularly evident. First, there has been a tendency, evident in both traditional British realist and American neo-realist approaches, towards complacency at once theoretical and historical – a turning of what is a legitimate refusal to be stampeded by the current and the immediate (what Martin Wight termed 'presentism') into an assertion of transhistorical verities. This is observable in much reaction to the Cold War and the end of the Cold War, but it is, more broadly, evident in the treatment of the history of the modern international system as a whole. Faced with the end of the Cold War, or with the transformation of the international relations brought about by the rise of modern industrial society, the task of the academic analyst is to recognise what is indeed new, as well as to identify that which is continuous. The second distortion has been more specific to the North American branch of IR and has taken the form of a search, as well funded and relentless as it is fruitless, or 'scientific' and 'professional' forms of analysis and theorisation. This feckless cult, born of the 'behaviouralist revolution', has dominated the most influential part of the IR community for the past three decades for more and continues unabated: but, as was well pointed out when this aberration first arose, such an approach, while pertinent to some areas of social science, cannot provide a general or comprehensive methodology for any area of human behaviour, that of international relations included. That it has so continued, with a dogmatism and exclusivism worthy of any self-protecting hegemonic doctrine, has been an almost wholly unmitigated catastrophe for the study of international relations, both as an academic discipline and in its ability to influence and attract interested attention from outside the field.

This 'scientistic' distortion has now been compounded by its apparent opposite, the more recent flight into various forms of relativism and post-modernism. As with behaviouralism, there is nothing specific to IR about this trend, which has pervaded much of the social sciences in the past decade. Beyond a set of suggestive, but by no means original, claims about meaning, discourse and the position of the speaker, this trend is remarkable above all for its abandonment of claims to rational analysis, and for an affectation of language and reference. Like behaviouralism, post-modernism makes great play of its methodological concerns, at the expense of substantive or particular analysis. It compounds this by a confusion of what are particular issues in the field of analysing the international with a discussion, of a rather unoriginal kind, of general methodological concerns.[2] The result is, too often, bad IR *and* bad philosophy of social science, or what Gellner, citing Clifford Geertz, terms 'epistemological hypochondria' (Gellner, 1992, p. 44). For this reason, much of the work produced in IR over the past decade has been of little value and has served further to isolate, and indeed discredit, the discipline. Its prevalence reflects the convergence of a number of contemporary trends: the reluctance of much of the professional intelligentsia to engage with substantive analysis of the real world, the belated discovery by British and North American intellectuals that their values are not the only starting point for social analysis, the misinterpretation by English-speaking academics of what was, in its original French and German contexts, a political and substantive approach.[3] Transhistorical complacency, a vacuous scientism, a mannered heteroglossia – these are the three sirens of the contemporary IR discipline.

Topics old and new

If IR to date has, therefore, had a mixed record, it would appear probable that its future will continue to exhibit comparable points of strength and weakness, in both subjects covered and theoretical approaches. Thus the range of subject-matters covered by the discipline will probably remain wide and perhaps grow even wider. International political economy, security studies, nationalism – there is every indication that these established concerns will remain major preoccupations, within the university and without.[4] One question that much preoccupied the international community in the post-Cold War period of the early 1990s was that of intervention, 'humanitarian' in the narrowest sense and political in a broader one: Kurdistan, Bosnia, Somalia, Rwanda were but some of the cases where this has arisen, with the likelihood that, as a subject of ethical and policy relevance, it would continue. Yet neither moral principle, nor political guidelines have been clarified by these instances, which have remained subject to the vagaries of domestic politics in the major states as much as to any calculation of obligation. In a post-Cold War context, there is much reason to re-examine the original subject-matter of the subject, what is mistakenly referred to as 'utopianism': if the naive belief that international law can prevent war has long been abandoned, two other aspects of that original Wilsonian vision are of considerable contemporary relevance – the building of institutions of global governance, and the relation of democracy to peace. The former encompasses not only the major global and regional institutions – UN, IMF, EU etc. – but also a range of other, relatively novel, issues of taxation, regulation and management. The latter, a classical theme much revived with the demise of communism, has manifold implications, political and theoretical, for the study of international relations (Doyle, 1986; Fukuyama, 1992; Halliday, 1994).

From the vantage-point of the mid-1990s other issues appear likely to attain importance, the product of changes in the international system rather than of any particular shifts accompanying the end of the Cold War. Ecology, migration and communications constitute three such instances: all identify transnational issues that go beyond the competence or domain of individual states and all involve political and ethical questions. Beyond recognising their importance, they also merit attention for the very complexity of the analytic and moral issues they involve: there is no simple answer to the question of how the role of states and the separation of societies have been affected by these processes, any more than there is to the moral, and hence political, choices such processes present.

A pessimistic listing of issues is not hard to establish: nuclear terrorism, wars between democracies, the fragmentation and break-up of trade blocs, the ecological destruction of states, transnational mobilisations of religious communities. There may well also, however, be issues that are not evident today but which will over the next decades come to prominence. Two topics that are on the horizon in the mid-1990s and which could acquire much greater prominence are 'civilisation' and demography: both were, of course, central components of inter-state relations in previous centuries and have now re-emerged, after some temporary displacement. Neither has ever left the ideology, the lived popular perception, of international affairs. 'Civilisation', although generally seen as encapsulating religion, ethnicity and distinctive national values, pertains not only to matters of belief and value, but also to economic organisation and performance, i.e. to competition. In regard to perception, inter-state behaviour and economic record the issue of 'civilisations' could acquire a central place, in public discourse as in academic reflection. The issue of demography is perhaps the most important single challenge facing the contemporary world, yet it is one that is side-stepped by much of the literature on ecology and is perceived as part of some 'Northern' conspiracy in much of the Third World. Its importance is also denied by two of the most powerful religious establishments – that of Catholicism and of Islam. As much as any other contemporary issue, it embodies concerns of state power, moral diversity and transnational consequence.

The future: theoretical prospects

On the theoretical plane, there is little prospect of the discipline attaining any methodological unity of the kind that it once had, and it would probably be undesirable for it to do so: in this IR to some degree replicates the diversification and fragmentation that has marked other disciplines, notably sociology, geography and history. While the principle that 'anything goes' is dangerous, a situation of theoretical pluralism is desirable, provided that each of the theories generates a research agenda that leads to substantive analysis. Realism cannot re-establish the monopoly it once had, but nor will it disappear: old paradigms never die, they just go marching on, and realism will be no exception.

This need not prevent other theoretical approaches from producing their own, alternative, agenda and analyses. Two of the potentially most fruitful areas are historical sociology and feminism. The former, encompassing the work of both Weberian and Marxist writers, provides the opportunity to address some of the most complex and under-researched issues in IR – the relation between domestic society and international relations, the role of culture in influencing and forming the system, and the historical periodisation of the international system. The domestic–international link, beyond its intrinsic importance, is an issue through which IR can develop its relationship to other areas of the social sciences, not least by looking at the evolution of the state and examining patterns of interaction at different periods in history. Indeed once the state is seen not as a legal abstraction, but as a political and social entity, then a reorientation of the subject becomes possible (Little, 1994). The second is the subject of much speculation about how international communications, by satellite, cable and fax, have broken down barriers between states and societies; beneath this lies another claim, about the role of culture in constituting systems of influence and domination. The least that can be said is that such claims require careful, comparative, assessment. The third of these issues, that of periodising the history of the system, allows us to examine how far changes in society, and most notably the advent of 'modernity', have restructured the international system (Rosenberg, 1994). All three questions abut onto the issue much suppressed in conventional IR, be it by realism or behaviouralism, of the historical evolution of the state and its altered powers and character.

For its part, feminism has already shown how a range of issues conventionally seen as gender-neutral do in fact have a gendered character: security, national interest, human rights, war, nationalism. As such it suggests a general reconceptualisation of much of IR, linked to the development of other, critical, approaches. But equally feminist engagement with the international suggests a range of issues on which the feminist perspective, hitherto focused on individual and social dimensions, may itself be affected by such a context – the international constitution of economies, gender images, social practices, legal possibilities. At the same time, the encounter of feminism with the international, as much as that of sociology, poses questions to both bodies of thought – the very complexities, analytic and ethical, of international issues force clarification and development of feminist approaches. Feminism too has not been immune to the distortions of post-modernism: its impact on the discipline has been reduced by this divisionary association. The conceit, prevalent throughout much of post-modernism, that it alone provides a means of examining structures of domination, and giving voice to the oppressed, is reproduced in the analysis of gender relations. As feminist critics of post-modernism have shown, the risk is one of self-marginalisations, often disguised as principle: too often methodological introversion prevails at the expense of ethical critique or substantive analysis.

The future: four hopes

As Macchiavelli and Carr have intoned, one of the abiding mistakes of IR has been the confusion of reality with wish: if this is true of international relations themselves, it would be equally mistaken to assume that the future evolution of the discipline will accord with one's own hopes. One is, however, still entitled to wish. So here in optative mood, I offer four guidelines, in the full awareness that these do and will bear only a small relation to what actually occurs.

1   *The philosophy of the social sciences*

Issues of methodology and philosophy of social science are central to the study of international relations; they need to be handled on the basis of an adequate grounding in the general literature on the subject. This should be a compulsory subject for all students of the international: this would provide IR students with a broad social science culture but also diminish the danger of IR specialists wasting their time, and that of others, with mediocre reflections on methodology. In addition, a grounding in the philosophy of social science might serve to reduce the influence of both behaviouralism and post-modernism. It might also counter the misconception, which seems to pervade much of the current methodological debate, about the degree to which the major issues in the philosophy of social science are particular to IR: there are a range of issues, analytic and moral, which are specific to IR, but there is no methodological singularity about the subject. Questions of ought and is, of perception and reality, of fact and meaning, of quantification and prediction are common to the social sciences as a whole and should be studied in this context.

2   *History*

The study of history has, it might appear, been central to the study of IR, and was indeed, in its diplomatic variant, the subject from which IR first emerged. In its British variant, realism invokes history as the prime referent, the authority and illustration for its assertions about the system. The first problem with this account of the history–IR relation is that it rests on a rather limited, if not dated, conception of history itself – that of diplomacy and wars, with little space for more recent developments of economic, social and popular orientation. The history to which IR relates needs to be re-thought in the light of changes informed by a richer social science culture in the study of history itself. But there is another reason why a historical dimension, suitably defined, is essential for the study of IR: it can help to place the present in perspective. On the one hand, where historical perspective has been lost or denied, as in much behaviouralism, it can serve to set contemporary events in that context, both to identify their origin, and to provide a perspective from which to assess how novel, or otherwise, particular events and processes may be. Far from legitimating transhistorical truths, it can serve as a corrective both to presentism (everything is new) and to transhistorical complacency (nothing is new). At the same time, a conception of history involving social and economic, as well as political, change, can address

the very question that realism denies, namely the historicity of the international system itself, and, in particular, the relationship of international
relations to the emergence of a modern social order.

3   Substantive analysis

The central criterion for the evaluation of any theory is its ability to
generate a research agenda, and, to identify and explain significant
issues. Thus it must be asked of any theory, or theoretical debate, how it
contributes to this goal. It has already been suggested that much of the
methodological debate, self-inflated as 'meta-theory', fails this test and
would indeed regard such a test as impertinent. Herein lies the great
failing of the 'third debate' – while it has made a positive contribution in
introducing discussion of critical and feminist theory, it has also marked
a regression in the subject of the discipline, insofar as it has detached the
argument on method from the identification and analysis of substance.
The self-proclaimed advance '*beyond* positivism' has disguised a retreat
into incoherence. On the other hand, the more conventional approaches,
notably realism, would argue that they do meet the criterion of being substantive: but they do so often by a sleight of hand, in that a range of what
would, on broad social science criteria, be regarded as indeed significant
issues are not deemed worthy of analysis. Two examples of realism's
suppression of substance have already been given: the character and end
of the Cold War, and the impact of industrial 'modernity' on international relations. This occlusion is achieved by the act of asserting a
transhistorical reality that allows of no specific epoch and which, indeed,
denies the possibility of change. The study of real history yields to the
myth of a recurrent, and so history-less, anarchy.

4   Ethics

Much has been made in recent theoretical debates, and critiques of
positivism, of the need to recognise the subjective, the hermeneutic or
meaning-related, character of IR. This recognition, common to all social
sciences, can, however, lead in two different directions: one is that of
relativism and subjectivism, most evident in the current variant of post-
modernism; the other is towards a careful, rigorous, study of the moral
issues present in IR, and the relation of these to other areas of moral
evaluation. That IR as a discipline, in the main, neglected ethical issues
is evident enough: realism's claim about the limited effectivity of
morality in international relations may or may not be valid, but it is far
from being equivalent to saying that moral questions are irrelevant. This

area of human activity, as much as any other, is one replete with moral issues – about legitimacy, loyalty, equality, obligation and the like. In reaction and frustration at this ethical science, the alternative, 'critical', literature has too often resorted to the opposite, making broad claims about how the international system ought to operate, with precious little indication of how practical or realistic this might be. In the non-academic, public, debate on international issues – war, sovereignty, foreign aid, migration – one is often hard pressed to identify anything other than claims about morality in what is being said. Over the past few years, however, there has been a remarkable efflorescence of work on normative issues, influenced by, but not simply derivative of, broader theoretical developments of the past two decades (Beitz, 1979; Nardin and Mapel, 1992; Hoffman, 1994). As such work has shown, the way to overcome this situation, to demonstrate that awareness of morality does not entail a collapse into relativism, and to anchor the debate about ethical choices in international politics within a realistic context, is to produce rigorous work on the ethical issues that pervade the international arena. Beyond sharpening the mind, and providing the context for an informed and creative relation to the history of thought on these matters, such work could also make its contribution to clarifying public debate.

Conclusion

IR as an academic discipline is, and will remain, creatively subject to changes outside its own subject, be these shifts in intellectual and academic culture, or changes in the real world. It can, however, respond to these in a more or less creative way and the above is designed to suggest ways in which this may occur: neither autarky nor imitation provide the way ahead – it is by accepting IR's place in the broader context of social science and then defining its particularity that the subject can best assure its future. If the next twenty-five years can certainly surprise us, by the ideas and events they occasion, we are also, in some measure, in control of our own intellectual and academic destiny. It would be the greatest of failings if the advances which IR has made over the first three-quarters of a century were to be squandered by aberrations and conceits in the quarter that ensues.

NOTES

1 Kennedy, 1988; Watt, 1989; Fukuyama, 1992; Kissinger, 1994.
2 As Gellner remarks of anthropology: 'It is also uncertain, why, given that universities employ people to explain why knowledge is impossible (in philosophy departments), anthropology departments should reduplicate this

task, in somewhat amateurish fashion' (Gellner, 1992, p. 29). The same could be said of our 'meta-theorists'.

3 Thus Gramsci analysed systems of class and national power, Foucault prisons, Bourdieu education – their epigones resort only to meta-babble.

4 For one overview of the programme facing IR see the proposals by the incoming editor of *International Organization* (Odell, 1992). Under the heading 'Traditional subjects and promising opportunities' he listed: general theories of international relations and foreign policy; political economy; war, peace, and security; institutions; negotiation; policy ideas. He also welcomed work on the domestic–international relationship, nationalism, and history.

REFERENCES

Beitz, Charles (1979), *Political Theory and International Relations* (Princeton: Princeton University Press).

Carr, Edward Hallett (1981), *The Twenty Years' Crisis* (London: Macmillan).

Doyle, Michael (1986), 'Liberalism and World Politics', *American Political Science Review*, 80 (4), pp. 1151–69.

Fukuyama, Francis (1992), *The End of History and the Last Man* (London: Hamish Hamilton).

Gellner, Ernest (1992), *Postmodernism, Reason and Religion* (London: Routledge).

Halliday, Fred (1994), *Rethinking International Relations* (London: Macmillan).

Hoffman, Mark (1994), 'Normative International Theory: Approaches and Issues', in A. J. R. Groom and Margot Light (eds.), *Contemporary International Relations: A Guide to Theory* (London: Pinter), pp. 27–44.

Kennedy, Paul (1988), *The Rise and Fall of the Great Powers* (London: Weidenfeld and Nicolson).

Kissinger, Henry (1994), *Diplomacy* (London: Simon & Schuster).

Little, Richard (1994), 'International Relations and Large-scale Historical Change', in A. J. R. Groom and Margot Light (eds.), *Contemporary International Relations: A Guide to Theory* (London: Pinter), pp. 9–26.

Nardin, Terry and Mapel, David (eds.) (1992), *Traditions of International Ethics* (Cambridge: Cambridge University Press).

Odell, John (1992), 'Editor's note', *International Organization*, 46 (2).

Rosenberg, Justin (1994), *The Empire of Civil Society* (London: Verso).

Watt, Donald Cameron (1989), *How War Came: The Immediate Origins of the Second Cold War* (London: Heinemann).

17   75 years on: rewriting the subject's past
– reinventing its future

Ken Booth

For much of the 75 years of its existence the Department of International Politics at the University of Wales, Aberystwyth, has both flourished and laboured under powerful foundational myths. In this regard it can be seen as an icon (albeit often a dusty one, ignored in the corner) for most of the subject in most other places. I mean 'myths' here in the weak sense of the term: not as absolute fairy-tales but as part fictions/part truths – let them be called half-truths – which help shape attitudes and buttress ideologies. To be myth a story has to be recurring, primordial, and appealing to a particular group's ideals, hopes and fears, and widely felt emotions. In this way, myths, as Robert Cox said about theories 'are *for* someone and *for* some purpose' (1986, p. 207). Myths are not easily ignored, and on the whole I believe that they tend to sustain primitive rather than complex understandings of human predicaments. This has been the case with our subject's foundational myths. They have helped discipline the discipline.

There are three separate elements in the foundational myths under which this Department has flourished and laboured. They focus on two individuals, whose differing opinions and acrimonious relationship became stereotyped and dramatised into a powerful story that gave meaning, a sense of direction and succour to the work of most students of international relations during the scary yet heady years of the Cold War. The individuals were David Davies and E. H. Carr.[1]

The first element in the story is obviously made up of David Davies, the industrialist/landowner/Welshman-believing-in-education/and Liberal Member of Parliament, who endowed the Woodrow Wilson Chair in 1919. Although Davies advocated the study of law, politics, ethics, economics, other civilisations and international organisations, what became lodged in the collective mind was the idea that the study of international politics, shocked into academic life by the Great War, must have the study of war as its overriding purpose.

The second element is made up of the work of E. H. Carr, who, twenty years after Davies endowed the Wilson Chair, published his classic book

The Twenty Years' Crisis (1939). Despite the fact that this book contains several strong defences of utopianism, regular criticisms of realism, and a definition of political science as 'the science not only of what is, but of what ought to be', Carr became stereotyped as the scourge of utopianism and the advocate of an unrelenting realism. Under the shadows of Hitler, the Second World War and then the Cold War, Carr was seriously and continuously misread (Booth, 1991).

The third element of the myth is made up of the belief that Carr's 'realism' triumphed in every sense over Davies' 'idealism', and that this represented a definite advance in the academic development of the subject. This belief about the subject fitted in well with familiar assumptions about the idealism and immaturity of youth evolving into the realism and commonsense of one's mature years. But 'idealism' was never crushed by 'power politics' (note post-war liberal internationalism in the United States, and the commitment to European integration) while realism (note its innumerable policy failures in the Cold War) hardly lived up to its name. What actually happened in the decades after the Second World War was that the ideas of realists about themselves and the world they had helped and were helping to create were congenial to the national security elites, and so academic power shifted in their direction; but this was not necessarily synonymous with one idea triumphing over another in a deeper sense. Even so, most students of the subject for the next forty years were taught that it was, and they learned to pass examinations accordingly.

The Carr/Davies story was simplified and twisted, and became a myth. It helped create and sustain the view that the academic subject of International Politics was about 'power politics' between states and could only be respectably studied from a 'realist' perspective. This belief, at times elevated to science, had disciplinary power and intellectual glamour. By the time I came to the Department as a student in 1961 – nearly half the lifetime of the Department ago, and seemingly all mine – the three elements had fused and disciplined what we studied. With hindsight I can now see that a stunted view of Carr had 'triumphed' over a superficial view of Davies, leaving the subject to develop, ostensibly in greater maturity. Here as in most other centres of the subject, theories other than realism were marginalised or quite simply ridiculed, and the method employed was implicitly or explicitly positivist. The academic hubris of Cold War international politics was characterised by elements of Sunday school (preaching and worship) and anti-intellectualism (a strict policy of non-intervention into the territory of other disciplines).

As a result of these developments, the subject focused, in Raymond

Aron's felicitous phrase, on what 'soldiers and diplomats' did. In the 1960s the subject taught in Aberystwyth was dominated by International History (which represented a continuation of Hans J. Morgenthau with an admixture of diplomatic archives) and by Strategic Studies (the precocious offspring produced by the pernicious coupling of the nuclear revolution and the Cold War).

By the 1960s, throughout the Anglo-American world, the discipline of International Relations was carried along by its perceived relevance, the superpower strategic concerns of the period, the momentum of its academic success, and the power of its foundational myths. But Cold War International Relations – ostensibly realist – lost sight of both reality and its roots. The subject had started out to combat human wrongs (in the obvious and important form of war) but it had developed into an activity which taught students to ignore other massive human wrongs (Booth, 1995b); it had started out with a broad disciplinary agenda – to 'tell the World about the World' as one early professor put it – but it had narrowed into the examination of the mini-worlds of military establishments and foreign offices; it had started out with the assumption that there were other ways for humans to live, but had shrivelled into the ethnocentric rationale that this is the best of all possible worlds; and it had started with a belief that theory could shape practice, but it evolved into a positivist cliché that what it was properly concerned with was the 'objective' description and explanation of self-evident international facts under a microscope. In short, it had developed from a concern to provide a comprehensive account of world politics as the basis for thinking about the creation of a better world, into a narrowly conceived and philosophically misconceived attempt to describe the world 'as it is' – interpreted as (political) relations between (reified) states.

Thinking about how academic International Relations has evolved over three-quarters of a century has recently led me to wonder about a counter-factual history of the profession and the Department. What, for example, would the subject look like today had its origins and development been guided by a radically different set of foundational myths? If, instead of being founded by a wealthy Liberal MP in Wales (and those like him elsewhere in the Anglo-American world) what if the subject's origins had derived from the life and work of the admirable black, feminist, medic, she-chief of the Zulus, Dr Zungu (Booth, 1995b, pp. 124–6)? When I have raised this provocation, there have been some smiles of recognition, but many more signs of unease. The responses have been more in body than in academic language. That the subject might have had a different origin and history to the one that now seems natural and commonsensical is profoundly discomforting for those whose work still derives all its meaning, sense of direction, and succour from the disciplinary norms of the 1940s–1960s. Nevertheless, it is interesting to speculate about the character of the 'International Politics' that would have developed from a different (non-Western, non-masculinist) foundational source. What would our syllabuses now look like? Would our students be different? What would have dominated the literature? Who would be our professors? Would their myths have led us to a more comprehensive account of the world, as the basis for thinking about and creating a better world? Would the subject be considered more or less relevant by policy-makers? One thing is certain, however: *it was not an accident* that the subject was created by David Davies (and his Anglo-American counterparts) rather than Dr Zungu's forebears. The institutionalisation of the subject and its development underlines simply and clearly the crucial relationship between the global distribution of power and the global production of knowledge. The subject of international politics as we have come to know it cannot be understood apart from its origins and growth as one of the production lines in the twentieth-century Western academic enterprise.

For 30–40 years after the Second World War the Department expanded with a very coherent view of the subject, but in more recent years it had been part of the struggle in what Holsti in the mid-1980s called the 'dividing discipline' (1985). That was and remains a good description, but I prefer the image of a South African colleague, Peter Vale, who after an absence of some years from British IR conferences, experienced his return as an 'intellectual Somalia'. He saw a collection of ontological clans, huddling under the authority of academic warlords, each vying for disciplinary power. And, like their counterparts in Somalia, these academic clans were all scrambling for financial support from foreign funding bodies. The distance between the disciplined discipline of the pre-1980s and the dividing discipline of today is evident from the contrasts between *The Aberystwyth Papers* – Brian Porter's inspired idea to mark the Department's 50th anniversary – and the agenda and book of the 75th anniversary conference. The authoritative sense in the earlier book about what the subject of International Politics *is*, and how it should be studied, is unthinkable today. Symbolising the change is the fact that the editor of the 50th anniversary volume commissioned a Foreword by His Royal Highness Prince Philip. Had they thought a Foreword suitable, the editors of the present volume would have been drawn towards Dr Zungu.

The subject of International Politics is much more confused today than it was twenty-five years ago, but I welcome the change without hesitation. Furthermore, I believe that those who do not feel confused, and who are not exploring their confusion, are missing out on exciting intellectual times, are letting down their students, and are abusing the privilege of being a teacher of this endlessly fascinating and important material, even if we are not as sure what the 'subject' is. As a result of developments since the early 1980s students in IR are provoked to think about what they are doing and why they are doing it in more fundamental ways than in the past. This is notable pedagogical progress. Everywhere, those of us who are teachers owe it to our students to show them that there is much more to politics on a global scale than the traditional assumptions and axioms of superpower academics. Those of us teaching in Aberystwyth, in particular, also owe it to the two key founders of our Departmental tradition, David Davies and E. H. Carr.

Paradoxically – in the light of the foundational myths that have grown up around them – I believe that Davies and Carr would have welcomed and fitted into the 75th anniversary conference much better than many of the 40 or 50 people who have worked in the Department over the past 75 years (there are, incidentally, more teachers on the staff now than there were during the whole of its first 40 years). David Davies, as a liberal reformer and believer in education, would have no trouble with constitutive theory, while his belief in interventionist international organisations would leave him quite unimpressed by stark (Wightian) distinctions between 'political' and 'international' theory and the niceties of the English School. E. H. Carr, as a utopian realist (Booth, 1991) would also have no trouble with constitutive theory. His views about political economy would make him comfortable about discussing structures and forces other than states, while his ideas about the relativity of thought and the subjectivity of (historical) knowledge would make him at home with the post-positivist turn.

The academic subject of International Relations is only now beginning to emerge from its powerful disciplinary myths. Nevertheless, they remain very powerful, since the misconceptions and simplifications on which they were based were congenial to the emotions and interests of the Anglo-American academic community in the era of hot and cold world wars. The subject is clearly at a crossroads, and I believe the Department is playing a role in the debate about the way ahead. With the recent developments in the subject in general, and new courses and new appointments in Aberystwyth, I see us trying to engage with the future and with the real by going back to the subject's roots. I applaud this, and believe the 75th anniversary conference is part of the process of reinventing the subject's future by, in part, rewriting its past.

A handful of us at the 75th conference were also at the 50th anniversary conference, and I for one intend to be here for the 100th. In the years until then, I would like to see the subject developing or continuing to develop in the following ways:

1   From 'international politics' to 'world politics'

This involves a continuation of the effort to break down the autonomy of 'the international'. If our task is to understand politics in a global perspective – 'who gets what, when, [and] how' (Lasswell, 1950) – then trying to understand relations between states is only one dimension of the task. Indeed, there is increasingly less justification for conceiving the 'international' as autonomous. This does not mean jettisoning the old agenda of diplomats and soldiers – foreign policy and strategy – but rather trying to see them in world political perspective. Individuals travel, consume and communicate globally. Today, in important respects, the global is local and the local is global. Understanding the world of states must concede precedence to understanding the state of the world.

2   From positivism to constitutive theory

In trying to understand the state of the world, one of the central debates in the subject is between explanatory and constitutive theory (Smith, 1995, pp. 26–8). The eclipsing of positivism following the post-positivist turn has lead to a more widespread recognition that there is no escape from theory: to paraphrase Trotsky, you might not be interested in theory, but theory is interested in you. The ideal of positivism is equivalent to the move from being a player to being a commentator in the same game. But players can never escape the theories of their own game (with internalised understandings of its purposes and meanings). Nor would the ideal of 'objectivity' be reached if the commentator were to be an individual from a different century or culture, with no understandings whatsoever of the game's purposes or meanings. As hard as we try, we cannot turn critical distance into objectivity. We look at evidence, but always from within a theory. Humans cannot transcend (the theories of) their own game(s). However, if positivism remains a false god – an understandable temptation and indulgence of the age of science – that does not mean that we can or need eschew the empirical world. Indeed, most of us got interested in the subject because we were interested in the world: we would think we were failing if what we said was not relevant to real people in real places.

3   *From 'soldiers and diplomats' to silenced voices*

International relations are not made by governments alone, and their stories are only part of what constitutes 'reality'. We need to ask who has controlled the facts of international politics, and why and how? Who has the discipline been *for*? Why has the literature taken on the shape it has? What image of politics on a global scale do we get if we bring in the perspectives of the hitherto marginalised and silenced, as opposed to the perspectives of the Cold War disciplinary managers? Silenced voices reveal a more sophisticated understanding of how power works in world society. Realism remains indicted for its crudity in this regard.

4   *From history to theory*

History will remain the data-base of students of international relations/ world politics, but the international history that we give students should be more theoretically self-conscious. Whatever theoretical positions we have, and even historians cannot escape them, it is an obligation to try to be self-aware, explicit and informed. As the subject makes whatever contribution it will to the way societies think about politics on a global scale in the next era of world politics, it is desirable that its exponents be more self-reflexive and open about their standpoints than was the case in the Cold War. This is not to advocate what might be called theory for theory's sake, but rather theory for the sake of better practice, since theory and practice cannot be separated in the way asserted by fact-fetishisers and policy-pundits. Scholarship which is explicit about values should also be transparent about its interests, especially when it involves unseen paymasters in military–industrial–governmental complexes.

5   *From strategy to security*

The study of strategic policy was the basis for IR's most powerful sub-discipline in the Cold War, namely Strategic Studies. To argue for a shift from strategy to security is certainly not to suggest that war and other forms of inter-group violence are not important. They must remain primary considerations. But it is to call into question the Cold War equation whereby security is synonymous with states, the military dimension and the preservation of the status quo. Instead, safety from inter-group violence is seen as only part of a broader conception of security which also includes safety from threats of political oppression, economic injustice and so on. The sources of human (in)security are far wider than those traditionally in the purview of strategists. Whose interests are being served by keeping the other issues off the agenda? But the agenda should not only be widened, it should also be deepened, in order to discover the ideas and structures from which we derive our particular conception(s) of security. This broadening and deepening – the task of a critical security studies – will reveal Cold War security studies as an Anglo-American, statist, masculinist and militarised ideology – not one calculated to deliver a more secure world by the middle of the next century.

6   *From micro-international history to macro-global history*

In order to think about where we are and where we might be going on a global scale there are decreasing returns from investing scarce academic resources into the accumulation of knowledge about the details of relations between governments. It is unlikely that we will learn through archival mining any more about the character of inter-governmental relations than we know already. Of far more potential value is the exploration of macro-global history, so that by stimulating our historical imagination we might gain insights into the meanings of the present and the prospects for the future. As we move into a century in which the global material circumstances will be quite unlike anything in the past, we would be better prepared by thinking about the seismic shifts in political consciousness which led to feudalism, nations, the Renaissance, the Enlightenment and so on, than by adding yet more details from yesterday's archives. Realist international relations theory has been hostile to the future (Booth, 1995a) but the future that is now on the horizon can only be ignored at our peril, and so demands priority over all but the future-relevant past.

7   *From the past to the future*

While the subject of international relations cannot but avoid history, the urgency of engaging with the next 50–75 years of world history should take precedence over the leisurely contemplation of the post-Second World War moment. Some of the economic and social conditions of the middle of the next century are already apparent – the huge population surge and varieties of environmental stress. We have barely begun to grasp the implications. If our subject is to be policy relevant, as opposed to merely interesting, we must provide ideas helpful to the contemplation of the future, rather than merely assuming there will be one. Which structures and processes might deliver a better world? What is a 'better' world? What are the material circumstances likely to be? For realism, the future tends to replicate the past, and so history is enough. For those for whom realism is not enough, the ways of the past must be challenged and unlearned, and alternative futures envisaged.

8   *From Cold War IR to Global Moral Science*

The 'dismal science' of Cold War international relations was narrow in focus and spirit. I would like to see the subject be informed by what I have called Global Moral Science in the future (Booth, 1995b, pp. 109–12). This entails systematic enquiry into how humans might live together, locally and globally, in ways that promote individual and collective emancipation in harmony with nature. All approaches are set in some ethical position, though whether it is recognised is another matter. The shift entailed here is from traditional realism's belief that 'this is the best of all possible worlds' to utopian realism's belief that 'we do not have to live this way' (Booth, 1991). What is being advocated here is not the transformation of the subject into an endless course of seminars on ethics, but of choices for teaching and research that speak to global predicaments rather than being driven by the research momentum of one's PhD.

9   *From 'romanticising' the state to problematising it*

The sovereign state portrayed in the standard textbooks of Western political science is not going to deliver humankind the best of all possible worlds. In its discussion of 'the state' the discipline is not persuasive, analytically or normatively. Academic international relations has the reputation of being 'state-centric' but its conception of states has been curiously limited and simplistic, parochial in both a temporal and geographical sense. What has been projected, particularly in neo-realist theorising, is the Western political science notion of a unitary entity standing as guard over the security of its citizens from within and without. In practice states have come in many varieties, and most have represented far greater threats to the lives of those who lived within their borders than the armed forces of neighbours. Under conditions of globalisation, mass consumerism, environmental decay, identity politics, burgeoning science and technology and so on, 'the state' – in the textbook conception of a territorial political unit with sovereign decision-making power and the primary focus of loyalty – might be seen as the problem of world politics, not the solution. If and when one comes to believe this, one's whole perspective on what one takes the subject to be opens up.

10   From high politics to deep politics

The definition of 'high politics' in terms of narrowly conceived security and diplomacy has been one tactic by which the Cold War disciplinary managers defended the subject's frontiers. While some parts of the latter are still strongly contested, substantial openings have been made by 'low politics' and the broadening of the security agenda. Trends in the global environment, for example, have been such that the narrow definition of 'the political' is less sustainable. Belatedly, international relations specialists are learning that politics is everywhere, and not just in the hands of governments. Deep politics means investigating the structures of thought and material circumstances from which derive the epiphenomena we call 'states', 'security', 'politics', and so on. This deepening of the concept of 'the political' in international politics will require a greater input of political economy, in which markets have more leverage over states than vice versa, and of the feminist insight that the personal is the international (Enloe, 1989). To illustrate the last sentence: my taste for a daily banana (multiplied many times by that of others) is of more import for world politics than anything that might have been said by Douglas Hurd, the British Foreign Secretary, and I find it easier to envisage a post-Westphalian and even post-Clausewitzian world – a world without sovereign states and war – than I do a world without gender. If valid, these insights say something fundamental about what makes the world go round.

11   From binaries to balance

Our thinking about world politics, and hence its practice, has been hampered by the familiar feature of Western thought whereby concepts are defined by their opposites. This has resulted in unhelpful polarities and over-simple categorisations. The problem has not disappeared as a result of the subject's post-positivist turn. Indeed, new binaries have become fashionable. More helpful theories and policies will require a more sophisticated and balanced understanding that key concepts are not necessarily political 'opposites', but rather are conditions which offer the scope for compromise. Indeed, world politics will be an arena of widespread violence unless a balance can be mediated between the local and the global, communitarianism and cosmopolitanism, fragmentation and integration, unity and diversity, foundationalism and anti-foundationalism and realism and idealism.

12   *From foundations to anchorages*

Humans are a meaning-creating species, and 'international relations' is one of the stories we tell ourselves, to give meaning to our lives. There has long been a desire to ground meaning in foundations that would last through space and time. But such archimedean points are too demanding for the complex and evolving human story. Consequently, we can only rely on the best anchorages for our ideas, which shift as the human journey continues, but which offer the best promise, in their own context, for trying to answer the central questions. In the move from the accumulation of knowledge to the search for meaning, the debate about the limitations and potentialities of the phenomenon we have come to call 'human nature' will be crucial. In this respect, students of international relations will have to see their subject not simply in terms of the outcome of the most recent happenings of the twentieth century, but as a stage in the evolution of the human race. Perspectives on evolution are a necessary part of thinking about 'human nature', which is an aspect of all theories of international politics. In this regard, there is far more for students of international relations to gain from studying the bones of the earliest 'humans' in the Rift Valley of Africa than from studying the sanitised entrails of governments in public records offices. Reinventing humanity's long-term future will require some re-writing of humanity's long term past.

As a junior lecturer at the Department's 50th anniversary conference, fully imbued with what one of the participants, Charles Manning, liked to call the 'conventional convictions' of the profession, I could not have predicted where the subject would be today. I could not have predicted the intellectual excitement, challenge, and fun of discovering that most of the things I had been taught were flawed. So it goes. Perhaps some of the directions just indicated will prove equally flawed (certainly some of my colleagues will hope so). I expect that much of it will come to seem to be wrong, in time, though not in the way traditionalists expect. Major changes will continue to take place in the subject, making it unrecognisable, and even more inhospitable for those who presided over its expansion in the middle years of its first century. It will change or die. It will become the site for considering all the most interesting and fundamental questions in the social sciences in global perspective, or it will become a diplomatic history backwater. It will have to evolve, since the assumptions and axioms of Cold War international relations will not fit the dynamically evolving global kaleidoscope. New times need new tunes.

I trust that those who will plan the Department's 100th anniversary conference – some of whom will have been present at the 75th conference – will remember the tunes I have just played, will remind the Woodrow Wilson professor of the day, and will insist that she gives me an invitation to account for them. I already have begun to plan my talk. It will begin like this: 'In the Cold War (1940s–1980s) the Department at Aberystwyth both flourished and laboured under its foundational myths. In the next period (1990s–2010s) it laboured to flourish under its foundational inspirations: to tell the world about the world, in a spirit of utopian realism . . .' How it will end remains to be invented, contested and written.

NOTES

I wish to thank the other editors for their comments on an earlier draft of this chapter, but in particular Tim Dunne.
1 For a more detailed and traditional reading of the history of the Department, see Porter, 1972, pp. 86–105, 361–9.

REFERENCES

Booth, Ken (1991), 'Security in Anarchy. Utopian Realism in Theory and Practice', *International Affairs*, 67 (3), pp. 527–45.
(1995a), 'Dare Not to Know: International Relations Theory versus the Future', in Ken Booth and Steve Smith (eds.), *International Relations Theory Today* (Cambridge: Polity Press), pp. 238–50.
(1995b), 'Human Wrongs and International Relations', *International Affairs*, 71 (1), pp. 103–26.
Carr, E. H. (1939), *The Twenty Years' Crisis 1919–1939. An Introduction to the Study of International Relations* (London: Macmillan).
Cox, Robert W. (1986), 'Social Forces, States and World Orders: Beyond International Relations Theory', in Robert O. Keohane, *Neorealism and its Critics* (New York: Columbia University Press), pp. 204–54.
Enloe, Cynthia (1989), *Bananas, Beaches & Bases. Making Feminist Sense of International Politics* (London: Pandora).
Holsti, K. I. (1985), *The Dividing Discipline. Hegemony and Diversity in International Theory* (Boston: Allen & Unwin).
Lasswell, H. D. (1950), *Politics Who Gets What, When, How* (New York: Peter Smith).
Porter, Brian (ed.) (1972), *The Aberystwyth Papers. International Politics 1919–1969* (London: Oxford University Press).
Smith, Steve (1995), 'The Self-Images of a Discipline: A Genealogy of International Relations Theory', in Ken Booth and Steve Smith (eds.), *International Relations Theory Today* (Cambridge: Polity Press), pp. 1–37.

18 'All these theories yet the bodies keep piling up': theory, theorists, theorising

Marysia Zalewski

What difference does it make that the contributors to this volume have varying understandings and conceptions of theory? Are the variations significant and if so to whom and why? Debates about theory sometimes bring out the worst in those of us involved in the discipline of International Relations. Academic conferences, and the resulting volumes, are often the places where insults get hurled both by those who consider themselves, or are considered, to be primarily concerned with theory (we can call these the 'theorists') and those who regard theory as something of a dubious, even self-indulgent, pursuit (we might refer to these as the 'real worlders'). The 'theorists' regularly claim that the 'real worlders' don't understand what theory is or how important it is. The 'real worlders' claim that 'the theorists' are stuck in their ivory towers and have little to say that can help us understand or do something about events such as the Holocaust, the Second World War or the contemporary war in the former Yugoslavia. These debates about theory are evident in the chapters in this volume as well as at the conference that preceded it.[1]

I think that underlying these central debates about theory is an important and significant layer of fear, which has institutional, intellectual and practical aspects. What I mean here is that there are serious differences of opinion about what it takes to enable politics to happen; in other words, how do we, and can we, think and act about the daily tragedies, inequalities and devastations in world politics? One question that arises out of this is partially implied by the title of this chapter. What are all these theories for in international politics if they do not help us to understand and act upon the problems we are currently witnessing internationally? A further concern regards those theories which are apparently far removed from policy constructions and international action. One might characterise this debate as paralleling the modernist/ post-modernist split; each side fearing the politics of the other giving rise to the insults and behaviours mentioned above.[2] Whilst I have claimed above that this fear has three aspects, in this chapter I will only consider the latter two, intellectual and practical.

In this contribution to the concluding section of this book I will address this debate about 'theory' versus the 'real world' and in particular look at three questions that weave through many of the contributions to this volume: namely, what exactly is theory? How does theory relate to the 'real world'? Which is the best or most appropriate theory, and why? In order to facilitate this discussion and spell out further what the fear is about I want to look at three different ways in which theory has been presented in this volume. It seems that some people write about theory as a *tool*, some who use theory as *critique*, and some who think about theory as *everyday practice*. Let me stress that I do not think all the authors in this volume can be easily slotted into each of these groups; indeed some will fit into more than one category. However, I do think that these three groupings capture some of the important differences in ways of thinking about theory and its presumed relationship to the 'real world'. What I think is significant here is that theory can be and is represented and thought about in rather different ways which, I go on to explain, have implications for our understandings about what is 'really' happening and what we can do about it. I am, of course, fully aware that specific contributors may well use theory in more than one of these three ways but my point is not one about the consistency of individuals but is rather one about the ways in which theory is used in international relations.

Theory as a tool

On this view theory is something that is used by those wishing to make sense of events in international politics. James Rosenau's exposition of theory in this volume is a good example of this perspective. He seems unpuzzled about what theory is, believing it to be a framework for understanding the world, a framework that can be 'fine-tuned' by returning to the 'theoretical drawing board' if one finds oneself over-puzzled by events in world politics. As such, theory is something that one uses to explain, for example, the Gulf War, the Holocaust or 'ethnic cleansing'. Some contributors to this book seem also to see theory as primarily a tool, including Barry Buzan, Stephen Krasner, Michael Nicholson and Michael Mann. Additionally, each of these writers seems clear about how theory relates to the 'real world'. Buzan, for example, suggests that theories of post-war realism emerged because of a need to study the world 'as it was', rather than as one might have liked it to be. To be sure there may be a tension between the need to study 'what is' and the danger of therefore reproducing 'what is', but this tension, according to Buzan, is unresolvable. On this view, 'what is' represents the 'real world' and particularly the continuities in that world, and although we might not like some of those continuities (such as wars) we have no choice but to accept them even if, ideally, we would like to change them.

According to Buzan, realism's concern with 'power' (as defined by realists) makes it the most adequate theory as such a concern can serve as a starting point for the construction of grand theory. Stephen Krasner speaks of 'theoretical tools' and of various theories, such as co-operation theory, which can be applied to issues such as finance, the environment and economic sanctions. The purpose of the various theories is to answer a set of questions about the international political economy. Michael Nicholson writes about theory as something which is testable, a model to describe the real world. In his defence of empiricist/positivistic theories, Nicholson argues that we need to be able to discern regularities in the world in order both to construct policy and to have some measure of control over it. He suggests that the morality of many of the issues international relations scholars are concerned with including wars, famines, poverty and gross inequalities makes it imperative that we have rigorous criteria for distinguishing between what is the case in the world and what we want to be the case. Michael Mann, although stating that he is not a fan of theory, nevertheless demands that theory fulfils specific requirements such as an emphasis on substantive issues, most centrally war and peace.

I would argue that envisaging theory as a tool is predicated on a number of significant assumptions which have several implications for our understandings and behaviours in international politics. The first assumption is that there is a separation between *theory* and *theorists*. Once again, Rosenau gives us a clear example of this. Referring to the work of Gaddis, Rosenau claims that Gaddis seems 'puzzled more by the conduct of *theorists* than by the conduct of *actors* who brought an end to the Cold War' (my emphasis). As such, according to Rosenau, Gaddis was not perplexed by a genuine puzzle – the end of the Cold War – but was instead puzzled by the failings of theorists which, for Rosenau, is not a particularly significant thing and certainly not one that touches on the lives of large numbers of people (the latter a theme which crops up regularly at BISA and ISA conferences). Rosenau goes on to use the example of Gaddis's preoccupation with 'theorists' to make the claim that 'the same criticism can be levelled at the organisers of the conference for which this paper has been prepared' asserting that 'the organisers' puzzlement concerns the activities of theorists rather than global actors'. On this view, theorists are people with academic positions and a propensity to write about theory and perhaps not an explicit or overt concern with policy making. What are the implications of this? One is that it implies that global actors, for example President Clinton or Prime Minister Major, are not theorists and conversely that academic theorists are not global actors and are perhaps not centrally concerned with 'real world' events such as the massacres in Rwanda, and are instead only interested in the minutiae of the supposedly separate enterprise of theory. This allows those who would wish to criticise 'theorists' to appear to claim the moral high ground by asserting that the 'theorists' are failing to pay attention to what is really believed to matter in world politics and instead are indulging in an intellectual pastime. These are points to which I will return.

A second assumption is that there is a separation between *theory* and the *'real world'*. Buzan frequently speaks of 'what is' in a way that implies that the 'real world' exists independently of our theories about it. This leads to a common criticism of realism but one that realists defend in a way that again seemingly captures the moral high ground. Kal Holsti, for example, exemplifies the realist's defence with the statement, 'what do reflexive turns have to do with . . . ethnic cleansing, fourteen new international peacekeeping efforts, starvation in Africa, the continued shadow of the Balkans and Middle East, and arms racing in Asia?' (Holsti, 1993, p. 407). This belief that events of interest to international scholars are ontologically prior to our theories about them has significant implications. One is that it is simply asserted that specific issues or events are legitimate areas of study. In practice this means that the continual (arguably arbitrary) decisions that are made about what gets included and what gets excluded are presented as 'natural' or 'obvious' choices, determined by the 'real' world, whereas they are instead *judgements*. James Rosenau suggests that it is 'sheer craziness to dare to understand world affairs' but 'dare we must'! He advises that we must approach this awesome task with a sense of humility and puzzlement. But following this admirable advice he claims that our sense of puzzlement should be disciplined, by which he means that 'one needs to be puzzled by observable outcomes' and to 'probe puzzles persistently' is not a 'license to investigate *trivial questions*' (my emphasis). But if these puzzles are not 'naturally obvious' then the boundaries between trivial and non-trivial are merely, but significantly, the result of value judgements.

A third assumption concerns the value of Enlightenment rationality. It is the faith in and commitment to the Enlightenment rationalist tradition that most clearly identifies those authors who write about theory primarily as a tool on the modernist side of the modernist/post-modernist divide. And it is around this divide, I have suggested, that the fear and disagreements about politics in international relations emerge. Stephen Krasner is most insistent that 'the achievements of international political economy have been generated by an epistemology that conforms with the Western rationalistic tradition, not with those versions of post-modernism that reject any separation between the student and the object of study'. Krasner's fear is that the loss of 'conventional epistemology' threatens to 'strip social science of the most important contribution that it can make to the betterment of human society: that contribution is to discipline power with truth'. He goes on to claim that to abandon Enlightenment epistemology for post-modernism would make it impossible to argue that apartheid in South Africa or Nazism in Germany were wrong. If this is correct then many would be tempted to agree with Krasner that post-modernism is indeed an 'evil development' (a claim he made at the conference). But what else does his claim imply? Krasner claims that 'we', presumably international relations scholars, need to hold on to the presumed strengths of Enlightenment reason and modernist methodologies because they allow the possibility of rationally judging between competing claims. Post-modernism (according to Krasner) does not have this ability and is therefore unsuitable for international politics. Again, judgement *per se* is not the issue, the point is that reason and rationality become the foundation for such judgements, on the assumption that these are neutral.

It is the debate about which is the most appropriate theory to study international politics that seems to be of most concern to those who write about theory as a tool, given that they seem satisfied about the nature of theory and its relationship to the 'real world'. Krasner's claims imply that it would be folly at best, and immoral at worst, to abandon the modernist theoretical enterprise. What might happen if Krasner's worst nightmare came true? That the Holocaust would happen again? That people (who? Jews, Gypsies, homosexuals, state officials, government leaders, international relations scholars?) would not have recourse to theories which enabled judgements to be made? Of course there is fear here. I cannot imagine any contributor to this volume who would not be scared if they thought that such a thing as the Holocaust could happen again, or that no one could say it was wrong to kill six million people because they were Jews. It is in this sense that I would claim that Krasner, and those who argue similarly, is implying that post-modernist theories are unable to deliver politics to international relations because they offer no grounds for making judgements about what is wrong or right, good or bad. This again seems to capture the moral high ground.

Theory as critique

On this view, theory is assumed to be actively interrelated with the 'real world' and, as a tool, is wielded with a different purpose. One example amongst the contributors to this volume who view theory as critique is Andrew Linklater. He is enough of a modernist to think of theory as a tool in the sense that one can *use* theory to understand the world but he takes theory much further than this. Linklater is clear and explicit about some of the purposes of theory, which imply a radically different relationship between theory and the 'real world' than that put forward by those who write about theory primarily as a tool. For Linklater, Critical Theory is not just a tool to make sense of the world 'as it is' but to make sense of how the world 'got to be as it is', with a central aim underlying such an endeavour being that of emancipation. Essentially, Linklater argues that we do not have to accept that the world is inevitably unequal and hierarchical. We can use theory both to understand how those inequities came to exist and as a base for changing them. Additionally, Linklater asserts that Critical Theory collapses the subject/object distinction which indicates a clear break from the belief that events in the world are ontologically prior to our theories about them.

Linklater explicitly discusses politics in a way that highlights the point I wish to draw out regarding the level of fear that seems to underpin some of the heated debates about the value of theory within international relations. He claims that the aim of using theory to manage the existing international order (as opposed to changing it) has the unpalatable political effect of neglecting marginalised groups and subordinated interests. He additionally argues that those observers who claim value-neutrality for their efforts to attempt to further the smooth running of the international system fail to understand that intellectual projects (one might include 'doing theory' of any form here) have important implications for the national and international distribution of wealth and power. In other words, simply seeing theory as an 'objective' tool one uses to make sense of ontologically prior events in the world (the world 'as it is') is not simply benign and has serious political and moral implications. Thus Linklater sees a moral and political imperative in both understanding the nature of theory and theory's relationship with the world. To this end he implies that theories such as realism are untenable because of their proponents' failure to understand its involvement in perpetuating gross inequalities. Equally, post-modernism is unsuitable as it fails to align itself to the emancipatory project of the Enlightenment.

Theory as everyday practice

Theory as critique and theory as everyday practice merge into each other at many levels but there are significant differences between theory as a tool and theory as everyday practice centring around the questions: 'what is theory?', 'who are "theorists"?' and 'what issues become counted as important enough to theorise about?' The authors in this volume that I want to introduce who have written about theory as everyday practice are Cynthia Enloe and Christine Sylvester. Let us take the first of those questions – what is theory for these authors? They certainly do not see it as an objective tool made up of rigorous criteria whose function is only to make sense of the world in order to manage it more efficiently. Indeed, I would suggest that these writers do not think of theory as a *noun* at all but as a *verb* (see Sylvester, this volume, also Christian, 1987). Thinking of theory as a noun, as I would argue is the case with those who write about theory as a tool, reinforces the impression that it is a thing which may be picked up and used and refined if necessary. But thinking of theory as a verb implies that what one does is 'theorise' rather than 'use theory'. There are several implications resulting from this.

First, it implies that theorising is a way of life, a form of life, something we all do, every day, all the time. We theorise about how to make cups of tea, about washing clothes, about using the word processor, about driving a car, about collecting water, about joking, about what counts as relevant to international politics and about how we relate to colleagues, students, families, friends or strangers. We theorise about each of these everyday activities, mostly subconsciously. This is relevant to international relations scholars because it means that first, we are *all* theorising (not just 'the theorists') and second, that the theorising that counts or that matters, in terms of affecting and/or creating international political events, is not confined either to policy makers or to academics. Cynthia Enloe's chapter helps us to understand what this means. In choosing to look at the Mayan Indians of Chiapas she knows that mainstream international relations scholars would think that she had chosen an obscure and marginal group to shed light on the negotiations about the North American Free Trade Agreement (NAFTA). But she argues that by taking seriously the voices of the people at the margins of life she has a clearer insight into understanding how the artifices of international politics are constructed than do mainstream observers of NAFTA. Such observers tend to concentrate on the negotiations between 'Mexico' and the 'United States', perhaps extending their analyses to speculate upon the side effects. Theories that might be drawn upon by such observers might include realist theories of power politics and sovereignty as well as theories from international political economy. To be sure these might give some guidance to policy makers, they might help smooth the implementation of NAFTA; but they don't really help us to understand much about how the whole situation came 'to be' or the magnitude of the 'reality' that underlies the 'negotiations' between 'Mexico' and the 'United States'. In this sense, mainstream theories allow us only a superficial glimpse of what is going on, which has serious consequences.

By way of contrast, Enloe's chapter allows us to have many more insights into the 'real world' of international politics, but she achieves this by using unconventional sources and unconventional 'theorists'. For example, her discussion of a male rancher's ability to bargain with central state officials over land reform shows how this depends on a host of interweaving social relationships, each in some way related to the other. The image she portrays is one of both fragility and power: fragility because each relationship is part of an interdependent chain; if one of the links breaks this may have devastating knock-on effects; power, because the links gain strength the more interweaved they become particularly as many of the links are deemed to be irrelevant to understanding international politics and therefore, to all intents and purposes, are invisible.

To understand theorising as a way of life implies that we must take into account many more human activities and behaviours than would be considered sensible by those who utilise theory as a tool. For example, an analysis of the jokes made at the conference that this book is based on might shed some light on the construction of international relations theorising. Consider this one told by Fred Halliday at one of the panel sessions. An American diplomat in Britain was asked what he missed most about home, his answer was, 'a good hamburger'. His wife's answer was, 'my job'. Most of the audience laughed. How is this an example of international relations theorising and how might it affect how we study international relations? First, it tells us something about the gendered nature of diplomacy and the sacrifices that countless women have made in order to tailor their marriages and lives to fit in with their husband's career and, by implication, the significant (unpaid) contribution that these women's actions have made to the workings of governments and inter-state relationships. One may disagree about what makes jokes funny but the fact that Halliday's anecdote elicited laughter and not shock tells a story about what we take to be significant and important in international relations.

How might this affect how we study international relations? At a recent British International Studies Association Conference, a senior Professor

(Prof A) reminded another senior Professor (Prof B) that 'we should not lose sight of the categories in which people think'. The comment was made because Prof B insisted that international relations scholars should pay as much attention to nurses and mothers as to soldiers and diplomats. Prof A, perhaps shocked at this urging, was at pains to warn Prof B of the dangers of not paying attention to those who make policy and those who enact international politics, namely soldiers and diplomats. It seemed to me that Prof A was right in one way yet missed the point of Prof B's remarks. Prof B was not implying that we should ignore soldiers, diplomats and policy makers but, rather, was arguing that placing them at the centre of our studies did not necessarily help us to understand why events (such as the war in the former Yugoslavia) happen, or what are the full consequences. Making them the core of our study merely reifies their position at the centre of the study of international relations. However, Prof A was clearly right in the general sense that we should not lose sight of the categories in which people think. But what this means for those who think of theory as everyday practice is rather different to that which, I think, Prof A implied. One effect of this for the study of international relations is that we have to acknowledge that there is a great deal more to the construction of international politics than what appears to be on the surface. What appears on the surface is not automatic, natural or inevitable – to paraphrase Enloe, the conventional portrait of international politics too often ends up looking like a Superman comic strip when it probably should resemble a Jackson Pollock.

This leads on to the second implication of understanding theory as a verb which is that it radically extends our understanding of who 'theorists' are. As noted above, James Rosenau gently chided the conference organisers for seemingly being more puzzled with the activities of theorists rather than with global actors. But if one believes that theory is everyday practice then theorists are global actors and global actors are theorists. Additionally, one might find these theorists/actors in many more places than conventional international relations theories would imagine. Christine Sylvester articulates this point in her chapter confirming that to understand international politics, and in the case of her contribution to this volume, to understand more about the gendered construction of international politics:

we must locate the people of international politics in their places of action, which are apt to be far less heroic and insufficiently abstract to qualify for usual attention in the field. Such places are lower than 'low politics', being households, factories, farms, remote rural areas and international immigration posts in lesser as well as great power settings. To suggest bringing such people into international relations is earthshaking for a field that admits only official decision makers, soldiers, statesmen, terrorists, kings, and the occasional 'crazed' religious group to the fold.

So it is indeed true that the conference organisers are concerned with the activities of theorists but we would insist that these are also global actors, though we would look for these actors/theorisers in a wide variety of places, not just at the reified core of what has become international politics. For example, in order to understand more about the Cold War we might want to pursue Farah Godrej's analysis of the sex industry in the Philippines (Godrej, 1995). Her description of a common T-shirt slogan worn by servicemen referring to the local women which reads, 'Mind Over Matter: I Don't Mind And You Don't Matter', might be a good place to begin. From such a starting point, which could be both that of the men who wore the T-shirts and that of the women who were the 'subject' of them, we can attempt to understand the construction of Filipino women's debasement and servile and compliant sexuality, which is inextricably linked to the construction of both the 'other' and militarism itself.

A third implication of thinking of theory as a verb concerns a question posed earlier – what issues are deemed important and relevant to the study of international politics? – in other words the issue of ontology. Many contributors to this volume stress repeatedly that scholars should be concerned with substantive issues in international politics. For example, Michael Mann insists on the production of substantive theory on war and peace; James Rosenau claims that we do not have a 'license to investigate trivial questions . . . we must consider genuine puzzles'; Fred Halliday argues that for a theory to be useful it must be able to generate a research agenda and to identify and explain significant issues. He continues by asserting that 'it must be asked of any theory, or theoretical debate, how it contributes to this goal'. But on what grounds does one identify substantive issues or what counts as a research agenda or what is genuine and non-trivial in international politics?

To many of those involved in the study of international politics it is obvious what the issues are and should be. But on this point consider what Martin Hollis has to say (in this volume) about the question of relevance:

He [Wittgenstein] suggests that . . . social facts are as they are intersubjectively taken to be, thus implying that to change the rules of the game is to change the reality of the social world. This line of thought might appeal to feminists . . . if the players [of the game of international relations] can be persuaded to take gender seriously as a relevant category for understanding action, then feminism is thereby vindicated by its very success . . . gender has whatever significance the players come to give it. Whatever is taken seriously is thereby serious.

Those writers with their feet firmly in the camp of modernism would probably want to take issue with Hollis's comments, claiming that what is taken seriously in international relations is so because it *is* serious or substantive or non-trivial, with the 'problem' of (inter)subjectivity regulated by the tools of reason and judgement inherited from the Enlightenment. Those on the post-modernist side might claim that such judgements do not yield to some overarching meta-narrative of 'reason' or 'judgement' and therefore are not innocent. This, I think, is where a major fault line appears, where a dispute about politics, and by implication power, ferments and frequently erupts. It is because of this fault line, I would suggest, that the worst sometimes emerges in the debates about 'theory' versus the 'real world' in international relations, with all proponents, in some way, claiming the moral high ground.

Modernists seem to have faith in the belief that the human condition can be understood scientifically. Such an understanding depends on the rigours of rationalist epistemology and methodology. To abandon these would, the fear is, lead to Krasner's nightmare scenario whereby we would all be floundering around in a world in which our theories could give no foundations for claiming that such events as the Holocaust were wrong, implying that such things could regularly happen again. As such, Krasner argues, we need to retain the tools of modernism to 'discipline power with truth'. On this view the relationship between knowledge and power is mediated by science. Those who hover in and around the post-modernist camp would claim that the epistemologies and methodologies of modernism do not provide us with *neutral* or indeed *innocent* tools to learn about the world but instead only provide us with the means to produce *meaning* in the world. These meanings are not the result of 'truth' but the result of agreement on what the rules are for producing 'truth'. As such, the choice of substantive issues to study in international politics is not the result of 'natural selection' or 'neutral judgement' but is a reflection of specific interests. Therefore to insist on consensus about what the 'issues' are in international politics is problematic since the implication of this is that the issues that will be 'agreed' upon will primarily reflect the interests of the powerful. The push towards consensus can therefore be seen as more of a coercive strategy to relegate the interests of the less powerful to the margins. Indeed, the whole project of modernity has been interpreted as being about conquest and control and about silencing others in a sort of theoretical imperialism. On this view reason is another weapon to exclude and silence (Marshall, 1994, p. 24).

There are two key interlocking points to emphasise here about the post-modernist approach.[3] The first is that events in the world, issues in international politics, are not ontologically prior to our theories about them. This does not mean that people read about, say realism, and act accordingly, but that our (and by 'our' I mean theorisers/global actors) dominant ways of thinking and acting in the world will be (re)produced as 'reality'. This is not simply about self-fulfilling prophecies but reflects a profound and complex debate about the existence of the world 'out there'.[4] The second point is that in the name of elegance and policy-relevance serious decisions are made about what gets included as a substantive issue in international politics. By serious I do not mean simply important, but rather with severe implications. In the words of Cynthia Enloe 'for an explanation to be useful a great deal of human dignity is left on the cutting room floor'. The loss of human dignity often manifests itself in its worst extreme, death. The loss of life, through war for example, has been a central feature of the study of international politics. Why not alter this core of the subject to consider seriously the leading cause of death in the world – coded by the International Classi-fication of Diseases as Z59.5 – or in more simple terms, poverty. It is surely a serious and substantive issue that this is the world's biggest killer.

All these theories yet the bodies keep piling up[5]

The 'real worlders' use a variety of tactics to delegitimise those forms of theorising which they see as either useless or downright dangerous to international politics. These range from ridicule, attempts at incor-poration, scare-mongering and claiming that such theories are the product of 'juvenile' whims, fads and fashions. The charitable interpret-ation of these manoeuvrings is that they are instigated by a sense of fear, with the 'real worlders' insisting that the 'theorists' and the plethora of theories do not relate to what is 'really' going on in the world and thus the 'bodies keep piling up' while the 'theorists' make nice points. Conversely, the 'theorists' accuse the 'real worlders' of being complicit in the construction of a world in which the 'bodies keep piling up' and the resistance to criticism simply reflects their institutional and, sometimes, public power as well as their intellectual weaknesses. Perhaps it is not surprising that we are having these debates about theory as 'the practice of theory has been deeply affected by the debate about modernism versus postmodernism and the attendant questions of a social theory which can foster human autonomy and emancipation' (Marshall, 1994, p. 1). But what is the future for the discipline and practice of inter-national politics if such a debate has the effect of bringing out the worst in people and which is often conducted within a spirit of 'jousting' verging on the hostile?

Richard Ashley's contribution to this volume attests somewhat to the
futility of and angst felt by many who are party to and witness to these
debates with his comments that there is little point in offering arguments
to a community 'who have repeatedly shown themselves so proficient
at doing what it takes not to hear'. In a paradigmatically masculinist
discipline such as international relations perhaps the sport of intellectual
jousting and parodies of bar room brawling is functionally inevitable.
Maybe the concentration on wars, foreign policy, practices of diplomacy
and the imageries of 'us' and 'them' that goes along with all of that
fosters a 'winners' and 'losers' mentality. So the 'theorists' do battle
with the 'real worlders' and the 'modernists' do battle with the 'post-
modernists'. So who wins? Perhaps nobody wins with the possible
exception of the publishers, especially in the context of contemporary
academic life, where an academic's value is measured by the quantity of
publications.

If research produced in International Relations departments is to be of
use besides advancing careers and increasing departmental budgets then
it surely has something to do with making sense of events in the world, at
the very least. In that endeavour it will be of supreme importance what
counts as an appropriate event to pay attention to and who counts as a
'relevant' theorist, which in turn fundamentally depends on what we
think theory is and how it relates to the so-called 'real world'. International politics is *what we* make it to be, the contents of the 'what' and
the group that is the 'we' are questions of vital theoretical and therefore
political importance. We need to re-think the discipline in ways that will
disturb the existing boundaries of both what we claim to be relevant in
international politics and what we assume to be legitimate ways of
constructing knowledge about the world. The bodies do keep piling up
but I would suggest that having a plethora of theories is not the problem.
My fear is that statements such as 'all these theories yet the bodies keep
piling up' might be used to foster a 'back to basics' mentality, which, in
the context of international relations, implies a retreat to the comfort of
theories and understanding of theory which offers relatively immediate
gratification, simplistic solutions to complex problems and reifies and
reflects the interests of the already powerful.

NOTES

Many thanks to the following people for their comments on earlier versions of
this chapter: Ken Booth, Tim Dunne, Steve Smith and Cindy Weber.
1 The 75th anniversary conference was actually marked by its good naturedness.
   Nevertheless, strong claims and debates did emerge concerning theory.
2 I realise that some may disagree with my characterisation of these debates as

paralleling the modernist/post-modernist split. For example there is the argument that Critical Theorists have said many of the same things that post-modernists say and indeed before the post-modernists said them! There are two points I want to make here. First, I think the debate about 'who said it first' is unfruitful. At some level we are all footnotes to Aristotle and Wollstonecraft (and a few others no doubt!). What matters is the use, implications, and manifestations of the debates and insights. Second, although Critical Theorists and post-modernists do seem to share many of the same insights, especially on the subjects of power/knowledge, politics and the construction of reality, the assumptions and beliefs underlying the post-modernist's representations of such things marks a radical departure from the beliefs and assumptions of modernism in ways that Critical Theory does not. In short, the modernist/post-modernist split fundamentally divides around what counts as political/politics, what counts as action/activism, what the 'point' of politics is and what the 'point' of theory is. Additionally, post-modernists reject the epistemological and foundational security which modernists rely on to legitimate their claims to knowledge. Of course it is this particular radical understanding of politics, action and epistemology that disturbs Critical Theorists (and others) about post-modernism.

3   I know that Critical Theorists also make similar points but their ultimate belief in Enlightenment methodologies marks a radical difference in the interpretations, assumptions and implications of the uses of these insights by post-modernists. See my earlier note 2.

4   This is part of a very complex debate. I suggest readers start with Jim George's book (1994), especially the first chapter.

5   My colleague, Nick Wheeler, has this phrase pinned up on his notice board in his office.

REFERENCES

Christian, Barbara (1987), 'The Race for Theory', *Cultural Critique*, 6, pp. 51–63.
George, Jim (1994), *Discourses of Global Politics: A Critical (Re)Introduction to International Relations* (Boulder, CO: Lynne Rienner).
Godrej, Farah (1995), 'Women and Post Cold War US Foreign Policy: The Case of Filipina Prostitutes', paper presented at the ISA conference in Chicago, 21–5 February.
Holsti, Kal (1993), 'International Relations at the End of the Millennium', *Review of International Studies*, 19 (4).
Marshall, Barbara (1994), *Engendering Modernity* (Oxford: Polity Press).

Index